ML

A Poor Harvest

The Clash of Policies and Interests in the Grain Trade

A Poor Harvest

The Clash of Policies and Interests in the Grain Trade

Richard Gilmore

Longman

New York & London

A POOR HARVEST
The Clash of Policies and Interests in the Grain Trade

Longman Inc., 19 West 44th Street,
New York, N.Y. 10036
Associated companies, branches, and
representatives throughout the world.

Developmental Editor: Irving E. Rockwood
Editorial and Design Supervisor: Joan L. Matthews
Production Supervisor: Ferne Y. Kawahara
Manufacturing Supervisor: Marion Hess
Composition: Intergraphic Technology, Inc.
Printing and Binding: BookCrafters Inc.

Library of Congress Cataloging in Publication Data

Gilmore, Richard.
  A poor harvest.

  Bibliography: p.
  Includes index.
  1. Grain trade—Government policy—United States.
2. Agriculture and state—United States. 3. Grain
trade—United States. I. Title.
HD9036.G54   380.1′4131′0973   81-19309
ISBN 0-582-28193-8   AACR2

Manufactured in the United States of America

9 8 7 6 5 4 3 2 1

*To Judy, Jennifer, Kate,
and my beloved grandmother*

Contents

Figures and Tables

FIGURES

TABLES

Foreword

A global food problem exists, and no one knows quite how to solve it. *A Poor Harvest* tackles the tough questions of channeling trade and marketing functions to reward producers and consumers to the maximum extent possible. The book outlines the present global food system as defined by major importing and exporting countries and the private sector. Instead of dealing with each set of policies and merchandising patterns separately, it approaches this complex mix as a whole, where initiatives in one country impact directly on another. At the same time, the book endeavors to integrate the workings of the trade in order to describe how governments and the private sector interact in the distribution and marketing of grains and oilseeds worldwide.

A second major section of the book presents a series of case studies in an effort to trace the evolution of government policies and commercial practices during the last decade. Because some of the material presented is new, it goes beyond previous works in this area. The events and policies are up-to-date and, therefore, relevant to current global food issues.

In addition to descriptive elements and case studies, Dr. Richard Gilmore offers a third section in which he presents a number of recommendations for consideration. While the author cautions that some of the proposals he advances would be difficult to implement, at least in the short term, he nevertheless raises some interesting approaches to the major food problems we are likely to face in the decade ahead and in doing so, inspires others to join in the debate.

Thomas S. Foley, Chairman
Committee on Agriculture
U.S. House of Representatives

Preface

In the last two decades the world has witnessed tremendous uncertainties about food resources. In 1972, it was the Soviet grain heist; 1973 ushered in the soybean embargo that threatened drastic reductions in an important food item for the Japanese; by 1974 the world's grain supply bins were close to empty, and developing countries were hurt most of all; 1975 revealed problems in the grain trade involving extensive shipping and handling abuses at the expense of American farmers and consumers worldwide; 1976 to 1980 were less dramatic years, when the quiet revolution in grain production and merchandising went ignored as food shortages were seemingly confined to regions of the nonindustrial world and prices were reduced by global surpluses; and 1980 once again started thunderously with the massive cancellation of U.S. export sales to the Soviet Union.

These events indicated a marked change in agricultural trade relations. For me, personally, there was a sense that each crisis subsided without resolution. As a staff member of the Senate Foreign Relations Subcommittee on Multinational Corporations, I recommended in late 1974 that we turn our attention to the agricultural sector. The subject was entirely relevant to foreign policy, particularly since Secretary of State Kissinger and Secretary of Agriculture Butz had so enthusiastically espoused a food weapon strategy for U.S. grain exports. Congress had picked over the 1972 Soviet sale without turning up significant new insights as to how the United States had fallen into such a predicament and how it could avoid its recurrence. With the endorsement and support of Senator Frank Church as Chairman of the Subcommittee, and Senator Dick Clark, I made some initial inquiries about the workings of the grain trade. After successive rebuffs couched in claims that the export business was too complicated for a nontrader such as myself to comprehend, I was convinced that the subject matter warranted a thorough review.

In the fall of 1975, I visited the Soviet Union on official business to attempt to ascertain how this important buyer contracted for the importation of grains from the United States and other suppliers. Normally this information could be obtained in corporate headquarters and the bureaucratic confines of Washington. Not so in the case of the grain trade. The Soviets were estimable clients of the world's largest grain-trading companies, whose interests were protected along with their own. My trip to Moscow proved more informative than my initial inquiries in the United States. Thanks to the imminent convening of the party congress, Soviet officials were in lively competition to claim credit for past successes and pass blame for failures. As a result, I was an unsuspecting beneficiary of this peculiar form of professional warfare.

In June 1976, the Subcommittee's hearings on the workings of the grain trade were launched. Representatives of major American grain houses were well prepared for the event and claimed victory at their conclusion. They were persuaded that their testimony had effectively discredited the fanciful notions of the staff, particularly myself, that an oligopoly existed in the grain trade that was potentially harmful to U.S. and other countries' economic interests. Industry lobbyists were buzzing pridefully over the fact that the hearings did not go into greater depth, and presumably that the lid was still clamped tight on information about the grain trade.

I was persuaded that they may have been right and that the matter was serious enough to warrant further research and review. With foundation grants, I had the luxury to pursue the subject from a scholarly distance that a public congressional hearing cannot afford. In the course of preparing this book, a tide of new events occurred and then subsided, which underscored my sense of the need to offer additional information and insights relating to the grain trade in an effort to modify public policies.

In this book I have attempted to fill a knowledge gap and, at some hazard, offer suggestions for reforms both in the United States and the international community of food importing and exporting countries. Above all, what I hope to accomplish is to dispel so many of the mysteries and myths that surround the grain trade, and to stress the urgent need for changes affecting both the public and private sectors. Food is, in my estimation, a semi-public resource and, as such, should be regarded as a public responsibility that no nation or company can hold on its own.

This book was begun under a Rockefeller Foundation grant from October 1977 to March 1978. This support as well as the personal encouragement from John Stremlau of the Foundation were instrumental in the most important stages of the study's development. I am also extremely indebted to the Overseas Development Council for inviting me to do the major portion of my work under its auspices as a Visiting Fellow. It was a rare opportunity, permitting me to learn a great deal and establish friendships with several members of the Council's permanent staff. During this time, ODC received a research grant from the CENEX Foundation in support of my work, for which I am most appreciative. The final writing phase of this book was conducted at the Carnegie Endowment for International Peace where I served as a senior associate. My tenure at the Endowment was a most fruitful challenging experience where, once again, I had a chance to exchange ideas with an extraordinary group of bright, dedicated individuals.

As much as a project of this kind depends upon institutional support, I found even greater nourishment from the ideas, work-related assistance, and psychological backing of my friends. In particular, I owe a great deal to my research associate Fred Blott, who also has collaborated with me on other projects. He withstood the pains of the birth and initial phases of this study, providing invaluable improvements along the way. His successor, Jade Barnett, deserves equal credit for the professional caliber of her work and personal commitment to the project. Heather Burridge, my secretary and editorial assistant, deserves a reward all her own for helping to transform the original manuscript into its present readable state. In addition, she propped up the author in times of travail and is in every way a unique person in my eyes. Irv Rockwood, my editor, also deserves a special note of gratitude for his skilled assistance.

There is no way to thank my friends and, in particular, my wife, Judy, for their time and genuine advice. The book is now finished, but these relationships continue to grow, inspire, and comfort.

Richard Gilmore

1

The Problems of Plenty

The decade of the 1980s has begun with food supplies in abundance and incidents of mass starvation on the wane. The United States and other suppliers are anxious to sell their surpluses to ready buyers, and the private sector, having undergone a period of intensive investment, is prepared to handle even greater volumes of grain imports and exports than in the past. These are signs that suggest the world's food producers and traders are poised to cope with the challenge of increasing global consumption. Such a view, however, minimizes the enormity of the problem. It also fails to recognize the risk that under present conditions food scarcities will continue. The world agricultural economy is as yet insufficiently stable to turn a time of plenty into a sustained period of food security.

Today's food problem is unlike that of the immediate post-World War II period. In 1945 the problem was not merely one of distribution, as at present, but of inadequate production. In the wake of World War II, global food supplies were simply inadequate in absolute terms. Increased production became the order of the day and a major policy objective of governments everywhere. Unlike some, it was a policy objective that was realized.

Ironically, we face a situation today, especially in the United States, in which the successful public policies of an earlier era, policies so successful that global food surpluses rather than shortages had become the norm within a decade of the close of World War II, are themselves the source of new problems. Thus the food issues of the future promise to have less to do with food production than with marketing, trade, and government policy. That some have too much food and others too little in a world in which global supplies are, as at present, either equal to or slightly greater than effective demand is not a problem that can be attributed solely to the quirks of nature. It is an outgrowth of structural change rather than true scarcity, a problem that is in large part the product of public and private institutions that dominate the grain trade and their relationship one to the other. Further, it is a problem that can only grow worse in the future if, as some fear, producers should become hard pressed to keep up with demand.

Today, as in the entire post-World War II period, we live in an era of agricultural nationalism. Each nation seeks to satisfy its own food requirements, competing with other nations for access to adequate supplies. Lacking the skills, information, and resources necessary to fulfill this objective unilaterally, most governments have turned to the private sector for assistance. The result has been a marriage of convenience between the public sector and an increasingly oligopolistic private sector. While offering certain immediate benefits to both partners, this alliance has not been without cost to producers and consumers. Most important, however, it has fostered a dependence of the public sector upon the private for the accomplishment of a vital public policy objective.

It is difficult to realize that a crisis may be imminent in an era when the benefits of the status quo seem so self-evident. For much of the world, and for Americans in particular, the era of agricultural nationalism has been a time of abundance and profit. Consumers with sufficient purchasing power have had all the grain they wanted, and at relatively cheap prices, while food aid programs—authorized by the public sector but implemented in large part, and quite profitably, by the private—have met the needs of many of those unable to pay. Producers have generally received an adequate return on investment and have been all but assured of prosperous, captive, domestic and foreign markets for their crops. Land has remained relatively cheap, energy has been plentiful—if not always inexpensive—and capital has been readily available. Small wonder that production has soared almost hand-in-hand with the profits of the international grain traders.

Yet numerous portents have appeared in recent years that suggest we are today faced with a food future less bright than the experience of the past four decades. Foreign demand for food and feedgrain supplies, which have been concentrated in a few industrialized countries, has grown to inflationary proportions. Free trade in the grain business has vanished following the emergence of an oligopoly of private companies. American producers, credited as the most efficient in the world, have become progressively more dependent on exports for their livelihood, but the return to the American farmer has declined in spite of record-breaking harvests. Under mounting pressure from large-scale production, some of the world's most fertile farmland has begun to suffer from erosion and degradation. American consumers have found themselves competing with unpredictable foreign giants like the Soviet Union for low-cost U.S. agricultural commodities. Developing countries, once able to obtain cheap food imports, have been forced to compete in the world market for these same resources as their food aid and purchasing power have dwindled. Market uncertainties have cast a pall over a once prosperous picture.

The underlying pattern is one of growth accompanied by structural weaknesses. In the United States the government's emphasis on foreign sales and benign neglect of related production and distribution issues has inadvertently reduced the influence of producers and consumers in the market. Other importing and exporting states, even those with biases toward protectionism, have fared no better. In Canada, for example, the government's efforts to respond to growers' needs for cheap transportation have backfired, leaving a highly inefficient national rail system badly in need of modernization. The European Community, which forged ahead in the difficult task of rationalizing agricultural production at a considerable burden to other sectors of the economy, has had to underwrite the costs of a highly subsidized farm program. Japan's cheap yen has not assured it access to supplies in times of scarcity, nor protected it from a cutoff in foreign supplies, while rising inflation has made its protected rice program all the more costly to maintain. In centrally planned economies and less developed countries bureaucratic roadblocks and public sector inefficiencies have taken their toll on domestic agricultural programs.

In the face of these difficulties, and notwithstanding the efforts of most nations to attain agricultural independence, the United States' role remains pivotal. The struggle for self-sufficiency among deficit countries has done little to reduce their dependence on the United States. Conversely, the effort to stimulate the American agricultural economy through exports has produced its own form of dependence on foreign markets. Other major exporters now face a similar dilemma. Canada and Australia peg their minimum foreign sale prices to the bids and offers barked from the trading pit in Chicago. Brazil and other countries trade directly on U.S. commodity markets in an effort to bolster the export prices of their own crops. The entire European system of variable levies and export subsidies could not run without an international price determined in the United States. Japan's Food Agency's American wheat purchases help pay for its heavily subsidized rice program; and the Soviet Union could not have built its livestock herds so rapidly if U.S. feedgrains had not been so affordable. American food aid, with all its pitfalls, has been an essential determinant of many developing countries' agricultural economies. But dependence by others on the United States has in turn bred U.S. dependence on foreign markets that account for at least half of its annual grain production. Agricultural nationalism has created agricultural interdependence.

With the rapid growth in international grain transactions which has characterized our era has come the equally rapid growth of the trading companies that now dominate the world market. Whatever the national marketing system or policy objective, the business of buying and selling grain worldwide has fallen into the laps of these companies. For example, the Canadian Wheat Board, although a centralized public agency, is not in a position to assume handling, shipment, and delivery expenses on its foreign sales contracts. The Soviet Union cannot acquire grain on the world market at favorable commercial terms without the assistance of the private sector, whose methods of operation help conceal the identity of the buyer and the size of purchases. When Japan's Food Agency acquires wheat or barley from abroad, it cannot circumvent the country's leading trading companies without cutting across Japan's economic tradition and exposing the Food Agency to considerable risk. The European Economic Community relies on information furnished by private traders to operate its complicated levy system. Most third-world governments still lack the commercial sophistication and requisite capital to procure their food requirements directly on foreign markets.

Thus, a small cluster of companies now exercises a tremendous hold over domestic and international grain markets. In fact, overreliance by public institutions on private traders has in turn reinforced the trend toward concentration in the buying, selling, and processing of grains and oilseeds, leaving increasingly less room for producers, consumers, and independent buyers and sellers to exert any influence on the market. Instead, an oligopoly of intermediaries now claims a disproportionate share of the profits in grain production, marketing, and distribution. Dependence on the private grain traders has cost exporting and importing countries alike in terms of revenue foregone and unfavorable prices, and has made agricultural planning difficult.

Efforts to counterbalance these trading patterns via the establishment of government-run trading organizations have offered little protection. Instead, such agencies tend to reduce the flexibility once associated with an open market and suffuse every significant international agricultural transaction with potential political tension, serving only to narrow the field among government and private players. Simultaneously, there has been a growing concentration of supply in a few countries. In recent years these trends have converged, transforming what was once an assembly of diverse markets and traders into a complex power game among fewer players. The impact upon the weaker participants has been brutal. The dynamics of the grain trade no longer conform to a classic economic trade model where supply is matched with demand through efficient intermediaries. Grain prices today do not ensure deliveries any more than they accurately register market conditions in terms of supply-demand relationships. Today's international grain markets are oligopolistic in structure and are dominated by a few powerful private firms and public agencies whose behavior often does more than producers and consumers to determine prices and the availability of commodities. This development, too, is a by-product of agricultural nationalism.

Grain and power politics are now merged. Today's private transactions are often laden with international political overtones owing to direct government involvement in the market, popular sensitivities in dealing with food-related issues, and the manipulation of grain imports and exports to serve national foreign policy objectives. When, in 1980, the United States cancelled the largest American grain sale in history intended for the Soviet Union, it was intervening for express political purposes. Washington was attempting to use food as a weapon, withholding access to American grain to retaliate against the Soviet Union's invasion of Afghanistan. Similarly, the European Community awards subsidies for its wheat exports according to long-standing political and economic relationships with importing countries, while food aid has routinely been dispensed, by all the major exporters including the United

States, in accord with political objectives. Importing and exporting states have struggled relentlessly with the blunt and sharp sides of the food weapon, withholding or consummating food sales and purchases for general or explicit diplomatic purposes. If war is the extension of a nation's foreign policy, so too, it would appear, is the conduct of its international grain trade.

Nor has the trade of foodstuffs been unaffected by domestic political considerations. In the United States, for example, the farm bloc is breaking down only to be replaced with new coalitions of specialized interest groups. In this kaleidoscope of domestic farm politics, the private grain companies have been quick to capitalize on the widely accepted presumption that more foreign trade in food and feed crops is a boon to American farmers and the national economy and thereby to carve out their own niche in the policy-making process. The popularity of this position and the effectiveness of its tactics have thus far helped the grain oligopoly fend off the criticism to which the corporate oil cartel is frequently exposed.

Like the United States, other countries must respond to their own set of pressure groups, which often create a highly charged political atmosphere whose effects spill over into the international arena. Increasing reverence for the European Community's Common Agricultural Policy by supporters who see it as the European manifesto of unification has had the practical effect of likening questions concerning internal prices or import tariff levels for individual agricultural commodities to a test of the legitimacy of the European Community's constitution. Similarly, any effort to change rail transportation rates in Canada is a contentious political matter that pits traditional supporters of the board system against opponents in the ranks of the private sector. Bridging these sensitivities leaves little room for international compromise and often exaggerates conflicts stemming from inherent differences in national or regional agricultural systems. Thus the international grain trade is affected by domestic political considerations.

It is also affected by a divergence of national interests. For the Canadian or Australian systems to work, a buoyant export market is essential.[1] A downturn in international wheat prices hits producers directly. Their centralized export marketing systems focus on price stability within a range sufficiently high to guarantee producers a fair rate of return and consumers an inflation-controlled food bill. Although increasingly dependent on exports, American growers can rely on a larger domestic market plus storage and crop-reduction programs for minimal protection. For the American agricultural economy volume is as important as value. This is less true for other exporting countries, and not at all the case for France, the main wheat producer in Western Europe. Importers who have a firm set of controls for basic commodities generally share the objective of strengthening the hand of local producers, securing access to foreign supplies whenever necessary, and capping inflation.

In sum, the structure of the international grain trade needs reforming, but the obstacles to that reform are formidable. The dependence of the public sector upon a powerful, entrenched, and oligopolistic private sector, the politicization of the trade, and differences in national interests all militate against change. Nonetheless, given agreement on the need for change—if only to cope with the problems now emerging—there is hope that some common basis for cooperation can be found by the major governmental actors involved.

The United States, for example, is less wedded in fact to noninterventionism on the part of government than its official espousal of free trade would suggest. The European Community has come to recognize the costly aspects of some of its protectionist devices and the Canadian Wheat Board has demonstrated a willingness to upgrade the country's transportation system with investment in modern rail cars and a change in rates. Japan and Australia, traditionally opposed to long-term, multilateral reserve plans, officially endorsed the American international reserve proposal of 1979. Developing countries, once adamant in their rhetorical insistence on favorable reserve and foreign assistance terms, have indicated a receptiveness to alternate ways of obtaining food resources to fulfill their minimal requirements.

Nevertheless, efforts to act upon common objectives have to date consistently failed. An international reserve system that would offer a mechanism to counterbalance global supply and price fluctuations has never gained international acceptance. Coordinated food assistance programs for development purposes have fared little better. When the massive cancellation of Soviet contracts threatened to depress farmers' prices in 1980, the United States suddenly opened its concessional window to friendly recipients like Pakistan, a moderate shift in policy, but one that tended to belie an American commitment to development. Japan, faced with embarrassingly burdensome rice stocks at roughly the same time, began a food assistance program of its own, that raised American ire. The United States claimed that Japan had violated international trade rules when, in fact, the Japanese maneuver bore a striking resemblance to earlier days of American food aid. And Western Europe has remained steadfast in its attachment to its politically weighted agricultural program and heavily subsidized export system.

Protecting traditional markets at whatever cost is the spirit of the times. Crimped industrial economies and marketing systems working at cross purposes constrain governments from acting otherwise. It should not be surprising, therefore, that when the United States invoked the 1980 grain embargo against the Soviet Union, its effort to enlist the participation of other supplying countries failed in spite of international outrage over events in Afghanistan. The Soviet Union, with the assistance and schooled instruction of the giant grain trade companies, knew well how to take advantage of agricultural nationalism. Instances of international cooperation in the realm of grain policy have thus far been few and far between.

What now exists is a world in which economic and political power rather than market forces are the prime determinants which match available food supplies to demand. This structural evolution is startling in its implications for public policy and the conduct of commercial business in the field; yet institutions dealing with agricultural export issues in particular have not kept pace with the change, allowing market distortions, inefficiencies, and inequities to become commonplace. Hence the benefits of technological breakthroughs in agricultural production and distribution during the 1950s have not been fully utilized. The remainder of this book is devoted to evidence on behalf of this conclusion, and to a further consideration of its policy implications.

NOTES

1. Richard Gilmore, "Wheat and Coarse Grains—Stabilization or Status Quo?" in *A New International Commodity Regime,* ed. Geoffrey Goodwin and James Mayall (London: Croom Helm, 1979), pp. 77-85.

2

From Farm to Market: U.S. Grain Production and Distribution

The American farmer is today called upon to raise ever-increasing amounts of grain to meet a growing demand. He depends on it. And the increase in consumption on which he depends originates not at home but abroad. The market for U.S. grain extends to all continents.

Less than 30 years ago, domestic consumption of American wheat was roughly double the amount exported, but by the late 1970s the situation had reversed dramatically. In 1980/81, for example, wheat exports were 41.1 million metric tons while domestic consumption was only 21.1 million metric tons. A similar trend is evident in the consumption of soybeans and other feedgrains, although exports of these commodities have yet to equal domestic consumption (see Table 2.1).

With this increase in exports has come a significant change in the structure of grain distribution and the farmer's relationship to the consumer. The massive export sales which have pushed grain prices up faster and higher than smaller domestic purchases are to fill large foreign orders often handled by government agencies such as the Soviet Unions's Exportkhleb and the Food Agency of Japan. These agencies usually purchase enormous quantities of grain, with their minimum shipments 10,000 metric tons. Even the largest American mills or feed processors cannot match these amounts.

One immediate result of the way export purchases are made is increased risk for the producer. Today's export-oriented market is a boom or bust market. Government programs designed to shield farmers are inadequate to afford the farmer full protection from the exigencies of swiftly changing market conditions. In earlier days, the farmer had a sense of greater direct control over the prices received for his crop, which he almost always sold to local buyers. But who can negotiate a contract with a powerful buyer overseas, particularly

TABLE 2.1   U.S. Grain Production for Domestic Use and Export, by Marketing Years*
(million metric tons)

	Marketing Year	Domestic Use	Exports
Wheat	1950/51	18.8	9.4
	1980/81	21.1	41.1
Feedgrains	1950/51	109.8	6.5
	1980/81	146.9	69.4
Soybeans	1960/61	12.1	3.7
	1980/81	30.1	19.7

*The marketing year for wheat, oats, and barley begins June 1; for corn and sorghum, October 1; and for soybeans, September 1.

SOURCE: U.S. Department of Agriculture, Economic Research Service and Economics, Statistics, and Cooperative Services.

when a foreign government is involved? The farmer and the small, independent handler cannot. Both must turn to larger intermediaries to conclude export sales. Inevitably their influence over the final sales price is reduced in the process.

Times have changed for the government, too. Except for wartime and the period of the Great Depression, the federal government's involvement in the exporting of grain used to be minimal. Today the government is buyer, supersalesman, and prop for private business. As export transactions have grown larger, the political and commercial stakes have become greater and more intertwined. The merchandising of grain for foreign markets is now big business and a matter of national security.

More has changed than simply the amount of grain being exported from American shores to foreign markets. American agriculture has responded remarkably to the surge of demand from abroad, but in the process the structure of grain production and distribution in the United States has been drastically altered. Some alterations have been beneficial; others less so. The era of exports has brought prosperity to some. It has also been accompanied by an expansion in the average size of farm units, concentration in the trading and marketing sectors, and the integration of export and import operations. These developments have changed the entire complexion of the U.S. agricultural economy. They have also added to the cast of characters involved in the production and distribution of grain, and so complicated this entire process that its workings are less and less intelligible to the layman. It is, therefore, worth examining in some detail what this increase in grain exports has meant to the major actors involved.

PRODUCTION

Over the years, farming has become more efficient and individual farms have increased in size. In 1960 the average farm size was 297 acres; by 1978 this had grown to over 400 acres. Yet total farmland in use has decreased, indicating improved yield per acre of land. Average farm incomes have also improved with average net income per farm family at nearly $23,000 in 1978.[1]

The number of farms in the United States has decreased by about 50 percent over the last 25 years as farm units have increased in size.[2] Total farm debt has kept pace with skyrocketing land values rising 16 percent annually, reaching a high point of approximately $120 billion in 1977. Nonreal estate farm debt for credit to finance farm machinery, fertilizer, and other inputs in 1977 increased 20 percent over the 1976 level. The U.S. government assumed proportionately more of this indebtedness as surplus crops were kept in storage under loan from the Commodity Credit Corporation (CCC). Rural banks had to increase their loan-to-deposit ratios in 1977 beyond the levels normally considered prudent in order to satisfy the cash flow squeeze of their biggest customers—family farmers who had become perilously over-extended.[3] Despite the export boom, these farmers were running a net loss from their return on production.

The magnitude of these financial pressures is an indication of the high degree of capitalization in American agricultural production, particularly in food and feedgrains. There is, thus, a growing concern over the long-term consequences of intensive farming in the United States. American agriculture, once built on cheap factors of production, now runs on high-cost inputs, and inflated real estate values, and, consequently, on high/asset ratios.

If it were merely a question of determining the relative cost of land, labor, and capital, the conclusion might be that the exodus from farms should be accelerated. The larger, corporate-owned farm would then be encouraged to proceed in the wake of family farm foreclosures. Without addressing the social costs, there are grave uncertainties about whether such a development is the most effective means to maintain a strong agricultural economy in the United States. Pressures to move in this direction increase, nevertheless, as export markets expand and commercial risks multiply in handling large-scale transactions with foreign buyers.

TRANSPORTATION AND STORAGE

Like the American farmer, the transportation system in the United States also faces a watershed period. The demands of moving huge quantities of grain to ports all year round requires an upgrading of the existing infrastructures and regulatory reforms. This transformation has begun, ushering in new efficiencies and at the same time real social and economic costs.

Transporting grain is costly. Transportation within the United States adds approximately 10 percent to the price of corn and wheat and 5 percent to that of soybeans. International freight expenses for shipping grain to Rotterdam in the Netherlands—the most frequently used grain-trading route in the world and hence the cheapest—adds another 10 percent to the price the farmer receives for wheat and corn and less for soybeans.[4] The expense is justifiable to the seller and purchaser as long as the system provides speedy, reliable pickup and delivery.

Inland transportation is by rail, truck, or barge. Normally, grain moves by truck from the farm to a local elevator, the first point in the delivery of grain to mills or export points. Trucks are also used to haul grain to domestic processing plants or larger elevators, generally referred to as subterminals, where the grain is received and sent on by barge or rail to ports for shipment abroad. With the exception of the Great Lakes, where trucks can pick up from grain-growing areas and carry loads directly to port elevators (known as terminals) on the lakes, barges and rail cars normally are cheaper for long-distance hauls and larger cargoes.

When grain leaves the farm it goes directly into either the domestic or the export stream. The handling process is the same. The farmer unloads his crop at the local elevator, which may be independently owned, part of a cooperative, or an affiliate of a private grain trading firm. Generally, these local facilities are not adequate to accommodate entire unit-train shipments; therefore, the grain has to be moved on to a larger elevator facility, a subterminal, where rail cars or barges can load and transport these larger hauls directly to port terminals.

These subterminals have certain built-in efficiencies. Located in rural areas and aided by new feeder rail lines or improvements in other modes of transportation, they can often service producers directly. Thus in some regions these new facilities are bypassing country elevators and driving them out of business. But the construction and operating costs of such facilities are beyond the reach of smaller operators. Size is the name of the game, and there is less and less opportunity for smaller producers or grain marketers to participate.

While rail is the most widely used grain carrier, barge loadings have increased in the last few years, particularly for feedgrains. In 1976 barge shipments to export terminals made up 40 percent of all deliveries, compared with 44 percent by rail.[5] Most barge traffic is on the Mississippi River to New Orleans and the Columbia River to Portland, Oregon—the main waterway arteries in the United States—where corn and soybeans are the big crops.[6]

Barge transportation rates have been low historically because the American taxpayer funds the Army Corps of Engineers, which maintains the U.S. waterway network. Barge rates as a rule have been more competitive than truck rates, even though maintenance for highways is also drawn from public funds. The main advantage of barge trafficking is the relatively low fuel cost. Barges can take smaller loads than rail cars, thereby reducing the pickup charges to smaller elevator owners and to farmers using these or comparable facilities belonging to co-ops. Barge transportation is still a relatively open, competitive industry, ·one that in theory should be characterized by price competition. In 1980 some 1,800 barge companies were registered in the

United States with no single firm or small group of firms dominating the market.

The biggest drawback to barge transportation is the seasonal limitation. In winter, the Mississippi is partially frozen, limiting access to the big user states in the north. During the drought of 1980 the river was too shallow to accommodate an average boat, fully loaded. Portions of the waterway system need widening for the more modern barges now in use.

Given the strengths and weaknesses of barge, truck, and rail transportation, it is clearly advantageous to have access to all three forms. In this respect the United States is all but unique, having relatively efficient transportation networks of all three types. The development of this triad which was essential to the conduct of domestic, interstate commerce in grain has resulted in a capability that is now ideally suited to service foreign trade as well. It is worth asking, however, whether efforts to service that trade do not also tighten further the economic squeeze on family farmers and reinforce the trend toward concentration in the production and merchandising of grain.

Shipping grain starts at the port where it is unloaded from rail cars or barges into huge terminal facilities. The grain goes by means of elevated conveyor belts into large bins, each having a minimum storage capacity of 10 million bushels. Grain is rarely stored at these terminal points for any length of time; there is more profit in moving it rapidly through elevators and loading it onto waiting ships. Port terminals are not generally the largest storage facilities because they are designed to move a large volume of incoming and outgoing grain fast. For example, one grain-exporting company owns an elevator in Chicago that can store as much as 23 million bushels of grain. On the other hand, in New Orleans, the largest grain port in the United States, the average storage capacity of any single terminal is 5 to 6 million bushels.[7] Their average throughput capacity is as great as 60,000 to 70,000 bushels per hour, however, which means they can unload a car or barge and fill ships with this quantity in one hour.

Ocean vessels have an average carrying capacity of 20,000 metric tons. They are tankers and very often are used interchangeably for transporting grains, oil, coal, iron ore, and cars. An ideal run for a shipowner is to have grain loaded at a port like New Orleans destined for either Rotterdam or Tokyo, with a return voyage transporting cars or other manufactured goods to the United States. The commercial advantage is that the ship arrives at an American port with a full load of cargo requiring minimum preparation before reloading.

In response to the demand for imported oil in 1973-74, owners of ocean vessels contracted with shipbuilders for larger tankers. Grain traders were also in the market, chartering for extended periods oil tankers, which could serve as grain carriers more economically than smaller vessels to long-distance markets in Europe and Japan. The market has since reversed itself, and a glut of tankers now floats on the high seas. The demand for oil was not as great as expected from 1975 to 1979 in the big oil-importing countries. To take advantage of the resulting oversupply of tankers and bargain short-term rates, grain traders shifted positions, chartering tankers by the voyage. This was a logical move for big international firms in the grain trade, but the extensive use of larger vessels meant higher commercial risks, which, once again, only the largest traders could afford.

International ocean freight rates for grain are also an advantage to larger traders and a disadvantage to smaller ones. At present, grain, along with other commodities, is regarded as "tramp tonnage," and its shipping rates are both unregulated and subject to fluctuation with changing market conditions. These rates, however, always favor larger volume shipments, thus placing smaller buyers and sellers at a disadvantage. Further, because grain traffic is heaviest in the United States-Europe-Japan triangle, grain-shipping rates favor routes between New Orleans, Rotterdam-Amsterdam-Antwerp-Hamburg, and Tokyo. In fact, the price of grain shipped from the United States to foreign ports is based on the cost of shipment to Rotterdam, the largest export-import port, and current rates favor American and Canadian producers. One consequence of this situation is that developing countries generally pay more for delivered grain from the United States than the Japanese. Therefore they are doubly disadvantaged by the terms of the grain trade. As smaller customers, they have less clout in the marketplace. Further, they will typically have to pay more for delivered grain than the more affluent Japanese or Europeans, even though the distance shipped from point of origin in the United States may, in fact, be shorter.

FARMER COOPERATIVES

As exports have become a critical factor in the U.S. agricultural economy, the role of cooperatives has come to a crossroad. Traditionally, they have attempted to be for farmers what labor unions were in theory for workers, allowing individual growers to compete collectively for a fair return on their production. When the bulk of the grain harvest was consumed domestically, the cooperative's primary task was to organize handling, distribution, and marketing at a local level. Now they are contemplating appropriate ways to launch effective export operations. The bulk of their operations, however, continue to be domestic.

Nonetheless, cooperatives are no longer smalltime operations. In 1975 there were approximately 7,500 co-ops and their collective membership was roughly 6 million, or three-fourths of the farm population, and they registered a total net business volume of over $42 billion.[8] Farmer co-ops resemble conglomerate enterprises; they embrace numerous local and state co-ops through a hierachy of financial and contractual relations. Some of the larger co-ops, like Farmland Industries or Farmers Union Grain Terminal Association, retain autonomous management and coordinating responsibilities with local cooperatives acting largely as stockholders in the central organization.

At present, co-ops account for about 40 percent of all off-farm sales of grain at the first-handler level and approximately 29 percent of export grain to final ports in the United States.[9] They have gradually improved their share of the grain export market over the last few years, but their real growth has been in handling grain and soybean transactions up to the phase of actual export. International grain trading intimidates even the largest co-ops because of the risks, complexities, and commercial barriers posed by the larger private exporting firms.

In spite of these hurdles, larger co-ops such as Far-Mar-Co, a subsidiary of Farmland Industries, do have a foot in the export door. In 1976 four co-ops handled 9.2 percent of U.S. wheat exports; three handled 8.2 percent of feedgrain exports; and three were responsible for 9.0 percent of exported soybeans.[10] These figures suggest a slow growth in the co-ops' share of the booming American agricultural export business. They handle almost half the initial domestic market transactions for grains, soybeans, and soybean products, compared with less than 10 percent of the export market. Measured another way, the co-ops' grain export business has grown from 220 million bushels in fiscal 1973 to 387 million bushels in fiscal 1976, but their share of the total export pie has grown only one percentage point over that period.[11] Even this figure is misleading because co-ops rarely handle an export sale door-to-door. They resort to private merchant services to cover actual shipments or enter into formal joint ventures with competing private companies.

GRAIN TRADING COMPANIES

The private grain trading companies control the majority of links in the agricultural chain. The farther downstream grain moves, the more predominant is the role these firms play. Although their role in marketing and processing grain within the United States has grown considerably over time, the bulk of their grain business is international. The grain traders have earned their reputations through specialization in the importing and exporting of grain on a worldwide scale. In the United States, for example, nearly 70 percent (the percentage varies by commodity) of the grain moving downstream for export is in the private, noncooperative sector by the time it is unloaded at the port terminal.

A major difference between the grain trading companies and co-ops is that the trading companies generally do not engage in production nor do they invest extensively in country elevators. Similarly, the trading companies, unlike co-ops which offer their members a commitment to purchase crops at a guaranteed minimum price and then to market them and distribute the profits or losses, have no formal links to producers and rarely purchase grain directly from farmers on a contract basis. The objective of the trading companies is to purchase grain supplies at the lowest possible price in a highly competitive market in order to sell in a market that they virtually dominate. In this way they gain the advantages of oligopsony as well as oligopoly power, and any effort to engage extensively in contract or direct corporate-run farming might well jeopardize the relations with American farmers and cooperatives on which the traders for access to grain which they did not produce.

Companies are much less timid about entering the next phase of the agricultural chain—inland grain handling and processing. Private grain trading firms own a majority of subterminal space in the United States,[12] but a minority percentage of country elevators. Subterminals allow the big grain trading firms to take possession of bulk quantities of grain, which enables them to fill large domestic or export orders from readily available inventories and to provide storage space under safe, efficient handling conditions.

Large grain traders, both private and cooperative, have also carved out an important role for themselves as processors, direct consumers of the grain they buy. Integration, a logical outgrowth of commercial accretion, aptly characterizes contemporary trends in the trade. Some firms have the largest mills in the world as affiliates. They may also manufacture feed, which they use in their own cattle feedlots as well as for sale to other users. A number of firms manufacture an array of soybean and other oilseed by-products while maintaining their principal line of business in the grain trade. Processing plants now play a critical role in the overall profit picture of individual grain exporters, especially the multinationals. Such plants may serve as "end-users" for grain purchased by any grain trading firm, but more frequently they give preferential treatment to the trading house with which they are affiliated.

Commercially, it is even more advantageous for private firms to have processing plants in foreign markets. When a company selling grain is affiliated with a foreign purchaser, the importer has an opportunity to purchase under flexible terms and undoubtedly at rates below the market. This is not true for firms with more limited operations.

Conversely, having an important facility—either an actual grain-processing plant of an import-export company—in a foreign country can offer commercial advantages from the exporter's point of view. Such an arrangement can provide sure buyers for the related exporting company's grain. Having affilitates in food exporting countries other than the United States offers yet other advantages. In particular, it helps keep the world's supply lines open, enabling the international grain giants to satisfy their customers, among which are their own subsidiary firms. Global integration on this scale helps ensure profitability.

The grain traders are also heavily involved in the operation and leasing of port elevators. Notwithstanding their commercial importance and the fact that they are owned and run by large private firms, port elevators are frequently semipublic facilities. Traders lease the land on which such elevators are constructed from the state, county, or municipality; actual construction costs in some instances are covered by public, insured bonds. The Federal Trade Commission found in 1923 that there was an inherently anticompetitive aspect to leasing grain terminals located at American ports: ". . . seaport facilities are so limited that all exporters must use them, and if they are leased to private operators, then the exporters who depend for their export facilities on the ports must put their grain through elevators handled by private competitors, and without any choice of selection."[13] Of 86 elevators located in major U.S. ports, only 13 are owned by cooperatives, and even the latter frequently sell the grain in their bins to international private shippers.

Finally, the grain trading companies are masters of the arcane world of commerce which constitutes the international grain transport system. Physically, the process of transfer is fairly straightforward. Grain is loaded from port elevators onto waiting ships and then transported to its destination. But between the initial purchase order and the final sale, the cargo may change hands several times, frequently between companies affiliated with one another. It is not uncommon to establish what the commercial lexicon refers to as a "string" of sales before shipment to the final destination. In such cases, the interchange of sellers and buyers may include international speculators and brokers, as well as companies that initiate the string, entering and later withdrawing from the same contract. These transactions do not improve the efficient handling of U.S. grain exports, but they do help to assure companies of securing additional quantities of grain at prices they otherwise could not obtain.

Single or multiple sales leaving from ports in the Gulf of Mexico, the largest export point for U.S. grains, are generally sold free on board (f.o.b.)—without shipping or related expenses included. The shipper then assumes the freight and service costs, including insurance for the cargo. In a full package deal the costs of shipment services, cargo insurance, and the freight itself are included; this is a cost, insurance, freight (c.i.f.) contract. In general, Gulf prices are on an f.o.b. basis with shipments destined for Western Europe because nonaffiliated European buyers (as well as affiliates of American firms) prefer to handle directly the remaining phases of the transaction. C.i.f. business, or a variation of this kind of contract, can be extremely profitable for traders with little direct participation in the big domestic markets of supplying countries. With a c.i.f. contract from the West Coast of the United States to Japan the shipper and domestic buyer are usually one and the same—the giant, highly integrated Japanese trading companies. The Gulf is the f.o.b. market and Rotterdam is the c.i.f. market of the world. These two basket prices are key terms in the language of the world grain trade.

Once freight is on board, the next step is to determine shipment destination. Shippers fill out a government customs form, designating the destination of their cargo, but this information does not always coincide with the final delivery. Total annual Gulf-origin exports to Rotterdam, for example, exceed actual imports for internal Dutch consumption. Thus, a load destined for Rotterdam may, in fact, be broken down into smaller units for shipment on barges down the Rhine or transshipped to points eastward. At the time of declaration, there is no way to confirm where commerical cargo will ultimately land, despite the economic and political importance of this information.

Grain profits depend on market flexibility. Unverifiable shipping destinations are one way to achieve this objective. Another way is through tolerance regulations, which are designed to account for changes in freight loads necessitated by unpredictable shipping conditions. These regulations are determined by an accepted contract form designed by a trade-run organization, the Grain and Feed Trade Association (GAFTA). To allow for varying conditions of the ship's load, a captain is generally permitted to take 5 percent more or less cargo—the tolerance threshold—than is allowed for in the contract. In commercial terms, this means the buyer may be obliged to buy the 5 percent margin at current market prices, which are often higher than the price agreed upon at the time of the sale. The resulting shortfall or gain for one transaction can be considerable. Rarely do accomplished shippers end up on the losing side.

COMMODITY EXCHANGES

Buyers and sellers use commodity exchanges to reduce their risks and improve their profits on any transaction. Because of its predominant position in the world grain market and its relatively open trading system, the United States is the hub of world hedging and speculation in agricultural commodities. There are three principal exchanges for grain in the United States: the Chicago Board of Trade, the Minneapolis Grain Exchange, and the Kansas City Board of Trade. Each specializes in certain commodities: Chicago, the largest of the three, deals principally in wheat, corn, and soybeans; Kansas City is the center for hard red winter wheat, Minneapolis for durum and dark northern spring wheats. Minneapolis and Kansas City are principally cash markets; the prices quoted there are intended to represent valid purchase orders at farmgate as opposed to futures prices. All three exchanges have developed additional price categories as a response to changes in trade practices. These may be nothing more than phantom or nominal prices, but their importance has become such that they are key words in the language of a burgeoning unsupervised trader's market.

Chicago's major market contribution is in futures prices. Its major commercial objective is to allow grain buyers and sellers—farmers, processors, merchandisers, foreign importing companies, and foreign government trading companies—to hedge against the price and supply risks they incur. Trading entities need to know that they will obtain their requisite quantity of grain at a predictable price, with a minimum cost for undertaking the transaction. One way they can obtain this assurance is via a futures contract executed at least three months in advance of the actual delivery date and offset by spot purchases or sales at the existing daily futures price. Taking out both a short, i.e., a spot or cash, and a long futures contract will reduce any risk to zero if the timing is right. By selling short and buying a long futures contract, the buyer can cover himself in the event the market swings upward. Conversely, by reducing his long position and making spot or cash purchases, the buyer can bet successfully, or hedge, against a bearish longer term.

The most ardent proponents of the present exchange system argue that it is the only true market mechanism left in the international agricultural chain. It is certainly true that without these exchanges there would be little opportunity for buyers and sellers to shop around for the most favorable prices, risk insured, and to calculate an appropriate value for a given transaction. What is clear, however, is that the influence of these exchanges is worldwide; the world's agricultural chain rattles when the Board in Chicago posts its prices. American producers look at the trend in Chicago futures as a firm indication of what demand will be for grain in the upcoming crop year, or what they can expect if they sell any surplus grain they may be holding in storage during the current marketing season.

Cash prices are theoretically pegged to spot prices in Chicago, and both are pegged to longer futures contracts. Similarly, traders in Minneapolis or Kansas City synchronize their purchases and sales to a large extent with price performance in Chicago. Prices tend to be harmonized among them, with any differentials reflecting relative transportation costs from one region to another. Ultimately, all these prices converge into what has become the international price for traded grains, the Chicago price. Chicago is unrivaled as the grain-pricing leader of the world. Foreign governments either directly or indirectly use Chicago. In so doing they can successfully hedge their crops or importing requirements against international price trends registered on American exchanges. Conversely, they can play the market to force up prices in commodities where they may hold a momentary advantage over those exporters.

Yet another exchange, the Chicago Mercantile Exchange, has begun to play an important role in the grain trade as a result of developments in international currency markets. It began to do so when the last remaining link between the price of gold and the value of the dollar was severed by the Nixon administration in 1971. At that time, every expectation was that the new arrangement, in which the dollar's value was expressed in terms of other currencies, would involve a modest adjustment in the relative values of different international currencies. The actual consequences of a freely floating system of exchange rates were far greater than anticipated. By 1978-79, in the wake of the oil embargo and the subsequent economic slowdown in the industrialized world, the dollar was cast off, very much at sea, and barely floating.

As a result, the grain export business grew riskier and more complicated. Virtually all grain transactions, whether they involve purchases of grain originating in the United States or elsewhere, are conducted in dollars. Although a little worn, the dollar remains the international passport currency for grain. With fairly wide daily fluctuations in the value of the dollar, a trader now has to engage in arbitrage—nonspeculative buying and selling of alternate currencies—synchronized with any spot and long futures position he may hold. Otherwise, the dollar gain from a well-placed hedge or a contract involving purchases or payments in foreign currencies could evaporate into losses if the dollar fell while other currencies appreciated before the grain transaction had been consummated. Then nondollar purchases would result in windfall profits, irrespective of the U.S. grain price—a recurring advantage to Japanese and European buyers (including well-placed foreign affiliates of U.S. firms).

The Chicago Mercantile Exchange (also called the International Monetary Market), the principal U.S. center for currency trading other than American commercial banks, registered a 166 percent increase in currency contracts during 1978.[14] While anyone can in theory trade on the "Merc," the chances of an average farmer taking out a futures contract in pound sterling, German marks, or Japanese yen are slim. This is not true for the grain trader, for whom the commercial risks of an open position unhedged against currency fluctuations are significant. If American grain were bought and sold strictly within the United States, relative currency valuations would not be as relevant to the trade. With the dominance of U.S. grain exports and the dollar worldwide, however, monetary movements have become hooked up to the agricultural chain.

FINANCE

The world of finance constitutes still another link in the agricultural chain. Credit availability has always been extremely important in financing American agricultural production. Soaring credit demands are easily explained by the real rise in costs of farm production. What is much harder to calculate is the total of commerical loans and lines of credit used for financing hedging, marketing, and distribution phases in the grain trade. On an average day in Chicago, the total volume of trading at the Board of Trade alone is 150,000 contracts. Since as much as 75 percent of the value of all grains and soybeans can be purchased on margin accounts, a prudent buyer would need ample credit to cover the total cost. With the trend toward larger individual contracts and unlimited transactions on commodity and currency markets, the financial stakes rise proportionately.

The number of contracts a company has in hand determines how its assets are calculated. Expert bankers estimate that almost 90 percent of a grain trader's assets lie in the contracts that commercial banks utilize in evaluating the firm's loan requirements. Larger export-import houses naturally have more contracts, and greater credit needs, than smaller operators. Accordingly, banks have to earmark greater funds for loans to the largest trading houses, whose clients are writing contracts for greater and greater amounts. It is riskier for banks to devote more funds to fewer clients because of the possibility of default. Commercial banks have ignored this potential danger while raising loan levels to service the increasing volume of grain transactions conducted by these firms.

Modernization of grain merchandising has raised capital investment ratios one step higher. Construction costs for subterminals and port elevators are mounting; loans are needed to rent hopper railroad cars or barges; bank financing is usually used for chartering ocean vessels. Virtually every phase in the agricultural chain involves substantial capital, which increasingly can be raised only by the largest firm.

GOVERNMENT

Government remains the first and last link in the agricultural chain. Grain does not move from field to market through the magic of Adam Smith's "invisible hand." Instead, government is a principal in all phases of the grain trade from its origination on the farms to final delivery. No group in the agricultural chain, including the largest grain merchants, could prosper without some government assistance.

Government standards for the quality and weighing of grain may help determine the price farmers actually receive. A producer may be offered a given price for a specified quality of grain and actually receive a premium or a discount, depending upon official standards for delivered grain. Buyers are similarly affected. The price they pay also depends upon quality and weight. Producers, merchandisers, warehousemen, processors, and consumers in the United States all accept the fact that enforceable standards for quality and tight regulation of weighing devices and procedures are in their interest.

The U.S. government, accordingly, has administered an inspection system for the application of official quality and weight standards for grain ever since passage of the Grain Standards Act of 1916. Now all grain moving in the export stream must pass Federal Grain Inspection Service (FGIS) authorized inspection for quality and weight. Washington's range of responsibilities in grain standards places it dead center in the grain trade.

In administering an inspection system for weights and standards, the government becomes a kind of arbiter of justice. When it regulates the flow and direction of exports, the government is more a spigot that a scale. Given its broad authority over commodity exports, it can determine whether grain should even be sold on international markets. A number of times in American commercial history, Washington has suspended foreign sales, declared an embargo on exports, and halted shipments. It can restrict sales to individual countries and thus selectively discriminate against certain buyers. Conversely, it enters into agreements that afford countries preferential treatment.

When the government clamps down on exports to lower prices to the American consumer and help control inflation, it generally resorts to one of three approaches: embargoes, quotas, or licensing. When there are shortages in one or more commodities, an embargo on sales and shipments of the affected commodities is the most likely approach. With moderate shortages, which require less Draconian measures than a total embargo, a licensing system to allow quotas for shippers and buyers is the preferred response. When political objectives are at stake, the government has a well-fashioned tool: selective embargoes. The blackball list may change, depending on shifting diplomatic sands. Shortages come and go. The American export control system is supposed to be more permanent, fully prepared to meet changing economic and political circumstances.

Administering this system on top of its other agricultural responsibilities puts the federal government out front as the supersalesperson of the nation, with an array of programs aimed at developing markets for U.S. grain. Export promotion devices open the spigot wide, while controls, in theory, can turn the faucet off. In both cases the purpose is the same—advancing U.S. economic and foreign policy goals.

The government's primary market promotion tool is Public Law 480, the Food for Peace program. Since its inception in 1954, PL 480 has provided an outlet in less-developed countries for American agricultural surpluses. While there was definitely a need for food in these countries to counter hunger and malnutrition, the United States was not motivated only by humanitarian concerns. New outlets had to be found for American grain surpluses after American relief efforts were completed in Europe as part of the postwar European Recovery Program and the Korean War had ended. The less developed countries were the most obvious targets, offering fertile new markets for U.S. commodities. PL 480 was the ideal vehicle.

In 1978 an official task force undertook a major study of U.S. food aid programs to assess their economic and political contribution after a quarter of a century in existence. In its report, which was far from critical, the group endorsed PL 480's past contribution and recommended only modest changes over time:

> In sum, meeting humanitarian needs and encouraging long-term agricultural and economic development in developing countries have been elevated from minor to major goals of the U.S. food aid program. At the same time, expanding agricultural trade and building and maintaining commercial markets for U.S. agricultural commodities abroad remain important to the program. Food aid also remains a means for achieving foreign policy objectives. *With the return to generally ample world supplies of grain and lower prices, food aid could play a larger role in domestic supply management.*[15]

The program remains primarily a trade promotion and foreign policy device and, to a lesser extent, an economic development tool. There are two main elements in the program—concessional sales and grants. PL 480 provides for food donations and the sale of agricultural commodities to developing countries on a long-term credit basis, repayable in dollars or local currencies convertible into dollars.

In both cases the U.S. government is the buyer. It either draws from its own stocks or buys grain on the open market to satisfy its PL 480 commitments. It is, in an indirect sense, also the seller. When grants are involved, the transaction is between Washington, private voluntary organizations, and the shipper that offers the best delivery terms. When handling concessional sales, the U.S. government offers loans to recipient countries, which in turn assume responsibility for their shipments. In both instances, the United States behaves as a grain merchant and, thus, as a critical link in the U.S. agricultural chain.

To coax people to buy American when grain from other countries may be cheaper, the United States has in the past offered export subsidies to make the American grain price competitive. Between 1949 and 1973, the last year the subsidy was applied, the U.S. Department of Agriculture paid a total of $4.3 billion in subsidies, applied to 10.5 billion bushels of wheat.[16] The authority to use subsidies still exists, but conditions have not required their reintroduction. Their use in the past, however, was critical in allowing the United States to corner the world grain trade.

Export credit sales are still another way in which U.S. surpluses move into the export stream. The difference in approach between commercial export financing and export subsidies is that the latter apply across the board, offering the same advantage to traders and foreign purchasing agencies alike. Export credits are short- and medium-term financing of commercial sales (as opposed to the longer-term credit arrangements under PL 480) and are offered to countries or private foreign buyers on an individual basis. Both approaches serve to increase American grain exports above the amount that would occur if there were not these "sweeteners" for foreign buyers.

When export demand is sluggish by comparison to domestic production, the federal government is promptly called upon to take remedial action. Government-held stocks have periodically played a critical role for farmers and the private trade. Production controls, income supports, crop insurance, and other programs figure directly into the agricultural sector. Apart from initiatives prompted by those groups most directly affected, Washington continues to flirt with the idea of transforming its comparative advantage in agriculture into a food weapon in foreign policy. In such cases, the government must have the cooperation of the private sector, multinationally based, and the American farmer.

Under the circumstances, the American agricultural chain is closely linked with a combination of economic and political forces. Grain in the United States, and in most other countries, is not merely grown and delivered to market. It is hedged and speculated against, linked to international currency alignments, and even constitutes a source of economic and political warfare. The fact that people eat grain seems incidental.

NOTES

1. U.S. Department of Agriculture, *A Time to Choose: Summary Report on the Structure of Agriculture* (Washington, D.C.: U.S. Government Printing Office, January 1981), pp. 42-44.

2. U.S. Department of Agriculture, *Agricultural Statistics 1977* (Washington, D.C.: U.S. Government Printing Office, 1977), p. 471.

3. Federal Reserve Bank of Chicago, "Agricultural Credit 1977/78," March 1978, p. 2.

4. U.S. Department of Agriculture, ECS Research Report 34, *Improving the Export Capability of Grain Cooperatives*, (Washington, D.C.: Farmer Cooperative Service, June 1976) pp. 30-39.

5. U.S. Department of Agriculture, Agricultural Marketing Service, "Grain Market News," 1980-81.

6. American Waterways Operators, Inc., *Inland Waterborne Commerce Statistics 1974* (Washington, D.C.: American Waterways Operators, 1975).

7. U.S. Department of Agriculture, Federal Grain Inspection Service, "List of Export Elevators in Each Grain Division Field Office Circuit," 18 May 1978.

8. U.S. Department of Agriculture, Farmer Cooperative Service, *Statistics of Farmer Cooperatives, 1974-75*, FCS Research Report 39 (April 1977), iv, 2 and 9.

9. Data supplied by the Cooperative Program, Economics, Statistics, and Cooperatives Service, U.S. Department of Agriculture. Also refer to U.S. Department of Agriculture, Farmer Cooperative Service, *Improving the Export Capability of Grain Cooperatives*, FCS Research Report 34 (June 1976), iv.

10. Donald E. Hirsch, "Cooperatives Directly Export $2 Billion in Farm Products," *Farmer Cooperatives*, 45 (May 1978): 9.

11. U.S. Department of Agriculture, Farmer Cooperative Service, *Regional Grain Cooperatives: 1974 and 1975*, FCS Service Report 150 (August 1976), Table 2; and U.S. Department of Agriculture, Economics, Statistics, and Cooperatives Service, *Regional Grain Cooperatives: 1976 and 1977*, Farmer Cooperative Research Report 6 (April 1979), p. 13, Table 4.

12. A study of elevator ownership in 12 midwestern states indicated that as early as 1968, six major grain exporters owned 3.3 percent of the country elevators located there, compared to 30 percent of the terminal elevators. Monte E. Juillerat and Paul L. Farris, "Grain Export Industry Organization and Facilities in the United States," Research Progress Report 390 (Lafayette: Purdue University, Agricultural Experiment Station, August 1971), pp. 7 and 12.

13. U.S. Federal Trade Commission, *Report on Methods and Operations of Grain Exporters*, 2 vols. (Washington, D.C.: U.S. Government Printing Office, 1922-23), vol. 2: *Speculation, Competition and Prices*, p. xl.

14. "C.M.E. Trading Volume for '78 Climbs 92% to 15.2 Million," *Milling & Baking News*, 23 January 1979, p. 38.

15. *New Directions for U.S. Food Assistance: A Report of the Special Task Force on the Operation of Public Law 480 to the U.S. Secretary of Agriculture*, May 1978, pp. 2-3. Italics added.

16. U.S. General Accounting Office, *Russian Wheat Sales and Weakness in Agriculture's Management of Wheat Export Subsidy Program*, B-176943, 9 July 1973, p. 1.

3

The Grain Traders:
Who They Are

THE BIG LEAGUE

Companies that hold the lion's share of world traffic in grain are monuments to commercial enterprise. The largest private traders have expanded and diversified their operations to cover a broad reach of business activities, but in most cases global grain merchandising is still the underpinning of their success. The guiding principle is to sell high volumes of grain anywhere to anyone.

Some private export-import houses are among the oldest corporate concerns in the history of international commerce. Still owned by their founding families, they continue to ride the crest of growing world demand for food.[1] Today's front-running firms were once local operations nestled in the smaller trading centers of Europe. Now they are global giants, based in all principal importing and exporting countries and with the capability to move grain supplies worldwide. In fact, the largest grain houses generate their own demand. Their biggest business does not come from sales to unrelated companies, but from affiliate transactions that are part of a web of vertically and horizontally integrated operations.

The Big League traders dominate the international grain trade, which is today a highly concentrated industry in which the six largest firms account for 96 percent of U.S. wheat exports, 95 percent of U.S. corn exports, and 90 and 80 percent respectively of U.S. oat and sorghum exports. Since at least the early 1920s when the Federal Trade Commission (FTC) reported significant concentration in the industry, the trend toward dominance of the industry by its largest members has continued to the point where the six largest firms—Cargill, Continental, Dreyfus, Bunge, Garnac, and Mitsui/Cook—now account for a larger proportion of U.S. grain exports than the 36 largest firms did in 1921.[2] (See Figure 3.1 and Table 3.1.) The difference is that today these

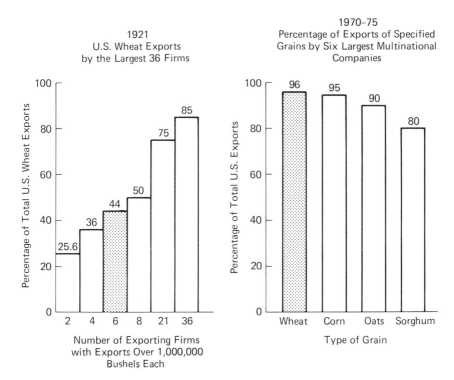

FIGURE 3.1   Company Participation in U.S. Grain Exports 1921 and 1970–75 Compared.

half dozen largest firms dominate not just the domestic but the international grain trade.

Cargill, Inc.

The largest member of the grain establishment is Cargill, Inc. Once a family-owned country elevator in Conover, Iowa, the firm grew impressively, establishing a secure base in storage, transportation, and finance. World War II was its springboard into the export business. At that point Cargill entered the class of well-established, international grain houses. Cargill among others handled wheat and flour shipments under the postwar European Recovery Program (ERP), which enabled them to nurture potential commercial buyers and learn the complexities of exporting grain while making substantial profits without risk. When the European economies recovered, the Big League traders, having gained experience from postwar relief programs, were well equipped to handle European import and intrastate transactions.

Typical of the trade, Cargill depends on high sales volumes, profits, and capital resources to sustain its vast operations and accelerated investment program worldwide. Cargill earned a net income of $121 million from sales of $11.6 billion for the fiscal year ended May 31, 1978.[3] Between 1965 and 1975

TABLE 3.1 U.S. Exports of Selected Commodities by Big League Exporters 1970–74 (million metric tons)

	Marketing Year[a]					Calendar Year[a]							Fiscal Year[a]		
		CARGILL		CONTINENTAL			DREYFUS		BUNGE		GARNAC			COOK INDUSTRIES	
	U.S. Total (marketing year)	Company Exports	% of U.S. Total	Company Exports	% of U.S. Total	U.S. Total (calendar year)	Company Exports/Sales[b]	% of U.S. Total	Company Exports/Sales[b]	% of U.S. Total	Company Exports/Sales[b]	% of U.S. Total	U.S. Total (fiscal year)	Company Sales[b]	% of U.S. Total
						CY 1970							**FY 1970**		
Wheat				3.18	18	17.44	(S) 1.24	7	.77	4	(S) .37	2	19.93	1.38	7
Corn				2.88	20	14.38	.36	2	1.45	10	.48	3	13.08	2.22	17
Soybeans				2.31	19	11.95	.42	3	NA[c]	NA	.53	4	11.56	1.57	14
Barley				.57	49	1.16	.06	5	.21	18	.02	1	1.80	—	—
Sorghum				.20	5	3.76	.16	4	.56	14	.05	1	4.20	.97	23
Oats				.01	4	.23	.01	4	.02	8	.01	4	.26	—	—
Total				9.15	18	48.92	2.25	4	3.01	6	1.46	2	50.83	6.14	12
	MY 1971–72					**CY 1971**							**FY 1971**		
Wheat	17.20	5.30	30	3.17	19	16.22	(S) .88	5	.81	4	(S) .52	3	16.91	2.68	16
Corn	20.20	2.90	14	9.96	77	12.87	.29	2	.64	4	.80	6	16.72	1.53	9
Soybeans	11.30	3.00	26	2.16	18	11.54	.49	4	1.51	13	.48	4	11.74	1.92	16
Barley	1.10	.43	39	.21	18	1.11	.06	5	.15	13	.13	11	1.02	.07	7
Sorghum	3.10	.71	22	.38	13	2.82	.10	3	.42	14	.02	0	2.64	.49	19
Oats	.34	—	0	.05	83	.06	—	0	—	0	—	0	.33	—	—
Total	53.24	12.34	23	8.93	20	44.62	1.82	4	3.53	7	1.95	4	49.36	6.69	14
	MY 1972–73					**CY 1972**							**FY 1972**		
Wheat	32.30	9.20	28	4.95	23	21.32	(E) 2.12	9	.76	3	(S) .93	4	31.77	2.47	8
Corn	31.90	5.00	15	6.11	27	22.36	1.61	7	1.68	7	.79	3	28.89	1.99	7
Soybeans	13.00	2.90	22	2.06	18	11.20	.78	6	1.07	9	.59	5	13.75	1.76	13
Barley	1.40	.65	46	.67	53	1.25	—	0	.06	4	.01	0	1.32	.20	15
Sorghum	5.30	1.20	22	.44	11	3.82	.27	7	.30	7	.02	0	4.86	.50	10
Oats	.32	.01	3	.25	75	.33	—	0	—	0	—	0	.29	—	—
Total	84.22	18.96	22	14.48	24	60.28	4.78	7	3.87	6	2.34	3	80.88	6.92	9

TABLE 3.1 (Continued)

	MY 1973–74						CY 1973						FY 1973		
Wheat	31.20	9.40	30	37.44	8.71	23	(S) 5.73	15	2.34	6	(S) 2.83	7	31.25	3.93	13
Corn	31.50	5.10	16	33.14	7.56	22	2.19	6	3.63	10	1.41	4	34.85	2.88	8
Soybeans	14.70	2.60	17	13.22	2.48	18	.55	4	1.18	8	.77	5	14.05	3.56	25
Barley	1.90	.80	42	1.99	.44	22	.09	4	.45	22	.01	0	1.91	.11	6
Sorghum	5.90	1.30	22	5.59	.43	7	.18	3	.70	12	.05	0	6.21	.64	10
Oats	.84	.32	38	.72	.08	11	.10	13	.24	33	.03	4	.82	—	—
Total	86.04	19.52	22	92.10	19.70	21	8.84	9	8.54	9	5.10	5	89.09	11.12	12

	MY 1974–75						CY 1974						FY 1974		
Wheat	28.30	7.40	26	25.13	5.84	23	(E) 6.25	24			(E) 2.46	9	28.29	4.82	17
Corn	29.20	5.80	19	29.80	6.37	21	3.05	10			1.88	6	28.38	4.27	15
Soybeans	12.60	2.50	19	13.94	2.92	20	1.60	11			.69	4	11.01	2.46	22
Barley	.87	.37	42	1.18	.31	26	.30	25			NA	NA	.85	.41	48
Sorghum	5.40	1.40	25	5.69	.29	5	.22	3			NA	NA	4.87	1.16	24
Oats	.15	.13	86	.40	.05	12	.12	30			NA	NA	.16	—	—
Total	76.52	17.60	23	76.14	15.78	20	11.54	15			5.03	7	73.56	13.12	18

aData on company exports and sales were collected from several different sources and thus were not comparable in all cases. For Cargill, export data are for marketing years, while for Continental, Dreyfus, Bunge, and Garnac, data are for calendar years. Percentages are based on the appropriate marketing or calendar year. For Cook, the available data are for its fiscal year, beginning June 1. While the available export data for the U.S. are for fiscal year beginning July 1, percentages are based on these slightly different fiscal years.

bFor Bunge and Cook, export data were not available, so volumes of grain sales to foreign countries were used as a substitute. For Dreyfus and Garnac, export data were available for only selected years. When not available, sales figures were substituted. To distinguish between sources of data, an (S) indicates sales data and an (E), export data.

cNA indicates that data is not available for use in the table; it does not imply that no exports were made for those particular commodities.

Source: U.S. Congress, Senate Committee on Foreign Relations, *Multinational Corporations and United States Foreign Policy.* Hearings before the Subcommittee on Multinational Corporations, 94th Cong., 2d sess., Jì Part 16, and various trade data.

Cargill's consolidated earnings grew from approximately $8 million to $250 million; assets in property, plant, and equipment increased fivefold, moving from the $130 million range to well over $600 million.

Even its huge earnings are not enough to service a firm of Cargill's size and diversity. Large grain trading enterprises require vast amounts of credit. Cargill is no exception. It depends on huge amounts of short-term capital to finance its grain operations as well as increasingly large credit resources to cover its wide range of fixed investments. Apart from profits, Cargill's internal capital resources are drawn largely from affiliated insurance companies,[4] where it can borrow on the basis of the cash-surrendered value of insurance policies plus direct lines of credit. In one year almost 30 percent of Cargill's long-term debt was in notes payable to affiliated and nonaffiliated insurance companies. Cargill's Summit National Holding Company owns the Summit National Life Insurance Company, a source of capital for the company's operations in Alabama, Delaware, Indiana, Louisiana, Minnesota, and Missouri. Horizon Agency and Horizon Underwriters are insurance firms that help finance operations in Minnesota.

Even these companies do not provide the requisite capital to fuel Cargill's global operations. The remainder must be obtained from outside. Cargill is a principal client of the main commercial banks in the United States and an important borrower in foreign lending institutions; its line of credit is in effect a fixed amount of capital open to the firm for an extended period. While the consortia of banks handling the Cargill account do not necessarily act together in deciding the level of this commitment, they are privy to one another's terms and to the amounts of credit available to Cargill. In fact, individual credit lines to the same firm are determined in part by how much of a commitment rival banks have made.

Cargill's line of credit is unsecured, which means that the firm's assets, inventories, working capital, and other receivables are less than the credit advanced. Bankers approve these loans for preferred customers on the basis of an evaluation of the firm's level of working capital, short-term risk versus equity position, foreign and domestic operations, and above all, contracts (including futures). In this amalgam Cargill's rating is outstanding, enabling it virtually to write its own ticket on the terms and size of its loans. Should a Cargill affiliate apply for a loan in a foreign country with a subsidiary or correspondent of an American bank and be turned down, the American parent bank can overturn the initial decision or provide the loan on its own. With Cargill's record as an exemplary client, this situation is unlikely to occur. Banks offer these exceptional terms because Cargill is a highly profitable investment.

In a representative year Cargill borrowed over $300 million in bank notes, with an additional "contingent commitment" of approximately $85 million. A credit line covers these debits as well as "contingent liabilities." Over the last five years the largest share of this form of indebtedness was in guarantees to Cargill's international subsidiary network, amounting to as much

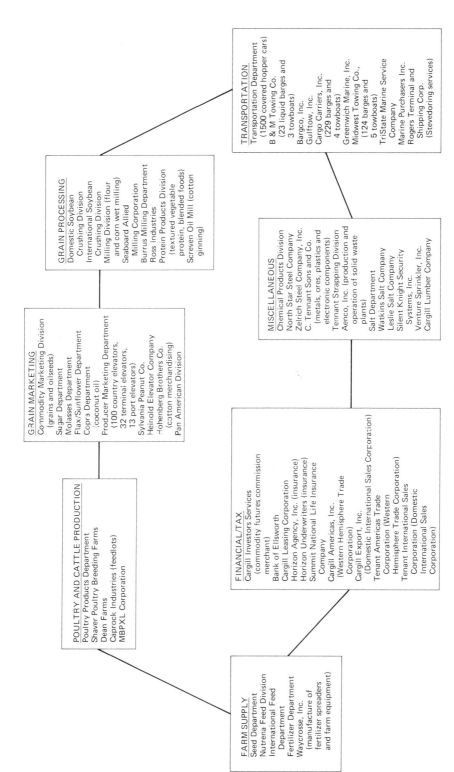

FARM SUPPLY
Seed Department
Nutrena Feed Division
International Feed Department
Fertilizer Department
Waycrosse, Inc.
(manufacture of fertilizer spreaders and farm equipment)

POULTRY AND CATTLE PRODUCTION
Poultry Products Department
Shaver Poultry Breeding Farms
Dean Farms
Caprock Industries (feedlots)
MBPXL Corporation

GRAIN MARKETING
Commodity Marketing Division
(grains and oilseeds)
Sugar Department
Molasses Department
Flax/Sunflower Department
Copra Department
(coconut oil)
Producer Marketing Department
(100 country elevators,
32 terminal elevators,
13 port elevators)
Sylvania Peanut Co.
Heinold Elevator Company
Hohenberg Brothers Co.
(cotton merchandising)
Pan American Division

GRAIN PROCESSING
Domestic Soybean
Crushing Division
International Soybean
Crushing Division
Milling Division (flour
and corn wet milling)
Seaboard Allied
Milling Corporation
Burrus Milling Department
Ross Industries
Protein Products Division
(textured vegetable
protein, blended foods)
Screven Oil Mill (cotton
ginning)

FINANCIAL/TAX
Cargill Investors Services
(commodity futures commission
merchant)
Bank of Ellsworth
Cargill Leasing Corporation
Horizon Agency, Inc. (insurance)
Horizon Underwriters (insurance)
Summit National Life Insurance
Company
Cargill Americas, Inc.
(Western Hemisphere Trade
Corporation)
Cargill Export, Inc.
(Domestic International Sales Corporation)
Tenant Americas Trade
Corporation (Western
Hemisphere Trade Corporation)
Tenant International Sales
Corporation (Domestic
International Sales
Corporation)

MISCELLANEOUS
Chemical Products Division
North Star Steel Company
Zelrich Steel Company, Inc.
C. Tennant Sons and Co.
(metals, ores, plastics and
electronic components)
Tennant Strapping Division
Aenco, Inc. (production and
operation of solid waste
plants)
Salt Department
Watkins Salt Company
Leslie Salt Company
Silent Knight Security
Systems, Inc.
Venture Sprinkler, Inc.
Cargill Lumber Company

TRANSPORTATION
Transportation Department
(1500 covered hopper cars)
B & M Towing Co.
(23 liquid barges and
3 towboats)
Bargco, Inc.
Gulftow, Inc.
Cargo Carriers, Inc.
(229 barges and
4 towboats)
Greenwich Marine, Inc.
Midwest Towing Co.,
(124 barges and
5 towboats)
TriState Marine Service
Company
Marine Purchasers Inc.
Rogers Terminal and
Shipping Corp.
(Stevedoring services)

FIGURE 3.2 Cargill, U.S. Products and Services.

29

as $40 million in a single calendar year. This imbalance is explained by the fact that Cargill's foreign subsidiary and affiliate family accounts for almost 25 percent of the firm's consolidated current liabilities.

The Tradax structure—the non-U.S. arm of Cargill—has grown significantly since it was established in 1953. In the 1950s Tradax subsidiaries sprang up worldwide, particularly in Western Europe, but they did not make a significant commercial contribution until the early 1960s. From 1963 to the present the Tradax group has represented an average of 20 percent of Cargill's consolidated total assets and 30 percent of its revenues. With more American and foreign grains sold through subsidiaries outside the United States, foreign-derived profits may eventually surpass parent company earnings. Tradax Internacional affiliates, exclusive of the United States, Canada, and certain companies in Latin America, have increased their assets to well over $130 million with at least 70 percent of the equity held by the parent company in the United States. When non-Tradax foreign operations are added to this sum, total assets, stated conservatively, are around $200 million. Although most of the equity holdings in the Cargill/Tradax complex are retained in the hands of the original family owners—the MacMillans and Cargills—informed sources have suggested that an increasing share of minority foreign equity in the Tradax group is held by individuals and corporations in OPEC (Organization of Petroleum Exporting Countries) member states. This trend would represent an effort to attract foreign capital, an increasingly important requirement in light of Cargill's expansion of foreign affiliates.

Cargill's investments have been directed at integrating its agricultural operations. At present Cargill is both a principal buyer and seller of commodities, a "fobber" (a grain handler responsible for moving the crop to port), an exporter and importer, a grain handler, a processor, and a livestock and poultry farmer; it is a broker for all modes of transportation and an owner of trucks, railroad cars, and ships; it is a speculator, hedger, and Futures Commission Merchant (FCM) on the commodity exchanges; and it is a borrower and lender in commercial credit. One measure of the success of Cargill's integration effort is that with its September 1981 purchase of Seaboard Allied Milling Corp., Cargill, already the world's second largest meat packer, became the world's largest miller as well.

Company representatives maintain that Cargill's success to date has less to do with its investment portfolio than with the legendary acumen of the accomplished trader. Cargill's size and the salience of its operations are, nevertheless, crucial to its position as captain of the Big League. It owns at least 12 major export elevators in the United States alone, with an average loading capacity (expressed in terms of the maximum number of bushels that can be loaded through the elevator in one hour) of almost 70,000 bushels. The firm also has sizable fixed investments in U.S. and foreign plants, and service agencies to integrate grain merchandising from the farm to consumption, including midway processing stages. Its international investments dwarf earlier grain company forays beyond national borders.

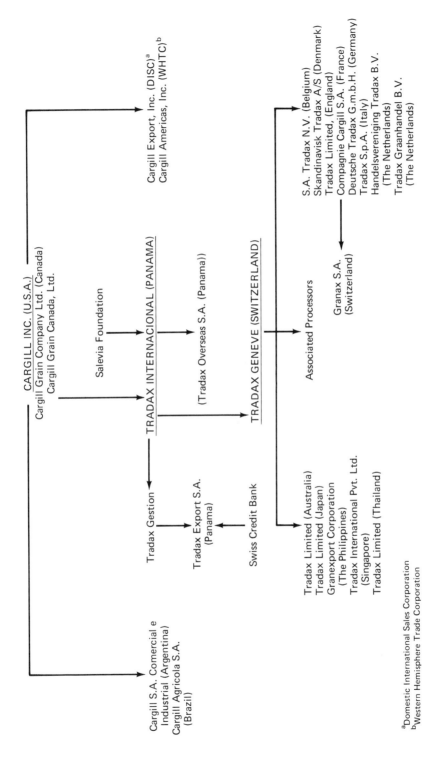

FIGURE 3.3 Cargill/Tradax Corporate Structure.

CARGILL INC. (U.S.A.)
Cargill Grain Company Ltd. (Canada)
Cargill Grain Canada, Ltd.

Cargill Export, Inc. (DISC)[a]
Cargill Americas, Inc. (WHTC)[b]

Cargill S.A. Comercial e
Industrial (Argentina)
Cargill Agricola S.A.
(Brazil)

Salevia Foundation

TRADAX INTERNACIONAL (PANAMA)

(Tradax Overseas S.A. (Panama))

TRADAX GENEVE (SWITZERLAND)

Tradax Gestion

Tradax Export S.A.
(Panama)

Swiss Credit Bank

Tradax Limited (Australia)
Tradax Limited (Japan)
Granexport Corporation
(The Philippines)
Tradax International Pvt. Ltd.
(Singapore)
Tradax Limited (Thailand)

Associated Processors

Granax S.A.
(Switzerland)

S.A. Tradax N.V. (Belgium)
Skandinavisk Tradax A/S (Denmark)
Tradax Limited, (England)
Compagnie Cargill S.A. (France)
Deutsche Tradax G.m.b.H. (Germany)
Tradax S.p.A. (Italy)
Handelsvereniging Tradax B.V.
(The Netherlands)
Tradax Graanhandel B.V.
(The Netherlands)

[a]Domestic International Sales Corporation
[b]Western Hemisphere Trade Corporation

31

Cargill went international primarily in response to the relative restrictiveness of U.S. tax law.

> . . . in late 1953, the owners of Cargill established a new corporate entity, Tradax Internacional, in Panama. Organizing the new company in Panama enabled us to conduct our trading activities in the international grain market on the same tax footing available to our major competitors.
>
> Taxes are a critical cost element in our business. Unlike firms involved in manufacturing operations, commodity traders possess no unique advantage like patents, trademarks, brand franchises, technology or product superiority which enable them to absorb higher tax costs. We all buy and sell the same commodities, dealing with the same sellers and the same buyers. To compete on equal terms we had to seek tax costs no greater than those accessible to established foreign-owned competitors.[5]

Given the relatively small average margin of profit on purchases and sales of grain, one means of increasing profitability is to reduce tax liabilities. Cargill's corporate organization reflects an effort to minimize its tax obligations, primarily in the United States where corporate tax rates are high.[6]

Cargill has established two affiliates outside the United States—Tradax Export and Tradax Overseas—whose primary purpose is to retain nontaxable income derived from sales of U.S. grain. This kind of company is often referred to as a "letter box" operation because its main function is to serve as a profit collection center rather than a productive form of investment. From 1972 to 1974 Tradax Overseas provided a haven from U.S. taxes on earnings of over $1.2 billion.[7]

Tradax Export's gross sales and other revenue were over $775 million in 1970-71, more than 25 percent of Cargill's consolidated earnings, jumping to roughly $2 billion annually by 1976. In those years, Tradax Export paid roughly $3.5 million in U.S federal income taxes.[8] It qualified for deferral of its U.S. income tax obligations on the basis of a special exemption to the normal corporate tax liability for earnings of foreign subsidiaries engaged primarily in the exportation of U.S. agricultural commodities.

Cargill also has a subsidiary within the United States that owes its existence to a specially designed tax incentive for exports. Cargill Export, Inc., is a Domestic International Sales Corporation (DISC), which means that a portion of Cargill's exports are funneled through its DISC in order to save on taxes. Cargill Export does not enter into any part of the grain export-handling process, but as a DISC, only half its export income is subject to U.S. taxes. As a result, Cargill Export was able to defer at least $16 million of its federal income tax between 1972 and 1975.[9]

The third leg in Cargill's international tripod is Tradax Internacional. Formally, Tradax Internacional owns and operates the Tradax network in Switzerland.[10] Cargill Corporation holds 70 percent and the Cargill-MacMillan families the remaining 30 percent of the Panamanian corporation through their Swiss foundation—the Salevia Foundation.[11] These interrelationships are tailored to tax convenience, but the Swiss-based Tradax system is also a work of commercial genius. Swiss headquarters offer the dual advantage of direct access to Eurocurrency markets in Western Europe and the commercial secrecy afforded by Swiss law. Tradax Internacional's operations are protected from foreign government surveillance and inquiries, including those from the United States, despite the extent to which those operations are closely intertwined with those of Cargill's American branches.

This is an arrangement with great advantages for both the company and its prospective customers. Many buyers prefer to operate secretly. Similarly, traders contend that the relative openness of the American system works to their disadvantage when competing with other countries for export markets. Revealing the identity of foreign buyers, they maintain, is a commercial albatross. The fact of the matter is that any purchaser or seller is likely to secure a better deal if negotiations and the contract itself are not disclosed.

Flexibility is another valuable asset built into the Tradax system; it enables the company to act swiftly and appropriately in the go-go world of the grain trade. If Cargill, U.S., had to handle directly all sales worldwide, it would have difficulty hedging transactions in commodity markets with only one source of supply. There would be less assurance that foreign purchasing contracts could be fulfilled reliably if the company were solely dependent upon the American market, and less opportunity for price management in the absence of both a buying and selling arm. Contracts would be more restrictive, foreign capital would be harder to obtain, and taxes would be higher.

Cargill has prospered in an imperfect economic climate distorted by government intervention and restrictive commercial trade practices. Much of its success is rooted in the relationship between the American parent firm and the Tradax group, paradoxically an outgrowth and cause of these imperfections. Tradax Internacional, via Tradax Geneva, is in fact Cargill's best customer. Cargill sales of U.S. grain to Tradax companies over a representative five-year period were as follows:

1970-71	1971-72	1972-73	1973-74	1974-75
50.7%	44.5%	37.3%	43.3%	35.6% [12]

Several commercial advantages stem from this arrangement. When Tradax, Geneva, makes a purchase of American grain from Cargill, U.S., or Cargill, Canada, the ultimate purchaser's identity and the final destination of the shipment rarely appear on the U.S. Customs declaration. The importing Tradax subsidiary may not even be named because these subsidiaries generally serve as agents to Tradax, Geneva, and therefore never take legal possession of the grain. As a result, a Tradax purchase offers the seller—Cargill, U.S.— and the real buyer foolproof camouflage.

This arrangement also provides Cargill or Tradax Internacional greater freedom in hedging prospective sales and purchases on the commodity exchange markets. Were the purchase to come from an identified foreign buyer, it would be harder for Cargill, U.S., to break up and phase its futures transactions in such a way as to avoid sending signals in the marketplace before its hedging and cash operations were completed in anticipation of sales. In other words, scattered futures positions placed by a Tradax group member in Chicago (usually through or in coordination with Cargill) tell market analysts little. They are hedges placed by a foreign company, and as such, they enjoy more freedom from U.S. disclosure requirements than if the same transactions were conducted by an American firm.

The Tradax system provides another hedge: multiple sourcing. Because the Tradax group is made up of autonomous foreign subsidiaries, Tradax companies or an analogous grouping of affiliates are under no obligation to buy grain from the United States. If the price is better elsewhere, the grain of a higher quality or more suited to a customer's specified requirements, or a foreign shipment of a certain grain can be carried out with better timing, Tradax may in theory buy that grain. But it may not. In order to maintain maximum flexibility in deciding where and what to buy, the trade has come up with an appropriate answer: the optional-origin contract. This means that a contract between buyer and seller is written without specifying the grain's origin. It is up to the seller to decide at the time of shipment. In the interim, the seller can juggle different purchases in several countries to fill an identical order. Therein lies the trader's hedge. He can hold a foreign-origin contract in Brazilian soybeans, for example, and switch to American beans if the terms are more favorable. The news of the trader's Brazilian purchase could result in a downturn in the futures price of American beans, and vice versa if the trader switches out of Brazilian and into American beans, as is his privilege under an optional-origin contract. With the right coordination, Cargill and the Tradax group can come out ahead, whether the futures market goes up or down.

The foreign purchaser gains because a portion of the cost reduction in this form of contract is passed on to the purchaser by the trader. Aside from price-hedging opportunities, the trader gains by being able to short-circuit restrictive national agricultural policies. If, for instance, a country suddenly enacts export controls or clamps an embargo on the export of particular agricultural commodities, a company with an optional contract can fill the contract from another source. Under these circumstances, the purchaser has the additional benefit of assured supply; otherwise, the actions of a single government could cut the foreign buyer off from the flow of grain for which he had already contracted.

To combat just such an export cutoff, international grain companies have developed still another tool. A seller such as Cargill, whether it enters into a transaction with an affiliated or a nonaffiliated buyer, is permitted to cancel the contract through mutual consent or international arbitration. With this "out," companies can deliberately sell beyond their foreign buyers' (most often members of the same corporate group) actual requirements as a hedge to ensure access to supply during the time export controls are in effect. Under a partial embargo, a portion of these contracts would normally qualify for shipment and under a complete cutoff would enhance a seller's claim for compensation. In the event that controls are lifted and world grain prices decline, the seller and buyer can cancel by mutual consent those contracts that did not correspond to real demand in the first place. American grain and soybean exports in the past few years show a high incidence of such inter-affiliate cancellations, particularly on sales contracts with no declared destination.[13]

A Tradax-like network affords additional flexibility by allowing foreign subsidiaries to purchase from parent companies under favorable pricing arrangements. Frequently, interaffiliate transactions leave final prices open until delivery. These "basis" contracts (based on current market prices plus a premium or discount at the time the shipment is received) are fairly standard among related companies. They are also, at key times, the most popular way to sell grain that is never bought.

Cargill's well-coordinated, multinational structure can accommodate different, often contradictory demands. Its organization, in fact, is best equipped to capitalize on varying interests and policies. Cargill has earned a record of being a reputable, efficient international grain trader. Its standing does not detract from the point that the international grain business today, as exemplified by Cargill, functions best in a climate of governmental restrictions and controls.

Continental Grain Company

If Cargill is captain of the Big League, then Continental is a star player. It is the oldest American grain exporting house, with roots deep in European soil transplanted during World War II.[14] The company was founded in 1813 in Arlon, Belgium, by Simon Fribourg and remains under control of the Fribourg family.

Continental was a pathfinder in modern marketing. Its investment strategy reflected from the outset an interest in balancing raw commodity handling services with processing facilities. When Continental set up its first American subsidiary in Chicago in 1921, which was quickly followed by a New York office incorporated in Delaware and a Canadian affiliate in Winnipeg, it was setting its sights on merchandising services relatively distant from the farm. Then it moved backward, inching closer and closer to the point of production.

Initially, Continental had certain advantages over Cargill and other American-based trading houses. It had an international superstructure in place, including a brokerage service for ocean vessel charters operating out of France, minority holdings in financial houses, and close ties to large European banks—then the world's money moguls. It held on to these ties when it was baptized a bona fide American company in 1946.

Continental had a trading arm in Switzerland as early as 1925, but the international clearinghouse function was not instituted until the birth of Finagrain (Compagnie Commerciale Agricole et Financière, S.A.) in Geneva in 1957, one year later than the founding of Tradax. Then came the establishment of an in-house financing facility, Fribgest (Société Continentale de Gestion Financière, S.A.), in which over 85 percent of the owning interest was held by Continental Grain, U.S.,[15] and its twin, Fribexport (Agricultural Export Corporation, S.A.). At one time, Finagrain and Fribexport were to Continental what Tradax still is to Cargill.[16]

Continental also has two holding companies in Panama. Central Overseas Corporation offers a potential tax haven for earnings related to Continental's shipping ownership and operations. Desarrollo Agricola, S.A., identified as a holding company for agricultural trade in Conti's nuclear family, is another toll-free tax avenue.

Continental's profit base, however, is clearly the United States, its adopted host country. It now conforms to the Cargill model, fully leveraged at all principal links of the agricultural chain. Continental ranks second to Cargill in grain merchandising worldwide. Its annual sales are at least $7 billion, with 65 to 70 percent of the company's assets in grain and other commodity inventories. Continental Grain, U.S., registered between 50 and 70 percent of its sales of U.S. wheat and barley to related foreign companies in a recent five-year period. In terms of Continental/"F" line consolidated assets, related non-U.S. companies account for almost 40 percent of the total, at a cost value of approximately $400 million. In the four years since its establishment, Conti's DISCs have had over $6.5 billion in sales, allowing it to defer a minimum of $55 million in U.S. taxes.

Like Cargill, Continental's capital requirements are immense. In a recent typical year Continental secured almost $60 million in foreign bank borrowings to cover one year's operating costs and investments. In percentage terms, foreign bank borrowings from the same year's operations were approximately 25 percent of Continental's bank borrowings, totaling close to $340 million. Above and beyond this amount were contingency forms of credit representing an additional 20 percent of the company's current liabilities or over one-third of its current bank debt. Long-term debt for the year was over $100 million, roughly 25 percent of the company's borrowings.

Louis Dreyfus Corporation

The third- to sixth-ranking stars in the Big League are foreign firms with extensive operations in the United States and Canada. None are newcomers. The family-owned Louis Dreyfus Corporation is based in Paris, but its American corporation has grown into the largest profit center. By 1980 it had replaced Continental as the largest seller of U.S. grain to the USSR and ranked third in sales to China, two of the largest importers of U.S. grains and oilseeds.

Louis Dreyfus and Company, Paris, although privately owned, is also a cooperative under French law. It owns 49 percent of the shares of the co-op UFC (Union Française des Céréales, better known as "La Coopérative

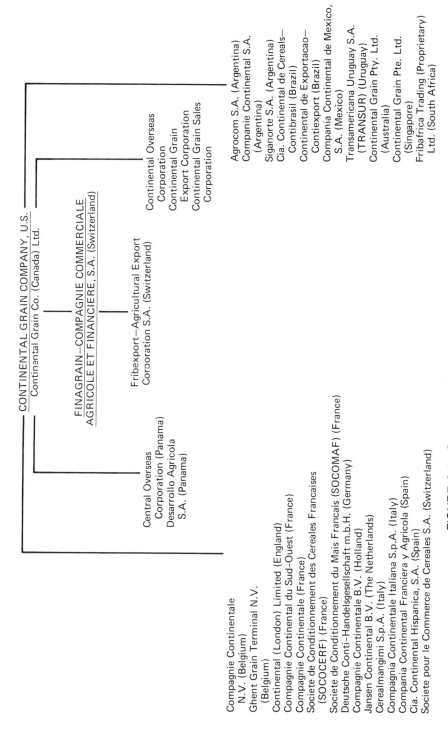

FIGURE 3.4   Continental Grain/"F" Line Corporate Structure.

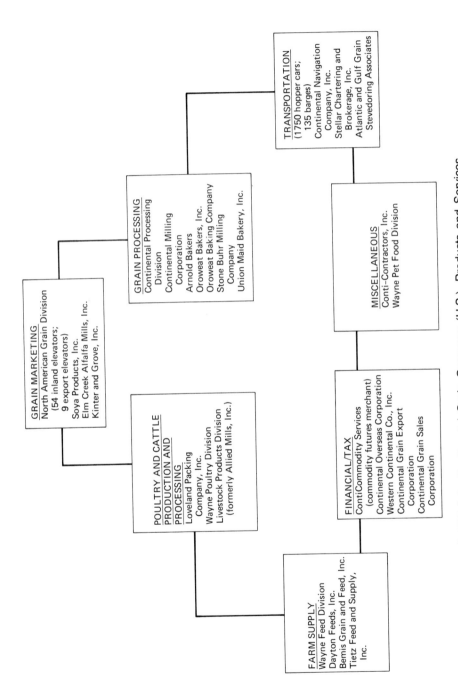

GRAIN MARKETING
North American Grain Division
(54 inland elevators;
9 export elevators)
Soya Products, Inc.
Elm Creek Alfalfa Mills, Inc.
Kinter and Grove, Inc.

GRAIN PROCESSING
Continental Processing
Division
Continental Milling
Corporation
Arnold Bakers
Oroweat Bakers, Inc.
Oroweat Baking Company
Stone Buhr Milling
Company
Union Maid Bakery, Inc.

TRANSPORTATION
(1750 hopper cars;
135 barges)
Continental Navigation
Company, Inc.
Stellar Chartering and
Brokerage, Inc.
Atlantic and Gulf Grain
Stevedoring Associates

POULTRY AND CATTLE
PRODUCTION AND
PROCESSING
Loveland Packing
Company, Inc.
Wayne Poultry Division
Livestock Products Division
(formerly Allied Mills, Inc.)

MISCELLANEOUS
Conti-Contractors, Inc.
Wayne Pet Food Division

FINANCIAL/TAX
ContiCommodity Services
(commodity futures merchant)
Continental Overseas Corporation
Western Continental Co., Inc.
Continental Grain Export
Corporation
Continental Grain Sales
Corporation

FARM SUPPLY
Wayne Feed Division
Dayton Feeds, Inc.
Bemis Grain and Feed, Inc.
Tietz Feed and Supply,
Inc.

FIGURE 3.5   Continental Grain Company (U.S.), Products and Services.

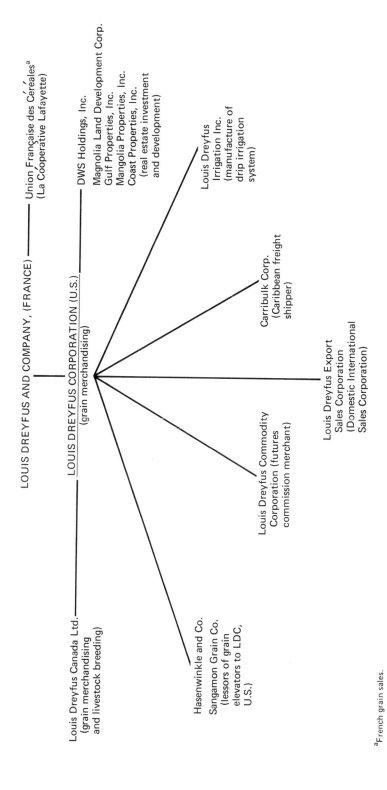

LOUIS DREYFUS AND COMPANY, (FRANCE) ——— Union Française des Céréales[a]
(La Cooperative Lafayette)

LOUIS DREYFUS CORPORATION (U.S.)
(grain merchandising)

DWS Holdings, Inc.
Magnolia Land Development Corp.
Gulf Properties, Inc.
Mangolia Properties, Inc.
Coast Properties, Inc.
(real estate investment
and development)

Louis Dreyfus
Irrigation Inc.
(manufacture of
drip irrigation
system)

Carribulk Corp.
(Caribbean freight
shipper)

Louis Dreyfus Export
Sales Corporation
(Domestic International
Sales Corporation)

Louis Dreyfus Commodity
Corporation (futures
commission merchant)

Hasenwinkle and Co.
Sangamon Grain Co.
(lessors of grain
elevators to LDC,
U.S.)

Louis Dreyfus Canada Ltd.
(grain merchandising
and livestock breeding)

[a]French grain sales.

FIGURE 3.6 Louis Dreyfus and Company, S.A./Louis Dreyfus Corporation
(U.S.), Corporate Structure.

39

Lafayette"). Under this seeming marriage of opposites, UFC sells French grain exclusively for itself and Dreyfus both within the European Community and to third markets.[17] This arrangement allows Dreyfus to obtain credit at low interest rates from the quasi-official French agricultural banking institution, Crédit Agricole. Such rates are not available to strictly private corporations. French laws and government policies endow both Dreyfus and UFC with other forms of preferential treatment as well.

Other than this unique feature, the mode of Dreyfus' operations differs only in degree from the two top firms. The transatlantic connection has proven as beneficial to Dreyfus as it has to Continental and Cargill. In 1975 Dreyfus, U.S., wrote five times as many contracts on an unfixed as a fixed basis price. At the same time, "buy backs" or cancellations between Louis Dreyfus, Paris, and its American affiliate amounted to over 2 million metric tons in just two months.[18] In six years, starting in the late 1960s, Dreyfus, U.S., increased its assets by roughly 400 percent to a figure of over $300 million, 90 percent of which related to its commodity business.[19] In 1976 one source estimated that it earned over $1.1 billion,[20] representing an average of 10 percent of Dreyfus' total consolidated sales.

Again tax minimization has boosted profits for the Dreyfus group. The tie with "La Coopérative Lafayette" offers certain tax advantages. In the United States, Dreyfus has set up a number of tax shelters, including a DISC. Over a two-year period the Dreyfus DISC, Louis Dreyfus Export Sales Corporation, reported sales of over $2.5 billion, on which a minimum of $14 million of U.S. federal taxes were withheld.

Bunge and Born Corporation

Like Dreyfus, Bunge is a foreign-based firm with an international affiliate superstructure including extensive representation in the United States. While Dreyfus had an American partnership in the 1920s, Bunge held controlling common and preferred stock in one of the largest American grain-exporting houses, P. N. Gray and Company. In 1921 Gray's share of U.S wheat exports was 5.5 percent, with an additional .5 percent from the Gray-Rosenbaum Grain Company of Portland, Oregon.[21]

Bunge was originally a Dutch and then a Belgian firm. Later, Ernesto Bunge and his brother-in-law, Jorge Born, set up shop in Argentina where the company was in a position to straddle the growing Latin American as well as European market. As the U.S. market took off, Bunge was ready. By 1960, expropriations of Bunge and Born elevators in Argentina and the promise of U.S. exports prompted another reorganization. N. V. Financieel Zaken Maatschappij "Los Andes," of Curacao, Netherlands Antilles, became the parent to all American and several non-U.S. subsidiaries. Los Andes is the holding company that owns Bunge Corporation, which was established in 1923 as the American arm of Bunge and Born. It is also the "letter box" for profits from the rest of the Bunge group; Cereals Export of Delaware, described as a firm merchandising and exporting Brazilian soybeans, and Bunge Export, the company's DISC, are two of the principal tax shelters for profits derived from operations in the United States. From a management standpoint, however, the reins are currently held in São Paulo, Brazil. With the exception of Spain, Western Europe—once an active market for Bunge— has declined in importance by comparison to subsidiary operations in intra- regional Eastern European trade.

The United States, nevertheless, is the profit center for the entire corpo- rate group. In an average year Bunge and Born's consolidated subsidiaries in the United States register a short-term bank debt of approximately $280 million, or almost 15 percent of reported total sales. Long-term debt over the past six years has averaged $33 million for Bunge Corporation alone, a figure that does not include all of Bunge and Born's borrowings for U.S. invest- ments. Bunge Corporation's long-term debt is smaller than Cargill or Conti- nental's; nevertheless, this form of borrowing has increased considerably,[22] to cover the wave of Bunge investments in the United States that have a book value of more than $450 million. U.S. sales were estimated in 1975 at $2.8 billion, excluding receipts from the salad oil division with working capital in excess of $60 million.

Mitsui/Cook

Mitsui and Company/Cook Industries, Inc., is unique among the Big League in several respects. Formed in 1978, when Mitsui and Company purchased the greater part of Cook Industries' grain assets at a reported net book value of $53.9 million, it is the only Big League firm with a Japanese parent.[23] The events leading up to this acquisition form perhaps the most interesting, and widely publicized, recent episode in the unpublic history of the grain trade.

Before its sudden fall in 1978, Cook Industries was the fourth largest grain trading firm in the world. It was also a relative newcomer to the Big League. Originally a conservatively managed cotton trading house that dated back to 1919, Cook Industries had by 1963 moved away from cotton and into soybeans under the leadership of Edward W. (Ned) Cook, who took over his father's business in 1951. In 1968, Ned Cook became director of what had become a publicly owned conglomerate. Then came the roller coaster ride.

In less than a decade, Cook became a Big League trader with assets to prove it. The company's net sales climbed in six years from $121.1 to $433.6 million in 1975. Assets were valued as high as $140 million.[24]

In Cook's peak year of 1975, its grain merchandising margins reached $62.6 million and oil-processing revenues (from both soybean and cotton seed) reached $213.3 million.[25] Cook Export Corporation, a DISC, had accrued income of about $34 million on sales of over $4.8 billion and accounted for approximately 17.2 percent of the company's pretax income.[26] In that same year, 1975, Cook sold approximately 6.5 million metric tons of U.S. wheat, 2.2 million tons of which went to the Soviet Union, Cook's best

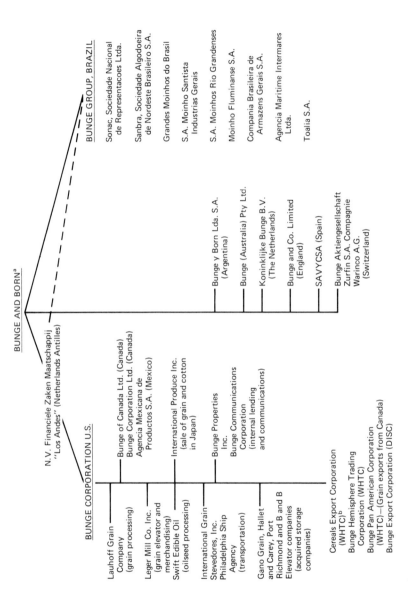

BUNGE AND BORN[a]

N.V. Financiele Zaken Maatschappij
"Los Andes" (Netherlands Antilles)

BUNGE CORPORATION U.S.

Lauhoff Grain
Company
(grain processing)

Leger Mill Co. Inc.
(grain elevator and
merchandising)

Swift Edible Oil
(oilseed processing)

International Grain
Stevedores, Inc.
Philadelphia Ship
Agency
(transportation)

Gano Grain, Hallet
and Carey, Port
Richmond and B and B
Elevator companies
(acquired storage
companies)

Cereals Export Corporation
(WHTC)[b]
Bunge Hemisphere Trading
Corporation (WHTC)
Bunge Pan American Corporation
(WHTC)–(Grain exports from Canada)
Bunge Export Corporation (DISC)

Bunge of Canada Ltd. (Canada)
Bunge Corporation Ltd. (Canada)
Agencia Mexicana de
Productos S.A. (Mexico)

International Produce Inc.
(sale of grain and cotton
in Japan)

Bunge Properties
Inc.
Bunge Communications
Corporation
(internal lending
and communications)

Bunge y Born Lda. S.A.
(Argentina)

Bunge (Australia) Pty Ltd.

Koninklijke Bunge B.V.
(The Netherlands)

Bunge and Co. Limited
(England)

SAVYCSA (Spain)

Bunge Aktiengesellschaft
Zurfin S.A. Compagnie
Warinco A.G.
(Switzerland)

BUNGE GROUP, BRAZIL

Sonac, Sociedade Nacional
de Representacoes Ltda.

Sanbra, Sociedade Algodoeira
de Nordeste Brasileiro S.A.

Grandes Moinhos do Brasil

S.A. Moinho Santista
Industrias Gerais

S.A. Moinhos Rio Grandenses

Moinho Fluminanse S.A.

Compania Brasileira de
Armazens Gerais S.A.

Agencia Maritime Intermares
Ltda.

Toalia S.A.

[a]Listing of foreign companies in Bunge group is incomplete. Companies are shown for representational purposes only.
[b]WHTC–Western Hemisphere Trading Corporation

FIGURE 3.7 Bunge and Born/Bunge Corporation (U.S.), Corporate Structure.

customer. Cook was also doing considerable business with Japan, India, Korea, and the People's Republic of China. By the summer of 1975, Cook had shipped over 1.2 million metric tons of wheat, soybeans, corn, sorghum, and barley to Japan, while shipments the previous year had exceeded 1.8 million metric tons. Thus Cook had between 10 and 12 percent of Japan's import market for U.S. grains. The firm was also handling almost 20 percent of U.S. wheat exports to India and more than 25 percent of grain exports from this country to South Korea. Its share of U.S. exports to China was lower than any of these percentages, but it was still one of the top four shippers to China at that time.

Throughout its period of rapid, almost tumultuous, growth from 1968 through the mid-1970s, Cook Industries' operations were determined by Ned Cook. His strategy was a combination of style and substance. An astute businessman, he saw the need for a network of affiliates to maximize and consolidate profits and nurture new markets. The result was the rapid-fire incorporation of one affiliate after another, including the creation of a central headquarters for foreign operations in Geneva and a letter box operation in Panama.

Trouble began in 1975-76, and by 1977 Cook's Agri-Products Group had lost $91 million. Another loss of $42 million was reported in the fiscal year ending May 31, 1978. Company management attributed these losses to hedging transactions. The official management explanation was that Cook was on the wrong side of its soybean hedges. It was holding high-priced futures contracts and selling short when the spot market was moving up and distant deliveries were moving in the opposite direction. It was a tame way of describing disastrous misjudgment. While Cook was hedging itself into oblivion, the Hunt family had succeeded in cornering the soybean market. Undoubtedly the Cook team's guesswork did not take account of the Hunt's temporary ability to turn prices in the opposite direction of what conventional indicators may have persuasively suggested. Although the Hunt factor could have exaggerated Cook's losses,[27] the firm's traders were still responsible for virtually placing the company's entire assets in jeopardy.

As late as 1978, Cook's bankers stood by the company, owing in no small part to their own exposure. When the company incurred is first big losses, a consortium of four American banks, with Chase Manhattan acting as agent, met to decide whether to provide additional loans. They elected to advance Cook another $300 million, bringing the company's total bank debt during the 1977-78 period up to $600 million. This was an exceptionally high debt level for a firm of Cook's size, but the bankers involved saw no alternative but to witness their grain accounts fall like a deck of cards. Chase, Citicorp, and Morgan Guaranty, in particular, simply could not afford to let Cook go out of business until its contracts had been resold or fully executed.

The bankers' objective, therefore, was to buy time. Other big firms—major clients of these banks—were tied up in Cook "strings." As is typical of the trade, Cook's contracts were strung together in such a fashion as to make

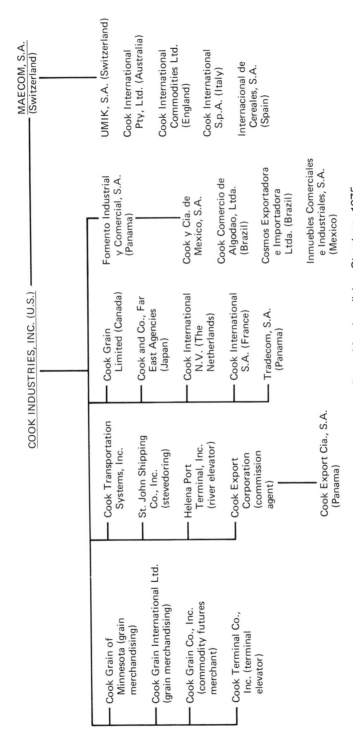

FIGURE 3.8 Cook Industries Grain Merchandising Structure, 1975.

MAECOM, S.A.
(Switzerland)

UMIK, S.A. (Switzerland)

Cook International
Pty. Ltd. (Australia)

Cook International
Commodities Ltd.
(England)

Cook International
S.p.A. (Italy)

Internacional de
Cereales, S.A.
(Spain)

COOK INDUSTRIES, INC. (U.S.)

Fomento Industrial
y Comercial, S.A.
(Panama)

Cook Grain
Limited (Canada)

Cook and Co., Far
East Agencies
(Japan)

Cook International
N.V. (The
Netherlands)

Cook International
S.A. (France)

Tradecom, S.A.
(Panama)

Cook y Cia. de
Mexico, S.A.

Cook Comercio de
Algodao, Ltda.
(Brazil)

Cosmos Exportadora
e Importadora
Ltda. (Brazil)

Inmuebles Comerciales
e Industriales, S.A.
(Mexico)

Cook Transportation
Systems, Inc.

St. John Shipping
Co., Inc.
(stevedoring)

Helena Port
Terminal, Inc.
(river elevator)

Cook Export
Corporation
(commission
agent)

Cook Export Cia., S.A.
(Panama)

Cook Grain of
Minnesota (grain
merchandising)

Cook Grain International Ltd.
(grain merchandising)

Cook Grain Co., Inc.
(commodity futures
merchant)

Cook Terminal Co.,
Inc. (terminal
elevator)

it virtually impossible to identify which receipt went with which loan or who was owed what. Further, a certain portion of Cook's debt was in unsecured loans, a factor which only complicated the picture and led to assertions by the American bankers that it was their loans which were either totally or partially secured, whereas the unsecured loans were held by "less informed" foreign banks. Which banks were, in fact, the most exposed and how some were better able to protect themselves than others is a story that remains to be told. What is known is that the banks and large trading houses caught up in Cook's strings were saved.

Cook, however, was not. In order to satisfy its creditors and remain solvent, it was forced to dispose of virtually all its assets. These found a willing purchaser in Mitsui and Company. Mitsui's involvement with U.S. grain exports extends back at least to 1921 when its market share was approximately .6 percent. In subsequent years, it gradually and quietly increased its share of the American market. Its purchase of Cook's assets in 1978 marked a turning point.

Prior to that acquisition, Mitsui, like the other major Japanese trading companies—Sogo Shosha—had played a continuing but limited role in the North American grain trade. Its major activities had been effectively confined to the purchase of wheat and soybeans from the United States or Canada for export to Japan. Its normal mode of operation was to enter the market as a c.i.f. contractor or as a participant in a string. As with other members of the Sogo Shosha, Mitsui's customary strategy was to run most of its contracts through more specialized grain trading firms with extensive operations in the United States and Canada. Mitsui had, for example, purchased 85 percent of United Grain Corporation in Portland, Oregon, and 50 percent of Pacific Grain of Illinois, but its principal purpose in so doing was to acquire a minimal base of handling facilities rather than to compete with the Big League traders.

With the Cook acquisition, Mitsui and Company was instantly transformed from a secondary trader whose grain operations in this country were largely confined to the West Coast and to shipping cargoes to foreign markets—principally Japan—into a member of the Big League. It remains to be seen how successful the new company will be. Despite a generally cautious posture, it incurred severe losses in the commodities market during 1980-81, much like those incurred by Cook earlier, losses which illustrate the risks inherent in such a move. On the other hand, the Cook purchase gave Mitusi a new entrance point into the U.S. market, a secure base for sales to third market countries, and may also constitute a lifeline to foreign food resources for the Japanese government to which the company is so closely linked.

Garnac Grain Company

One of the most consistent and unobtrusive team players is Garnac Grain Company, a fully owned American subsidiary of the André holding company, which in turn is owned by the André family of Lausanne, Switzerland. André and Company, Switzerland, is putatively a legal correspondent to Garnac Grain, meaning that it can sign an interaffiliate contract in its own name or can confirm a contract with related or nonrelated companies for Garnac. This type of contract now represents 50 to 80 percent of Garnac's total sales in soybeans; between 30 and 50 percent in corn; and approximately 20 percent of Garnac's total sales of U.S. wheat.

Garnac's capital requirements are proportionately as great as any other member of the Big League. Its short-term loan position in a recent, typical year was about 2 percent of its consolidated profits, or more than $4 million. Its line of credit in the same year totaled over $55 million, or approximately 37 percent (as compared to an estimated 42 percent for Cargill) of total sales. By any definition—sales, investment, international affiliate system, capital resources—Garnac qualifies as a major international grain trader, albeit the smallest in the Big League.

Together, these six firms which make up the Big League account for as

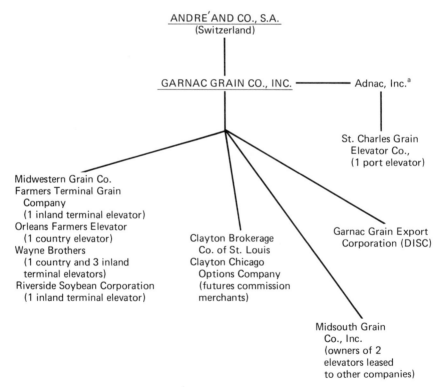

aAdnac is a joint venture holding company with
Archer-Daniels-Midland Company.

FIGURE 3.9 André and Company, S.A./Garnac Grain Company, Inc., Corporate Structure.

much as 60 percent of the world's traffic in grain (including shipments under food assistance programs). Their singular influence on the world grain market is undeniable. Despite differences in their patterns of growth, operations, and commercial strategies, these firms share many characteristics. They have proven themselves to be efficient, profitable companies. Since 1972 all have grown bigger. Their general tenaciousness has inspired them to diversify and integrate. They have the confidence of a firmly ensconced aristrocracy.

If the continued survival of the aristocracy is all but assured, however, the survival of any single firm is not. The Big League has lived through one recent revolution with the loss of Cook. There is no guarantee that a similar fate could not befall another member of the team, as the shocks which have buffeted the international grain markets since Cook's demise have made abundantly clear. Several smaller firms are at the moment jockeying for a leading position in the trade, and their rise to the inner circle is likely to come about only in the wake of another Cook-type failure.

The emergence of the smaller contenders is thus a source of potential concern to the Big League even as it is also sometimes used to substantiate the claim that the grain business is, in fact, perfectly competitive. That competitiveness will be limited, however, for as long as the continued prosperity of the second-order firms depends upon their receipt of business from the Big League. Such conditions contribute to the perpetuation of the existing oligopoly, whose continuation will in no way be threatened should one of the veterans die only to be replaced by a smaller firm.

THE MINOR LEAGUE CONTENDERS

Archer-Daniels-Midland (ADM)

Among the firms seeking to enter the ranks of the Big League, none would appear more suited to the challenge than Archer-Daniels-Midland (ADM). Established in 1902 as the Daniels Linseed Company, ADM assumed its current bullish position in 1965 under the management of Dwane and Lowell Andreas. Although the company is publicly owned, the Andreas family holds the biggest block of stock and dominates ADM operations. The firm's spectacular growth differs from that of other large international grain trading houses; it backed into the classical parts of the grain business, starting as a processor buying grains for its own plants which primarily manufactured soybean products. Global expansion and diversification came once it had gained a strong position at home. ADM now offers almost every merchandising service and product provided by the majors.

It holds enough patents to serve an entire soybean menu. Its corn fructose, an expensive sugar derivative, is competitive with sugar beet and cane. As the United States groped for self-sufficiency in energy, gasohol was hailed as an attractive fuel supplement. ADM was ready as the nation's number-one producer to upgrade its production to a level of 150,000 gallons

FIGURE 3.10 Organizational Characteristics of the Minor League Contenders.

Companies (in Order of Size)	Benefited from the "Game of Courtship"	Not Primarily A Grain Trader	Very Strong Capital Resources	Management Changeover	Strong Producer Ties	High Level of Integration	Govt. and Commercial Union	Large Subsidiary Network	Buys F.O.B. for C.I.F. Sale to Parent Co.	Particular Area of Independence	Specialized in Commodity &/or Market	High Degree of Dependence on 6 Major Cos.
Archer–Daniels-Midland (ADM)[a]			✓			✓		✓				
Phibro Corp.		✓ Oil Trade	✓								✓	
Toepfer International	✓				✓ Farmers Co-Ops Own 50 Percent			✓ Follows Cargil/Tradex e.g.				
Ditta Feruzzi Serafino and Company						✓				✓ Ravena, Italy		
The Sogo Shosha (Japanese Trading Companies)[b]		✓					✓	✓	✓		✓	
Tradigrain			✓	✓ Formerly with Cook								
Coprasol			✓	✓ Formerly with Continental								
Van Stock										✓ Dutch Based	✓ Wheat/Europe	✓ [c]
Z. B. Fox											✓ Latin Amer.	✓ [c]
Joseph										✓ Minneapolis	✓ Feedgrain/Europe	✓ [c]
Farmers Export Co.					✓ Owned By U.S. Farmers Co-Op							
Union Equity Cooperative Exchange												✓
Pacific Grain Corp.												
North Pacific Grain Growers[d]												

[a] ADM is also the largest producer of gasohol in the United States.

[b] Market shares of the smaller firms are sustained by the Japanese Food Agency.

[c] Although all "Minor League" firms are dependent in some way on the majors, these specialized firms in particular provide regional ties in return for the supplies and markets necessary for their own survival.

[d] These farmer-owned exporting companies have between 5 and 10 percent of the world export pie. Some have special arrangements with Zen-Noh, the National Federation of Agricultural Cooperative Associations, Japan.

per day. Higher prices plus special government tax writeoffs and exemptions minimized the risk.

To capitalize on these commercial and political developments, ADM foresaw the need for vertical and horizontal integration. Given the vagaries of the grain market, it was no longer satisfied to depend on Big League members for grain purchases. Moreover, they had become ADM's most worrisome competitors in agricultural by-products. Self-defense dictated that ADM follow the tested pattern of backward and forward integration, moving its operations closer to the farm to maintain profitability for its expanding product lines. With the acquisition of Tabor Grain Company in 1975, ADM made a giant step toward developing a self-contained infrastructure of facilities and services for handling grain. In addition, ADM's processing plants at home and abroad became a captive market for Tabor Grain's sales, transforming arm's-length sales to more flexible interaffiliate transactions.

The firm's subsequent growth has followed the classic pattern of expansion in the grain business. ADM now boasts a network of foreign subsidiaries with the usual corporate shells in tax haven countries like Panama and the Cayman Islands. It has broken new ground by entering into a joint venture with Nestle, a Swiss owned company, for soybean-processing and oil-refining plants in Brazil. Expansion at home and abroad, greater global integration of its operations, rich capital resources, and new foreign partnerships make up ADM's life insurance policy for the future.

Phibro Corporation

Looming large on the horizon is a giant commodity-trading firm, Phibro. Formerly a subsidiary of Engelhard Minerals & Chemicals Corporation, Phibro (formerly Philipp Brothers) has engaged in the commodity business since 1914, and handled sales in 1980 of approximately $24 billion with earnings above $450 million.[28] With Engelhard, it handled more contracts for metals and oil than for grain, but it has since strengthened its position so that now it accounts for a significant share of agricultural commodity transactions. Although less integrated in its grain operations than some, Phibro is a huge and accomplished trader that could very well become the Cook of the next decade. In August of 1981 it staged a highly dramatic merger with one of the world's largest and most prestigious investment houses, Salomon Brothers. It gives Phibro its own sophisticated financing arm whose capitalized net worth at the time of the transaction was above $300 million. What Phibro still lacks is grain handling facilities to qualify as a bona fide grain merchandiser, but the Salomon acquisition could facilitate an eventual move in this direction.

Toepfer International

Toepfer International's uniqueness lies in its present ownership. Once privately owned and under the strong management hand of Alfred Toepfer, it is now a joint venture with ownership divided equally between the founding company, Alfred C. Toepfer Export, Inc., and European and American cooperatives.[29] Toepfer's growth was in large part attributable to extensive personal contacts nurtured by Toepfer and his associates with government officials in East and West Germany. While there have been suggestions of questionable payments to East German officials, which the firm denies, Toepfer's dominance of the East German trade is at least as noteworthy as its origins are obscure. What is clear is that Toepfer has secured an estimated 50 percent of East Germany's grain imports, most of which are contracted through its American subsidiary.

Most of Toepfer's investments in processing plants and handling facilities were concentrated in Europe, whereas its strength in the United States lay with marketing techniques fortified by strong customer relationships abroad, especially in both Germanies. Noteworthy among its investments was over 70 percent of the equity in two French firms—Compagnie Européene de Céréales and G. Muller—the remaining quarter of which was held by the Rothschild Group in France. These companies and Toepfer directly owned at least ten large elevators in France and the Federal Republic of Germany, including one in the free zone of the port of Hamburg, a key shipping point for Toepfer's largest customers in Eastern Europe. Its own bank, the Bankhaus Hesse Newman, was icing on the cake.

Toepfer's success continued until the late 1970s when the firm became overexposed in ocean vessels. It purchased its fleet when shipbuilders could not keep up with orders for tankers and oil/cargo vessels. As the world recession hit between 1977 and 1979, there was a sharp turnaround and a glut of ocean vessels. Chartering became cheaper than owning ships and carrying finance charges. Toepfer was caught. During this two-year period, joint ventures with the Rothschild Group, plus outstanding relations with reputable German banks, helped keep the firm solvent, much like the Cook rescue operation.[30]

When the cooperatives stepped in, they were not exactly purchasing a moribund company.[31] Toepfer brought extensive assets, marketing skills, and personal contacts to the joint venture. The cooperatives contributed much needed working capital, roughly equivalent to the market value of Toepfer's assets, to the enterprise. Moreover, their participation offered the new company's marketing arm direct access to production in several countries. In effect, Toepfer gained assured supply from its producer members, presumably on favorable terms. In return, the co-ops obtained at least a minimum of implicit preferential treatment from Toepfer International for merchandising their members' production refunded at a premium from the joint venture's earnings. In addition, the investment provided the cooperatives with expanded marketing capability, made possible the exchange of valuable information, and provided a means of coordinating producer commodity positions in the world market.

Each party has high hopes for the joint venture. It is a bolder initiative than the Dreyfus-UFC connection in that the cooperatives share fully in any liability as holders of 50 percent of the equity and there are no geographic limits to its sales operations. Its members straddle the Atlantic, permitting multiple sourcing comparable to that done by most private international grain houses. Should it work, the Toepfer acquisition could well establish a precedent as one way, perhaps the only way, for cooperatives to enter successfully into the export business. At the least, the move has fortified Toepfer's position as a leading contender.

Feruzzi Serafino & Company

Feruzzi Serafino & Company is an Italian firm owned by Serafino Feruzzi of Ravenna. The company operates mainly in the United States and Italy and is putatively the largest Italian importer of U.S grain. Argentina is the other main source for the company's imports of corn and wheat. Feruzzi reportedly once had carte blanche in Argentina, courtesy of his close friendship with Juan Peron, the country's former dictator.

The company is buyer, seller, shipper, and end-user rolled into one, servicing Italian livestock and processing customers of which Feruzzi is a prominent member. Several competitors as well as EC officials complain about the difficulties which Feruzzi's stronghold pose for non-Feruzzi grain entering Ravenna for shipment to other points in Western Europe. Yet Feruzzi's position remains unassailable in the Italian market.

The Sogo Shosha

In the grain trade, Feruzzi may have Ravenna, but the Sogo Shosha—the large trading companies—have the Japanese government. These are the giants of the commodity trade world. Mitsubishi Corporation, for example, exceeded Mitsui in global sales. In 1973 it handled about 14 percent of Japan's total imports and 10 percent of its exports. In 1978, its American subsidiary alone registered sales of $7.8 billion.[32] Koppel Grain, a Mitsubishi subsidiary, offers handling facilities on the West Coast. To date, however, Mitsubishi has conformed to the traditional Japanese pattern of working through well-established American companies in procuring U.S. grain and, unlike Mitsui, has made no move to enter the Big League.

Marubeni adheres to the same philosophy, moving more cautiously than Mitsui in the American and Canadian markets. Columbia Grain, its grain handling subsidiary in the United States, has recently expanded with its lease on Cook's large elevator in Portland, Oregon, but it has not taken the plunge of openly competing with the Big League in the United States or elsewhere other than Japan. Nevertheless, the Sogo Shosha as a group have moved more aggressively of late in the grain markets than ever before. In recent years they have expanded their trade of U.S. grains and oilseeds to include the entire Pacific region where they now function on equal footing with the Big League.

As their volume has increased their futures purchases have begun to have ripple effects on food markets around the world. Their potential to have an even greater impact will depend on whether or not they follow Mitsui's lead.

THE SMALLER FIRMS

Unable to match the resources of the Japanese Goliaths, smaller firms stand a better chance of survival through market specialization. Rather than engage in all aspects of the trade, most of the second-tier contenders prefer to piggyback their operations onto those of the large export-import houses. Among these are Van Stolk, which specializes in importing wheat, primarily from the United States and Europe, for resale to European millers, C. B. Fox, which sells primarily to Latin American buyers, and Peavey, an old Minneapolis firm, which is also strong in Latin America.

I. S. Joseph, an old family firm, trades in lower-quality coarse grains that make up compound feed for livestock, and now has stepped up its investment in processing plants. Cargill, which lured Minnesota farmers in the Red River Valley into sunflower seed production to feed its new processing plants, did most of Joseph's costly spadework. Today the two companies have the biggest plants in the region, turning sunflowers, a wonder crop of the 1980s, into oil. In 1976 Joseph tested the water for a possible joint venture with North Dakota's state-owned elevator and participating cooperatives. It was an abortive effort, but could be revived somewhat along the lines of the Toepfer deal. In the meantime, new investments and new markets such as Egypt offer Joseph a promising future.

In Toledo, Ohio, The Andersons, a family-run firm, rules supreme. It bears a striking resemblance to Peavey in that both entered the export business via a symbiotic relationship with Big League traders. In such a relationship, the small need the big to stay alive, and the majors gain from regional ties that firms like The Andersons provide.

> During 1977 approximately 86 percent of the grain sold by the Partnership (The Andersons) was purchased by exporters for shipment to foreign markets. Direct foreign sales, primarily to Canadian purchasers, accounted for about 8 percent of the Partnership's 1977 grain sales, and the remaining 6 percent was sold to domestic millers and grain processors. Customers of the Partnership who accounted for 10 percent or more of its grain sales during 1977 are as follows: Louis Dreyfus Corporation—16 percent; Cargill, Inc.—17 percent.[33]

Like other firms of a roughly equivalent size, The Andersons is engaged in a tough balancing act. Its roots are in Ohio, Illinois, and Indiana, and for the moment its place is secure. But at least one other firm, Tabor Grain, had similar standing before its acquisition. Paradoxically, the stronger such firms become, the greater their vulnerability to takeover. This possibility may effectively be forestalled as long as the world grain market remains dynamic. Under such conditions, there is room for all. Nevertheless, the other trend in the grain business is accelerated concentration. Acquisition, always a possibility for the smaller firms, looms larger than ever now that the majors' profitability increasingly hinges on obtaining a satisfactory return on their longer-term investments. In an industry whose structure resembles that of the grain trade, competition has its limits.

THE COOPERATIVES

The obstacles that confront the smaller private firms also beset cooperatives attempting to elbow their way into the export business. In the United States cooperatives account for over 40 percent of domestic grain sales. Their percentage share of the market is even larger in other countries, but their major export role is everywhere that of supplier to the international houses, despite the fact that traditionally they have received preferred treatment at the hands of government.

Grain-grower cooperatives around the world have been unable to break into the export business on their own. Their share of the world export pie continues to hover in the 5 to 10 percent range, depending upon the source of supply and the individual commodity. As was noted by the U.S. Department of Agriculture's chief economist in 1979:

> Dominating competition in this industry [grain marketing], especially at the export level, are several large multinational firms. Five of the largest of these exported 60 to 70 percent of total U.S. wheat exports during 1974-77. For feedgrains, the five largest exported from 50 to 60 percent of the U.S. total during 1974-77. Within this general structure [the sale of grain directly to export outlets by regional cooperatives] accounts for less than 4 percent of U.S. grain sales and only about 7 percent of total grain exports.[34]

Most governments, both in exporting and importing countries, tend to favor cooperatives in their agricultural programs. The degree of their protection and support generally has been limited, however, to their function as producer groups with domestic marketing capabilities. The United States in particular has shied away from preferential treatment of co-ops over the private sector in the export business. Instead, federal government policies have traditionally focused on their domestic role, deferring to the private sector to carry the torch of American grain sales abroad. In this sense, official policy inadvertently has circumscribed the role of producers in the export market.

American and foreign cooperatives as a rule have been sellers or, at best, 'fob'ers, which are highly dependent on the giant grain firms as their biggest customers. As the export share of grain production eventually surpassed domestic utilization in the United States, this unlikely alliance has been strenghtened. The seeming complexities of international transactions were beyond the traditional scope of most cooperatives. The contagion of this initial timidity has spread so that only in rare instances have cooperatives ventured into such deep foreign waters alone.

Farmers Export Company (FEC) was among the biggest cooperative-exporting firms in the United States, reporting in 1978 approximately $700 million in export-related transactions of wheat, feedgrains, and soybeans (60 percent of sales were on an f.o.b. basis). Under management stolen from the biggest of the accomplished grain houses, FEC was soon catching the trade's attention as a possible contender. Spirited by its own successes, FEC assumed more and more risk exposure until its limb broke à la Cook. In 1980, FEC management seriously miscalculated commodity prices and the state of barge traffic on the Mississippi. As a result, it lost an estimated $30 million in soybean futures and in damaged, undelivered corn backed up on the river route to the port of New Orleans. To recoup financially FEC had to sell leases on port terminals and other assets. The fallout is an overall retrenchment with dimmed prospects for an early recovery. Secondarily, this rude experience will undoubtedly reinstill all the earlier fears shared by cooperatives in taking the plunge into the direct, more profitable c.i.f. export business.

To overcome this reluctance rooted in the American cooperative movement, the U.S. government would have to reduce the risks in direct participation in international transactions. Certain inducements along these lines were introduced by the Carter administration, but to date, they have proven insufficient. The U.S. government ruled in 1977 that a cooperative export marketing association could receive price support loans for grains from the Commodity Credit Corporation (CCC) on behalf of its producer members.[35] The whole idea was to encourage pooling for export purposes. Loan money could be used as an advance payment to farmers agreeing to participate, committing a portion of their crop to the pool. This incentive has not been enough to convince co-ops that its use represents a viable option, in part because of contradictory export policies, but also because of the FEC experience.

Other cooperatives have fared better than FEC, but their role in the c.i.f. export business remains limited. Zen-Noh is Japan's National Federation of Agricultural Cooperative Associations. It has a highly integrated operation both in the United States and Japan. As the largest manufacturer of feedgrain compounds in Japan, it is also Japan's biggest single buyer of coarse grains in the United States. UNICO-OP, its American trading susidiary, traditionally has divided its purchases between American cooperatives like FEC or Producers Grain Corporation and the Sogo Shosha. Recently, however, it has undertaken construction of a huge terminal elevator of its own, which suggests more direct participation in the American market for servicing its member cooperative requirements in Japan.

In Canada there is XCAN or United Grain Growers; in France, INTER-AGRA. These cooperatives are permutations of their American counterparts and in general endure the same obstacles to their entry into the export business. There are, of course, exceptions, such as INTERAGRA, which is probably more successful because it is fundamentally a private concern. Its status as a co-op is derived from the fact that its shareholders are producers belonging to U.C.A.S.O. (L'Union de Coopératives Agricoles du Sud Ouest).

They are an odd admixture, producers of everything from fruits and vegetables to wine, wheat, and corn. Leaders of the French cooperative movement contend that U.C.A.S.O. is nothing more than a consortium of large private growers in a marriage of convenience. The inspiration for this alliance rests with INTERAGRA's and U.C.A.S.O.'s president, M. Jean Doumeng, France's "Red Millionaire," who earned his title from his personal wealth, his alleged financial backing of the French Communist party, and the corporate personality of INTERAGRA.

The firm specializes in import-export traffic with East Europe. As official sales and purchasing agent for Hungary, Czechoslovakia, and the German Democratic Republic, INTERAGRA in effect has an exclusive franchise for their bilateral agricultural trade with France.[36] The exclusive terms are favorable to all parties. INTERAGRA gains a protected market with substantial profits derived from contracts that are mostly on a barter basis. Eastern European countries obtain a bridgehead for exports to France and other hard-currency countries.

Doumeng is openly courting American cooperatives, but they remain skeptical. Most are convinced that INTERAGRA is a bona fide cooperative in name only. Nevertheless, the firm's efforts in the United States may eventually take off, given its favored position in trade with Eastern Europe.[37]

The few successes involve compromises, as demonstrated in the Zen Noh and INTERAGRA examples. In the case of American cooperatives, radical changes in management strategies, organization, and member decision making are necessary. Government support, already provided inadvertently to the private sector, is almost a prerequisite for success. A third promising ingredient would be close coordination with counterpart organizations in other countries. This prospect, however, is unlikely as long as the state-run organizations that currently proliferate the market continue to prefer dealing with the Big League for import-export transactions.

State-run grain trading organizations may thrive on every continent (see Appendix A, "National Grain Trading Organizations"). Exportkhleb, a state trading company, exercises a complete and effective monopoly over grain imports in the Soviet Union. Japan maintains a Food Agency for the importation of wheat and barley. Canada and Australia have government boards that serve as monopolies for their grain exports, and virtually all developing countries have exclusive national procurement organizations.

Despite their monopolistic powers within each country, none of these organizations single-handedly can predetermine an outcome in the international market for an extended period of time. They are further limited by the fact that in most cases they are reluctant to engage in the entire game of the grain trade. Instead, they prefer to transfer the largest portion of the risk onto the shoulders of the private sector. The eventual recipients of this business are invariably the Big League. Just like the co-ops, these strong market organizations are a force to contend with inside their own borders, but a willing partner of the oligopoly in the grain trade. The net result is a degree of pluralism among different groups—the private companies, cooperatives, and state organizations—competing against each other on the margin only to reinforce the dominant position of the six major companies.

NOTES

1. The UN Food and Agriculture Organization's basic projection for world demand for wheat is 441 million metric tons in 1985, from 355 million in 1972-74. United Nations Food and Agriculture Organization, *Commodity Projections 1985* (ESC: PROJ/78/8), June 1978, p. 4.

2. U.S. Federal Trade Commission, *Report of the Federal Trade Commission on Methods and Operations of Grain Exporters,* 2 vols. (Washington, D.C.: U.S. Government Printing Office, 1922-23), vol. 1, *Interrelations and Profits*, pp. 41-43.

3. This figure does not include all earnings of Cargill affiliates outside the United States and Canada.

4. Cargill owns one bank—the Bank of Ellsworth in Ellsworth, Wisconsin.

5. U.S. Congress, Senate, *Multinational Corporations and United States Foreign Policy*, pt. 16, p. 101.

6. Cargill reported in 1975-76 an effective tax rate of 31.5 percent on its earning in the United States and an effective worldwide rate of 30.3 percent. Its actual rates are lower when subsidiary earnings outside the consolidated corporate family are included.

7. U.S. Congress, Senate, *Multinational Corporations and United States Foreign Policy*, pt. 16, p. 234.

8. Ibid.

9. This figure is also on the conservative side since Cargill Export, Inc., reported sales in one year alone of over $270 million.

10. Since this writing, Cargill's, as well as other traders', corporate structures may have been modified.

11. U.S. Congress, Senate, *Multinational Corporations and United States Foreign Policy*, pt. 16, p. 136.

12. Ibid., p. 120.

13. U.S. General Accounting Office, *Issues Surrounding the Management of Agricultural Exports,* Report to the Congress by the Comptroller General of the United States (Washington, D.C.: General Accounting Office, 1977), 2: 60.

14. Refer to Dan Morgan, *The Merchants of Grain* (New York: Viking, 1979), p. 89; and James Trager, *Amber Waves of Grain* (New York: Arthur Fields Books, 1973), pp. 23-25.

15. Under the terms of a December 1971 Swiss court ruling, Continental Grain (U.S.), Finagrain, and the other principal Fribgest shareholder, Banque de l'Indochine, agreed to settle on Fribgest's outstanding financial obligations prior to its dissolution.

16. Finagrain's importance subsequently declined when roughly 90 percent of its management and trade staff moved over to a new Lebanese-owned firm, Coprasol, in the late 1970s. Management oversight was reasserted by Mr. Fribourg in New York.

17. As far as can be determined, this line of ownership and management relationship does not apply to Dreyfus U.S.'s operations within or outside the United States.

18. This figure is for all commodities exported by Dreyfus to Louis Dreyfus, Paris.

19. Less than 15 percent of consolidated U.S earnings and 10 percent of assets in a record year were for DWS Holdings.

20. "The (Strictly) Private Sector," *Forbes*, 1 November 1976, p. 39.

21. U.S. Federal Trade Commission, *Methods and Operations of Grain Exporters,* 1: 44.

22. Bankers Trust Company Chase Manhattan Bank, Chemical Bank, and Morgan Guaranty Trust Company are the principal banks for Bunge Corporation.

23. Cook Industries, "Notice and Proxy Statement," submitted to the U.S. Securities and Exchange Commission, 10 May 1978, p. 5. A U.S. affiliate of another large Japanese trading firm Marubeni, Bunge, and Farmers Export Company acquired the remaining grain-related assets.

24. Cook Industries, Inc., *Annual Report 1975*, p. 5; and *Moody's Industrial Manual 1978* (New York: Moody's Industrial Service, 1978), p. 1531.

25. Cook Industries, Inc., *Annual Report 1975*, pp. 3-4.

26. Ibid., p. 56.

27. The Hunt case involving Commodity Futures Trading Commission proceedings against Nelson Bunker Hunt, W. Herbert Hunt, and members of their families was initiated in April 1977. The position of the CFTC was upheld in a final court ruling on 21 July 1981. Four Chicago brokers have independently filed suit against the Hunts concerning the same matter.

28. Engelhard sets Philipp Brothers as a new company, *Milling & Baking News,* 7 April 1981, p. 11.

29. "Major New Entry Into Grain Exporting," *Milling & Baking News*, 19 December 1978, p. 49.

30. Michel-Louis Debatisse, *Le Commerce International Des Céréales* (Paris: Centre Français Du Commerce Extérieur, 1979), p. 142.

31. The agreement to assume a 50 percent share of Toepfer's grain division went into effect July 1979, with the following participating cooperatives: (a) U.S.—Gold-Kist and Indiana Farm Bureau Cooperative Association; (b) The Netherlands—CEBECO (Central Dutch Cooperative); (c) Germany—D.R.W.Z.; (d) France—U.N.C.A.C. (Union Nationale des coopératives agricoles de céréales).

32. Ray A. Goldberg, *Agribusiness Management for Developing Countries: Southeast Asian Corn System and American and Japanese Trends Affecting It* (study prepared by Harvard University for the U.S. Department of State, Contract AID/csd 3153, 1979), p. III-58.

33. The Andersons, "Form 10-K," submitted to the U.S. Securities and Exchange Commission, 31 December 1977, p. 4. Cargill also leases space from the Andersons' largest elevator.

34. Affidavit of Howard W. Hjort, Director of Economics, Policy Analysis and Budget, U.S. Department of Agriculture, filed in *Hiatt Grain & Feed, Inc.*, v. *Bob Bergland, Secretary of Agriculture,* 602 F. 2d 929, U.S Court of Appeals, 10th Circuit (16 July 1979).

35. *Federal Register*, 42, no. 135 (14 July 1977): 36234.

36. This exclusive licensing arrangement actually may be in violation of European Community laws, notwithstanding the fact that it is sanctioned by the French government.

37. Farmland Industries, a regional cooperative, and the Cyrus Eaton Group formed a joint venture in early 1981 specializing in barter transactions with Eastern Europe. Former Secretary of Agriculture Bob Bergland is president. It is, thus, a potential rival for INTERAGRA.

4

The Grain Traders:
What They Do

Proponents and defenders of the Big League argue that these firms have arrived at their present situation because of their operating prowess and efficiency, and that the size of their operations reflects economies of scale. No doubt they do offer many efficiencies in distributing and handling large volumes of grain, but the question remains as to whether the current industry structure favors the exploitation of producers and consumers, and makes it all but inevitable that at least a portion of the Big League traders' profits are generated at the expense of these two groups.

The Big League and their smaller brethren have played an indisputably important role in opening up new overseas markets for U.S. agricultural products since the conclusion of World War II. The resulting export sales have constituted both a plus factor in the American balance of payments and a seemingly providential solution to a chronic overproduction problem. Because of these sales, encouraged by government but carried out by the private trade, the American taxpayer has largely been spared the burden of expensive income and price support payments to farmers while farmers have been provided with a commercial outlet for their excess production.

In the best of all possible worlds, the grain traders' activities would be beneficial in at least one other important way. The prices received by producers and paid by consumers would reflect the true market price. In such a world of perfect competition none of the parties involved—producers, traders, or consumers—would have sufficient power to distort the workings of the market, affecting both the availability of supplies and prices. Reality, however, is quite different due to the fact that a few companies now have enough market power and institutional strength to limit effective competition at the very least to their own ranks. The Big League is now in a position to dictate its own terms to producers and consumers, particularly with the assistance of the U.S. and foreign governments.

These same firms are also in a position to limit entry into the industry. New entrants like Cook or Farmers Export have to wrestle not only with the Hunts but the strength of the Big League within the United States and abroad. Although the U.S. government has granted American cooperatives special anti-trust exemptions, their members continue to compete fiercely for sales, with the largest portion going to the grain trade oligopoly. Rather than diminishing the Big League's overwhelming share of the export market, the co-ops, thanks to this lower order of competition, have reinforced the "elite's" position.

Actual industry profit levels are difficult to ascertain with any precision, but they are generally higher than acknowledged and made in ways not generally understood. Industry representatives often point to the low profit margins on their sales contracts and cite such figures as evidence of the competitiveness and efficiency of the industry at large. Such arguments, insofar as they are effective, undoubtedly perform two useful functions simultaneously. They serve in the first instance to deflect public criticism, and scrutiny, and in the second to understate average industry profit levels.

One common misconception is that grain trading companies must buy from growers at inordinately low prices and sell high to foreign buyers if they are to make money. Such a view is completely false. These firms can make as much, if not more, money in a period when export prices are down as when they are at a peak. The key to profitability in the grain trade is not the price itself but a host of other factors including the variation in price levels for a commodity *at any given point in time,* the spread between cash and futures prices, interest rates, the state of the money markets, and transportation costs. Many of these parameters are established quite independently of export price levels, which are determined in large part by the amount of production available for export and actual foreign demand. But the amount of production available for export does not solely determine the amount of profit a trader can make. Volume is essential to profitability, but not to profit margins on individual transactions.

Farmers associate higher profits with a bullish market and hence higher prices. Not so the grain trader, who may well prefer an interaffiliate transaction at a below-market price to a contract that offers an ostensibly higher cash return. The largest international grain houses, in fact, are individually the biggest buyers of their own product, for the benefits of interaffiliate transactions often outweigh the apparently lower profit margins such contracts entail. Tax considerations and volume are more important to the Big League than are price differentials. Those higher prices so important to the American farmer may be counter to corporate interests if the result is reporting more income in the United States, where corporate income taxes are effectively among the highest in the world. And deals involving the most favorable of price differentials may be rendered unattractive if they involve operating a high volume elevator at less than full capacity or delaying the departure of a chartered ship. Small wonder that in the world of the grain trade export price levels are almost irrelevant to profitability. And small wonder, too, that reported profit margins on sales contracts constitute something less than the full story.

One set of implications of the high degree of concentration and mode of operations in the grain trading business is, therefore, that the largest firms in the industry are in a position to dictate prices, to limit entry, and effectively to conceal their profit margins. The same group of firms is likewise able to pursue its own interests at the expense of producers from any single country and without regard to national concerns. Still, their strength is rooted in their access to fertile sovereign food resources. Their profits are by no means derived solely from the sale of United States' exports, for they are also the outlet for the bulk of Brazil's soybean oil and meal and much of Argentina's wheat and corn, to name but a few commodities that compete directly in the world marketplace with American agricultural products. As long as global demand is adequate, American producers may not suffer, but such is not often the case. Instances when sizable purchases from one country do not have a negative effect on the receipts of producers in other countries are rare. From the standpoint of producers, the world of the grain trade is a Hobbesian one, and the Big League is Leviathan.

Despite the potentially, and sometimes actual, negative effects of the behavior of these firms on the fortunes of individual countries and their producers and consumers, the international grain traders' operations are essentially undeterred by national regulatory efforts. A firm with an efficient international corporate structure and active representation in the major importing and exporting countries can, in fact, make money by playing off one set of government restrictions against those of other nations. It is necessary only that there not be so many restrictions as to create a worldwide reduction of trade and that prices not be effectively regulated within defined limits. It is the variation in daily prices registered on the commodity exchanges, along with the ability to purchase and sell huge volumes of grain throughout the world, that is the gold in the grain and not the grain itself. As long as international trade flows are not arrested over an extended period of time or variation in grain prices constrained, the profits of the Big League traders are unlikely to be curtailed by the actions of national governments any more than they would be enhanced by a truly free trade environment.

The high degree of concentration in the grain trading business worldwide thus has important implications for most national economies, particularly for a major exporter such as the United States, where the level of government intervention has been relatively moderate. Even if governments recognize this relationship to national economic interests, few have attempted to restore the private/public balance of power with regard to grain. Indeed, most governments have found it convenient, if not necessary, to court the favor of the Big League in order to satisfy their country's import/export requirements. Inevitably, these immediate requirements preempt any development of a uniform international grain trading system for importing and exporting countries alike.

The resulting clash of national interests ensures that the most agile grain houses will continue to make money and that shortsighted food policies among sovereign states will prevail.

FRANCÉRÉALES

In January 1970 a group of 12 grain exporting companies in France signed a formal agreement establishing an economic consortium that was legal under a 1967 French law allowing companies to join in a common trust to promote French exports. The consortium, Francéréales, was effectively a cartel, and its membership included such Big League representatives as Société Française Bunge, Compagnie Contanentale France, Société Granax (Tradax/Cargill subsidiary in France), and Société Louis Dreyfus. One of the purposes of the cartel was to divide up the market for French grain exports among its members, and Compagnie Continentale France was allocated the largest share while the other companies' quotas reflected their traditional share of French wheat and barley exports.[1] Among the subsidiaries of Big League firms, only Maecom, Cook's subsidiary, was absent from the membership list. Later Maecom was to claim that it, along with two smaller firms,[2] had been ostracized.

Such a cartel, while legal under French law, was of questionable legality under European Community law. Similarly, the participation of subsidiaries of companies in a venture whose collective purpose was, in part, to undercut the market for American products left the companies involved open to prosecution under U.S. antitrust law. It was, in short, an arrangement of dubious legality and a party to international trade tensions.

One of the purposes of the cartel was to divide up the market among its members. The other was to seek increased sales of French grains in 16 targeted countries, most of which were in Asia and Eastern Europe.[3] When a prospective foreign buyer, having qualified as a government-controlled organization under a very loose set of criteria, entered into negotiations for French wheat or barley, the cartel was given exclusive rights by the French government to conduct and handle the transaction. The French government's role was crucial in giving Francéréales a competitive edge in sales to state monopoly-run markets. ONIC (Office National Interprofessionel des Céréales), a special bureau within the French Ministry of Agriculture, helped put package deals together with special financing from COFACE (Compagnie Française d'Assurance Pour Le Commerce Extérieur), an agency whose function was to offer credit on favorable terms for private foreign investment and trade.

Although active in setting up this special arrangement in 1970, the government did not make participation in Francéréales a precondition to selling French grains in foreign markets other than the targeted countries. Moreover, prior to 1970 a voluntary agreement existed much along the lines of the formal venture with the tacit acceptance of the French government. Representatives of Big League members maintain that they had no choice but to participate if they wanted to trade French grains and retain representation in Paris. Records of the group suggest otherwise. Minutes of their meetings show an effort to jockey for a larger quota on the part of each firm, but no sign of moral outrage or even disgruntlement over the cartel's existence.

The formal agreement was signed in 1970, but the cartel's operations actually began at least two years earlier. One of the cartel's first acts was the August 1968 sale of French milling wheat and barley malt to Japan, which had been considered a traditional American and Canadian market—off-limits to France—up to that time and which was not included on the list of target countries in the 1970 agreement. The 1968 Japanese sale involved 58,000 tons of French milling wheat at a price well below the levels established by the recently concluded Wheat and Food Aid Convention and the Common Agricultural Policy (CAP) of the European Communities. The price was made possible only via incentives granted by the French government, and the transaction led to strident objections from both the United States and Canada. The U.S. Secretary of State, Dean Rusk, observed that

> EC apparently intends to take on pricing in Japanese market so aggressive as to undermine foundation of IGA (International Grains Agreement). If so U.S. cannot stand by and lose market to French wheat. We have no choice but to remain competitive in Japanese market. Prices reported will force us to go below IGA minimum to compete. EC and French must understand that we will do so as soon as reported price is effective.[4]

Both the United States and Canada argued that France was selling its wheat and barley to Japan and Taiwan, where most of the French wheat was ultimately diverted, and Egypt, where the cartel had also shipped grain at roughly the same time, at predatory prices that undercut the Wheat Agreement and, more importantly, intruded into their traditional markets. Sargent Shriver, the U.S. ambassador to Paris, protested to President Pompidou that EC-subsidized wheat shipments of French origin to Japan were undercutting U.S. exports in a market that "it had developed if not created over a long period of years."[5] Canada echoed this claim with regard to French barley shipments.[6] Both governments directed their protests toward the EC and the French governments, not the private traders, apparently unaware of the traders' role and understanding with the French government.

The incident was never completely resolved, and the private companies were never called to task. The European Commission was at the time in a weak position. Hopes for European unity rested largely on the success of CAP, whose success in turn depended on French endorsement and cooperation. Some former EC commissioners later claimed they were shocked to learn of the existence of Francéréales[7] and would have brought the matter before the European court as a violation of the Rome Treaty had they known about it during their tenure. Under the circumstances at the time, however, the European Community had neither the capability nor the inclination to examine closely or otherwise question the role of the French government and the private traders with regard to the Japanese and Taiwanese shipments. Similarly, the United States and Canada, satisfied that their protests had effectively staved off any similar future undertakings by the EC, moderated their criticism. All the governments involved were content to leave the International Wheat Council, whose enforcement of uniform wheat export prices under the 1967 Wheat and Food Aid Convention had been seriously undermined by the incident, in a semi-moribund state.

A near trade war was thus averted, yet the veil of secrecy surrounding Francéréales was never lifted. By the summer of 1973 it was dissolved, having failed to meet the expectations of its members. In the end, it was undone at least in part by the actions of Maecom, the Cook subsidiary, and the two other "outcast" firms that felt left with no other solution than to move aggressively and undercut Francéréales' export prices. Undoubtedly, the insiders concluded that they could offer equally favorable terms to foreign buyers of French grains and still retain their share of this market without Francéréales.

The French government apparently was of two minds. Clearly the International Grains Agreement in 1967 and the total harmonization of member states' agricultural policies under CAP was a boost to the French farmer. Their income security was now underwritten by the entire Community instead of France alone. These two initiatives did not, however, stave off the downturn in prices the following year. Francéréales' foray into Japan and Taiwan worked sufficiently well to justify its formal establishment. Its subsequent lackluster performance did not convince the French government that it could not be tried again.

In 1975 the cartel was resurrected, again without the government coercing the private sector to participate. This time the target of opportunity was the Soviet Union, and the effect of the proposed transaction would have been to undercut thoroughly a threatened moratorium on sales of American grain to that country. Only days before that moratorium was announced by the U.S. government, the head of ONIC and representatives of two participating French cooperatives, whom the French government attempted to put out in front, were in Moscow negotiating a contract for French grain on behalf of the reconstituted cartel. On the insistence of the French agricultural exporters' association, Synacomex (Syndicat National du Commerce Extérieur), two-thirds of the deal was to go to the private companies that had comprised Francéréales. Had the deal gone through, the net effect would have been to undercut the American moratorium and weaken U.S. efforts to negotiate a bilateral agreement assuring the Soviets of access to American supplies in return for limitations upon the amount of those purchases. Once again, however, the profits of their foreign affiliates weighed more heavily on the minds of the Big League. The companies did not withdraw out of any moral compunction or special allegiance to the United States. Quite simply, the Soviets did not bite, as they were in the midst of negotiating an agreement that was more favorable to them over the long term. As far as the Big League was concerned, the 1975 incident—like the earlier period—demonstrated that the profits of their foreign affiliates superseded any obligations or loyalty to the United States, which was negotiating a grain agreement with the Soviets that the companies did not welcome enthusiastically. And, as before, they found their path widened by the conflicting national interests that characterize international politics.

BRAZILIAN SOYBEANS

The divergence of national and private interests, and the ability of the large traders to circumvent the regulatory efforts of any single national government and prosper while doing so, can be clearly discerned in the case of Brazilian soybeans during the 1970s. This was a period of rapid growth in Brazilian soybean production, which grew from 1 million metric tons in 1967 to over 12 million metric tons in 1977, some 80 percent of which went into the export stream with almost 70 percent in the form of soybean meal. This rapid growth in production and the ensuing export campaign was in large part the result of policies pursued deliberately by the Brazilian government with the assistance of several of the largest traders. These actions led directly to a clash between the United States, Brazil, and the European Commission, precipitated in part by the actions of the Big League but from which they emerged the only clear winner.

In the early 1970s, Brazil was a rapidly growing market, especially for soybean feed products, and one highly attractive to the international grain houses. They did not want to lose out on Brazil's agricultural prosperity. Moreover, Brazilian soybeans offered an alternative to U.S. supplies, something that caused considerable anxiety among American producers but something the companies were eager to obtain. The American-based investors were inclined to take advantage of Brazil's soybean incentive program constructed to foster rapid growth and development. A clash became inevitable.

By the time of the U.S. embargo on soybeans in 1973, all the major traders were sufficiently well-entrenched in Brazil to service their customers' contracts from that country, as opposed to the United States, if necessary. They had already secured one hedge by overselling to their affiliates, but access to highly subsidized processed Brazilian beans offered still another opportunity for profit and a means of keeping supply lines open. Although such tactics were perfectly legal, they indirectly hurt American growers and manufacturers. One immediate result was that Brazilian soybean products were sold, by the majors, at a premium price while American prices were depressed by the embargo and a flood of soybean contract cancellations. Inevitably, the foreign buyers and investors looked at Brazil's growth potential as an alternative supply source.

At this time, the United States was the world's largest grower and processor of soybeans and had therefore a vested interest in maintaining its dominant position. Presumably it would have also preferred to limit the growth of Brazil's share of the soybean export market. Nonetheless, in keeping with the traditional American philosophy that foreign subsidiaries of domestic trading firms promote U.S. agricultural exports by generating additional demand and penetrating national tariff barriers, American policies had been conducive to investing in Brazil.[8] Thus when some American-based companies complained in the summer of 1974 to the U.S. Department of Agriculture that they were deliberately excluded by the Brazilian government's export-licensing arm, CACEX, from obtaining licenses, the federal government dutifully protested to the point that U.S. Secretary Butz was reported to have raised the issue during a visit to Brazil. However, other official communications to the Brazilian government voiced American displeasure over the invasion of traditional U.S. markets, particularly Western Europe, by subsidized Brazilian soybean meal and oil. It was a contradictory policy that argued on the one hand for nondiscriminatory treatment of U.S. firms specializing in the export of soy products to their affiliates in Europe and, on the other, for the reduction or limitation of those exports.

If the United States had reason to be apprehensive about the rapid increase in the volume of soybean products from Brazil which were finding its way into the export stream, so did the European Commission. It was concerned because of the threat to the region's own soybean processing industry. Continental, Cargill, and Unilever owned the biggest, most modern crushing facilities in Western Europe, where profitability depended on cheap soybean imports that could enter the EC duty-free. The EC had agreed, in response to intensive U.S. efforts, to exempt raw soybeans from its normal levies. With a growing processing industry, it was to the EC's advantage to import duty-free, unprocessed beans. Highly subsidized Brazilian meal and oil, however, were a direct threat.

FEDIOL, the European soybean processor's association, filed a complaint against Brazil for dumping, which allegedly forced FEDIOL's member plants to operate at a loss.[9] Among the complainants in the case were Cargill Soya and Central Soya in the Netherlands.[10] Noticeably absent were the other large international crushers and their corporate trading arms, whose affiliates figured prominently in Brazil.[11] They were instead lobbying the U.S. government to insist that Brazil award them export licenses commensurate with their long-standing dominant market there. In this conflict the majors were at an advantage whatever the outcome, but they had nothing to gain by supporting FEDIOL's case for relief based on principles of free trade. The United States, however, chose to ride with FEDIOL. The grounds for FEDIOL's complaint were clear-cut, and the case was rapidly resolved. Brazil backed down, and agreed to reductions in its subsidy program to avoid the countervailing duties which would otherwise have been imposed by the EC. In so doing, Brazil was admitting that it had been engaging in practices that were a flagrant violation of the trading system established by GATT.

As with the Francéréales incident, none of the governments involved evidenced any recognition of the role played by the international grain houses when they had given them a relatively free hand to advance or abuse their national interests. In both instances, these firms were in no way hampered by a protectionist-inspired trade conflict. Indeed they gained from it, while the countries involved lost in varying degrees. Brazil's aggressive pursuit of the export market was only partially successful and not without significant costs. The establishment and maintenance of a large subsidy was in itself costly, and in the end the bulk of these subsidies went not to the local cooperatives the program was ostensibly designed to protect but to the largest international firms which, as a result, strengthened their position in Brazil. The EC's competitive posture was eroded as independent European crushers were gradually forced to surrender a greater share of the market to the international grain lords. They could not compete with these global giants with their subsidies in Brazil, special protection in Europe, and easy access to relatively cheap American soybeans. As for the United States, it suffered both losses for its producers and processors and a discrediting of its agricultural export policies at home and abroad. Few seemed to notice that of all the participants, only the international traders had had nothing to lose.

EUROPE

The EC Common Agricultural Policy (CAP) has proven to be an extremely costly form of protectionism straining the Commission's budget but at the same time a very profitable environment for the veteran international grain traders. The nuts and bolts of CAP's machinery are import levies, export subsidies, and intervention prices, which are the minimum internal prices supported by member governments for most commodities (including grains but excluding soybeans under the Trade Agreement of 1965). The domestic or intervention price always has been pegged above the international price to provide income security to producers and achieve self-sufficiency. Now that surpluses prevail, the internal price serves mainly as an income guarantee. In order to enforce this price structure, CAP operates on a system of import protection and export subsidization. Import levies and export subsidies are the mechanisms winding the internal clockwork. The former are essentially tariffs, adjusted daily in such a way as to bring c.i.f. grain prices in line with the EC threshold price (the target or wholesale price above the intervention level set to account for transportation differentials between intervention centers in member countries) for grains of comparable quality and use. When external prices are lower and the EC is holding costly surpluses—a persistent trend in the last decade—the EC offers restitution payments on supplies available for export. These refunds redirect grain from domestic to export markets, reducing the burden on states' intervention agencies to continue buying in times of excessive production. Following textbook rules, subsidized exports reduce stocks, and prices stay at the minimum EC support level.

To operate effectively, the European Commission needs daily market information that accurately reflects the international price of traded grains. The Chicago-Minneapolis-Kansas City futures market triangle tells only half the story, since it does not report the price of a commodity shipped to a foreign port. Amsterdam-Rotterdam-Antwerp (A-R-A), as the busiest grain shipping center in the world, has become an essential source of information on c.i.f. transactions. The combination of U.S. f.o.b. and A-R-A c.i.f. news completes the price picture which the Commission needs to post its daily levy. If the information is skewed, the levy will be too high or too low, resulting in revenue losses and long-term market distortions for the EC as well as other importing and exporting countries.

Since A-R-A has no central exchange that parallels the Chicago Board of Trade, the Commission has relied on intervention agencies in each member state to poll the trade on daily c.i.f. prices, coming mainly from A-R-A, the primary import point for Western Europe. Companies report the lowest bids on their cargoes as to actual, certifiable transactions, on the theory that this enables the Commission to post the highest possible levy that corresponds to market trends and thereby to protect fully the internal European intervention or purchase price. A maximum of 20 companies are polled in Europe's principal ports, but generally the list is confined to the elite of the trade: Cargill/Tradax, Bunge, Continental, Dreyfus, Garnac-André, and Toepfer.[12] These firms actively engage in interaffiliate transactions that do not necessarily depend on true market prices. Moreover, depending upon their own position, they may have a vested interest in securing a certain posted levy.

To alleviate burdensome bureaucratic controls and at the same time instill relative stability within the EC, it was first thought that the most appropriate way to administer the system would be to allow grain traders to pre-fix their levies, or reserve their shipments, at a fixed tariff level for as long as 90 days ahead of the import date. With such a substantial lead time, companies could pin down their import costs by securing a designated amount for import at the levy posted on the day that they fixed, or registered with the Commission. In effect, they were getting at minimal cost a guarantee on a designated amount of imports into the EC for a fixed entry price, which facilitated their hedging operations and other export commitments. They lost no flexibility in the process because they could back out of the original fixed levy, replacing it with another in the future, incurring only a relatively small penalty. Part of a good levy play depends on the level a trader is able to fix in relation to his futures position and cash holdings. With the Commission's loose price reporting system and the extended grace period for holding a levy on a predetermined amount of imports, it could be to the shipper's advantage to register higher c.i.f. bids with the Commission in order to obtain a lower levy for grain he had already purchased. On the other hand, if the grain merchant anticipated a bearish trend in world grain markets and was short in inventories or futures, it could be to his advantage to lock in a portion of his business with a relatively high levy.

By definition, such a system is vulnerable to manipulation and, to a large extent, the companies hold the cards. In 1967, just prior to CAP's harmonization in all member countries, the U.S. agricultural attachés described some of the main loopholes, many of which remain to this day.

> This intentionally deceptive reporting which occurs frequently is done to influence applicable EEC levies, i.e. to increase or decrease them according to the desires of the reporter. . . . Incidentally, firms will also often sell a small quantity of a commodity at an unrealistic price if they feel sure that they can influence the levy in the direction they want.[13]

The U.S. government, on the other hand, felt assured that the price information it obtained from identical sources in the private sector was not open to the same kind of rigging: ". . . we are trusted not to report information to any German or EEC reporting agency, which is often being given incorrect prices in an effort to influence EEC levies."[14]

Ironically, it was almost as important for the U.S. government as for the European Community to obtain reliable price reports mirroring actual market conditions. Otherwise, American calculations of export subsidies (when they are in effect) or food assistance allocations would be seriously off base. Government payments for these two programs were directly related to c.i.f price levels, and the main source of this information was the same as the European Commission's—the international grain houses operating out of A-R-A. Without a true reading of the market, Washington may have offered more subsidies than might otherwise have been warranted. Similarly, PL 480 allocations depended on cash prices, which, for government review purposes, were a combination of Rotterdam c.i.f, Gulf f.o.b., and exchange spot prices. The higher the price when the government went into the market to make its purchases, the less quantity would be available for food aid purposes. Mixed signals from Europe could skew the whole process and end up costing the federal government and, ultimately, aid recipients a great deal of money.

Despite the system's vulnerability to manipulation, Washington and Brussels have generally preferred to tackle the problem as a question of minor adjustment in the levy or price polling apparatus and leave the overall system intact. When Commission officials found that giving the companies the widest lattitude possible for prefixing levies coupled with a 90-day period resulted in allowing them actually to import grains below the threshold or minimum internal EC price, the Commission's response was to shorten the time period for levy fixing. Even this minor step has been modified, for on occasion the Commission has reextended it. Nothing has been done to address the fact that the levy rules allow the biggest importers to monopolize the market. By pre-fixing large quantities sufficiently in advance, no matter how long the time period, the large traders can leave little opportunity for other suppliers. The present system is inherently biased in favor of the Big League.

The EC system also offers special subsidies or export restitutions for different parts of the world. Traders can pre-fix their restitutions for specific amounts much as they are allowed to do with levies. On a number of occasions the Commission's announced export tenders have all been picked up in advance of the export date. This phenomenon is permissible, but it produces the same net effect as the EC's handling of imports in that the major international grain houses have consistently managed to dominate the market with little possibility for smaller competitors. The Commission is acutely aware of this problem, but, again, it has taken the limited response of shortening the time period in which a company can hold an export license at a pre-fixed restitution level. This step has neither arrested the immediate buying up of EC export tenders at the most favorable restitution levels possible nor fostered any degree of competition. In fact, the entire CAP system has served to reinforce the dominant market position of the majors.

Today, the private sector argues that these possibilities are remote, that everything changed in 1967 when CAP was harmonized and that, over time, levy plays and other balancing acts have become a footnote in history. In reality, the system has changed little, and from the perspective of an open market, conditions have worsened to the point that some Commission officials have argued that the trend is irreversible toward greater concentration as long as CAP remains in its present form. As CAP grows increasingly complex to administer, the scale of investment necessary for a company to operate successfully is more than most smaller grain traders can afford. This explains in large part the rise in the number of bankruptcies and acquisitions in the European grain business in recent years. For its part the United States has done equally little to foster competitive, open market conditions. It continues to rely on Rotterdam c.i.f price information reported by a select group of traders for its own operations, and relies upon this information as an accurate indication of current market trends, the questionable integrity of the data notwithstanding.

Such a system involves a double risk. On the one hand, the Big League's subsidiaries in Europe can report out arbitrary c.i.f bids, which are then picked up in Brussels, translated into posted levies, and transmitted to other capitals around the world. Alternatively, the companies can influence the market more indirectly by the mere fact of their size, and achieve virtually the same results at considerable cost to the broader scope of public concerns. Big League purchases in the United States have a disproportionate weight on short-term price movements (cash and futures) with attendant effects in other grain trading capitals. If a large trader wants to influence Rotterdam c.i.f. prices, and hence the EC levy, he does not necessarily have to rig reported bids in A-R-A. Instead, he can enter the American market in such a way as to have an impact on a daily report in Europe, since Rotterdam generally registers the pulse of the exchanges in the United States more than the other way around.[15] If the news out of Chicago in the early morning, which precedes Brussels' announcement of a daily levy position, is bearish (or bullish), an experienced trader can anticipate a jump or decline in the levy and act accordingly.

The other side of the coin results from the fact that there are instances when Rotterdam c.i.f prices or Brussels' levy announcements affect American price movements the following day, as the exchanges open.[16] If bids reported out of Rotterdam are unusually low, the news could dampen cash and futures prices in the United States, allowing a knowledgeable buyer an ideal opportunity to pick up cheaper contracts. Under such circumstances, no one would have a better sense of proper timing than the Rotterdam reporters themselves, namely, the Big League traders.

Governments tend to be more parochial in their national agricultural policies than grain traders. Their narrow focus on production or domestic farmer income problems results in various protectionist devices that ultimately play into the hands of the grain traders, whose interests and operations transcend national borders. The net result is that the dexterity and market influence of the Big League, instead of reducing protectionism, may actually foster it.

When EC levies or restitutions do not achieve their purpose, the grain firms must share in the blame. The Commission response has not been to reduce their influence and the potential for manipulation. Instead, it has been to raise the intervention price for European farmers and the export subsidies to alleviate resulting surplus production. The United States has likewise resorted to export subsidies in the past, notwithstanding the fact that the grain traders's participation in an organization like Francéréales or Brazil's export program can precipitate the need for such action. Rarely do these subsidies offer long-term assistance to producers or consumers, but they do ensure, at a minimun, windfall profits for those grain houses that are the most internationalized in their operations.

When the EC steps up its own subsidy program necessitated by the inherent weakness of its own system, which encourages production totally independent of existing demand, the United States, Canada, and others frequently find it necessary to respond. One result can be a trade war with untold long-term consequences, far more damaging in terms of production, consumption, and general equity considerations than the original initiative. Less dramatic scenarios occur frequently, the cost of which are analogous if proportionately lower. But the least likely to be scathed are the grain traders, even though it is their efforts to circumvent protectionist measures which may precipitate those very policies that trigger international trade conflicts and disruptions.

NOTES

1. Quotas or shares assigned for the fiscal year ending 31 July 1970 were as follows:

Name	Percent Share
Société Française Bunge	4.88
Compagnie Algérienne de Meuneria	4.65
Compagnie Continentale France	14.16
Compagnie Européenne de Céréales	6.12
Compagnie Grainière Paris	8.48

Name	Percent Share
Comptoir Commercial André	5.66
Société Louis Dreyfus	11.12
Société Goldschmidt	10.67
Société Granax	3.76
Etablissements G. & P. Levy	4.21
Union Générale des Coopératives Agricoles Françaises	12.35
Union Nationale des Coopératives Agricoles de Céréales	13.94

Cited in "Francéréales Règlement Intérieur: Généralités," unpublished document of Francéréales' Internal Regulations.

2. The two smaller French firms referred to are Soules and Soufflet.

3. China, North Korea, Sudan, Syria, Egypt, Brazil, Tunisia, Algeria, Morocco, USSR, Poland, Romania, Bulgaria, Hungry, Czechoslovakia, and East Germany. "Francéréales, Règlement Intérieur: Généralités," Art. 8.

4. Secretary of State Dean Rusk to American Embassy, Brussels, U.S. Department of State, Telegram 216431, 7 August 1968. (FOIA material.)

5. Sargent Shriver, American Embassy, Paris, to Secretary of State, Washington, D.C., U. S. Department of State, Telegram 11266, 23 July 1969. (FOIA material.)

6. U.S. Mission, Brussels, translation of a Canadian note to the European Commission on the subject of "Canadian Protest Against EEC Barley Export Subsidies," transmitted 29 April 1969. Unpublished.

7. They claimed no knowledge of the cartel until their discussions with Richard Gilmore in 1978.

8. Richard Gilmore with the assistance of Frederick Blott, "U.N. Food and Beverage Industry Report," UN Center on Transnational Corporations, United Nations, January 1978, pp. 153-220. Mimeographed.

9. FEDIOL, EEC Seed Crushers' and Oil Processors' Federation, "Request for the application of Council Regulation EEC 459/68 on Protection Against Dumping or the Granting of Bounties or Subsidies by Countries which are not Members of the European Economic Community," 3 January 1977.

10. FEDIOL, "Request for the application of Council Regulation EEC 459/68," Annex 1, p. 3.

11. Cargill Agricola, S.A.; ADM, Do Brazil Produtos Agricolas LTDA; Anderson Clayton CIA Industria E Commerciao; CIA Continental DR; Cereais Contribrasil, NV, Bunge; Tradax Export; Alfred C. Toepfer; Finagrain; Cook Industries; Panchaud Frères, S.A. (André).

12. U.S. Congress, Senate, Committee on Foreign Relations, *Multinational Corporations and United States Foreign Policy, Hearings before the Subcommittee on Multinational Corporations,* 94th Cong., 2d sess., pt. 16; 18, 23, and 24 June 1976, pp. 187, 200. (After 1 July 1967 the CAP was completely harmonized, but the price-polling practices have remained virtually unchanged.)

13. Ibid., p. 194

14. Ibid., p. 188.

15. Ibid., p. 113.

16. U.S. Department of Agriculture, Economic Research Service, "Relationship Between Daily Grain Price Movements on Rotterdam and U.S. Markets and EC Levy," submitted to the Senate Foreign Relations Subcommittee on Multinational Corporations, June 1976. Unpublished.

5

The U.S. System: History of U.S. Farm Policy Since World War II

The recovery of American agriculture after the Great Depression was made possible by a dual policy of farm support programs and government-engineered development of foreign markets. Washington's assumption of an active role was an act of necessity that was generally well received by the farm community writ large. Under successive administrations the federal government wrote a new chapter for American agriculture. The ensuing near-miraculous turnaround in production and boost to farm incomes appeared the perfect remedy. Only gradually did the underlying problems of this structural shift from a domestic to a foreign demand-based economy surface.

The cornerstone of American farm policy since the Roosevelt administration has been the Agricultural Adjustment Act (AAA) of 1933. The AAA was a piece of New Deal legislation that fashioned the principle of parity whereby the government agreed to support crop prices at the parity level. The original definition of parity was an assured price for individual commodities that maintained their value in relation to other goods and services for the same base period of 1909 to 1914. The concept was to provide farmers with adequate purchasing power or an indirect income guarantee. Parity was, and is, an indirect income guarantee to farmers. Viewed as such, it could be expected to arouse powerful antagonisms. In 1933, however, the pressing need for adequate farm income and crop prices outweighed any philosophical misgivings about an expanded role for government.

It may be said that the AAA is an example of a governmental initiative that was too successful. The promise of absolute (100 percent) parity, while highly attractive to producers, inspired overproduction that ultimately became a drain on government resources. Finding a way to reduce that drain without openly attacking the parity principle has been a major objective of every subsequent administration's farm policy.

The first such effort was the Brannan plan, unveiled in April 1949 by the Truman administration. Secretary of Agriculture Brannan proposed to reduce the government's obligation to ensure parity through high prices. Instead, he offered a formula by which the government would underwrite a minimum average farm income level through direct government payments, whereas prices would be allowed to reflect the real supply and demand forces of the marketplace. This plan was ill-fated for the principle of parity was seen as an all but nonnegotiable item by the politically powerful farm bloc. Accordingly, Secretary Brannan's effort to separate the issues of agricultural income and farm prices failed. The deep-rooted consequences of this failure, however, were obscured for a time. The Korean War, which began in 1950, depleted commodity surpluses and kept prices above the minimum parity support levels, thus deferring further difficulties until after the election of a new administration.

President Eisenhower was elected on the promise of peace in Korea. His success on the diplomatic front, however, was a bad omen for American agriculture. The war, as with World War II, had stimulated demand abroad for U.S. grain. Its sudden end, coupled with good harvests, ushered in a new cycle of mounting government stocks and depressed farm prices. As a stopgap measure, the administration turned to the new U.S. food assistance program, "Food for Peace" (PL 480), as a means of channeling some of the excess supply into foreign markets. It also initiated new government payments under the Soil Bank program for idling land as a means of cutting back production.

Neither outlet, however, was used effectively enough to have the desired effect for American farmers. Eisenhower's Secretary of Agriculture, Ezra Taft Benson, had hopes of tackling the problems largely through freeing prices from the parity anchor. The Agricultural Act of 1954 did establish a flexible pricing system whereby basic commodity price supports ranged from 75 to 90 percent of parity. Although a significant departure from the earlier fixed support provisions during the Korean War, the range was not wide enough nor sufficiently flexible to respond to prevailing market conditions. Demand had softened after the Korean War without a corresponding decline in production. As a result, surpluses continued to mount with the government acting as the buyer of last resort. The Benson era was extremely unpopular with the farming community, not only because of its heretical rejection of the parity principle but also because of mismanagement of existing programs.

Left with the failure of Benson's attempts to bolster farm income and reduce government stocks, Kennedy's Secretary of Agriculture Orville Freeman restored parity to its sanctified position in the hope that wheat growers would support an enforced lid on production. They turned it down in a referendum, leaving the administration with no choice but to introduce an inherently less effective voluntary system of production controls. Nonetheless, it did result in a return to the New Deal concept of linking price supports to production levels.

In the absence of stringent controls on domestic production, Secretary Freeman sought recourse in expanded food aid under PL 480 as a means of relieving the pressure of mounting surpluses. Benson had been reluctant to tamper with the export sector, but he too used PL 480 as a tool to develop export markets for future commercial sales. Unable to limit production effectively, the Kennedy administration leaned heavily on the concessional food aid program to draw down stocks accumulated under the Eisenhower period. Thus, despite their espousal of different market philosophies, both the Kennedy and Eisenhower administrations resorted to the use of food aid for virtually identical domestic purposes.

Although Lyndon Johnson was least inclined to disavow the New Deal agricultural heritage, the Johnson administration's farm policies did not noticeably differ from those of its predecessors. During the Johnson years, price support levels were still pegged to parity, albeit at lower levels than before. Voluntary production controls remained in effect, but a severe drought in India did more to relieve the surplus problem in the United States than did any domestic program designed to curb production. Surplus reduction through exports remained a feature of the Johnson years, particularly since the main proponents of such a policy—Orville Freeman and Hubert Humphrey—held key positions in the administration.

Emphasis was placed on sales promotion, a characteristic of all American agricultural policies since World War II. Throughout the farm policies of the Eisenhower, Kennedy, and Johnson administrations ran a consistent thread. Unable, and in varying degrees unwilling, to limit domestic production or to afford the expense of purchasing and storing massive surpluses, the government turned to the export market as a means of bringing demand into balance with supply. The importance of export volume was emphasized above everything else. Yet in each case the role of government was limited to expanding the food aid program. All other aspects of export policy were left in the hands of the private trade. Federal involvement in the management of the farm problem was concentrated on the domestic arena.

In contrast, President Nixon and his Secretaries of Agriculture, Hardin and Butz, set out to develop a more integrated agricultural export strategy, one linked to domestic as well as foreign policy objectives. Although the differences between the Nixon administration's farm policy and that of its predecessors were at the time more rhetorical than substantive, the Nixon years were marked by two major developments: a surge in commercial export sales of American grain, and the passage of the Agriculture and Consumer Protection Act of 1973.

The promotion of exports, this time in the form not of food aid but of commercial sales encouraged and sometimes subsidized by direct government action, was a solution that Secretary Butz found congenial. It suited his philosophy of reliance upon the private sector. It seemed the simplest solution to a chronic problem. Within a very short time commercial sales replaced concessional transfer as the major vehicle for U.S. agricultural exports. How rapidly this change was effected can be seen in the fact that government subsidy payments to private exporters leaped from $55.6 million to nearly $127 million in a single year (1970 to 1971).[1]

In order to make cash sales of American grain affordable to all but the poorest buyers, the Butz program utilized three readily available tools: export credits, barter, and subsidies. None of these were novel devices. All had been used to some extent by previous administrations. What was new in the Nixon/ Butz years was the concerted application of all three tools to commercial sales. The period of surplus disposal through food aid was over.

As indicated, Secretary Butz made increased use of export credits. These had been used extensively under the Marshall Plan, and between 1948 and 1954 the U.S. Export-Import Bank, an autonomous government bank established to finance foreign purchases of American goods, served as a major source of credit for food transfers to Western Europe. During the peak years of PL 480, the Export-Import Bank declined in importance and was eventually replaced by the Commodity Credit Corporation (CCC), which had become part of USDA in 1939 as the federal government's primary agricultural credit arm and risk insurance vehicle.

Export credits had also been utilized by other major exporters, notably Canada and Australia, which had for some years been offering favorable credit terms to importers with nonconvertible currencies (for example, China and the USSR). Further, they had been used to good effect in 1963 by the Kennedy administration, which offered the Soviets export credits to finance a grain deal, a move stimulated in large part by competitive pressure. This last action was generally regarded as successful and the credits as money well spent. U.S. export credits grew rapidly thereafter from their relatively modest 1962 level of $32.8 million, doubling in each of the two succeeeding years,[2] in large part because of the Soviet sale.

It was against this background that the Nixon administration offered the Soviets a new credit package in 1972. It amounted to over $750 million, or 75 percent of total 1973 CCC credits earmarked for wheat and feedgrain purchases. The decision proved to be a major blunder.

Credits had been designed as an incentive for foreign buyers, but in 1972 the Soviets needed no incentive. They purchased over 22 million metric tons of grain to meet their own consumption needs, compared with 7.8 million in the previous year. Moreover, the United States was the only country with a surplus sufficient to supply such a quantity. Nonetheless, proceeding on the basis of faulty information and a certain naiveté, the United States offered the Soviets a double bonus in the form of credits and subsidies, the net effect of which was to reduce the export price below domestic levels. The government spent the next three years trying to disentangle itself from the situation it had helped create. American growers and exporters had even greater difficulty recovering.

The Nixon administration's use of the barter exchange program was not notably more successful than its use of export credits. However, it did drastically increase the volume of transactions taking place under this program. By 1973 barter sales reached the $1.2 billion level and represented almost 11 percent of total U.S. agricultural exports.[3]

The barter program, established in 1954 at roughly the same time as PL 480, was designed to enhance prospects for future commercial sales. Under the authority of the CCC, bartered U.S. agricultural products were traded with qualified foreign countries at a discount below the international price in exchange for goods or supplies produced by these countries. Theoretically, the United States gained in the process by securing access to scarce resources as well as to convenient local supplies. For participating countries, the advantage was clear: access to agricultural commodities at artifically low prices without any expenditure of scarce foreign currency.

Private companies also benefited, particularly the veteran traders.[4] In 1969, for example, Cargill was the second-largest participant in the barter program, with contracts worth over $36 million; Continental ranked sixth with nearly $14 million; Cook, eleventh, with $5.7 million; and Bunge, seventeenth, with $2.3 million.[5] The program was a source of risk-free profits as well as a means of obtaining government financing at noncommercial rates. But few indeed were the transactions under this program that would not or could not have taken place in any event.

By 1973 it had become manifestly clear that the barter program contributed more to private enrichment than public welfare, and the program was suspended. Policy makers had earlier reached a similar conclusion about the subsidy program, which was suspended after the Soviet sales fiasco earlier in the fall of 1972. A series of official investigations concluded that programs to promote export growth in the agricultural sector had been grossly mismanaged by the Department of Agriculture and misused by the private sector.

Domestically, the most significant development during the Nixon years was the Agriculture and Consumer Protection Act of 1973. This administration-sponsored legislation introduced a market-oriented pricing system balanced by government incentives for production controls. In effect, if offered a deficiency payment type approach with assured commodity prices at high enough levels to gain wide acceptance among farmers. It did what Benson and Brannan were unable to do: gradually move away from guarantees of parity and closer to prices that reflect true market conditions.

A new target price system was established, under which the government paid farmers whatever difference existed between the cash price they received for their crop and a fixed target level (adjusted periodically to account for increases in the cost of production). In comparison with guaranteeing farmers' income on the basis of straight parity prices, this method had the ostensible advantage of guaranteeing farmers a minimum income without making the public sector responsible for underwriting production at artificially high prices. The new policy was less costly to the government than a scheme based on full parity because the payments covered only the difference between the loan rate price of the grower's crops used as collateral for federal loans and the fixed target level. To avoid abuses and an overdose of protection, any individual farmer could qualify for a maximum of only $20,000 in support. Even so, the new system could not escape the peril of the old—a tendency to stimulate overproduction.

In the final analysis the Nixon/Butz policies, like the tools of their implementation, were flawed. Indeed, the U.S. position as the world's largest reliable food supplier was imperiled by the 1972 Soviet sale. What started out as a concerted strategy of drawing down stocks and building up export markets crumbled into a succession of ill-conceived, mismanaged initiatives— the subsidy, barter, and credit programs. In the long run, the growth in export volume credited to these policies merely reinforced an inevitable trend toward export dependence that was an outgrowth of American post-World War II policies.

Even the short-run consequences were less than beneficial. With the help of certain outside forces—cyclical shortages, population increases, and changes in dietary habits—Secretary Butz was extremely successful in reducing U.S. grain surpluses, even to a point where there was very little margin between U.S. production and consumption requirements at home and abroad. Domestically, the resulting situation would have been enviable to every Secretary of Agriculture from Wallace in the early 1930s and onward, but internationally it represented an extremely perilous position. Operating so close to the margin meant that any severe food shortage could send the markets into pandemonium. Ironically, the "success" of the new Nixon/Butz export policy has been most evident in the high degree of price volatility and periodic instability displayed by grain markets since the Soviet sale of 1972.

When the Carter administration came into power, events had come full circle. The pendulum had swung back to a position where agricultural production once again exceeded the rate of growth in U.S. grain exports. In 1976-77, America's end-stock position in wheat and course grains had increased almost 60 percent over the previous year. The global grain picture had also improved enough so that the amount of carryover stocks had reached levels equivalent to those in 1969-70, which had represented roughly 16 percent of total grain utilization.[6] At the outset of the Carter administration, the problem was once again one of oversupply. Paradoxically, it was a predicament to which one of the contributing factors was the success of the Butz sales campaign. As a result of the effort, U.S. wheat prices had reached an all-time high in 1974-75. This was followed by higher loan levels which, in turn, raised farmer expectations for the following crop year so that by 1976 U.S. wheat production jumped over 9 million metric tons, prices at the farm dropped approximately 15 percent, and exports dipped by almost 2 million metric tons.[7] A rapidly depreciating dollar compounded the problem. Although U.S. grain became cheaper to foreign buyers as a consequence of the dollar's weakness, their capacity to purchase additional grain imports was limited, particularly in the wake of the energy crisis which left many food-importing nations with a severe balance of payments problem. When, as happened during 1977-78, the value of the dollar dropped faster than exports grew, the government was left with the two-fold task of tackling surpluses and sluggish prices.

Thus the Carter administration's principal domestic farm policy objective upon taking office was to help farmers ride out a period of stagflation—characterized by rising production costs and sluggish demand—in anticipation of an eventual surge in exports. In response to a gloomy price and supply picture it announced a new policy that, like so many before it, proved to be more new in its emphasis than anything else. In part, the need to proclaim a new policy stemmed from the unacceptability of so many of the old measures. PL 480, for example, was no longer an ideal vehicle for disposing of surpluses, given changing attitudes in the United States and in recipient countries. Further, such a program is a creature of the domestic budgetary process, requires relatively long lead times, and cannot easily be utilized as a remedy for sharply decreasing prices.[8] Subsidies were still associated with the 1972 Soviet sale in many minds and would only have put the United States in competition with itself as American grain prices were below those of other suppliers by 1976. Export credits were less objectionable and, with the support of the Department of Agriculture, new legislation was passed in 1978 that provided special credit for foreign buyers toward purchases of U.S. grain, livestock, and construction of facilities designed for storage or distribution of American agricultural commodities. But the bulk of the administration's efforts went into two areas: the negotiation of government-to-government agreements and the establishment of a farmer-held reserve program.

The Carter administration endorsed the bilaterals it inherited from its predecessor and was receptive to enlisting additional countries into similar long-term purchasing arrangements. Secretary Bergland traveled extensively to foreign capitals in search of big buyers. The most dramatic result of this campaign was in the form of increased sales to China after the Secretary's visit in the fall of 1978. Mexico also emerged as a foreign buyer of importance, and the Soviet Union remained America's most important customer. In 1980 American wheat and coarse grain exports had climbed to over 94 million tons *excluding* the contracts for 17 million metric tons to the USSR that were subsequently cancelled in the wake of the Soviet invasion of Afghanistan.

Nonetheless, exports alone were not the answer. Grain exports grew steadily during the 1970s, but it would have taken a booming international economy or severe foreign crop damage to create a foreign demand for American grain sufficient to raise prices above the rate of inflation during this period. Nor is there any reason to believe that, in the depressed international economy created by OPEC's price hikes, even Earl Butz's hard-sell formula would have produced better results. Clearly, domestic measures were needed to remedy the situation.

Secretary Bergland attempted at an early point to modify subtly the parity principle by pegging government support payments to production costs instead of income requirements while otherwise leaving the 1973 target-loan system intact, but this effort quickly failed in Congress, as had the Brannan plan which it most closely resembled. The principle of parity was reaffirmed by Congress, not only in this instance but again in 1979 and then 1980 when support prices were increased at the urging of farm groups. The administration had little choice but to go along with these congressional measures while promulgating at the same time its most novel contribution to American farm policy, a farmer-held reserve system.

A system of reserves and set-asides was instituted by Secretary Bergland under the Food and Agriculture Act of 1977. The administration's objective in introducing this program was to reduce surplus stocks to affordable levels. Set-asides were voluntary and did not involve the more complicated administrative procedure, which had been previously used, of designating quotas for each crop based on prior land use. In the first year of the set-aside program, 1978, farmers had to "set aside" a minimum of 10 percent of their feedgrain and 20 percent of their wheat acreage planted in the previous year in order to receive certain government loans and subsidies, including deficiency payments (the difference between target and "free-market" prices). Fifty-one percent of all eligible farms, which accounted for 72 percent of the national crop, participated.[9] This rate of participation, the government calculated, translated into a 10 percent increase in prices, but it fell short of the boost agricultural producers needed to keep pace with inflation. Producers were hit particularly hard by the rapid surge in energy-related expenses following the 1973 oil embargo, and for most the relatively small increase in earnings created by the set-aside effort was inadequate to offset their increased production costs and capital requirements.

Perhaps in anticipation of the limited success of the set-aside program, the administration combined it with a new reserve program in early 1978. With minor adjustments in the 1977 act, Bergland issued regulations placing the 1976 surplus wheat and feedgrain crops into what was called a "farmer-held" reserve. Under these regulations and beginning with the 1978 crop year, farmers received government payments and waivers of interest on their government loans, enabling them to store their grain for up to three years in exchange for an agreement to hold the grain in reserve until the market price rose to 125 percent of the average loan rate for feedgrains and 140 percent for wheat. (Soybeans were not included in either the reserve or set-aside program because their market remained strong.) At these levels, the farmer was free to sell and pay back his loan, or he could sell earlier and incur a penalty in the form of a requirement to pay back his loan with interest and storage charges. He had a third option of keeping his crop in reserve until it reached the "call price level" of 140 percent of the loan rate for feedgrains and 175 percent for wheat, at which time he would be required to sell.

By placing his grain in reserve, the farmer was entitled to loans covering his crops held as collateral, plus advance storage payments and loans for the construction of farmer-owned storage facilities. In this fashion the government attempted to encourage the construction of on-farm and local elevator storage, as opposed to the use of large facilities owned by the major trading houses. In this way farmers potentially could increase their market influence, assuming they held control of a significant amount of supplies and controlled their availability.

These various incentives proved effectual in the sense that, as with the set-aside program, a substantial proportion of American farmers chose to participate in the reserve program. By 1978-79, on-farm stocks of wheat under the farmer-held reserve accounted for 42 percent of total stocks. Nonetheless, the program proved to be a reserve more in name than in fact. Only temporarily did it remove a portion of excess production from the market and provide relief from downward pressure on prices. But, given the design of the program, when market prices hit the call level they triggered a sudden massive release of surpluses, the effect of which was to depress prices.

This was demonstrated in 1979, when the system was tested for the first time. During the summer of that year, prices climbed to the release level, at which point prices would have dropped precipitously had all the farmer-held reserves been released. The government accordingly stepped in, raising the call level to stabilize the market and shortly thereafter issued a change in the program ending wheat set-asides for the crop year 1979-80. This action was undertaken on the theory that it would bring more production on stream, discouraging any speculative futures buying that would force the release of farmer reserves and dry up supplies at inflationary prices. As a third and final corrective measure, the administration undertook to persuade Congress to authorize government purchases of a maximum of four million metric tons of wheat as a food security reserve. However, this last measure failed, only to become an issue once again after the 1980 Soviet embargo.

These stopgap measures did manage to avoid breaking the dam on reserves and thus flooding the market with new supplies to the detriment of farm prices. Still, prices had climbed high enough to trigger the release of large quantities of corn, wheat, and sorghum with an attendant sharp downward pull on prices. By August 1979, the following amounts of commodities entering into the reserve had reached the call level, at which point participating farmers had to redeem their government loans by selling the crops they were holding under the "reserve" program:

Grain	Total Originally in Reserve	Amount Redeemed	Percent Redeemed
Corn	732.0 million bu.	138.0 million bu.	18.9
Barley	41.2 million bu.	4.7 million bu.	11.3
Wheat	413.0 million bu.	144.0 million bu.	34.9
Oats	39.2 million bu.	6.7 million bu.	17.2
Sorghum	44.3 million cwt.	13.8 million cwt.	31.1[10]

Wheat futures quoted in Kansas City had gone up above the call level from the legislated target range of $3.07 to as high as $4.50 in June 1979, a jump of almost 35 percent. At that point, they stopped climbing and started winding down, partially in reaction to releases from the reserve and government modifications in the set-aside and reserve programs, as well as to shifting assessments of market prospects for the coming marketing year.

Clearly, the government had exercised more foresight than in the past, intervening at a crucial time to help stabilize prices and avoiding a precipitous decline. By adapting the regulations of the reserve system to changing market conditions, the Department of Agriculture moderated the price effect. Washington's response in general helped to keep prices from plummeting, but their bullish pace in the summer of 1979 had less to do with supply management than with a host of other factors outside of Washington's control. At best, the government had effected a short-term rescue operation which prevented the bottom from falling out of the market that was by this time extraordinarily sensitive to events from abroad.

In the wake of the Soviet grain embargo of 1980, the set-aside/reserve program was once again used to keep prices from plummeting. When the commodity exchanges reopened after being closed for two days following President Carter's announcement of the suspension of sales to the USSR, grain prices fell to their daily limit. To prevent a rout by speculators scrambling to take advantage of the sales cancellation by buying at depressed prices, the government intervened to protect farmers. After considerable pressure from Congress, the Carter administration opened up the reserve program to both wheat and corn growers who had previously been ineligible because they had not participated in the original 1979 set-aside program. Prices steadied close to the release price level, shielding farmers from the worst effects of the Soviet embargo. These price levels were, however, below those registered on the market prior to the announcement of the embargo.

When it was introduced in 1978, the farmer-held reserve system was trumpeted by Secretary of Agriculture Bergland as a major innovation in agricultural policy that would boost farmers' income while stabilizing domestic agricultural prices. If it had succeeded, it would have responded to the major concerns of producers and consumers simultaneously. Unfortunately, it did not, in part because it was too limited in scope to obtain its desired effect. In those instances when the new system was most vigorously applied, the "reserve" stocks were accumulated *and* depleted over a very short interval. In this sense the program had little to do with the establishment of a reliable food reserve system. Its contribution to price stabilization at levels which could assure farmers a fair return was equally questionable. Fixed "call" prices triggering the sudden release of supplies created artificial dips in the cash market during the redemption period. Even the Carter administration recognized this pitfall, but its efforts to correct the situation by changing the rules and reserve price levels created only bureaucratic tangles and more market uncertainties.

At best, the program offered only a partial solution. In effect it placed a lid on farmers' earnings and, if anything, put them at a further disadvantage vis-à-vis the private trading firms, who remained free to buy and sell as they chose. Nor were the incentives offered sufficient to redress the initial imbalance between the on-farm storage capacity of participating farmers and that of the private trader, whose warehouses are able to hold twice the amount stored on farms.[11] Thus, even at its peak, the on-farm reserve constituted less than a majority share of total reserves.

The Carter administration promised a sound management approach to agricultural policies and, to a limited extent, it kept its pledge. Production controls were coordinated with domestic and foreign consumption patterns. Secretary of Agriculture Bergland attempted to orient American farm policies in favor of family farms and cooperatives. The administration's programs, however, did little to reverse the trend begun in the late 1950s when U.S. agricultural prosperity was linked to exports. The farmer-held reserve program failed to moderate the inflationary effects created by large, unanticipated export sales. Government efforts to regulate the commodity exchanges and export transactions did not match Secretary Bergland's declared objective of favoring independent operators and the most efficient farm units. A continued export boom diverted attention from these important aspects of national grain policy.

Throughout the Carter years, production and marketing units in the United States continued to grow in size, while the growth of export markets affected every aspect of American agriculture, from issues of farm income and production levels to increased land competition, regional shifts in crop plantings, and livestock feeding patterns.[12] Agricultural production and prices were increasingly determined by the volume of grain exports. Yet, philosophically, America was still bound to the notion that this development was the result of an evolutionary process as natural and beneficial as Adam Smith's law. The government did not hesitate to push sales in foreign markets but was extremely reluctant to consider the domestic consequences of this effect or to develop an integrated policy. American agricultural policy remained primarily a reflex to political pressures and short-term crises.

As the American agricultural economy's export dependence has grown, so has the reliance of government and producers on the private companies dominating that sector. The hold of the major firms on this portion of the market has only been reinforced by the benefits they have been able to reap from the array of government programs laid at their feet—PL 480, barter, export subsidies, credits, insurance, and tax incentives.

Today the link between continuously increasing grain exports and American agricultural prosperity seems unbreakable. Yet the implications of export dependency are enormous. They include questions relating to land use, efficient farm production, transportation, and merchandising—questions that affect the entire production and marketing system. Nonetheless, the governmental response to date has been piecemeal. Thus has a major strength of the U.S. economy (its comparative advantage in agriculture) become a serious weakness.

NOTES

1. U.S. Department of Agriculture, Commodity Credit Corporation, "Quantities and Value of Export Payments Made on Agricultural Commodities for Fiscal Year 1971 through 1976 Transition Quarter," Data prepared by ASCS/FDM/FRAB. Manuscript.

2. U.S. Department of Agriculture, CCC Export Sales Credit Program, Grants for Fiscal Year 1956-1977. Figures provided by the Office of the General Sales Management. Manuscript.

3. Ibid., pp. 3-7.

4. U.S. Department of Agriculture, Office of Audit, *Barter Exchange Program,* Audit Report No. 60158-1-Hq. (Washington, D.C., 1974) p. 16.

5. Ibid., *Exhibit M*, p. 1. This ranking underestimates the value of the contracts awarded to the major grain trading houses because it does not register receipts of companies acting as barter agents for another contractor.

6. U.S. Department of Agriculture, "World Grain Situation Outlook for 1979/1980," *Foreign Agriculture Circular,* FG-11-79 (16 July 1979), pp. 2-3.

7. Ibid., p. 16; and U.S. Department of Agriculture, *World Agricultural Situation,* WAS (July 1979), p. 34.

8. U.S. Department of Agriculture, Food Aid Task Force, *New Directions for U.S. Food Assistance: A Report of the Special Task Force on the Operations of PL 480 to the Secretary of Agriculture* (Washington, D.C., May 1978), p. 104.

9. U.S. Department of Agriculture, *Agricultural Outlook* (Washington, D.C., July 1978), p. 14.

10. U.S. Department of Agriculture, *News*, USDA 1892-79 (Washington, D.C., 10 August 1979).

11. U.S. Department of Agriculture, Agricultural Stabilization and Conservation Service, *USDA Reports Grain Loan Activity through July 31, 1979* (Washington, D.C., 14 August 1979).

12. Philip M. Raup, "Competition for Land and the Future of American Agriculture," in *The Future of American Agriculture as a Strategic Resource, Papers Commissioned for A Conservation Foundation Conference,* eds. Sandra S. Batie and Robert G. Healey (Washington, D.C.: Conservation Foundation, 14 July 1980).

6

The U.S. Export Campaign

The New Deal wrote the constitution for contemporary American agriculture and World War II ensured its rapid economic recovery. The surge in foreign demand gave the needed stimulus to production and ushered in a period of prosperity for farmers. Each successive administration since Roosevelt's, while attempting to develop its own farm policies, has sought to encourage exports as a means of underwriting the U.S. agricultural economy. They have been successful in that the demand for U.S. food resources abroad has grown to exceed consumption requirements at home. The problem Washington has witnessed continually is that when foreign demand falls off, U.S. agriculture and the entire American economy is hurt severely. No way has been found to synchronize production levels with annual demand requirements. The result has been cycles of food shortages and surpluses despite efforts to redress the problem.

Surpluses first emerged in the immediate postwar period, but did not assume major proportions until after the close of the Korean War. In 1951 closing stocks of wheat, feedgrains, and rice had reached 28 million metric tons, but food aid shipments to Korea helped control the further growth of surpluses until the close of that war. Shortly thereafter surpluses began to skyrocket and by 1960 had reached 120 million metric tons, nearly four times the 1951 level.[1] The mounting surpluses of the 1950s led directly to what ultimately became a two-phased U.S. export campaign. Food aid came first, followed by a joint private and public commercial sales drive that included government-negotiated long-term export-import agreements with foreign buyers. Throughout, it has been a campaign planned in Washington but implemented, in no small part, by the private sector. In some ways it has been remarkably successful. In others, it has been remarkably costly.

FOOD AID

The first step in the export campaign took place in connection with the European Recovery Plan (ERP) of 1948, also known as the Marshall Plan. A major element in that bold initiative was a food aid program under which American grain surpluses, already mounting in 1948, were exported to food-hungry Europe. It was a happy marriage of good intentions and self-interest, responding effectively to Europe's immediate food requirements and the U.S. surplus problem as well as its long-term export strategy. ERP food aid shipments in 1948-49 were greater than average annual commercial wheat exports in preceding years, thereby helping rapidly to draw down expensive carryover stocks. Perhaps even more significant, the U.S. share of the world wheat market during this same period increased from roughly one-fourth to approximately one-half of the whole.

Food aid shipments to Korea during the Korean War provided a temporary respite from what would have otherwise been a major surplus problem following the termination of ERP's food program in 1951. By the time of the signing of the Panmunjon truce agreement in June 1953, the potential dimensions of the surplus problem had become sufficiently evident that the Senate Committee on Agriculture and Forestry reported out a major food assistance bill the following month. Commonly referred to as PL 480, this new legislation was heartily endorsed by farm organizations already suffering badly from depressed prices. Put into effect in 1954, it quickly became the linchpin of U.S. efforts to use food aid as a means of surplus disposal.

Since its genesis, PL 480 has undergone several policy facelifts. During its initial phase, the program's primary function was surplus disposal. In 1958, it received a new lease on life when it became known as Food for Peace, following a successful effort by Senator Hubert Humphrey to incorporate market development into the program's objectives. Finally, PL 480 was explicitly acknowledged as an instrument of foreign policy under the Johnson administration following passage of the revised Food for Peace Act in 1966.

This last piece of legislation may well have disappointed President Johnson, who had initially hoped to rename the program "Food for Freedom" and effectively add it to the arsenal of weapons with which the administration sought to conduct the Vietnam War. Nonetheless, the 1966 measure did include several significant modifications to the program. Previously, commodities shipped under food aid had first to be declared "surplus" by the Secretary of Agriculture. Foreign currency generated from food aid sales in the foreign country was initially accepted by the U.S. government for repayment purposes on dollar loans. The revisions eliminated the surplus provision and required concessional transactions handled under Title I of PL 480 to be conducted exclusively in dollars. In addition, food was made conditional upon new "self-help" requirements with certain political criteria added.[2] The net effect of these changes was more direct White House and State Department involvement in food aid decisions via the Department of Agriculture and the Agency for International Development (AID). Foreign policy objectives thus assumed greater prominence in the determination of allocations under PL 480.

Although the political quotient of PL 480 programs, especially Title I transfers, has been on the rise beginning with Johnson, the mechanics of the program itself have remained virtually the same. The U.S. government through budgetary review conducted jointly by the executive and legislative branches decides on an annual dollar amount for PL 480. Within this total package individual countries are targeted for specific amounts, presumably based on the economic requirements of the recipient country as well as American foreign policy and long-term commercial interests.

In the case of the Title I program, the Commodity Credit Corporation advances a loan to the aid recipient country which in turn uses the money to finance its own purchases of PL 480 agricultural commodities and by-products in the United States. Under Title II, which is designed to respond to emergency food requirements and promote self-help programs in developing countries, the U.S. government either buys directly on the open market or draws from CCC stocks for its donations. In both cases, the process originates in dollar allocations as opposed to quantitative commitments with the result that the level of transfers in any given year fluctuates with changes in the market price. An aid recipient country may receive an increase in its CCC loan from one year to the next and still not appreciate any actual gain in the amount of imports.

The main handlers of Title I contracts are private trading companies. In the case of Title II transfers, private voluntary organizations and the United Nations World Food Program have principal responsibility for food deliveries as well as the design and administration of their use in specific projects. Once the allocation process is completed, Washington's profile fades into the private sector and voluntary organization programs. Only the silhouette of national economic and political interests remains.

From any number of perspectives, PL 480 has been a remarkable success. Since its inception, the program was designed to do at least four things: to provide a mechanism for surplus disposal; to bolster domestic farm prices; to develop overseas markets for American agricultural products without simultaneously displacing current commercial exports, thereby paving the way for later commercial sales; and, finally, to effect real budgetary savings at the federal level in the form of reduced storage costs and price support payments.[3] In general, all of these objectives have been realized. The extent to which the last can be measured in dollar terms is limited, but few would deny that such savings have been realized.[4] As for the others, there is ample evidence of their achievement.

The program's surplus disposal effects, and the importance of PL 480 to the overall American export campaign, are evident in the data provided in Tables 6.1 and 6.2 below. As these tables suggest, food aid shipments in 1954—PL 480's kick-off year—represented 33 percent of total wheat exports. (Wheat accounted for an average of 50 percent of total PL 480 shipments annually in the initial years and at present is 65 percent of the total quantity shipped.) As surpluses continued to climb, PL 480 shipments increased at an ever faster rate, but never so fast as to displace commercial exports which they were designed to enhance.[5]

The extent to which PL 480 transactions have bolstered domestic grain prices has been publicly documented on several occasions, most notably in 1958 and again in 1978. The first of these years saw the release of the Humphrey Report, "Food and Fibre as a Force for Freedom," which cited the following Department of Agriculture conclusions and statistics:

1. The 1956 average farm price of wheat was increased by about 9 cents a bushel.
2. The program raised the average farm price of corn by 1 cent a bushel in both 1956 and 1957. Barley crops were 1 to 2 cents a bushel higher.
3. . . . cottonseed and soybean oils . . . by 1½ to 2 cents a pound in 1955 and 1956.
4. Because of the program, soybeans were 15 cents a bushel higher than support in 1955, and 7 cents a bushel higher in 1956.
5. Estimated cash receipts increases received by farmers as the result of exports under Title I, PL 480, were as follows:[6]

	(in millions of dollars)		
Commodity	1955-56	1956-57	1957-58
Wheat	—	70	60
Rice	10	—	15
Tobacco	45	30	30
Corn and other feed grains	—	10	15
Fats, oils, and other seeds	100	85	50
Meat	15	50	—
Cotton	—	—	60
Total	170	245	230

The Humphrey report further concluded that these figures underestimated the actual price effects of the program. It suggested that had the impact of production controls and CCC purchases been added to the analysis, the reported price effects would have been even greater, especially for 1957.

A blue ribbon review in 1978, some 20 years later, reached essentially similar conclusions. The 1978 panel reaffirmed the importance of food assistance, and of PL 480 as an instrument of that assistance, as "an integral part of U.S. efforts to promote exports and expand markets for its agricultural products."[7] The committee went on to conclude that even with then current trends toward greater wheat production, if necessary increased PL 480 shipments could raise the price of wheat by anywhere from 10 to 20 cents per bushel.[8]

From the beginning market development was, and remains, an important objective of the PL 480 program. During the initial phase the majority of PL 480 contracts were handled on a concessional loan basis with repayment to be made in local currencies over an extended period. The objective in offering

TABLE 6.1 U.S. Grain Exports Under PL 480[a] as Percentage of Total U.S. Exports 1950-78[b] (million metric tons)

	1950	1951/52	1952/53	1953	1954	1955	1956	1957	1958	1959	1960	1961	1962	1963
Wheat														
Total U.S. Exports	9.4	13.2	9.0	5.8	7.3	8.8	14.7	11.4	12.2	13.7	17.8	19.5	17.7	23.0
PL 480 Exports	0	0	0	0	2.4	4.8	8.6	6.0	7.7	9.9	11.9	13.7	13.5	13.4
PL 480 Exports as % of U.S. Total	0	0	0	0	33%	55%	59%	53%	63%	72%	67%	70%	76%	58%
Feedgrains														
Total U.S. Exports	5.8	4.4	4.9	3.4	4.9	7.2	7.2	8.7	11.2	11.7	11.6	15.4	15.5	17.0
PL 480 Exports	0	0	0	0	.7	4.2	3.4	2.0	2.4	3.0	2.9	3.6	1.9	1.5
PL 480 Exports as % of U.S. Total	0	0	0	0	14%	58%	47%	23%	21%	26%	25%	23%	12%	9%
Total Wheat and Feedgrains														
Total U.S. Exports	15.2	17.6	13.9	9.2	12.2	16.0	21.9	20.1	23.4	25.4	29.4	34.9	33.2	40.0
PL 480 Exports	0	0	0	0	3.1	9.0	12.0	8.0	10.1	12.9	14.8	17.3	15.4	14.9
PL 480 Exports as % of U.S. Total	0	0	0	0	25%	56%	55%	40%	43%	51%	50%	50%	46%	37%

	1964	1965	1966	1967	1968	1969	1970	1971	1972	1973	1974	1975	1976	1977	1978
Wheat															
Total U.S. Exports	19.7	23.2	21.0	20.8	14.8	16.4	20.2	16.6	30.9	33.1	27.7	31.9	25.8	29.9	32.5
PL 480 Exports	15.4	14.7	8.3	10.7	6.9	7.6	6.6	6.4	4.0	1.4	3.4	3.9	4.7	3.9	3.0
PL 480 Exports as % of U.S. Total	78%	63%	40%	51%	47%	46%	33%	39%	13%	4%	12%	12%	18%	13%	9%
Feedgrains															
Total U.S. Exports	19.6	26.5	20.1	21.2	16.7	19.0	18.8	24.6	39.1	40.4	35.7	50.0	50.6	51.6	60.2
PL 480 Exports	1.4	2.3	3.8	2.1	1.0	1.4	1.4	1.5	1.6	.9	.3	.3	.4	.8	.4
PL 480 Exports as % of U.S. Total	7%	9%	19%	10%	6%	7%	7%	6%	4%	2%	1%	1%	1%	2%	.6%
Total Wheat and Feedgrains															
Total U.S. Exports	39.3	49.7	41.1	42.0	31.5	35.4	39.0	41.2	70.0	73.5	63.4	81.9	76.4	81.5	92.7
PL 480 Exports	16.8	17.0	12.1	12.8	7.9	9.0	8.0	7.9	5.6	2.3	3.7	4.2	5.1	4.7	3.4
PL 480 Exports as % of U.S. Total	43%	34%	29%	30%	25%	25%	21%	19%	8%	3%	6%	5%	7%	6%	4%

aPL 480 includes Titles I and II.

bPL 480 figures are for fiscal years; total export figures are for marketing years.

SOURCE: U.S. Department of Agriculture, *New Directions for U.S. Food Assistance: A Report of the Special Task Force on the Operation of Public Law 480*, May 1978, Appendix C.

TABLE 6.2 U.S. Wheat Exports Under PL 480[a] as Percentage of Total U.S. Exports 1950-1978[b] (million metric tons)

	1950	1951	1952	1953	1954	1955	1956	1957	1958	1959	1960	1961	1962	1963
SUPPLY														
Beginning Stocks	13.5	13.4	9.0	18.3	27.1	30.2	30.8	27.3	26.2	37.2	37.7	40.9	38.6	34.6
Production	27.8	26.9	35.5	31.9	26.8	25.5	27.3	26.0	39.7	30.4	36.9	33.6	29.7	31.2
Supply	41.5	41.1	45.2	50.4	53.9	56.0	58.3	53.6	66.0	67.9	74.8	74.6	68.6	65.9
UTILIZATION														
Domestic Use	18.7	18.9	17.9	17.5	16.5	16.4	16.3	16.0	16.6	16.5	16.1	16.5	16.3	15.8
Total Exports	9.4	13.2	9.0	5.8	7.3	8.8	14.7	11.4	12.2	13.7	17.8	19.5	17.7	23.0
PL 480 Exports	0	0	0	0	2.4	4.8	8.6	6.0	7.7	9.9	11.9	13.7	13.5	13.4
PL 480 Exports as % of U.S. Total	0	0	0	0	33%	55%	59%	53%	63%	72%	67%	70%	76%	58%
ENDING STOCKS														
Total Ending Stocks	13.4	9.0	18.3	27.1	30.2	30.8	26.2	26.2	37.2	37.7	40.9	38.6	34.6	27.1
CCC Stocks	5.3	3.9	12.8	21.1	26.6	25.9	22.4	22.7	31.2	32.5	33.8	29.8	29.5	22.6
PRICE														
Average per Bu HRW #1 Ordinary Protein f.o.b. Gulf	NA	NA	NA	2.46	2.49	2.37	2.43	2.35	2.19	2.23	2.18	2.25	2.40	2.31

	1964	1965	1966	1967	1968	1969	1970	1971	1972	1973	1974	1975	1976	1977	1978
SUPPLY															
Beginning Stocks	27.1	25.1	18.0	14.0	17.1	24.6	26.8	22.4	26.8	16.2	9.3	11.8	18.1	30.3	32.0
Production	34.9	35.8	35.5	41.0	42.4	39.3	36.8	44.1	42.1	46.6	48.5	57.8	58.3	55.1	48.9
Supply	62.1	60.9	53.6	55.0	59.5	64.0	63.6	66.5	68.8	62.9	57.8	69.6	76.5	85.4	80.9
UTILIZATION															
Domestic Use	17.3	19.7	18.6	17.1	20.1	20.8	21.0	23.1	21.7	20.5	18.3	19.6	20.4	22.6	23.3
Total Exports	19.7	23.2	21.0	20.8	14.8	16.4	20.2	16.6	30.9	33.1	27.7	31.9	25.8	29.9	32.5
PL 480 Exports	15.4	14.7	8.3	10.7	6.9	7.6	6.6	6.4	4.0	1.4	3.4	3.9	4.7	3.9	3.0
PL 480 Exports as % of U.S. Total	78%	63%	40%	51%	47%	46%	33%	39%	13%	4%	12%	12%	18%	13%	9%
ENDING STOCKS															
Total Ending Stocks	25.1	18.0	14.0	17.1	24.6	26.8	22.4	26.8	16.2	9.3	11.8	18.1	30.3	32.9	25.2
CCC Stocks	16.5	7.1	3.4	2.8	4.4	8.2	10.1	10.0	5.7	.5	0.0	0.0	1.3	.06	.0004
PRICE															
Average per Bu HRW #1 Ordinary Protein f.o.b. Gulf	1.76	1.78	2.02	1.76	1.54	1.54	1.68	1.74	2.44	4.74	4.46	4.05	3.14	3.00	3.75

aPL 480 includes Titles I and II.
bData is for marketing years except PL 480 figures which are for fiscal years and CCC stocks figures which are for crop years.

SOURCE: U.S. Department of Agriculture, New Directions for U.S. Food Assistance: A Report of the Special Task Force on the Operation of Public Law 480, May 1978, pages 249–251, and U.S. Department of Agriculture, U.S. Agricultural Exports Under Public Law 480, 1980.

such exceptionally favorable terms—which at times created serious problems—was not altruism but the conversion of aid recipients into faithful
commercial customers for U.S. grain. Thus food transfers were concentrated
in those countries most receptive to U.S. investment and that constituted
promising markets for eventual commercial sales of American agricultural
commodities.

Unsurprisingly, "graduates" of PL 480 have frequently become big commercial customers for American grain, as demonstrated in Figures 6.1 and
6.2. In 1976, Taiwan and Brazil, both former food aid recipients, were among
the leading ten commercial customers. And India, once the largest food aid
recipient, was by 1976 one of the biggest cash buyers of American agricultural commodities.

The transition from aid recipient to commercial buyer was not, however,
merely a natural ontogenetic process whereby developing countries went off
the food dole as they grew more prosperous. Rather, inducements to conversion were written into PL 480 contracts from the beginning. Eventual commercial purchases were, therefore, in many cases a precondition for the
receipt of aid.

In the wake of PL 480, commercial sales had by 1977 come to represent
almost 95 percent of total U.S. grain exports. Earl Butz's vision of a world in
which commercial sales supplanted food aid had virtually come true by the
time he became Secretary of Agriculture during the Nixon administration. Yet,
despite PL 480's diminished role today, its price effects remain nearly the
same as during the years when food aid transfers surpassed cash sales abroad.

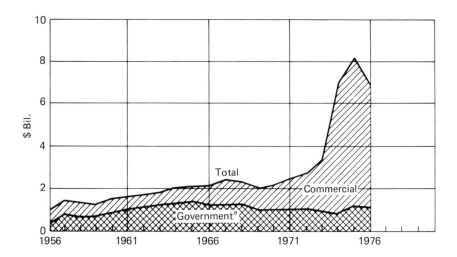

a Includes Public Law 480 and Mutual Security Programs.

FIGURE 6.1 U.S. Agricultural Exports to Developing Countries, 1956–76.

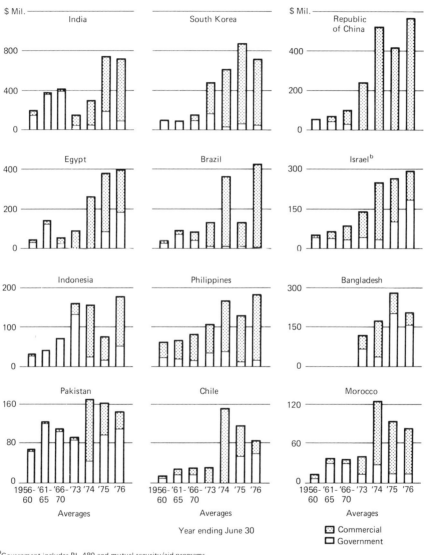

FIGURE 6.2   U.S. Agricultural Exports to Developing Countries, Government and Commercial, Fiscal Years.

[a]Government includes PL 480 and mutual security/aid programs.
[b]Until the last few years was considered developing.

PL 480's market impact in this regard was underscored between 1977 and 1979 when domestic grain stocks were reduced to a historic low.

Under the circumstances, the program retains a broad base of political support. Among its most ardent backers, farmers certainly appreciate the contribution PL 480 continues to make to commodity prices. The private sector has gained from the program, and those groups genuinely interested in the economic and social concerns of developing countries remain generally satisfied. Aid recipients certainly have their complaints, but few would deny PL 480's benefits. As much as this incredible admixture of interest groups recognizes the positive effects of the U.S. food aid program, the groups share at least one major grievance that relates to the political motivations of PL 480.

Criticism on the use of food aid as a foreign policy tool was particularly strong in the Johnson and Nixon administration. When Earl Butz, long an advocate of reducing food aid, proceeded to pare the PL 480 budget, the Nixon White House attempted to use food aid as a weapon to fight the Vietnam War. The former move may have indirectly facilitated the latter, for with Mr. Butz's budget reductions went the effective transfer of the food aid program from the Department of Agriculture and AID to the White House, where foreign policy objectives were more likely to intrude on food aid decisions. In any event, when Nixon and Kissinger, faced with congressional funding constraints on expenditures related to Vietnam, hit upon the Johnson precedent of attempting to use Food for Peace to wage war, many important program supporters were outraged. The administration was rebuffed, and in 1975 a new version of the PL 480 act reintroduced the principle of directing food aid to those countries with the most severe shortages and lowest per capita incomes. Even so, there are those who would maintain that the 1975 legislation represented a symbolic rather than a substantive response, and that the real threat perceived by PL 480 supporters in the Nixon/Kissinger actions was that such blatant use of the program would undermine its broad-based support and mark the end of its effectiveness as an economic instrument.

This debate surrounded PL 480 because of the size of the program and the foreign policies with which it became associated, but other national food aid efforts share similar weaknesses and strengths. Canada, the member states of the European Community, Australia, and even Japan—a food deficit country in every grain or oilseed except rice—have developed their own national programs. Each of these programs has a set of objectives much like those of PL 480—surplus disposal, market development, and the strengthening of the domestic agricultural economy. And each, again like PL 480, depends heavily upon the activities of the Big League, which has in turn found its involvement a most profitable activity.

When food aid dominated the U.S. export market, PL 480 was essential to individual trading companies' profits. Assured shipments under government contract offered low-risk sales plus an introduction into rapidly growing markets among aid recipient countries. During the peak 1962-67 period, the six major grain houses handled $329.9 in grain shipments annually, ranging from 50-75 percent of each year's total value of commodities exported under the Title I program of PL 480 (see Appendix Table B.2). Despite the decline in total volume of PL 480 shipments since 1967, the percentages have remained roughly the same with the seven largest grain houses handling between 70 and 90 percent of Title I contracts (including rice).[9] By contrast, cooperatives handled virtually no wheat or feedgrain sales and only 5 percent of rice exports under PL 480.[10] The six major firms, especially Cargill, Continental, and Bunge, have consistently been the most active bidders for PL 480 contracts. Their eager participation demonstrates the importance they attach to the program, less now for the direct profits than for the market development potential.

The role of the private sector always has been essential to implementing PL 480 sales negotiated between the United States and the aid recipient. Governments arrive at understandings on levels of aid commitments; companies handle the contracts. (Appendix Tables B.1–B.6 identify the principal exporting companies of every PL 480 commodity and product from the inception of the program to 1975.) Recipient countries either turn to their official agencies or directly to private importers to fulfill purchasing authorizations issued by the U.S. government. When an official agency takes charge of PL 480 imports, it usually enters into a secondary contract with private firms, which at a minimum handle the c.i.f. phase. In this sense, a PL 480 contract is like any other grain export-import transaction, except that characteristically there are more bureaucratic regulations. The process is, as a result, slower and more tedious. At the same time, corporate risk is minimized. Shippers are paid in dollars with a guarantee secured by an American bank, which processes a foreign bank's letter of credit. This practice, ensuring prompt reimbursement in dollars, allows an exporter to bypass the normal currency hedge. Although a recipient country's tender or offer of a contract is supposed to be public and open to competitive bidding, frequently it is little more than a pro forma exercise with the contract already agreed upon prior to its public announcement. LDC governments often prefer to avoid the intricacies of the marketplace by dealing with one or two firms consistently.

Once converted to commercial buyers, developing countries have been inclined to remain loyal to their traditional suppliers. Under PL 480, individual companies became associated with sales to one country or another. Nothing suggests that this evolution reflected any particular efficiencies or corporate specialization because all members of the Big League were selling virtually the same product. If price were the sole determinant, buyers would have gone with the firm that offered the best bargain. The glue that made these alignments stick was more likely an early introduction through PL 480 combined with mutual respect among members of the Big League for each firm's territory. (Appendix Table B.7 identifies the largest exporting companies by commodity and country under PL 480, Title I.) PL 480-sponsored programs, such as the "cooperator," Cooley loan, and Private Trade Agreement (PTA) programs in recipient countries, further entrenched the Big League in these new markets. Like Title I contracts, these special programs, proved highly profitable for the grain companies in carving out and securing special long-term relationships in aid "graduate" as well as aid recipient countries.

The cooperator program was an ingenious way to soak up excess capital, distorting local economies in aid recipient countries while, at the same time, encouraging commercial export of American grains. It arose in response to a problem which developed during the early years of PL 480. At that time, the majority of PL 480 contracts were handled on a concessional loan basis with repayment in local currencies over an extended period. As a result, American embassies in aid recipient countries were eventually awash in foreign currency receipts that were less expensive to spend locally than to convert to dollars and return to the United States. The problem of what to do with these monies was solved by channeling a portion of them to producers and nonprofit private trade associations ("cooperators") for the purpose of promoting the sale of American agricultural products in promising foreign markets. This program served to drum up business for member companies of participating associations by generating increased export sales and laying the groundwork for future investment. It was also a precursor of a shift among key aid recipient countries to commercial sales, and it was instrumental in easing that transition for both the recipient countries and the grain companies, as is suggested by the fact that Big League subsidiaries proliferated in these countries just as the volume of food aid transfers began to decline.

The Cooley loan (named after the chairman of the House Agricultural Committee in 1957, Harold D. Cooley) and PTA programs spured this investment trend. Cooley loans were tapped by major grain trading companies and U.S. agribusiness firms to help finance storage and processing facilities in aid recipient countries.[11] The loans rarely covered the cost of their total investment in individual projects, but the credit terms were highly advantageous and the sums involved substantial enough to reduce corporate risk exposure. During the life-span of the program, which went into a dormant state in 1976, Cooley loans amounted to a total of $423 million. At this level corporate borrowers gained a foothold in aid recipient countries that later became substantial commercial buyers.[12]

PTAs served as another device by which the United States could absorb some of its foreign currency holdings generated by PL 480 sales, and at the same time secure these growing foreign markets for U.S. agricultural products. PTAs were different from Cooley loans in that they were available for specifically defined joint ventures between American companies and their counterparts in aid recipient countries. Although PTAs were not crucial to their overall investment strategy, grain companies did not decline the opportunity of making full use of this option as well as the Cooley loans.[13] From the U.S. government standpoint, budgetary costs were nonexistent, since the loans were funded from LDC currency holdings abroad and were far outdistanced by the presumed benefits. The general assumption was that what was good for U.S. business, especially the Big League, contributed to the country's economic health.

As successful as PL 480 was in catapulting the United States to a preeminent position among the grain-exporting nations, it also served to sustain and enrich the private traders, especially the Big League, and to create a condition of export dependence in the American agricultural economy. The time came, however, when PL 480 was only of marginal use in sustaining American dominance of the international grain trade. Import requirements in developed as well as developing countries had grown to such proportions and the United States had so surpassed other competing suppliers in food and feedgrains that concessional food transfers diminished in importance relative to standard commercial transactions as a means of satisfying foreign food requirements. As long as buyers were willing to pay the higher prices, it was in U.S. interests to sell on the most favorable commercial terms possible. Food assistance was an investment of sorts. Commercial sales were the harvested return. The next phase of American agricultural export policy, therefore, was to maintain this momentum without foregoing PL 480 completely. Long-term bilateral purchasing and sales agreements appeared a convenient formula for achieving this objective. These agreements, it was thought, could respond to the needs of both the importers—for access to food suppliers—and the United States, whose agricultural economy was by the early 1970s virtually dependent on continued growth in export volume. By 1977 such multiyear agreements accounted for at least 25 percent of all U.S. wheat exports.

BILATERAL AGREEMENTS

Throughout the 1970s, the marketing boards of Canada, Australia, and Argentina entered into long-term selling/purchasing agreements with counterpart organizations in importing states. (Refer to Appendix Table B.8 for a listing of the principal bilateral agreements between the major grain suppliers and importing countries.) The boards sought, at the cost of reduced flexibility, to stabilize their markets through a plethora of multiyear bilateral agreements. By contrast the United States was reluctant to move in this direction out of an abiding faith in an open market economy coupled with an assessment that concessional sales would produce more satisfactory long-term results. Although decrying its competitors' use of these agreements as a form of trade restriction, the United States justified its reliance on high volume concessional transfers as a means of countering this export strategy.[14] The distinction was really an artificial one in that both arrangements—concessional and commercial transfers on bilateral terms—offered fixed guarantees on a portion of existing supplies whatever changes might occur in actual market conditions.

Eventually, Washington came to this realization. U.S. agricultural trade policy effectively began shifting in the early 1970s as competitive pressures mounted, eroding the U.S. and Canadian dominance. Further, it was perceived that the level of food aid transfers varied markedly from year to year in a highly erratic market, thereby contributing to rather than reducing instability. The bilateral option thus became increasingly attractive to U.S. policy makers as a means of handling sales to developed and developing countries.

The first major bilateral agreement, and the model for most subsequent agreements of this type involving the United States, is the U.S./Soviet agreement of October 1975. Upon signing, this agreement was extolled by the White House as a major achievement:

- The additional assured demand will assist farmers in making their planting decisions.
- Reduce fluctuations in world markets by smoothing out Soviet purchases of U.S. grain.
- Protect U.S. livestock producers and consumers and other foreign customers from large purchases of U.S. grain by the USSR without prior consultation.[15]

Even Secretary Butz, an outspoken opponent of government intervention, seemed persuaded: "This [the grain agreement] goes a long way, I am convinced, to iron out the wide fluctuations in Soviet purchases—not alone in this market, but in the world market too—from year to year."[16] That the U.S./USSR Grain Agreement has fallen far short of these publicly expressed hopes may not be surprising. Even so, it has been an agreement of singular importance, one that represents a turning point in American policy.

The historical impetus for this agreement can be traced back to the 1972 Soviet buying blitz that set the stage for a domestic inflationary spiral already in a vertical climb from oil price hikes. Retail food prices in the United States shot up an average of 12 percent above the previous year.[17] Nonetheless, those who profited from the Soviet purchases were few. The only farmers whose incomes increased appreciably were large wheat growers who could wait to sell their crop as prices reached all-time highs. The majority of farmers were not in this position and were hit broadside by the inflationary impact on the cost of their production inputs. As a result, realized net farm income in the wake of the 1972 sale dropped 7 percent in 1974 and an additional 25 percent the following year.[18] The 1972 Soviet grain purchases also had a deleterious effect on U.S. grain stocks, which remained hazardously low for wheat and feedgrains as late as the crop year of 1974. After 1972 it was increasingly clear that the Soviet Union had become the world's most unpredictable and, at the same time, most highly sophisticated grain importer. It had also become a highly disruptive influence in the international grain trade, fully capable of turning its own recurrent production shortfalls into major crises for other countries, including the major suppliers and most especially the United States. Clearly some response was in order. Close on the heels of the 1972 experience, in 1974 came rumors of renewed large-scale purchases by the USSR.

Between June and October 1974 hard red winter wheat prices increased by approximately $1.45, reaching a high point of $5.04 per bushel. Such price trends offered a grim reminder of 1972-73. In the face of tight supplies, escalating prices, and mounting political pressure, the U.S. government called a halt in the summer of 1974 to further grain exports to the USSR. At a White House breakfast, President Gerald Ford and Secretary of the Treasury William Simon prevailed on the chief executives of Cook and Continental, who together held signed contracts for 5.2 million tons of wheat and corn, to cut back their export contracts with the USSR. Mr. Cook quoted President Ford as saying that "the people of the United States . . . would be irate at the fact that grain was going to Russia in this magnitude."[19] The government's handling of the 1974 sales dramatized once again the need for a systematic approach to Soviet sales, as it was evident that the USSR was not going to transform itself of its own accord into a more responsible grain buyer. Events in the following year simply forced matters to a logical conclusion.

In early May of 1975, U.S. estimates of Soviet grain production ranged between 215 and 225 million metric tons, and projected Soviet import requirements were anticipated to be 10 to 15 million metric tons. Since American carryover stocks in wheat and corn were higher than in 1972, and since Canada was also in a surplus position, the threat of shortages and sharply higher prices induced by Soviet purchases seemed remote. Then came downward estimates of the Soviet crop as the growing season in the USSR wore on without any rainfall. U.S. intelligence, based principally on fancy guesswork by the CIA and a special task force from the U.S. Department of Agriculture,[20] concluded that the Soviet grain harvest would be only between 155 and 165 million metric tons. Projected Soviet import requirements escalated sharply at this point. The news sent tremors through the market. Prices began jumping to their daily limits on the commodity exchanges.

By 31 July 1975 U.S. sales to the Soviets of wheat, corn, and barley alone climbed to 10.3 million metric tons. Cook held a contract for 2 million tons of wheat. Cargill had contracted for an additional 1.2 million tons of wheat. The largest commitment was Continental's; it had contracted for delivery of 4.5 million tons of corn and 1.1 million tons of barley. In addition, the Canadian Wheat Board also registered a large purchase order of 2 million metric tons.[21] These facts were known and carefully monitored by Washington.

What was not known were such things as how much would the Soviets eventually buy in 1975? On what terms? For what markets? Without accurate data on Soviet stocks, estimates of Soviet import requirements were not wholly reliable. Further, little was known about Russian purchases on behalf of CEMA (Council for Economic Mutual Assistance) countries, yet the extent to which Soviets juggled their own imports and domestic supply with Eastern Europe's would naturally affect the calculation of total imports.[22] There was, finally, a dearth of information about sales contracts held by overseas subsidiaries of American corporations.

Such were the uncertainties and the potential for disruption that U.S. export sales to the Soviet Union were suspended in August 1975. This action, ostensibly taken to placate the Longshoremen's Union, which had refused to load grain destined for the USSR until the Maritime Agreement was renewed on more favorable terms, was followed shortly thereafter by President Ford's announcement that negotiations for a long-term bilateral grain agreement were underway. In the summer of 1975 the United States finally had come to the realization that government action would be required to moderate the disruptive effect of erratic Soviet grain purchases. Although they could not have been pleased by the sudden suspension of sales, the Soviets had a sufficiently pressing need for a guarantee of access to U.S. grain supplies that they, too, could appreciate the benefits of a long-term agreement with the United States.

Other considerations suggested to each side that an agreement would be in their mutual interest. The Soviets had experienced several moratoria on U.S. sales in the past, motivated either for political or economic reasons. A treaty could provide some protection against such action. Further, the USSR had embarked on an effort to build up its livestock herds and was devoting a greater share of the national budget to storage facilities. Both of these shifts in agricultural policy necessitated access to a constant and larger quantity of grain supplies than previously, supplies whose availability an agreement could help ensure in the event of a shortfall in domestic production. A bilateral treaty would also help the USSR avoid the embarrassing situation of competing against its Eastern European satellites, who had turned to the West—particularly to the United States—for supplies in times of scarcity. At the same time, such an agreement would not preclude the Soviets' signing additional bilateral contracts independent of the United States. For the United States, a U.S./USSR bilateral agreement offered a way of stabilizing the domestic market, increasing export volumes to Eastern Europe and the USSR, and simultaneously expanding its traditional export territories with minimal objection from competitors.

Under the terms of the treaty signed on 20 October 1975, the USSR agreed to purchase from private commercial channels a minimum of 6 million and a maximum of 8 million metric tons of U.S. corn and wheat annually for a period of five years, with purchases above this level to require consultation with and the approval of the U.S. government.[23] The Soviets further agreed to purchase the corn and wheat in roughly equal proportions and to schedule purchases and shipments as evenly as possible over each 12-month period. In return, the United States consented to exempt these shipments from export controls as long as American supplies exceeded 225 million metric tons.[24] From the American standpoint, the major purpose of the agreement was to turn the USSR into a responsible buyer and thereby stave off disruptions of the sort that occurred in 1972 and threatened again in 1974 and 1975.

Since the agreement went into effect, there have been fewer mishaps attributable to Soviet buying and shipping practices. Such a welcome development, however, had less to do with the treaty itself than market conditions where global surpluses could comfortably accommodate heavy Soviet import requirements. Except for the first year, actual U.S. grain sales to the USSR were far in excess of the initial 8 million metric ton ceiling, as shown in Table 6.3.

What the table cannot show, of course, is the extent of compliance with the terms of the agreement and its overall effects. In both cases, the results are mixed.

Neither country has been totally compliant or proven willing to meet the more difficult, albeit ambiguous, provisions of the agreement. The Soviets, who were supposed to spread their purchases and shipments throughout the year to reduce market disruptions and port congestion, have simply ignored this provision of the agreement. They have accepted and used the consultative machinery set up to implement the accord, but have generally proven no more forthcoming than before in such sensitive areas as contract information or carryover stock statistics.

For its part, the United States may be said to have honored the agreement at least until 4 January 1980, when, in response to the Soviet invasion of Afghanistan, President Carter announced an embargo on all grain sales to the Soviet Union in excess of the annual maximum of 8 million tons guaranteed under the 1975 agreement. As authority for imposing the embargo, the president cited the Export Administration Act, provisions of which allowed for such an action to be taken provided it was, as he stated, in the national security and foreign policy interests of the United States.

Depending on one's point of view, the 1980 embargo did or did not constitute a direct violation of the 1975 U.S./USSR grain agreement. The official Soviet position was that it did, that the resulting wholesale cancellation of contracts for some 17 million metric tons of wheat and corn in excess of the 8 million tons amounted to unilateral abrogation. Washington saw things differently, arguing that, at the time of the embargo, the Soviets had yet to clear any of the cancelled sales with the U.S. government, as they were obligated to do. In the end, the U.S. embargo was publicly denounced by Brezhnev, but perhaps because they anticipated a continued need for U.S.

TABLE 6.3 U.S. Sales to Soviet Union—First Through Fifth Agreement Years (thousand metric tons)

Year		Wheat	Corn	Total
1st	(10/76-9/77)	3,064	3,052	6,116
2nd	(10/77-9/78)	3,453	11,132	14,585
3rd	(10/78-9/79)	3,988	11,595	15,583
4th	(10/79-9/80)*	6,667	15,096	21,763*
5th	(10/80-9/81)	780	738	1,518

*Only a total of 7,939 thousand metric tons (2,171 wheat and 5,768 corn) was permitted to be exported under the sales suspension announced by President Carter on 4 January 1980.

SOURCE: USDA FAS/ESD/6/13/80

grain in the future, no direct retaliatory action was undertaken by the Soviets other than to seek long-term agreements with other suppliers.

In the summer of 1981 after the embargo had been lifted the Soviets crept quietly back into the U.S. market and resumed negotiations for a new bilateral agreement. The consensus in the United States appeared to be that the earlier agreement had had a stabilizing effect. Yet it is not at all clear that this was the case. In the years since 1975, the United States has had little need of a bilateral framework to increase its exports to the USSR or its European satellites. Similarly, the USSR's need for American grain throughout this period has been less than acute, with the exception of 1980/81 when production fell 60 million metric tons below its planned target. During these years the American crops were excellent, the dollar had depreciated significantly against the price of gold, and grain prices were depressed until the spring of 1979. Under the circumstances, the Soviets were willing to buy the 6 million metric ton minimum . . . and more.

Significantly, however, the agreement did little to alleviate American grievances about the Soviets' handling of their purchases and did not deter the United States from its sudden cancellation of Soviet contracts for 17 million metric tons of American grain in 1980. Despite the discord of 1980, both sides are receptive to signing a new agreement. The Reagan administration eventually lifted the embargo and began courting the Soviets to return to the American market. With the prospect of huge surpluses in wheat and, to a lesser extent, in other feedgrains, purchasing commitments within the framework of a new long-term agreement became increasingly attractive. The Soviets, although experiencing a better harvest in 1980/81 than the preceding year, undoubtedly were attracted to the idea of secure access to relatively cheap American grain to compensate for past shortfalls and the inevitable depletion of their own stocks.

While many domestic producers at one time opposed the 1975 agreement, arguing that it effectively put a lid on U.S. exports to the Soviet Union, many of them are now receptive to renewal, preferably with the provision for a higher annual minimum than under the earlier agreement. The producers' earlier objections, like those of the National Association of Wheat Growers, which argued at one time that the three-month moratorium on Soviet grain sales in 1975 depressed domestic grain prices and benefited other suppliers, notably Australia and Canada, have simply paled by way of comparison with their criticisms of the 1980 embargo.[25] The thinking of American producers has, in short, come full circle since 1975 to the point where many now favor the proposed five-year renewal of the U.S./USSR grain agreement.

Labor and consumer groups have come to accept the agreement, albeit for different reasons. Both groups have been persuaded by the argument that the agreement contributes to price stabilization and helps the U.S. balance of payments. Further, both groups supported the 1975 agreement from the time of its inception, a time in which there were many public rumors of large new sales to the USSR and a possible repeat of 1972. Consumer groups were heavily influenced by the widely publicized claim of the American Bakers Association that the rumored Soviet purchases would, if allowed, raise the price of a loaf of bread to one dollar. And George Meany, the powerful AFL-CIO president, wrote to the other officers of his union that governmental action was essential to prevent another "billion dollar rip-off."[26] (Meany may, of course, also have welcomed the idea of inflicting a certain amount of economic and political humiliation on the Soviets.) Thus, both labor and consumer groups have joined forces in supporting a bilateral U.S./USSR grain agreement, primarily as a means of keeping a lid on inflation-ridden food prices. Whether it is renewed or not, however, the 1975 U.S./USSR Grain Agreement has marked a major turning point in the agricultural policy of the world's largest grain exporter. As such, it has since its inception been a matter of concern to nations other than the United States and the Soviet Union. The international reviews have been mixed.

In general, exporters have viewed the agreement with more equanimity than importers. Among the major exporting nations, the European Community was not and is not in a position to supply more than a small proportion of Soviet needs. Both Canada and Australia already had negotiated long-term purchase agreements with the Soviets prior to October 1975. Thus none of these nations saw the agreement as an effort to displace them from their traditional markets. In fact, by 1981 Canada, Australia, and Argentina took advantage of the USSR's being ostracized from the American market and signed new long-term agreements with the Soviets at record amounts.

The potential consequences of the 1975 accord between the superpowers were much greater for importing nations, who responded more vigorously. In October 1975 grain importers around the world had just lived through a four-year period during which the Soviets wreaked havoc on the international grain market. The new agreement was interpreted widely, in effect, as a license to import on preferential terms. Those importers who felt they could afford to do so immediately set out to negotiate a similar arrangement with the United States. Those who could not, the less developed countries (LDCs), sought other means of gaining access to food from America.

From the LDC perspective, the U.S./Soviet accord was unsatisfactory on the one hand, because of the discrimination involved and, on the other, an opening to be exploited. It represented a turning point in U.S. agricultural export policy toward greater acceptance of long-term commitments to individual countries. The prospect of obtaining such a commitment was attractive to most LDCs, yet their ability to manage their side of such a bargain was limited. From the standpoint of the LDCs, bilateral accords with the United States suffer from one major drawback. These agreements establish only the quantity of grain to be delivered over a specified period of time, not the price. In certain instances, special credit arrangements are part of the package, but the cost of interest payments plus relatively high export prices still make commercial purchases under any terms prohibitive for many of the poorer food-importing nations. The problems of these nations were only exacerbated by the energy crisis, which adversely affected their export earnings—and thus their balance of payments—while depreciating their currencies even faster than the U.S. dollar. As a result, the imported food bills of many LDCs began climbing rapidly in the wake of the first OPEC oil embargo of 1973, and bilateral agreements patterned after the U.S./USSR model offered relatively little compensation.

Despite the short-term victory these nations had won at the 1974 World Food Conference in Rome when they successfully obtained supplemental pledges of food aid from the United States and other donor countries, by 1975 it was abundantly clear that such aid alone would be insufficient to cover their deficits. Yet at the same time they could not afford to purchase grain at commercial prices and thus could not avail themselves of the benefit of a bilateral agreement. For these nations, the only clear benefit offered by the U.S./USSR Grain Agreement was that it promised to alleviate some of the pressure on food prices that had been occasioned by continuing, sudden, large Soviet grain purchases prior to the agreement. These purchases siphoned off scarce food resources from other buyers, especially those least able to afford the resulting losses.

The U.S. response to the plight of the LDCs has been to establish a food security reserve of 4 million metric tons of wheat as a backup to PL 480, and a multiyear credit facility under Title III of the present food aid program.[27] Neither measure, however, is a substitute for long-term supply commitments at affordable prices. Recipients of food aid have much less certainty that promised supplies will be forthcoming than do commercial buyers under the terms of most bilateral agreements. Despite national pledges under the international Food Assistance Convention (FAC), assistance to individual countries can vary to an extreme from year to year. Moreover, donors do not always meet the target levels specified in the food convention. The EC, for instance, honored only 56 percent of its pledge in 1977 and 60 percent in 1978.[28]

Rich buyers have suffered less. They were quick to seize upon the U.S./ Soviet initiative as a formula for their own food security. For these more affluent countries, price is less an issue, and some bilateral arrangements can respond to most of their concerns for continued access to supply. The first such nation to seek and obtain an agreement patterned after the U.S./Soviet accord was Japan. Ironically, the resulting agreement was announced just as the U.S. government suspended sales to the USSR in 1975.

Under the terms of the Butz/Abe accord,[29] the two countries agreed informally on annual trade targets of a minimum of 3 million metric tons of wheat, 8 million of feedgrains, and 3 million of soybeans for a duration of three years. Japan agreed to notify the U.S. government of its purchasing plans prior to executing any transactions. The United States in turn offered an unwritten commitment to make available to Japan the quantities listed above. These amounts were only slightly below Japan's average imports from the United States, which in the previous three marketing years had totaled approximately 14.7 million metric tons per annum. Although nonbinding, the agreement was in fact more effective than the Soviet agreement. The Butz/ Abe understanding covered the major share of U.S. grain exports to Japan, whereas the 6 million metric ton minimum under the agreement with the Russians represented only 54 percent of average U.S. grain exports to the USSR between 1976 and 1980. Sewing up a vital market with a reliable buyer was a net plus economically and politically for both countries. The gentlemen's agreement gave the desired flexibility to both Japan and the United States. Japanese concerns over food security were satisfied, after having been heightened by the 1973 soybean embargo when the United States cut off shipments to all importers. The agreement allowed the United States, in turn, to save face from what had proved to be a disastrous economic and political decision.

These motivations notwithstanding, Japan was more insistent than the United States on making the bilateral agreement voluntary. Had Japan entered into a more formal arrangement, it would have constrained the Japanese Food Agency and the trading companies, uncustomarily subjecting their dealings to detailed review. Japan faced rice surpluses it knew would not disappear overnight, so wheat was less essential as a food import item than as a commodity sold at high prices domestically to help fund the Agency's rice subsidy program. The Japanese government and Sogo Shosha were also prepared to invest huge sums in the fertile Minas Gerais of Brazil, primarily for soybean production. Such new alternative sources of production were another safety valve for Japan's food supply needs, reducing the necessity for an inflexible long-term purchasing agreement.

Recent Japanese investments in the United States also militated against Japan's making fixed-purchase commitments. The acquisition of additional storage space by Japanese trading companies and Zen-Noh and a change in U.S. law, which until the Farm Act of 1981 exempted foreign government stocks held in the United States from export controls, gave the Japanese government potential access to supplies that a formal pact never provided. A gentlemen's agreement was equally congruent with Japan's political objectives. Japanese leadership was apprehensive about getting caught by another humiliating American "shoku" like the soybean embargo. They saw the accord with the Soviets as demeaning, because it allowed the United States more freedom than the Soviet Union to maneuver out of its obligations. From the Japanese perspective the terms of the U.S./Soviet accord were evidence that the United States would do what it wanted in times of shortages, treaty or no treaty. Thus, unlike the Soviets, the Japanese saw no advantage to a formal, written agreement.

Even this most informal of understandings ultimately proved itself unnecessary from the Japanese perspective. They did not seek renewal in 1979. By that date, global grain surpluses had strengthened the Japanese hand, underlining the importance of Japan's purchases to the entire American agricultural sector. During this three-year period, Japan had obtained voluntary sales commitments from Australia and Canada. In Indonesia a consortium of companies with Japanese backing had invested in a corn-producing project. The large-scale agricultural development project in Brazil was well underway, and negotiations were opening for a joint soybean venture in China. Further, Japanese public opinion had been aroused by the tone of the trade talks, which, from the Japanese perspective had been at times acrimonious, with the United States placing ever greater demands on Japan. A different policy structured more in accord with American liberal, free trade rhetoric offered the Japanese an opportunity both to avoid the appearance of asking for favors and a ready defense against U.S. criticism.

In short, by 1979 even the Butz/Abe voluntary model had outlived its usefulness to Japan. During Prime Minister Ohira's first official visit to the United States, the American host team tried to obtain a renewal but had to accept an even more fluid arrangement in the form of bilateral consultations. The two governments agreed to confer annually on their sales expectations and import requirements. Conferral became the substitute for targets, analogous to the Food Agency's dealings with Canadian and Australian wheat boards.

Among the major importers, however, Japan's situation was atypical. Other nations in this group have responded to the policy shift represented by the U.S./Soviet accord by seeking firm agreements of their own. As non-market economies with rising import requirements that could be satisfied only by supplies from the West, and with Soviet encouragement and financial backing, the Eastern European group of countries quickly sought bilateral agreements with the United States. Prior to 1972, the Soviet Union had accounted for an average 1.5 to 2 million metric tons to Poland, but by that year a severe shortfall in the USSR, coupled with poor harvests in Eastern Europe, forced Poland and other CEMA countries to turn to the United States. Poland's shortage in 1975 was estimated at almost 3 million metric tons vis-à-vis consumption needs.

When the USSR in 1975 took the Draconian step of canceling its supply contract with Poland, Rolimpex (the Polish grain-purchasing agency) immediately went on a shopping spree in the United States. American grain stores were officially closed to the Russians in August of that year, and the Poles were notified that by the last week of September they, too, would have to face a moratorium. Before the clock ran out, Rolimpex scurried to contract for roughly 4 million metric tons. American officials feared that this heavy buying, rumored to be financed largely by the USSR, was partially on behalf of the Soviets. To stop this potential leak and raise pressure on the Soviets to reach an agreement, the United States also tried to turn off the spigot for Poland. Nine days after the U.S. government notified the Polish Ambassador in Washington of the upcoming moratorium, the United States and the USSR settled on new rates for the Maritime Agreement. Less than a month thereafter, the two countries agreed upon their bilateral grain treaty. Then, on 27 November, the United States and Poland exchanged letters spelling out annual export-import obligations in the range of 2.5 million metric tons and a vague commitment for CCC credits. This arrangement, which is still in effect, was expanded along with special credit and even PL 480, Title I sales under the Carter and Reagan administrations when Poland was in a state of economic turmoil and virtual seige by the Soviet Union.

Other bilaterals patterned after the Polish and Japanese models were signed by the United States in 1975 and helped shore up damaged trade and political relations after an American record of poor supply management. An arrangement with Israel was a "best endeavor" commitment by the United States to satisfy Israel's import requirements over a period of three years, targeted at 1.7 million metric tons of grains and soybeans annually. What America had guaranteed to its major global antagonist, it could hardly refuse to an ally.

Other such agreements were complicated by their implications for U.S. relations with its allies. An East German understanding was made nonbinding because of the political implications. The United States could not afford to undercut its close ally, the Federal Republic of Germany, nor suffer the embarrassment of accounting for loosely identified American-origin grains transshipped via West Germany as "inter-German" trade. To avoid upsetting such a delicate balance, the United States had to tread lightly. The solution adopted was to simply acknowledge the German Democratic Republic's expressed interest in purchasing 1.5 to 2 million metric tons of grain annually and opening up consultative channels for this purpose. There could be no formal treaty in such a case, but the result was effectively another bilateral agreement.

Interestingly, the Japanese and Soviet agreements scrupulously avoided any mention of commercial arrangements but others did not. A case in point is the agreement with Romania. Under the terms of that agreement, Romania agreed to submit a shopping list of commodities and the quantities it desired to purchase from the United States in return for a U.S. best endeavor commitment to make these commodities available, with the possibility of terms involving unspecified amounts of CCC credits. The Romanian "protocol" contained an explicit reference to the role of private exporters in implementing the agreement: "To introduce more stability into commodity markets, the parties will encourage the conclusion of long-term purchasing arrangements between private exporters in the United States of agricultural commodities and Romanian foreign trade enterprises."[30] Although the U.S. government claims no knowledge regarding the status of these market-sharing arrangements between private exporters and the Romanian foreign trading arm, Agroexport, it has indirectly sanctioned them.

There are several other examples of commodity agreements to which private exporters are obligated. Iran, under the shah's rule, had an exclusive agreement with Tradax, Australia, and was likely to favor analogous arrangements with U.S. companies or their subsidiaries to handle American grains. Other centralized economic systems, especially in Eastern Europe, hosted similar arrangements. The shift to bilaterals has reinforced this trend. Orderly marketing on a state-to-state level stands a better chance of enforcement when rooted in parallel agreements between governments and the private sector.

The manner in which such arrangements work is illustrated by the agreements between the United States and the Norwegian and Taiwanese governments. In the Norwegian case a group of American grain companies entered in November 1974 into a three-year grain trade agreement, subsequently renewed, for the sale and purchase of U.S. grains with the Statens Kornforretning, Norway's national grain corporation. One of the U.S. companies is a cooperative, Producers Grain, while the remaining five are members of the Big League: Bunge, Cargill, Continental, Cook—(after liquidating its grain assets, Cook was dropped from the list)—and Louis Dreyfus.

The agreement requires individual bidding under an open tender system to fulfill the annual purchase and shipment targets. The Norwegian Grain Corporation, nevertheless, has reserved its right to negotiate with individual sellers over bids and retenders. Like the Japanese Food Agency, it has broad discretionary powers and favors those companies listed in the agreement. Both the American and Norwegian governments accept this arrangement, although it contradicts a stated policy preference for a nonpreferential, competitive marketing system.

The arrangement involving the government of Taiwan is a more important example because of the quantities involved. Whereas the Norwegian agreement involved 500,000 to 1 million metric tons of grain (wheat, rye, corn, sorghum, and barley), the 1976 agreement with Taiwan involved an average of 2.04 million metric tons per annum for four commodites (wheat, corn, barley, and soybeans). Taiwan's Trade Mission to the United States and the respective commodity associations in Taipei jointly signed agreements with nine grain companies: ADM, Bunge, Cargill, Continental, Cook, Garnac, Koppel, the National Federation of Grain Cooperatives,[31] and Peavey.

The Taiwan agreements of 1976 and 1981 have been less competitive than the Norwegian arrangement. The participating commodity associations do not explicitly reserve any right to entertain bids from companies other than those mentioned in the agreement. The Norwegian understanding does provide for more flexibility in this regard, although both sets of agreements are decisively preferential in nature. Japanese trading companies with operations in the United States viewed the 1976 Taiwanese accords as a deliberate attempt to exclude them from an important market. In an effort to defend U.S. acceptance of these potentially extralegal arrangements, American officials maintain that the Taiwanese actions were beyond American control and motivated by Taiwanese bitterness over Japan's decision to offer exclusive recognition to mainland China. These assertions respecting the 1976 agreement were clouded by the inclusion of Koppel, a Mitsubishi affiliate. By 1971, several Soga Shosha American subsidiaries appeared on the list (see Table B.8). Under any circumstances, the U.S. government's sanction of the earlier and later agreement raises serious questions.

Any long-term agreement between private firms and a foreign government agency, particularly one blessed by the U.S. government, contravenes the long-espoused American policy of preserving an open agricultural trading system. Moreover, it could be inconsistent with U.S. antitrust laws and in violation of the General Agreement on Tariffs and Trade (GATT) principles. Unsurprisingly therefore, the tendency of the U.S. and other governments has been to skirt this issue. Preferential arrangements between foreign buyers and private companies are rarely encouraged on an official basis in agreements between so-called market economy countries.

Even so, it has become an accepted pattern for governments to help lay the groundwork for the emergence of such relationships or to tolerate them as an inevitable, if not positive, consequence in the law of commerce. American protests to the contrary, the United States is no exception in this regard. Knowledge of firm understandings between foreign government trading agencies and American grain houses is one of these closely held well-known secrets. Such understandings are a likely outcome of bilateral agreements, especially those involving countries whose governments control the agricultural sector. Each example of a bilateral purchase-sales commitment presents a set of problems. Among agreements between the United States and other countries, the Taiwanese and Norwegian agreements are exceptional in that they directly involve the private trade. Such arrangements are undoubtedly a more common feature of agreements between exporting countries with less restrictive antitrust laws.

Government-to-government arrangements, however, have their own drawbacks. Rarely have they ushered in additional sales for an exporting country that would not have been made under normal circumstances. In the case of the United States, they have tended to confirm minimum, not maximum, trade flows. Instead of ensuring greater stability in world grain supplies and prices, they have had at best a neutral impact on the market. Potentially, they constitute a destabilizing force, depending upon how much of the total volume of international trade is ultimately handled under some form of bilateral arrangement. The greater the amount accounted for by bilateral arrangements, the more chance for wide price fluctuations. Countries that opt not to participate, or that experience a significant increase in their import requirements, will bid intensively against each other for the small margin of grain not already committed. Bilaterals, by themselves, are no insurance against arbitrary unilateral action on either the importer's or exporter's side.

There is, however, no gainsaying the political attraction of these arrangements. Bilateral agreements offer a potential source for greater coordination of agricultural policies. In addition, the symbolic value of such arrangements can be important, as illustrated in the 1975 U.S./Soviet accord. Undoubtedly it was a combination of these factors plus the interplay of domestic politics that prompted Secretary Bergland to entertain publicly the idea of committing a larger share of U.S. grain exports via bilateral agreements and led the Carter administration to pursue this alternative. One of the results of that pursuit was a U.S. commitment to Poland, which was sealed by credits offered during

President Carter's visit in December 1977. The Carter administration also secured new grain agreements with China and Mexico. Each such agreement has been reaffirmed by the Reagan administration in contrast to its avowed dislike of government intervention in the grain trade.

Although China was openly courted by the United States after recognition in 1978, it was not until the fall of 1980 (at which time the continuation of the Soviet grain embargo was still unresolved) that serious negotiations began over a U.S.-China agreement. The agreement, signed 22 October 1980 and similar in format to the U.S.-USSR accord, guarantees 6 to 9 million tons of grain annually through 1984 to the PRC (15 to 20 percent of which will be in corn). Each country is required to notify the other if it cannot meet, or wishes to exceed, these levels.

The U.S.-China agreement illustrates clearly the political utility of bilaterals, as China's grain imports from the United States have grown steadily since 1978, and by 1980-81 had already exceeded the 9 million benchmark specified in the treaty. Traditionally, China's grain imports have been handled under long-term purchasing guarantees with Canada, Australia, and, more recently, with Argentina. If, as assumed, the China market does grow steadily, it is logical to conclude that Canada, Australia, and Argentina together will at some point no longer be able to satisfy China's import requirements while meeting their other export commitments. Under such a scenario, China would inevitably have turned more and more to the United States, with or without a bilateral treaty. Thus it seems reasonable to suggest that it was the political rather than the purely economic advantage of such an arrangement that made it attractive to both parties.

A similar assumption may be made about the purchasing agreement with Mexico, signed in 1978 and renewed annually thus far. The history of that agreement is particularly interesting in that it was consummated only following rejection of an American proposal to swap grain for Mexican oil.[32] Like the similar 1975 American effort to barter grain for Soviet oil, the Mexican barter proposal never reached the stage of serious negotiations. With the price of oil appreciating much more rapidly than that of grain, the terms of trade work against such an agreement.

Other politically inspired efforts have brought about closer bilateral and multilateral consultations among exporting countries, particularly the United States and Canada. In the context of a relatively successful history of working together, American and Canadian representatives in 1979 met periodically in an effort to devise a joint supply policy that would produce higher export prices. Throughout 1979, the United States remained skeptical, particularly as global supplies increased and little progress was made. Following suspension of U.S. sales to the USSR in 1980, such a joint strategy became more attractive to American policy makers. The United States then needed the cooperation of other exporters to tighten the vise around the Soviets. It was no more successful in this attempt than the Canadian and American politicians with predominant farm constituencies were in their attempt to revive a joint export strategy for income purposes. The United States and Canada could not bring about in the period between 1979 and 1981 what they had successfully accomplished ten years before. Competing wheat suppliers were in a surplus position, undermining any effort by the world's two largest producers to secure a monopolistic hold on the market and, hence, on the pricing of supplies available for export.

Bilaterals between exporters and importers were seen as a second-best solution to the problem of income and food security. For the United States, however, the agreements have been so ambiguous that they limit the gain to political symbolism. Bilaterals that contain a reference to prices can offer limited protection against the wide swings in grain prices so characteristic of the years immediately following the Soviet sale of 1972 and the soybean embargo of 1973. Even informal understandings between sellers and buyers, reached either directly between governments or between representatives of the private trade, could ensure relative price stability for some portion of the world's grain supply. As long as these agreements are honored, they would assure the availability of needed supplies for participating countries and a guaranteed market for the exporter. In so doing they might relieve some of the strain on prices for the importer in times of shortages and the costs of holding stocks for the exporter. Unless prices are specifically dealt with in any such agreement, however, the stabilizing effect can be neither long-lasting nor mutually beneficial. If price is not dealt with, the participating importer gains during shortages because the prices he pays are lower than they would be on the open market. In times of surplus, however, the importer pays more than the going international price, which, assuming excess production is concentrated in one or several of the most important exporting countries, will be depressed. There are, of course, other factors that influence commodity price movement, but without specific agreements on price ranges, even a bilateral undertaking will do little to cushion the roller-coaster ride.

Bilateral arrangements would produce price stability only if they governed all but a few marginal transactions in the international grain trade. In this hypothetical situation, in which every supplier and every customer was a participant in one or more bilaterals, then and only then might a proliferation of bilaterals offer a comprehensive solution to the problem of world food security. Even in such a radically altered situation, there would be little incentive for importers to seek bilateral commitments from suppliers in the absence of sizable reserves.[33] Paradoxically, however, these reserves would themselves act as a disincentive to buyers who might then be likely to conclude that they could obtain more flexible purchasing terms on the open market than under any bilateral agreement.

Bilateral agreements are national instruments, and their success is the function of another country's failure. For exporters, their economic contribution is derived from displacing competitors; for importers, the gain comes from preferential treatment over competing countries' import requirements. Moreover, they are reactive rather than constructive measures, and as such are only fully appreciated during periodic agricultural booms and busts. Existing bilateral agreements constitute an uneven patchwork, too weak to fashion an international food security system. They do not offer either food security or long-range price stabilization in grains. In attempting to redress certain problems, they may have the net effect of creating others, and, although narrow in scope, their potential danger to individual countries and to the world food system is extensive. They are, at best, an imperfect solution in an imperfect world. For the United States they have done little to redress the problems that its agricultural economy now faces. Their tendency to reinforce the position of the grain trade oligopoly and distort the functions of the market to an even greater degree may, in fact, aggravate the American farm problem.

NOTES

1. U.S. Department of Agriculture, *New Directions for U.S. Food Assistance: A Report of the Special Task Force on the Operation of Public Law 480 to the Secretary of Agriculture* (Washington, D.C., May 1978), Table C-1, p. 246.

2. Mitchel B. Wallerstein, *Food for Peace–Food for War: U.S. Policy in a Global Context* (Cambridge, Mass.: MIT Press, 1980), pp. 44-45.

3. Ibid., p. 6.

4. U.S. Department of Agriculture, *Report of the Special Task Force*, p. 116.

5. U.S. Senate, Committee on Agriculture and Forestry, *Extension of Public Law 480, Hearings on S. 671, S. 1127, and S. 1314*, 85th Cong., 1st sess., 1957, pp. 41-42.

6. U.S. Congress, Senate, *Food and Fibre as a Force for Freedom, Report by Sen. Hubert H. Humphrey to the Senate Committee on Agriculture and Forestry* (Washington, D.C.: U.S. Government Printing Office, 1958), pp. 12-13.

7. U.S. Department of Agriculture, *Report of the Special Task Force*, p. 101.

8. Ibid., p. 114.

9. U.S. General Accounting Office (GAO), *Competition Among Suppliers in the P.L. 480 Concessional Food Sales Progam* (Washington, D.C.: GAO, 19 December 1980), pp. 2-3.

10. Ibid.

11. Richard Gilmore with the assistance of Frederick Blott, "U.S. Food and Beverage Industry Report" (United Nations Center on Transnational Corporations, United Nations, January 1978), pp. 45-56. The last Cooley loan was granted in fiscal year 1976 and PTAs were terminated in 1972.

12. Ibid., p. 47.

13. Ibid., pp. 52, 55; and Wallerstein, *Food and Peace–Food for War*, p. 37. Wallerstein notes that "these [Cooley loans] . . . became a major source of largesse for U.S. multinational corporations and their overseas affiliates which received 90% of the funds loaned."

14. Statement of Fred Hugo Sanderson, director of the Office of Food Policy and Programs, U.S. Department of State, during a meeting of 4 June 1965 of the Committee on Surplus Disposal (CSD) of the Food and Agriculture Organization of the UN.

15. The White House, *Fact Sheet*, Office of the White House Press Secretary, 20 October 1975.

16. White House Press Conference, Earl Butz, Secretary of Agriculture, 20 October 1975.

17. National Commission on Supplies and Shortages, *The Commodity Shortages of 1973-1974* (August 1976), pp. 82-83.

18. U.S. Department of Agriculture, Economic Research Service, *Farm Income Statistics*, Statistical Bulletin No. 576 (July 1977), p. 53.

19. Confidential Memorandum from the law firm of Arent, Fox, Kitner, Plotkin & Kahn, to the Board of Directors of the National Association of Wheat Growers; also refer to U.S. Congress, Senate, Committee on Government Operations, *Sales of Grain to the Soviet Union, Hearings before the Permanent Subcommittee on Investigations,* 93d Cong., 2d sess., 1974.

20. U.S. Congress, Senate, Committee on Foreign Relations, *USSR and Grain, by Richard Gilmore, Committee Print. Staff Report prepared for the use of the Subcommittee on Multinational Corporations* (Washington, D.C.: U.S. Government Printing Office, 1976), pp. 4, 20-21.

21. U.S. Congress, Senate, Committee on Government Operations, *Grain Sales to the Soviet Union, Hearings before the Permanent Subcommittee on Investigations,* 94th Cong., 1st sess., July and August 1975, pp. 117, 122-24, 133-37.

22. U.S. Department of State, Bureau of Intelligence and Research, Report No. 33, 18 July 1975. Confidential, declassified under the Freedom of Information Act request; and secret cable from Secretary of State Henry Kissinger to Undersecretary of State Charles Robinson on "Soviet Grain Crop," 1 October 1975. Declassified under Freedom of Information request. U.S. Congress, Senate, *USSR and Grain*, p. 21.

23. "Agreement Between the Government of the United States of America and the Government of the Union of Soviet Socialist Republics on the Supply of Grain," 20 October 1975, Art. 3.

24. The United States took a more limited interpretation of its obligation when it canceled its sales contracts with the USSR in response to the Afghanistan invasion in January 1980.

25. National Association of Wheat Growers, Letter to Congressman Paul Findley, 23 July 1976.

26. Letter from George Meany, president of AFL-CIO, to the officers of AFL-CIO state bodies, regional directors, COPE directors, and department heads, 29 August 1975.

27. PL 96-494, Agricultural Act of 1980 (the security reserve); and Agricultural Trade Development and Assistance Act of 1954, as amended, Title III, Sec. 304.

28. Commission of the European Communities, *The 1978 Cereals, Skimmed Milk and Butteroil Food Aid Programs*, COM (77) 512 final (Brussels, 26 October 1977), p. 2.

29. Shintaro Abe, Japanese minister of Agriculture and Forestry.

30. Protocol on Development of Agricultural Trade between the Department of Agriculture of the United States and the Ministry of Agriculture and Food Industry of the Socialist Republic of Romania.

31. The National Federation of Grain Cooperatives is a Washington association for cooperatives and not a bona fide exporter.

32. U.S. Department of Agriculture, "Thoughts on a U.S.-Mexican Bilateral Grains Agreement," Internal Memorandum. Manuscript.

33. Dan Morrow, "Analysis of Bilateral Agreement," 3 May 1978, p. 6. Manuscript.

7

The Rusting American Agricultural Chain

U.S. grain exports are booming. Each year more annual production of most grains and oilseeds goes to foreign markets. For the past ten years almost half of the American wheat crop was consumed abroad, thanks in the early 1960s to PL 480 and later to such big commercial buyers as the Soviet Union, Europe (East and West), and most recently China. The percentage of wheat production currently entering the export stream, as demonstrated in Table 7.1, is close to 65 percent, which represents an increase of approximately 15 percent in the last decade. This improvement is all the more startling when taking into account the spectacular growth of U.S. production over the same period. Wheat harvests today are at least 100 percent greater than ten years ago, and export volumes have leaped proportionately to a record level of 52 million metric tons.

Were it not for additional demand abroad, the United States would be left with either vast amounts of carryover stocks and/or expensive production curtailment programs. Domestic consumption of wheat alone has increased roughly 10 percent between 1962 and 1980/81, while in the last two years the U.S share has actually declined. This trend could continue as long as wheat prices remain significantly higher than other grains in the United States.

What is true for wheat also applies to other grains and oilseeds, as shown in Table 7.1. Production is up in all commodities and domestic consumption has leveled off relative to foreign demand. This trend is in some respects even more noteworthy than in the case of wheat because PL 480 traditionally accounted for the major portion of shipments in wheat and wheat flour, but very little in coarse grains and relatively insignificant amounts in soybean products. In other words, the steady, upward shift to exports in coarse grains and soybeans is largely a commercial phenomenon that is accelerating at a faster rate than wheat exports. Eventually, the prognosis is for the ratios in all these commodities to tilt in favor of foreign markets over consumption at home.

TABLE 7.1 Increasing Share of U.S. Production That Goes into the Export Stream (U.S. Exports as Percentage of Total Domestic Production, Crop Years 1960–61 to 1979–80)

	WHEAT (June–May)[a]	COARSE GRAINS (June–May)[a]	CORN (Oct–Sept)	BARLEY (June–May)[a]	RYE (June–May)[a]	GRAIN-SORGHUM (Oct–Sept)	SOYBEANS (Sept–Aug)
1960–61	49	8	7	19	24	11	24
1961–62	59	12	11	21	29	21	22
1962–63	58	12	11	16	50	22	27
1963–64	74	12	12	18	33	18	27
1964–65	55	16	16	18	6	30	30
1965–66	64	18	16	19	11	40	30
1966–67	58	14	11	15	15	35	28
1967–68	50	13	13	9	13	22	27
1968–69	34	10	12	2	5	15	26
1969–70	41	12	13	2	3	17	38
1970–71	54	13	12	20	9	21	38
1971–72	37	13	14	8	4	14	35
1972–73	72	21	22	16	23	26	38
1973–74	71	22	22	22	—	25	35
1974–75	57	24	24	14	2	34	35
1975–76	55	27	29	6	6	30	36
1976–77	44	26	27	18	—	34	44
1977–78	55	28	30	14	—	27	40
1978–79	66	28	30	6	1	28	40
1979–80	62	27	28	13	21	34	36 (proj.)

[a]Excepting years 1960–61 through 1964–65 which are July–June crop years.

SOURCE: Compiled with data from the USDA, Foreign Agricultural Service.

115

PRODUCERS

Among the most important of the unintended effects of the success of the export campaign has been the impact on producers. If all markets were identical, there would be no distinction from the producer's point of view between a foreign and domestic sale. The return on production would be equal. However, all markets are not identical. In the export business forces are at play that tend to reduce receipts for American farmers. Producers are thus squeezed between a new-found dependence on export sales that seem essential, yet for which they receive a lower return on their harvests.

So far relatively few farmers seem to realize the nature of the double bind in which they find themselves as a result of export dependence. Most American farmers attribute their livelihood to a steadily growing foreign demand for their crops.[1] Many, however, are discontented about the degree of control they think the grain trade exercises over the export market at their expense. When asked, "Do you believe that effective competition exists in the U.S. export market among the grain traders?" an overwhelming majority answered no.[2] Nevertheless, the major farm groups still seem to equate an increase in exports with greater farm income, in keeping with the long-held official view that greater overseas sales volumes must lead directly to higher farmgate prices.

In actuality, as Table 7.2 demonstrates, there has not been a significant relationship between increased export volume and higher farmgate prices. In 1962, when wheat exports were little more than half what they were in 1977, average farm prices were only 14 percent less, and real wheat prices (the value after inflation) were actually higher in the low-export year.[3] A similar pattern can be seen by comparing prices in 1978 with those of 1975. Despite higher export shipments in 1978, posted prices in 1975 were above those in 1978. And when prices surged in the wake of the 1972 Soviet sale, producers' cash receipts did not increase at the same rate. Therefore, while it is not true that export volume has no influence on the prices farmers receive for their crops, the point is that there is no one-to-one correlation between farmgate and f.o.b. export prices in the same time frame. Moreover, farm prices tend to respond more directly to a downturn than to an increase in foreign sales. Farm prices consistently lag behind f.o.b. export prices by at least one crop year. The lead time of almost an entire year can wipe out any of the anticipated future earnings from large export sales contracted for the previous year's crop.

This is because many factors other than exports enter into the price a farmer actually receives. For example, when the buyer takes delivery of the crop and tests its quality, the farmer may be paid more or less than he was originally offered. Transportation rates and delivery times also affect the cash price. Hidden costs, such as financing and inflated operating expenses, eat away at farmers' cash receipts. Nevertheless, whether taken separately or together these factors alone do not explain why farmers receive a diminishing

TABLE 7.2 Wheat Exports and Prices (figures are by marketing year, June 1–May 31)

	U.S. Wheat Exports (million metric tons)	Average[a] Farmer Prices ($ per bu.)	Average Price[b] Hard Winter #1 Ordinary Protein f.o.b. Gulf ($ per bu.)	Average Price[c] U.S. Hard Winter Ordinary Protein c.i.f. Rotterdam ($ per bu.)
1960	17.79	1.74	2.18	
1961	19.48	1.83	2.25	
1962	17.67	2.04	2.40	
1963	23.01	1.85	2.31	1.95[d]
1964	19.67	1.37	1.76	1.95
1965	23.18	1.35	1.78	1.75
1966	20.99	1.63	2.02	1.93
1967	20.83	1.39	1.77	1.88
1968	14.81	1.24	1.55	1.82
1969	16.41	1.25	1.54	1.67
1970	20.16	1.33	1.68	1.81
1971	16.59	1.34	1.74	1.76
1972	30.89	1.76	2.44	2.42
1973	33.12	3.95	4.70	5.24
1974	27.72	4.09	4.46	4.90
1975	31.92	3.56	4.06	4.25
1976	25.84	2.73	3.17	3.41
1977	30.59	2.33	3.08	3.30
1978	31.97	2.97	3.75	4.14

[a]R^2 = .5646.
[b]R^2 = .6854.
[c]R^2 = .1591 (1973–78).
[d]Figures before 1973 are not meaningful in terms of supply and demand because an export subsidy existed until that time.

SOURCE: USDA, ESCS, *Wheat Situation.* WS-244 May 1978 and WS-248 May 1979 and other price data.

share of the profits derived from a thriving export sector or, more precisely, why the linkage between export performance and producers' receipts is so loose that a majority of farmers realize no increase in earnings from higher export volumes.

The true beneficiaries of increased export volumes have not been producers but intermediaries. In a trade dominated by a few buyers and sellers—a combination of an oligopsony (buyers) and an oligopoly (sellers)—the farmer is isolated from the market, and it is the merchandisers who capture the largest share of any net gain derived from an increase in f.o.b. prices. The resulting plight of the producers is one attendant effect of the structure of the contemporary American export-based agricultural economy. With appropriate institutions and programs, efficient growers would not have been at a disadvantage, but ignoring this dimension of the farm problem has resulted in a situation in which the export engine works at the expense of the producers.

Instead of correcting this imbalance, the public and private sector has responded in such a way as to exaggerate the problems.

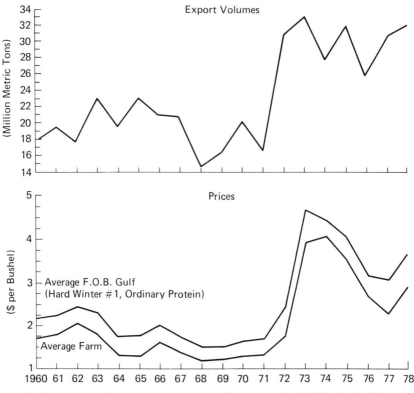

FIGURE 7.1 U.S. Wheat Exports and Prices, 1960–78 Marketing Years.

TRANSPORTATION

Throughout the 1970s, railroads failed to keep up with new demands created by the surge in exports. The rail companies and the Interstate Commerce Commission (ICC), which is responsible for regulating the railroads, were caught totally unprepared. During peak export periods, such as occurred in 1972 and 1977, there was a shortage of railcars; at other times of even heavier volumes the difficulty was one of car allocation. Neither the private sector nor the government seemed equal to the task. Railroad management blamed the inefficiencies on ICC's inflexible rate structure and other restrictive rules for rail transportation that do not apply to trucks and barges, which operate in an unregulated market. No doubt the ICC and the regulatory statutes for railroads needed revising, but the rail companies themselves must share the blame.

During the 1970s many lines fell under conglomerate ownership that chose to utilize assets for purposes other than running a railroad, leaving shoddy rail tracks, roadbeds, and financing conditions.[4]

Growing dissatisfaction over the railroads' ability to service grain-hauling requirements caused private companies to enter the business, with Cargill in the lead. Citing the need for efficiency and modernization, these companies organized a campaign in the late 1960s to change the rate structure to favor unit car trains instead of the old boxcars. The new trains were made up of as many as 100 hopper-covered cars, which are larger and easier to load and service than the old boxcars and, hence, are particularly well suited to the new terminal elevators the major companies owned.

Grain company strategy was to develop a privately owned fleet of hopper cars under a long-term lease agreement with the railroads backed by favorable government-regulated rates for the use of these cars to minimize their capital risk. Initially this seemed an ideal solution from the viewpoint of almost all parties, including farmers and consumers. Through construction and leasing contracts with the grain companies, railroads received an infusion of sorely needed capital and were assured of high-volume use of the new cars by the largest grain handlers.

There was, however, a debit side to the ledger. Smaller grain merchandisers could not risk committing capital to cover the minimum of five consecutive hauls (to take advantage of ICC's lower tariffs) when they had no certainty that they could fill such a huge string of cars.[5] The unit train was an example of modernization that created both efficiencies and gross inequities. It was a development that benefited the railroads, large traders, and the government in their joint effort to move as much grain as possible into the export stream. Its effects on small traders and producers were less beneficial.

An example of the impact of unit trains on producers can be seen in the period from 1972 to 1974 when demands on the U.S. transportation system were heaviest. During this period the unit train arrangement often proved discriminatory against growers. Before the Soviet sale, there had been a series of good harvests coupled with a sluggish demand for grain. Farmers were reluctant to sell their stocks, at bearish prices, but when the wheat and corn harvests of 1972-73 broke all records, they had little choice but to dispose of their surpluses. It was therefore essential that they sell quickly before prices dipped in response to the news of surpluses and transportation backups. Storage facilities in the countryside were full, and many farmers and country elevators were totally dependent on small branch rail lines to pick up their crop. The major grain houses held the leases on most of the unit trains, which gave them effective control of inland shipping. These grain houses had more privately owned and leased cars available for grain transport than the railroads did, and they were purchasing cars at a faster rate (see Table 7.3).

Such a large share of the transportation system in the hands of a few companies, especially at a time of rail-car shortages, was an invitation for commercial abuse. Producers and smaller buyers in need of access to rail

TABLE 7.3 Covered Hopper Car Equipment

Year (as of Jan. 1)	Private	Percentage Change	Railroads	Percentage Change
1971	38,972	—	130,954	—
1972	41,045	+5.3	138,099	+5.4
1973	43,910	+7.0	141,672	+2.6
1974	53,771	+22.4	150,499	+6.2
1975	64,081	+19.2	154,302	+2.5
1976	70,029	+9.3	156,850	+1.6
1977	70,145	+.2	158,850	+1.3
1978	73,103	+4.2	159,766	+.6
1979	80,775	+10.5	161,885	+1.3
1980	98,643	+22.1	164,959	+1.9

SOURCES: Economics and Finance Department, American Association of Railroads (A.A.R.); A.A.R., CS-54A; *Yearbook of Railroad Facts.*

transportation had to turn to the large firms: ". . . entire areas of the country are unable to secure shipments of vitally needed feedgrains because of these car distribution practices, thus creating great economic loss."[6] The response of the large companies was not always generous. Instead of following the normal practice of charging a flat fee for transportation, several major companies released their cars for use on a conditional basis. In exchange for picking up the grain, they often added charges for equipment costs over and above the normal tariff rates. As a result, farmers without alternate transportation who had to unload their grain on the market were frequently penalized by the large companies who discounted or deducted artificially high transportation costs from their original cash bids. An ICC investigation furnished evidence that discounting was widespread and concluded that Continental and the Illinois Central Gulf Railroad in particular were in violation of the law.[7]

The unit train arrangement between the railroads and the grain companies thus fostered a predatory business practice in which artificial car shortages allowed the companies to profit unfairly at the expense of producers. While the commodity exchanges posted soaring prices in the wake of the Soviet sale, many farmers sold in cash markets at a discounted price. The official statistics registered higher farmgate prices. In fact, however, a large portion of American farmers had to sell their produce below the published price while several of the large trading companies reaped windfall profits.

A similar situation arose when the ICC ruled in 1978 that wheat flour moving from midwestern mills to the East Coast could be shipped in 55-car unit trains at a lower rate than the single-car rate. Following that ruling Cargill decided to go ahead with its plan to construct a $2.5 million storage terminal in Maryland to receive the flour. Ross Industries, Cargill's main milling subsidiary, rested its case on efficiency and competition. It argued before the ICC that individual cars were not as practical as unit trains, that with more favorable rates midwestern millers could compete with their counterparts on the East Coast and could offer additional services to the eastern bakery business. Cargill's position was grounded in a legitimate claim that the current rate structure discriminated against midwestern firms by unduly protecting millers on the East Coast. At the same time, other midwestern millers complained that the ICC decision in favor of Ross Industries gave Cargill an unfair advantage because few other firms could afford unit trains and thus benefit from the new lower rate.

Such situations were and are inevitable as long as a governmentally endorsed export campaign is carried out with great enthusiasm while the equally important problems of internal production, price, and distribution are virtually neglected. In theory, the development of the world's most efficient and least expensive transportation system was the key to the competitiveness of American agricultural products in the export market. In this context, the unit train and the accompanying low tariff rate seemed appropriate. And these developments in transportation did reduce the cost to the point that f.o.b. prices were only marginally above farmgate prices. In this sense, regulatory decisions and private-sector initiatives together had a catalytic effect in developing a transportation system ideally suited to an export-oriented agricultural economy. At the same time, the structural transformation of the grain-merchandising industry weakened the market influence of growers and smaller independent handlers.

Eventually the ICC recognized that inefficiencies in the unit train rate structure worked against an equitable distribution of rail cars and transportation services nationwide and in favor of the export grain business. In 1979 it called for a comprehensive review of rail rates and immediate remedial action respecting the distribution of hopper cars and their uninterrupted use as unit trains by the grain companies.[8] The ICC's ability to carry out this policy, however, was reduced in March 1979 when the government took the first steps toward rail deregulation that was adopted by Congress in the following year.[9] Budgetary concerns, past regulatory abuses, and the specter of Canada's transportation difficulties convinced legislators of the need for deregulation at the very time when the ICC was moving to curb the abuses of the private system.

The new law ushered in a phased deregulation of the rail sector over a period of five years. After an initial transition period of ICC-monitored tariff adjustments, the railroads will be allowed to adjust rates without regulatory review and abandon those branch lines that proved too costly to maintain. Since the passage of the new law in October 1980, railroads have abandoned many feeder lines in the countryside, servicing only the principal lines that hook up to subterminals owned by the big traders. When the Chicago, Milwaukee, St. Paul & Pacific Railroad ceased operations over portions of its lines in November 1979, some shippers lost their only rail service and threatened not to move their grain at all until spring. Similarly, the bankrupt Chicago, Rock Island & Pacific Railroad Co. abandoned lines in the Midwest where it was the only railroad to service approximately 1,700 locations.

A special advisory task force[10] recommended measures to protect grower interests threatened by the initial reform package. These measures, which covered truck, barge, and rail transportation, include federal assistance to finance rail rehabilitation projects; ICC standards for upgrading lines whenever possible in lieu of abandonment; and a demonstration project to test the feasibility of rural transportation cooperatives in areas where abandonment was in prospect as an alternate means of making local lines more viable.

The task force made other recommendations to protect farmers and independent shippers who would otherwise be at the mercy of a few rail and grain companies. The key was to ensure enough competition in rates and access to rail cars. From developments so far, it would appear that the task force's suggestions will not be fully implemented and that predictions of the new deregulation approach reinforcing the position of subterminal companies and concentration in grain merchandising will be confirmed.

The net effect of these governmentally sanctioned changes in the railroad system has been to make alternate forms of transportation more attractive to producers. Trucks, in particular, became increasingly competitive for inland transportation after growers began storing more of their crop on the farm in response to the Carter administration's farmer-held reserve program. Timely deliveries on the resulting larger but fewer sales transactions were crucial to maximizing the return for growers. A virtually unregulated trucking industry for agricultural commodities theoretically gave producers and country elevator operators more power to influence rates. And as railroads cut back on branch lines, and subterminals became the magnet delivery points, trucks were ideal for traveling back roads to pick up the grain and making short hauls to a delivery point on the Mississippi or one of its arteries for barge or rail loadings. With the buildup of subterminals at strategic points along the rivers, both trucks and barges could hook up with rail cars as the grain moved to port.

Still, there are drawbacks to truck and barge transportation that make use of the rail system inescapable. Navigating barges during the winter months is treacherous and sometimes impossible. The Great Lakes are frozen from December to March, which closes export traffic from Duluth, Minnesota, via the St. Lawrence seaway to Europe. The Missouri River is shallow, and other rivers need dredging for barges to pass. Barges are more fuel efficient than railroads, but trucks consume between three and four times as much fuel per ton mile as railroads, making truck costs for long hauls almost twice as high as those for either barge or rail.[11] Moreover, barge transportation costs are likely to increase as a result of the passage of recent waterway user-tax legislation.

Traditionally, the U.S. Army Corps of Engineers maintained the inland river system at government expense, based on the principle that rivers were part of the public trust. This thinking gave way in 1978 to a completely different concept, one that was more in keeping with the fashionable notion that government expenditures and intervention meant inflation, whereas private sector self-rule meant commercial equity and efficiency. The 1978 Inland Waterways Revenue Act introduced a fuel tax for "commercial waterway transportation" that would reach 10 cents per gallon in 1985.[12] The tax, raised again in 1981, was meant to introduce self-financing from tax revenue for construction and maintenance of the U.S. waterway system. As with the deregulation of the railroads, gains in efficiency from a flow of new funds to improve the barge system were accompanied by certain costs. A barge tax inevitably is passed down the agricultural chain to wind up in the form of a reduction in the purchase price that is subtracted from cash bids on farmer crops.

Such a users' fee creates a ripple effect throughout the transportation system. Any increase in barge rates is likely to inspire proportionate increases in the trucking and rail sectors. Rail rates are pegged to water transportation, and truck rates are pegged to rail shipping costs. Synchronizing rate hikes in the transportation triad tends to hurt the farmer disproportionately. Current deregulation reforms and volume-related fee structures geared toward competition in the transportation sector may thus result in a paradoxical situation of increased concentration.

GOVERNMENT INSPECTION AND STANDARDS

The recent reductions in federal regulatory control over transportation have been based on the belief that such regulation hinders the export sector. Interestingly, the same concern has led to increased federal involvement and controls in grain inspection. Sophisticated foreign buyers have always been unwilling to accept inferior-quality grain at prices equivalent to those for high-standard crops. Wheat or corn, for example, can vary in grade; can be useful for milling or feed; can be moist or dry, broken or whole, or diseased. These distinctions are extremely important from a commercial and even a political standpoint. Cheating the system at any point along the distribution line can mean substantial windfall profits or losses for the parties involved depending on which side of the fence one stands.

Between 1965 and 1975, as U.S. export volumes were soaring, foreign buyers continually registered formal protests with the Department of Agriculture concerning grain quality and, to a lesser extent, shortchanging practices among shippers.[13] The Department's Agricultural Marketing Service received 26 complaints against Cook's elevator alone in Reserve, Louisiana, for selling inferior grain at higher-quality prices. In 1976, India sued several major companies, including Cargill, for deliveries that failed to meet the quality and weight standards specified in their contracts with the government. When China was first introduced to the American grain market in the early 1970s, it turned back U.S. shipments because of cargo infestation. These complaints were tame by comparison with reports Department of Agriculture officials received from other foreign buyers about the substandard state of grain shipments upon delivery.[14] They came from every region, from important commercial buyers, and food aid recipients, who could least afford to complain but at the same time who were affected the most. The complaints mounted, and reports filed by Department officials after on-site inspections of ships and terminal operations were finally brought to public attention, raising sufficient pressure for a full-scale investigation.

The inspection system then in effect had been established some three decades earlier. Under the U.S. Grain Standards Act (USGSA) of 1940, all grain destined for export had to be officially approved in accordance with government standards, and grain stored in facilities licensed by the Department of Agriculture was subject to official inspection. The purpose of all this cross-checking was to protect buyers and sellers, as well as the government. It was assumed, and rightly so, that the farmer who produced a high-quality crop would want to be justly compensated when selling it to the country elevator, which in turn would want to protect itself by ensuring the integrity of the grain for future sales. Banks that finance large export transactions need dependable certification of warehouse receipts, which they accept as collateral, and buyers naturally want to ensure that the terms of their contracts are satisfied. The federal government also has a stake in neither giving higher price supports than regulations allow nor making purchases in fulfillment of its own programs without proper documentation on quality and weight.

However, the 1940 system and the government's enforcement of it proved inadequate to preserve the integrity of American grain sales and protect those involved in grain production and distribution. This system was abused to such an extent that by 1975 none of these interests was satisfactorily protected. Over $13 billion worth of "inspected" grain was exported in 1976; by the spring of that year 16 firms—including all the Big League companies with the exception of Cargill—and 146 individuals had been indicted under the Grain Standards Act of 1968, resulting in a total of $1 million in fines, 31 years of incarceration, and 111 years of probation.[15]

Conflict of interest was the biggest single problem. Grain-exporting houses hired private firms or the local board of trade to certify inspections and weighing procedures. Federal licenses were not enough to ensure an arm's-length approach, and these firms falsified loading and shipping documents in virtually every major grain port in the country. If a ship was approved without proper inspection, the exporter gained by not having to suffer costly delays. Similarly, if a seller could blend high-grade with low-grade wheat and be paid for premium value, it was understandably a tempting and quick way to make a profit. Producers, on the other hand, might be paid for lower-quality grain than the actual quality of their crop warranted. Without government intervention, the grain-merchandising sector was unable to protect its own interests equitably over the long term. It stood to lose the most because of a threat by foreign buyers to seek alternate food sources if such fraudulent practices continued.

The impact of inadequate inspection was most significant near the end of the agricultural chain. The increase in export volume had exacerbated the weaknesses of the system, and a continuation of the status quo threatened to reduce this volume over time. Despite the need for reform, the large exporting companies, many of which had been indicted or had accepted out-of-court settlements for infractions of the USGSA,[16] vociferously opposed new legislation. Not one principal grain house endorsed a federal takeover of the inspection system at the ports and greater enforcement powers for oversight of licensed private and state agencies. After the USGSA was amended in 1976 and the new, expanded Federal Grain Inspection Service (FGIS) had been in operation for less than two years, these same companies launched a successful effort to reduce the stringency of controls mandated under the 1976 act. Their representatives maintained that the system was blocking the efficient, rapid handling of shipments and impeding sales.[17] Farm groups also criticized the FGIS, arguing that the new inspection fees were too high and the system represented too much government intervention.[18] The private sector generally shared these views, as demonstrated by a letter from The Andersons to the USDA, protesting fees charged by FGIS.

> . . . the bigger, more efficient shippers are being penalized and discriminated against.
> Industry is already reacting to your announcement and is doing everything possible to avoid the usage of FGIS. . . . we are working very hard to sell our rail grain without FGIS grades and weights (domestic sales could legally be sold without FGIS inspection certificates).[19]

In part as a result of these complaints, the law was amended in 1977. Authority for supervision fees was rescinded and detailed elevator recording provisions eliminated, but federal management of the system was not dismantled. Although the system is not now and never will be foolproof because of the export volume involved and the complexities of the trade, the post-1976 reforms still constitute a significant improvement over the past without being an obstacle to rapid turnover in port terminals.

Government procedures for setting grain standards, on the other hand, have never been subject to close review, despite their inherent vulnerability to abuse. Acceptable, uniform standards are as important commercially to the grain trade as is the certification process. For producers, they are a form of insurance that prices received will reflect the quality of a crop; for buyers, they offer price protection as well as a reliable way of identifying the commodity. Kernel defects or water content levels that do not meet premium requirements translate into millions of dollars. Unless grain standards are defined by unbiased experts, they also can become a barrier to trade. There is a decisive role for government in this area, which to date the Department of Agriculture has been reluctant to assume. Instead it has deferred repeatedly to outside specialists whose independence from grain trade interests is open to question. Grower and trade associations have grading committees set up for the express purpose of getting the government to use standards that will benefit their members. The stakes are enormous, and the influence of traders who deal directly with high-level officials to initiate changes in standards is powerful.

The Grain Standards Act of 1976 called for a study of all standards to determine their adequacy and to make them both more compatible with foreign buyers' needs and also easily certifiable by FGIS. No comprehensive investigation was conducted, however. In lieu of a comprehensive reevaluation of how these standards are determined, the government limited itself to a commitment for review every five years. As a result, the process remains very much the same as prior to the 1976 Act and continues to be viewed unfavorably by producers. When asked whether they believe that farmer interests regarding U.S. grain standards are fairly represented in the standards established by the USDA, polled farm organization members replied with a resounding no.[20] Despite this skepticism, the government continues to play a modest role, relying mainly on technical advice from the private sector.

COMMODITY EXCHANGES

American commodity exchanges were established to bring more orderly marketing to the agricultural sector by providing a forum where buyers and sellers could meet to conclude transactions. Without the exchanges, how would farmers in Kansas know what farmers in other states were getting for their wheat so that they could sell their crop at a competitive price? How could buyers commit themselves for purchases of undelivered grain and resell those commitments unless they had some contractual guarantee that the grain would be delivered at a price that bore an accurate relationship to supply and demand? Ideally, futures markets, which are run under the auspices of the commodity exchanges, offer a competitive system for pricing grain and, hence, for guidance in distribution and marketing. But their actual record has been blemished, not least by the fact that farmer involvement in the hedging system, purportedly designed for their benefit, has remained severely limited.

The exchanges functioned for many years with very little government regulation. Market manipulations, which culminated with a scandal in 1973 surrounding a New York firm engaged in the sale of options, and the push of U.S. exports in the 1960s and '70s, however, eventually made increased government involvement inevitable and led in 1975 to the establishment of the Commodity Futures Trading Commission (CFTC). Commodity exchange operations, however, are still subject to perhaps even less government control than is grain inspection. This is so because, traditionally, the exchanges have been viewed as the ultimate domain of commerce, to be left relatively unhampered from any public interference.

The exchanges, no less than the other links in the agricultural chain, have been affected by the growth of export volumes. The number of contracts traded on the exchanges went from slightly more than 4 million in 1957 to over 92 million in 1979, when corn and soybeans together accounted for 25.8 percent of total trading.[21] Despite this growth, the traders remained primarily an assembly of speculators and grain-merchandising firms to the exclusion of producers whose interests were directly linked to the outcome of daily trading in futures. Today only 1 percent of farmers actually hedge their own production. In 1976 less than 6 percent used the futures market.[22] Fewer than 10 percent of America's farmers used the futures market in the five-year period from 1970 to 1975.[23] Market complexity and an element of distrust kept them away from hedging their sales just when the need for this kind of backup was felt most strongly as a result of the uncertainty of cash markets.

Membership on the exchanges is open to anyone able to pay the requisite fee and pass the membership committee's review. Compared to the more restricted list of brokers of Futures Commission Merchants (FCMs), today's general membership looks like a well-balanced roster of industry representatives. Yet almost 42 percent of new members on the Chicago Board of Trade in 1976 were affiliated with large brokerage firms or commodity houses.[24] Nor does representation fully indicate the degree of power wielded by the large international grain houses over the exchanges. When Continental Grain enters the market, its affiliate Conticommodities does not necessarily handle the trades. In fact, to allow itself maximum flexibility, Continental is more likely to parcel its business out to a number of FCMs rather than its own affiliate. Size, then, is a principal indicator of influence on the exchanges (as well as in all other aspects along the agricultural chain); but because futures figure so prominently in grain operations, the Big League is equally attentive to the management side of the exchanges. A smoothly functioning hedging and speculative system is essential to overall profitability, and the large companies' preference has always been for self-regulation as opposed to federal regulation of the exchanges.

When the grain trading houses enter into large-lot foreign sales, such as those with the Soviet Union, they begin a delicate balancing act. A company whose orders are not covered through sufficient and well-placed futures contracts, cash purchases and existing inventories would have to go into the open spot (cash) market close to the date on which a large sale was to be concluded. Under these circumstances, the firm would face a severe risk of being caught short (unable to buy enough grain at the right price to complete their immediate foreign contracts). It would have to buy as basis prices were mounting in response to the trade news of a forthcoming large foreign purchase. Assuming the sale was at a flat price, the resulting losses would represent the difference between the purchase cost of more expensive spot contracts and the lower fixed or basis price (the difference between the cash and designated futures price) that had been offered to the foreign buyer.

To avoid this kind of squeeze, exporters endeavor to maintain a net long futures position sufficient to cover expected sales. For the largest sales made between 1975 and 1978, exporters as a rule hedged less than 10 percent of their total commitments.[25] Instead, they built up their futures position gradually in advance of these sales. To build up this kind of security in futures, exporters need an accommodating exchange system. Full public disclosure of the relevant details of these transactions would make such a strategy extremely difficult to implement, particularly if it identified all interaffiliate transactions. Conveniently from the Big League's perspective, reporting of a foreign subsidiary's hedging or speculative activities on American markets currently differs from the reporting requirements applied to U.S. companies, including the affiliates or parents of overseas firms. This discrepancy is not an accident; it allows the international grain houses the needed room to maneuver. A successful large trader almost by definition must now be a multinational organization in order to coordinate the placement of foreign and domestic hedging transactions.

Discrepancies in government reporting regulations to export transactions offer these multinationals a distinct advantage over U.S. firms. The CFTC only requires registration of a sale when the price is fixed, because it then becomes a specific sales commitment and, thus, part of the calculation of a trader's overall hedging position. Until that time, an American exporter and the foreign subsidiary buyer are free to enter into contracts unreported to the CFTC where the price is left indeterminate. Such an open contract allows foreign subsidiaries as much time as necessary to pin down the terms of a contract with another buyer and arrange the most advantageous hedging position possible. Timed correctly, the futures transaction can precede the sales registration with the CFTC and avoid any likely price penalty if news of the large export transaction breaks before the foreign subsidiary and its U.S. affiliate have time to place their hedges.

Registering the export sale with the USDA comes later than the firm's report of its hedge to the CFTC and gives the international grain firm the additional advantage of total secrecy until the very last minute. An export sale, no matter what the size, thus has a built-in camouflage resulting from discrepancies in the official interpretation of what qualifies as a bona fide hedge and what determines a sale at any given point in time.

As a consequence of the loopholes in present U.S. reporting requirements, many affiliate transactions go undetected. In theory, government reporting procedures encompass all futures contracts by a U.S. corporation and its affiliates. But what happens when the foreign affiliate assumes a futures position on its own or through another FCM representative on the commodity exchanges in the United States? These transactions are not necessarily reflected in government reporting forms that aim at gathering the company's total position, including its overseas affiliates. What happens when the lines of ownership are sufficiently stretched so that companies' legal obligation as foreign corporations to report their futures transactions is less than it would have been if they were treated as American corporations?

Regulating the activities of foreign traders in the United States, including foreign affiliates of American corporations, has been a thorny problem for the CFTC:

. . . attempts to collect information from foreign traders on a broad basis generally produced little useful information and then, only at great expenses of time and resources.[26]

Our feeling is that the Commission needs at least the same amount and type of information from all market participants. The current situation in which foreign traders provide less information than domestic traders is questionable in that the Commission is less able to detect large foreign market positions than it is large domestic positions.[27]

In an effort to correct the foreign trader loophole, the CFTC has in recent years concentrated on actions designed to prevent foreign governments or their agents from abusing the commodity trading system in the United States. The considerable apprehension that foreign traders could deal in futures beyond legal speculative limits without the CFTC's having any power to prevent such transactions is not without foundation. COBEC, the government of Brazil's trading arm, was rumored to have hedged periodically on U.S. commodity markets. In bad crop years, such as occurred in 1977-78, Brazil imported soybeans from the United States for processing and export. Either a direct hedge by COBEC or an agent private firm help reduce costs in such circumstances. Conversely, when there is a bumper crop of U.S. and Brazilian soybeans, it is in Brazil's interest to force the price up; this can be done through the commodity markets in the United States. In 1981 COBEC declared its intentions of participating directly in the newly established New Orleans Commodity Exchange, making any more speculation on the subject a foregone conclusion. Other buyers and sellers have similar interests in hedging their domestic positions on the U.S. market, which would constitute speculation in the United States and remain outside the CFTC's control.

Today, the CFTC is still struggling to balance the principle of equal treatment for foreign and American nationals against the necessity of preserving orderly commodity markets. The agency's working assumption is that foreign affiliate operations are accounted for under existing reporting requirements and that current revisions in foreign trader regulations need not specifically address the question of non-American subsidiary transactions.[28] More frequently than not, however, these foreign affiliates, in effect, are agents for a foreign government and synonymous with that government in many respects. In dealing with these buyers, the Big League has learned to turn to its subsidiaries, a lesson that was driven home by the 1972 experience, when American exporters sold directly to the Soviets (generally on a fixed-price basis) without long enough futures and cash positions to cover these and other sales commitments. The post 1972 arrangement is mutually beneficial. Foreign buyers are not subject to the disclosure requirements they would face if they entered the market directly. The majors gain more contractual flexibility and therefore greater profitability.

Many of the major foreign buyers have sought refuge in purchasing arrangements through foreign subsidiaries. Exportkhleb has preferred this procedure, and so has Canada's Wheat Board. Given the Board's self-imposed restrictions on direct participation in world commodity markets, it has used its exporting agents for the same purpose. The Board's sales to these companies, which are for the most part affiliates of American firms, are made with the express purpose of having the private sector hedge what amounts to the Board's own futures transactions to protect the Board against the hazards of price fluctuations. In a similar fashion, Japan's Food Agency issues weekly tenders with the full knowledge that the Sogo Shosha will synchronize their hedges in such a way as to offer the agency the best possible price.

It is clearly advantageous for all the major grain houses with U.S. and foreign affiliates to operate in a climate of minimum government oversight. American representatives of non-U.S. firms like Bunge or Dreyfus have argued that any modification of requirements for foreign traders would be discriminatory and would force them to transfer their trading to commodity markets outside the United States. Such arguments have to date persuaded the CFTC against enacting changes such as special-position limits for foreign traders, the continued and current threat of market manipulation or bias in favor of foreign accounts notwithstanding. Instead, the CFTC has concentrated on tightening the reporting requirements for foreign owners of accounts on American commodity exchanges. Recent efforts in this area include an agent-for-service rule, effective June 1980, to facilitate communication between the CFTC and foreign brokers represented by domestic agents on the exchanges. Another proposed rule would allow the CFTC to liquidate the position of a foreign trader who refused to respond within 24 hours to the Commission's request for information regarding trades. Although these rules are aimed at the problems of uniform accountability, the new disclosure laws still do not reliably identify foreign accounts. The Commission's reluctance to move any further in this regard is primarily a recognition that in closing one loophole, it will inevitably open another, because of the present structure and international character of the grain trade: ". . . the Division notes that requirements which contain position limits may be circumvented if a person distributes his holdings among several foreign brokers or FCMs (futures commission merchants) and is successful in not revealing the true ownership of these accounts."[29]

Aside from this seemingly arcane issue, official government policy since the inception of the CFTC is that the commodity exchanges are performing their proper function and that there is little necessity for additional government intervention. According to this logic, there have been no serious market disruptions linked to foreign trader activities: the Soviet sale was a Soviet problem; the 1973 soybean embargo a result of severe shortages in Peruvian anchovies; the 1974 and 1975 Soviet sales again a Soviet problem combined with U.S. mishandling of it; the Hunt family's cornering of the soybean futures market and the simultaneous miscalculation by Cook Industries in soybeans in 1977 were regarded as two unrelated domestic events; the 1980 tumbling of prices after the announcement of the embargo against the USSR was viewed as an inevitable consequence of a political decision; and the 1981 soybean futures miscalculation by Farmers Export Company was seen as still another example of poor judgment by management, but not in any way related to the foreign subsidiary loophole. Ostensibly, each case arose for different reasons, none of them having to do with unidentified foreign purchases; in fact, they all shared this common problem.

The 1973 soybean embargo illustrates the integral role that foreign subsidiaries play in a domestic and international supply crisis. As events unfolded prior to the decision to embargo all foreign shipments of U.S. soybeans in June 1973, interaffiliate transactions between American exporting companies and their subsidiaries overseas took a quantum jump in anticipation of the cutoff. Bona fide foreign sales were confused with paper transactions; as a result, the picture of what was happening to the soybean market was clouded to such an extent that shipments were halted on the assumption that a real shortage existed.

When President Ford met with leaders of the export industry at the White House in 1974, he was concerned that the Soviets might be buying on a scale comparable to the amounts in 1972. He invoked a moratorium because he could not establish with certainty what Soviet buying intentions or existing contracts were, since foreign subsidiaries served as intermediaries.

In 1980, the Carter administration struggled for over two and a half months to work out an arrangement whereby the U.S. government would reimburse those trading companies whose contracts were cut across when the suspension of grain to the Soviet Union was announced. A big part of the problem was in identifying actual Soviet contracts, which had been comingled with other interaffiliate transactions. The government was caught in the embarrassing position of not knowing who had sold what, notwithstanding CFTC reporting regulations on sales over 100,000 tons.

Each of these situations is a revealing illustration of the critical role foreign subsidiaries have in playing the U.S. commodity market. Thanks to ambiguities in existing law, their futures positions cannot be fully identified. Under such circumstances, they can conceal big sales by quietly building up a long futures position whose size neither other traders nor the government can divine. This provides ample lead time to buy at reasonable prices before the market finally registers an increase in prices resulting from a surge in demand. Depending on how long they are able to seal off the news, the companies may be able to establish all the futures they need for an extended period of time. If the foreign sales are large enough in the short term, their disclosure can bring pandemonium to the marketplace. When this has happened in the past, the large trading houses have rarely been identified as the culprits because, as they explain it, their interests lie with a stable, well-run exchange system. Nevertheless, the Big League's mode of operations is such that the margin of transactions they do not account for is more likely to show wide price variations when their share of the futures market is largest. The Big League's interests are certainly linked with a predictable market, but their hedging practices inevitably induce a high degree of market instability.

Ideally, futures are supposed to be a consistent barometer for cash sales, and vice versa, so as to provide buyers and sellers with a reliable signal of actual as well as probable market conditions. A concealed foreign sale of any magnitude means that the prices received by local producers' sales are not likely to reflect increases normally associated with such news. The absence of any reported new developments in the cash sector is likely to produce an equally flat response on the commodity trading floor.

The problem is not confined to the futures market. Whenever cash sales are bogus, they, too, can have a misleading effect in the futures market. The problem worsens with the degree of misrepresentation, and thus the accuracy of price information is essential to making the system work.

The CFTC has carved out a vague role for itself in tracking the cash markets as part of its surveillance of futures transactions, notwithstanding the insistence of interests in the trade that the commodity markets are perfectly capable of self-regulation: "The Commission has the responsibility to see that futures prices are not distorted away from value. Without accurate cash price information, the Commission and the Exchange are at a disadvantage in identifying price distortions in the futures market."[30] Despite this vital inter-relationship, the Commission obtains only weekly reports on individual cash grain commitments, identified as fixed or unfixed, without any reference to value. Under federal regulations the CFTC needs to ascertain the level of these commitments in order to determine speculative limits for an individual trader. A speculative transaction is not backed by inventories or contracts, but, at best, by these cash obligations. The higher the cash commitment, whether in storage or on paper, the proportionately greater room for speculation. Although the CFTC views its role as keeping speculation under control and distinct from normal hedging operations, the information it obtains on cash transactions, by definition, limits its effectiveness.

By ignoring other aspects of cash markets, the Commission has been unable to establish adequately stable conditions. It continues to rely on the commodity exchanges and the USDA for daily price information. But the latter mostly relies on the exchanges for its price reports, plus an unsystematic daily polling of traders about their bids and transactions while the exchanges are open. The two sets of prices rarely differ significantly, and the USDA has not yet devised a method to weigh one source against the other. Its published price, therefore, is usually not distinguishable from the one disseminated by the trade; any differences are usually subjective judgments by the official market news reporter. This situation leaves the government without a truly independent or critical source of price intelligence.

What exchanges report as current cash prices (actual transactions concluded during the course of a day) is essential to any institution or group— domestic or foreign—touched by the workings of the American agricultural chain. A wheat grower in Kansas needs to know what an equivalent crop is selling for in nearby Oklahoma before he concludes his own contract. What he receives will influence his planting decisions for the next year—how much of his acreage he will devote to wheat production and how much capital he will stake in improving his yield. The foreign buyer looks more to the futures market, but indirectly he is much affected by what occurs at the level of reported cash transactions. Buyers and sellers alike stand to lose if the U.S. marketing system does not effectively bring together the cash and futures markets. No one suffers more than the American farmer, whose earnings today are so closely linked to his cash receipts.

How, then, do the exchanges record prices and disseminate them? Minneapolis and Kansas City are the principal cash exchanges for wheat in the United States because of their proximity to production and midpoint location in transportation routing, whereas Chicago acts as the global center for futures and cash corn transactions. The exchanges operate differently but share similar systems for gathering information on daily prices. Each has a constellation of committees with the responsibility for recording sales prices and reporting them before the closing of the day's trading. This information is for publication in the exchanges' own daily journals as well as on the news wires and with the Department of Agriculture's grain-marketing service. The committees themselves are small in membership, but their task is critical because they are, in effect, a monopolistic source of information concerning the price of purchases scheduled to arrive at a later date than the time of their recorded purchase, transactions in the countryside for delivery elsewhere in the United States, house trades—purchases and sales by traders that are supposed to reflect wheat already in their own inventories—and nominal prices which substitute for actual prices in the absence of any recorded commodity transaction for the day.

This system has been in effect almost as long as the principal exchanges themselves, all of which were founded in the late nineteenth century. Until 1977, the rules governing committee procedures were extremely informal, if not anachronistic, in comparison to the dramatic evolution that has occurred in the grain business. The exchanges themselves were originally more commercial clubs than quasi-public service agencies. Their membership was limited to a fairly rarefied selection of traders seeking a place to confer on commercial conditions as well as conduct business in a "gentlemanly fashion." The exchanges have sought to keep one foot in traditional anonymity, but without losing their function as price discoverers and disseminators in the world market. Until very recently, official policy accepted this proposition, rarely intervening in exchange operations. The working assumption in Washington was that for government to get privileged information from the trade, it had to protect its sources: "We 'live' constantly on confidential information from companies and business and without full trust of private industry we would be unable to accomplish our work."[31]

As early as 1963, the vulnerability of the price-reporting system was put to the public test when the U.S. government filed a complaint against Cargill for manipulating the market in Chicago. Although the USDA's main objective was to point out that Cargill had cornered the spot market for soft red winter wheat, which is traded extensively in Chicago, court testimony pointed out that the system of price reporting was highly discretionary. Because Chicago accepted delivery only on soft red winter cash wheat, the duties of the Department of Agriculture's market news reporter were limited to conducting an informal poll among traders to determine the daily spot basis price for this wheat. The reporter then relayed these subjective findings as definitive polling conclusions to Washington and to other market news reporters posted at the big cash wheat exchanges in Minneapolis and Kansas City.[32]

This public disclosure of the looseness of a system that had proven vulnerable to preferential treatment notwithstanding, the U.S. government and the private sector undertook no actions to alter the status quo. In the absence of hard-and-fast rules for reporting cash prices, the system continued to invite price manipulation and general havoc, especially as transactions grew in size and number.

However, in 1976 the legal arm of the CFTC recommended that the Minneapolis Grain Exchange eliminate certain discretionary practices of its spot cash quotation committees.[33] It had found a discrepancy between actual trades reported in an independently published newspaper, the *Daily Market Record,* and those prices issued (or reported) by the cash closing committees. Under such circumstances, the determination of final sales prices was highly subjective. Committee prices were gathered by midday at an informal meeting of committee members and reported to interested parties including traders, farmers, country elevators, and the USDA.[34] (The Department's Market News Service reports in Minneapolis were consistently identical to committee prices even when they varied significantly from published prices of actual transactions.) Those few buyers and sellers selected to serve on the committees could, in effect, quote arbitrarily higher or lower prices, depending upon whether they wanted cash and future prices to respond the next day. For instance, if a big buyer bid more at around noon than was reported in the *Daily Market Record* by 4:30 p.m., he could attract more sellers; alternatively, he might want to engineer a lower committee price to compensate for earlier higher purchases.

> The Committee consisted of two durum (durum wheat) buyers, and two durum sellers, one of whom was absent. The Committee Chairman (one of the buyers) suggested that the spread on the highest quality durum be quoted down a nickel from the previous day's quotation. The Chairman's suggestion was accepted readily. Once the quotation for the highest quality durum was ascertained, the quotations for the lower qualities were set based upon it. The next step was to report the quotations to interested parties.[35]

Government investigation of multinationals in the grain trade in 1976 confirmed that in Minneapolis the largest trading houses—Cargill, Dreyfus, Bunge, and ADM—rotated their memberships on the cash wheat closing committees. Kansas City and Chicago had more balanced representation on their market reporting committees at the time of the government review, but companies specializing in grains and oilseeds still were disproportionately well represented. This raised a basic question about the neutrality of the price discovery system in the United States and the extent of its control by the largest trading firms. Although these companies' interests rest with a stable, orderly market, this common objective need not preclude attempts to influence the performance of cash markets.

In response to these public disclosures, the draft CFTC recommendations called for immediate remedial actions in Minneapolis to reduce the potential for anticompetitive practices. Specifically, the CFTC would have required the Minneapolis Exchange to change its method of ascertaining spot cash quota-

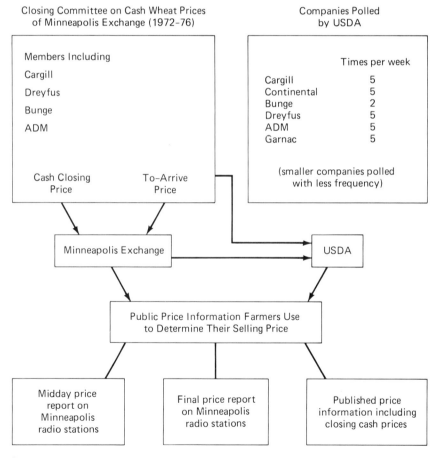

[a]Minneapolis is the largest cash grain exchange in the United States.

FIGURE 7.2 Flow of Wheat Price Information in Minneapolis. (*Source:* U.S. Congress, Senate Committee on Foreign Relations, *Multinational Corporations and United States Foreign Policy.* Hearings before the Subcommittee on Multinational Corporations, 94th Cong., 2d sess., June 1976, Part 16, p. 93.)

tions by (1) eliminating all discretion and judgment of committee members in the process; (2) developing a formalized procedure by which cash prices are directly reported on actual sales instead of committee judgments; (3) establishing a procedure of reporting actual bids and offers rather than the committee nominal price when no sales occur on a given day; and (4) distinguishing between reported prices that are representative of the day's trading and those that are not.

These recommendations fell short of what the Justice Department concluded was necessary, but the private sector managed to prevail over both the antitrust division and the much weaker CFTC. The final result was a softer line that left many of the most questionable practices still intact. The Commission's draft proposals would have effectively eliminated the Minneaplis committee practice of reporting "to arrive" prices—purportedly, the highest bid for grain scheduled for delivery generally within 90 days—on the grounds that they were too often fictional prices. The final recommendations, however, required only a justification for the continuation of to arrive pricing. Although CFTC hearings and other government investigations had established that this form of price reporting was a major loophole for manipulation and had to be closed, the Minneapolis Exchange threatened to halt all operations unless the Commission accepted its mild counterproposals as final. And the CFTC was too weak and the commissioners too divided to do otherwise.

Nominal pricing was another danger zone. Along with to arrives, nominals afforded overly discretionary forms of price reporting. In this instance, the CFTC urged both Kansas City and Minneapolis to establish concrete written guidelines for this category in order to minimize potential abuse that was likely to occur in informal deliberations among committee members. It concluded that "the development of more specific criteria than currently exist for the establishment of these nominal quotations will serve to minimize the role of discretion in the establishment of quotations.[36] The response from Minneapolis promised no such criteria: ". . . the Price Reporting Committee is to take into consideration current bids for the commodity, the previous day's price and its judgment of the current market value for the commodity had it been available and sold on the market that day."[37] The response from the Kansas City Board of Trade was similarly vague and was never approved by the CFTC.

In Minneapolis in 1976 it was common for traders to engage in transactions that went unrecorded by the cash closing committees. They were called house trades—transactions between members for their own accounts as opposed to commitments held by other sellers or buyers—and accounted for as much as 80 percent of total trades on a given day.[38] Despite exchange officials' explanations to the contrary, these transactions were signficant enough to have an important influence on the market. By not recording them, traders could engage in purchases and sales at prices that were unavailable to nonprivileged traders. The CFTC recommended that more complete records be kept, which presumably would have included the official registration of house trades; but the Exchange to date has not significantly altered its treatment of these transactions.

Cash markets continue to grow, and government surveillance is now little more than a pro forma exercise. The overly modest reforms called for somewhat reluctantly by the CFTC were rejected for the most part by the trade. The whole exercise produced little effective defense against a continued abuse of the system. In fact, the review process and subsequent procedural changes in the exchanges' operations may have actually legitimized many questionable activities heretofore exempt from governmental oversight. CFTC's minimal approach to its regulatory duties did little to foster competition and, if anything, may have passively engendered a greater concentration of the grain merchandising business in yet one more area.

The Justice Department recognized this danger in 1981 when it wrote an opinion subsequently overruled by the CFTC against the National Farmers Association's (NFA) mandate defined to assume exclusive responsibility for self-regulation of the commodity business on the grounds that it would violate U.S. anti-trust laws.[39] The NFA members are now empowered to apply rules for exchange members and nonmembers alike which, by definition, place important surveillance and enforcement responsibilities in the hands of the exchanges with minimal "interference" from the CFTC. The declared objective of this approach is to preserve competition, but the actual result is likely to preserve the status quo, which is, in effect, the very opposite of competition.

EXPORT INCENTIVES AND INFORMATION

If government involvement, or noninvolvement as the case may be, with transportation, grain inspection, the establishment of standards, and even the commodity exchanges, has bolstered the position of the Big League, so too have many of its efforts to promote exports. Government-sponsored programs such as PL 480 did as much to help create an oligopoly in the grain trade as to stimulate foreign demand for U.S grain. And the export subsidy program was a complete windfall for the big traders, a fact that was dramatically exposed by the Soviet sales in 1972.

Subsidies were initiated in response to the fear that the United States could be displaced from its world market position by competing suppliers offering grain exports below the international price. Washington was so intent on making the Soviet sale in 1972 and drawing down burdensome stocks that it set subsidy levels on exports below the domestic price. The result, of course, was to reduce the purchase cost to the Soviets, but the direct recipients of the subsidy payments were the shippers.

Official regulations for determining which transactions qualified for government subsidies were deliberately ambiguous regarding interaffiliate sales. The USDA perceived foreign affiliates of American companies as the vanguard in a national campaign to promote U.S. agricultural exports. When the subsidy program reached full throttle under the Nixon administration, the regulations regarding the definition of a bona fide transaction involving U.S. exports to a foreign country were liberalized.[40] This action reflected the belief that multinational grain exporters' interaffiliate sales contributed to the country's agricultural economy and its balance of payments.

The 1972 Soviet sale challenged this assumption. A series of audits and congressional investigations concluded that the sale had cost the government over $300 million in subsidies, primarily to cover Big League export contracts to the Soviet Union and other foreign countries in fiscal year 1973.[41] Because of poor management and private-sector abuse of government subsidy regulations during the final weeks of the program in the fall of 1972, the largest exporters made substantial windfall profits.

As Russian wheat sales forced up domestic prices, the Department of Agriculture finally concluded in September 1972 that subsidy payments to maintain the export target price had grown excessive. Besides, Russian purchases were long completed by that date. Before the cut-off of subsidy payments, the Department allowed exporters one week to cover their remaining sales commitments at peak payments, which represented the difference between rising domestic prices and the fixed, low export price. Export companies' sales registrations flooded the Department during this time. The windfall came from the fact that several firms, having made sales to their foreign affiliates before the government's notice of the forthcoming termination of the subsidy program, subsequently registered these sales at the peak subsidy rates. USDA had no way of distinguishing these early interaffiliate transactions from the registered sales. The Big League acted legally and profited liberally in taking advantage of the confusion in Washington.

> . . . the bulk of the $36 million registered after September 2, 1972, may represent payments to exporters for wheat sold at world prices requiring no subsidy. *In addition, by registering months before actually making sales, exporters will collect sizable carrying-charge increments. In short, Agriculture's failure to require evidence of a sales contract before registration gave exporters the opportunity for windfall profits.*[42]

The original plan had been to calibrate subsidies to U.S. supply and farm income goals. The end result was an isolated windfall to the largest grain houses with little spillover effect, except in the negative sense, to other sectors of the American economy.

Recognizing the havoc wrought by the subsidy program, the Department of Agriculture suspended it on 22 September 1972. The official justification for the suspension was that foreign demand had picked up because of recurring poor harvests in the Soviet Union, changes in agricultural economic policies in China, and new income-related patterns of consumption in other parts of the world. However, when foreign sales leveled off in 1976-77 and again in 1978-79, the government chose not to reintroduce subsidies but instead to use CCC credits in an effort to obtain the same results at less cost.

Thus credit sales for feedgrains alone jumped from $270.4 million in fiscal year 1977 to $525.1 million in the following year; similarly, the dip in sales during 1978-79 prompted another government credit infusion, which again surpassed $500 million.[43] The government's new medium-term financing program gave exports an additional boost in 1980, pushing sales over the record-breaking 1972-74 period.

Despite continuing increases in export volume, support for a return to subsidies has gained ground in recent years. In 1980, for example, foreign markets were not consuming surplus grain at a rate equal to the growth in U.S. production, and the cancellation of 17 million metric tons in grain sales to the Soviet Union heightened concern. In addition, farmers were earning less on each bushel sold abroad because of the depreciated dollar. Although mounting pressure for government price supports from the early 1970s on had led to Agriculture Secretary Bergland's target-set-aside-reserve package, still exporters argued that the U.S. export position was eroding. Trade spokesmen raised the specter of a price war in a world awash with surpluses and called for a resumption of the subsidy program.

> The United States should have immediately available a standby export subsidy (or restitution) policy. When other nations undercut United States prices, the United States should be in a position to tell them that we are immediately prepared also to price aggressively if they continue to undercut U.S. prices. During the past marketing year the United States stated, on the contrary, that it would never again resort to the use of export subsidies, leaving the field completely open to the other exporting countries, which ran away with the business.[44]

The reinstitution of such a program remains a legal possibility, since Congress reaffirmed the Secretary of Agriculture's authority to reinstate an export subsidy program under the Farm Act of 1981. The political appeal of such an action, however, rests largely on the myth that exports, with an assist from subsidized prices, could pull American agriculture out of the doldrums. Clearly, however, such payments have primarily benefited international grain houses in the past, and nothing has changed to suggest that a new subsidy program would do more than reinforce the well-established trend toward industry concentration and an inequitable distribution of the profits derived from increased exports.

In recent years the United States has arrived at a watershed period regarding its agricultural policies and programs. The major grain companies, through a careful strategy of internationalization and integration of their operations, have become sufficiently ensconced that there is little the government can do, short of major reform, to displace them from their firm hold on the global business. Thus far government intervention, however limited, has frequently produced results counter to its stated objectives. Deregulating the railroads did little for the growers and fell short of its efficiency goals. New CFTC regulations have not as yet introduced greater stabilization through market mechanisms any more than they have improved the exchanges' function in price discovery.

Efforts to upgrade supply information by bringing export news and analysis up to par with domestic crop reports have been equally unproductive. On the domestic front, the Crop Reporting Board of the USDA operates a highly respected statistical survey on domestic production every month. To gather the requisite data, the Board relies heavily on farmer appraisals of crop conditions and estimates of their crop yields. With this information and actual field observations, the Board makes extremely reliable predictions about crop prospects in every state. It has earned the well-deserved status of an invaluable resource. When the monthly crop report breaks around harvest time, its conclusions reverberate around the globe. For traders, its predictions and final surveys are critical to their operational decisions. Although the largest companies have sophisticated market intelligence capabilities of their own, the crop report serves as an accurate cross-check to their independently drawn conclusions. For other groups, it is virtually the sole national yardstick with any credibility, accessible to all on an equal basis.

Government reporting of export information is much less reliable and well-respected. American farmers complain that they voluntarily labor over the government forms essential to crop estimates, only to receive inaccurate and tardy information about foreign sales. The news of export sales published by the government is subject to frequent revision and is often out of date before publication. Producers and local processors argue that exporters have valuable information on domestic production, which allows them to close the most favorable deals possible, whereas farmers are kept in the dark about grain company contracts until it is too late for them to take appropriate steps. Were matters different, if news of large foreign purchases were available immediately and in sufficient detail, farmers could delay selling until market prices reflected the momentary surge in demand. Millers could buy before the price hike. The current information scarcity concerning export sales is inherently biased against producers and consumers and favors the largest grain houses and their major foreign clients.

Unlike his immediate predecessors, Secretary Bergland realized that the current dependence of American agriculture on ever-increasing export volumes presents serious problems that neither information nor regulation alone can resolve. Accordingly, the USDA under his leadership endorsed a more activist policy in support of farmer participation in the export sector. For example, he initiated the 1977 USDA regulation allowing cooperative marketing associations to obtain price-support loans on behalf of their members for wheat and feedgrains. The idea was to give cooperative pools, such as Promark, an opportunity to expand their export operations. This modest regulation was contested in a class action by Hiatt Grain Company—a small, private grain dealer—which filed as an industry representative for noncooperative, private grain dealers including Cargill, Continental, and other large grain-exporting houses. (The Big League traders had formed a corporation called Form G, specifically to fund a challenge of Bergland's regulation. To strengthen their case, they wisely selected an unknown small company to argue it formally as the plaintiff.) Hiatt argued that the government's decision was both anticompetitive and harmful to the public interest,[45] because it gave cooperatives a competitive advantage in the form of access to tax-free loans unavailable to the private sector. The USDA countered by arguing that the existing industry structure in the export sector effectively excluded cooperatives and that the secretary's decision was taken to give co-ops an opportunity to compete and not, as Hiatt maintained, to secure for them a monopoly position.

The courts upheld the government's position in 1978, and the decision stuck. As the USDA predicted, there was no sudden sprouting of pools nor any marked erosion of the strength of the majors. What the government did not foresee was that Promark would encounter subsequent problems and a disenchantment among its members with the whole idea after the Farmers Export Company debacle in 1981. The Bergland effort to encourage cooperative pools was far from adequate as a measure to make cooperatives competitive in the export sector. As the Department of Agriculture noted in the Hiatt case, there were other factors that would determine the co-ops' success or failure:

> The competitive impact of this action depends on the degree of control cooperatives may gain of United States grain supplies and advantages in obtaining operating capital. Grain is produced and traded in an international market with instantaneous communication of production, stocks, movement and price information.[46]

In all these areas the Big League continues to maintain an effective oligopoly that has not yet been successfully challenged.

In retrospect, the Bergland initiative was a relatively minor action. It merely extended to feedgrains what had already existed for the marketing of wheat and other commodities abroad. In all other aspects it left the American marketing system intact with the Big League retaining a firm hold. If anything, the erosion process of the independent farmer and cooperative as a market force may have been hastened by the fact that the Justice Department and Congress announced their intention to review the status of cooperatives. Studies were launched for the purpose of revising the Capper Volstad Act, the Magna Carta of American cooperatives, just when Secretary Bergland was attempting to facilitate cooperatives' entry into the export business. This act specifically exempts co-ops from U.S. antitrust laws governing combination and restraint of trade on the grounds that they would be unable to compete or even exist otherwise. Without this exemption, co-ops could harbor no hope whatsoever of competing with the Big League, notwithstanding any positive assistance they may derive from the Hiatt decision.

The increasing concentration of the grain business in the hands of a few vast corporations works against farmer cooperatives that are trying to gain a stronger foothold at the end of the agricultural chain. Such concentration remains a fact of life throughout the American agricultural economy. It pervades transportation, grain inspection, the daily activities on the commodity exchanges, and even some actions of government. It affects even the dissemination of information, which is crucial to any effort by farmers to gain a more direct role in marketing of grain and to the U.S. government as it attempts to regulate the grain trade. Structural inefficiences and inequities in the grain trade strengthen individual interests while they weaken others; ultimately, they work to corrode the entire agricultural chain.

NOTES

1. Richard Gilmore, "Producer Questionnaire," mailed in August 1978. "Do you believe that the volume of U.S. exports of wheat, feedgrains, and soybeans is the single most important factor in determining the price the farmer receives for his production?" National Association of Wheat Growers—80 percent yes; National Farmers Union—no significant response; Illinois Farm Bureau—61 percent yes; National Grain Sorghum Producer Association—57 percent yes; North Dakota Farm Bureau—no significant response; National Farmers Organization—82 percent no; Iowa Farm Bureau—63.5 percent no.

2. Ibid., National Association of Wheat Growers—60 percent no; National Farmers Union—62.5 percent no.; Illinois Farm Bureau—62 percent no; National Grain Sorghum Producer Association—77 percent no; North Dakota Farm Bureau—62.3 percent no; National Farmers Organization—90 percent no; Iowa Farm Bureau—62.3 percent no.

3. U.S Department of Agriculture, *World Agriculture Situation*, WAS 19 (July 1979), p. 34.

4. James Krzyminski, "Agricultural Transportation: The National Policy Issues," National Planning Association Report No. 168 (Washington, D.C., 1978), p. 7.

5. The National Farmers Organization leased a unit train in an effort to reduce transportation costs, but the market had changed from the period of car shortages in 1972-73. As a result, the venture proved to be a near disaster for the NFO, which could not maximize its use of the costly train.

6. Interstate Commerce Commission, *Ex Parte No. 307*, "Investigation into the Distribution and Manipulation of Rail Rolling Stock to Depress Prices on Certain Grain Shipments for Export." Decided 18 July 1977, p. 16.

7. Ibid., p. 96.

8. Ibid., *Ex Parte No. 270 (Sub-No. 9)*, "Investigation of Railroad Freight Rate Structure—Grain and Grain Exports." Decided 1 February 1979, pp. 3019-29.

9. Public Law 96-448, 14 October 1980.

10. U.S. Department of Agriculture and U.S. Department of Transportation, *Agricultural Transportation Services: Needs, Problems, Opportunities, Final Report of the Rural Transportation Advisory Task Force* (Washington, D.C., January 1980).

11. Krzyminski, "Agricultural Transportation," p. 11.

12. Public Law 95-502, 21 October 1978, sec. 4042, "Tax on Fuel Used in Commercial Transportation on Inland Waterways."

13. U.S General Accounting Office, *Report on Irregularities in the Marketing of Grain: An Evaluation of the Inspection and Weighing of Grain. Prepared for the U.S. Senate Committee on Agriculture and Forestry and the House Committee on Agriculture,* 17 February 1976 (Washington, D.C.: U.S. Government Printing Office, 1976), p. 57.

14. U.S. Congress, Senate Committee on Agriculture and Forestry, *Grain Inspection Hearings before the Subcommittee on Foreign Agricultural Policy and the Subcommittee on Agricultural Production, Marketing, and Stabilization of Prices*, 94th Cong., 1st sess., 19 June 1975, pt. 1, p. 48.

15. U.S. Congress, House Committee on Agriculture, *Federal Grain Inspection Service Operation, Hearings before the Subcommittee on Department Investigations, Oversight and Research*, 95th Cong., 2d sess., 12 April 1978. Statement of Leland E. Bartelt, administrator, Federal Grain Inspection Service, p. 5. And U.S. Department of Agriculture, "Summary of Current Grain Special Indictment/Information Status." Manuscript.

16. U.S. Congress, Senate Committee on Agriculture and Forestry, *Grain Inspection*, pt. 1, p. 63. In 1979 Cook agreed to pay $4 million to the U.S. government to settle a fraud suit concerning Food for Peace grain shipments allegedly diluted with inferior grain, dirt, weed, seeds, stems, chaff, and straw.

17. U.S. Congress, House Committee on Agriculture, *Amend the U.S. Grain Standards Act, Hearing on H.R. 6135 and Similar Bills*, Serial No. 95-F, 95th Cong., 1st sess., 29 April 1977. Statement of Joseph Halow, executive director, North American Grain Association, Inc., pp. 129-30.

18. Gilmore, "Producer Questionnaire."

19. T. L. Sam Irmen, general partner, The Andersons, to Mr. Jerry Cotter, Grain Inspection Section, U.S. Department of Agriculture, 27 December 1977.

20. Gilmore, "Producer Questionnaire." The National Association of Wheat Growers and the Illinois Farm Bureau were the exceptions, registering a thin majority in support of USDA's administration of standards.

21. "Futures Trading Rose 21% in 1980 to Record 92,096,109 Contracts," *Wall Street Journal*, 9 February 1981, p. 29.

22. Commodity Futures Trading Commission, *Economic Bulletin #1*, "Grain Pricing," September 1977.

23. Ibid.; and Gilmore, "Producer Questionnaire."

24. Norman H. Jones, Jr., and Allen R. Ferguson with James Booth and Thomas Yockey, *Competition and Efficiency in the Commodity Futures Market, Executive Summary* (prepared for the Commodity Futures Trading Commission by the Public Interest Economics Center, May 1978), p. 50.

25. U.S. Department of Agriculture, Economics, Statistics, and Cooperatives Service. "A Study of Relationships Between Large Export Sales and Futures Trading," by Richard Heifner, Kandice Kahl, and Larry Deaton, 8 June 1979. (Mimeographed advance copy.)

26. U.S. Congress, House Committee on Agriculture, *Extend Commodity Exchange Act, Hearings before the Subcommittee on Conservation and Credit*, Serial No. 95-QQ, 95th Cong., 2d sess., 21, 22, and 23 February and 11 April 1978. Statement of Mr. William T. Bagley, chairman, Commodity Futures Trading Commission, p. 106.

27. Commodity Futures Trading Commission, unpublished internal document.

28. U.S. Congress, House Committee on Agriculture, *Extend Commodity Exchange Act,*, pp. 89, 98.

29. Commodity Futures Trading Commission, staff document, "Regulation of Foreign Traders," 23 January 1979, pp. 47-48. Manuscript.

30. Commodity Futures Trading Commission, Division of Economics and Education, "Inquiry into Operations of Spot Price Committees on New York Coffee and Sugar Exchange, Minneapolis Grain Exchange, and Kansas City Board of Trade," June 1977, p. B-3. (Mimeographed.)

31. U.S. Department of Agriculture, Grain Division, confidential document distributed to Grain Market News Offices, 26 September 1975.

32. U.S. Department of Agriculture, Commodity Exchange Authority, Docket No. CEA 120 regarding: Cargill Incorporated, Erwin E. Kelm, H. Robert Diercks, Walter B. Saunders, and Benjamin S. Jaffray, Exhibits 12-17, 3 June 1964.

33. Commodity Futures Trading Commission, Office of the General Counsel, *The Antitrust Implications of Spot Cash Quotation Committees,* Memorandum, 18 November 1976; and U.S. Congress, Senate Committee on Foreign Relations, *Multinational Corporations and United States Foreign Policy, Hearings before the Subcommittee on Multinational Corporations,* 93d Cong., 1st sess., pt. 16, pp. 73-96.

34. Commodity Futures Trading Commission, *Antitrust Implications,* p. 4.

35. Ibid., pp. 3-4.

36. Commodity Futures Trading Commission, "Inquiry into Operations of Spot Price Committees," pt. 4, Kansas City Board of Trade, p. D-6.

37. Minneapolis Grain Exchange, *Guidelines for the Price Reporting Committees of the Minneapolis Grain Exchange,* for approval by the CFTC, 15 August 1977.

38. U.S. Congress, Senate, Committee on Foreign Relations, *Multinational Corporations,* pt. 16, pp. 84-85.

39. U.S. Department of Justice, Antitrust Division, *Comments in the Matter of the National Futures Association on the Application to the Commodity Futures Trading Commission for Registration under Section 17 of the Commodity Exchange Act,* 2 July 1981. Unpublished.

40. U.S. Department of Agriculture, Office of Audit, *Review of Subsidy Payments Involving Sales to Foreign Affiliates of Wheat Export Program (GR-345),* Foreign Agricultural Service, Audit Report No. 60212-3 Hy. (Washington, D.C., 26 June 1975), p. 2.

41. U.S. General Accounting Office, *Russian Wheat Sales and Weaknesses in Agriculture's Management of Wheat Export Subsidy Program,* B-176943 (Washington, D.C., 9 July 1973), p. 14.

42. Ibid., p. 37. Italics added.

43. U.S. Department of Agriculture, Office of the General Sales Manager (OGSM), *Quarterly Report of the General Sales Manager,* 1 April-30 June 1979, pp. 9, 27; and data supplied by the OGSM.

44. U.S. Congress, House Committee on International Relations, *Agricultural Exports and U.S. Foreign Economic Policy, Hearings and Markup before the Subcommittee on International Economic Policy and Trade,* 95th Cong., 2d sess., May, July, and August 1978. Statement of Joseph Halow, executive director, North American Export Grain Association, Inc., Appendix 7, p. 299.

45. "Suggestions in Support of Plaintiff's Motion for a Preliminary Injunction," p. 7, submitted in *Hiatt Grain & Feed, Inc. on behalf of itself and others similarly situated* vs. *Hon. Bob Bergland, Secretary of Agriculture, United States of America,* Civil Action No. 77-4161, case filed in August 1977, U.S. District Court, District of Kansas.

46. Affidavit of Howard W. Hjort, Director of Economics, Policy Analysis and Budget, U.S. Department of Agriculture, filed 2 September 1977 in *Hiatt Grain & Feed, Inc. on behalf of itself and others similarly situated* vs. *Hon. Bob Bergland, Secretary of Agriculture, United States of America,* Civil Action No. 77-4161, case filed in August 1977; litigation ended by Supreme Court on 19 February 1980.

8

The American Food Weapon: A High-Risk Strategy

The steady growth in volume of American agricultural exports since World War II has been accompanied, perhaps inevitably, by an increasingly prevalent belief that America's foodstuffs represent a significant source of national power. The reliance of other nations on American food supplies, it has been argued, provides the United States with a powerful diplomatic tool, the food weapon. Those who hold to this view see the food weapon as a means by which American agricultural productivity can be translated into bargaining power in the international arena. Recent American administrations have been urged to employ this weapon against targets as diverse as the Soviet Union, OPEC, Iran and other OPEC members, the Third World, and selected American allies. Although it has failed to produce the desired results in every instance in which it has been employed, the food weapon remains, in the eyes of many, one of the most powerful devices in the American foreign policy arsenal. Certainly its political allure is considerable.

Yet the historical evidence suggests that confidence in an American food weapon is, at best, misplaced. A larger share of the global agricultural export market does not automatically translate, as virtually every administration since World War II seems to have assumed, into increased American diplomatic leverage. On the contrary, there is ample evidence to suggest that efforts to use the food weapon are more likely to endanger than foster U.S. interests and that, in the past, the food weapon has proven more harmful to the user than the ostensible target. The debate over the food weapon does not, as some would have it, come down to a simple disagreement over ethics. It must also be an argument over effectiveness. The food weapon is a weapon that has been tried without success. It is a weapon that does not work and which, under present circumstances, cannot be made to work as is demonstrated so dramatically in the case of the soybean embargo of June 1973.

THE SOYBEAN EMBARGO OF 1973

The total embargo on soybean exports announced by the Nixon administration on 27 June 1973 is a special case. Unlike the other embargoes considered in this chapter, it is not an instance of a deliberate Washington attempt to employ the food weapon for foreign policy reasons. The administration's major purpose in declaring the 1973 embargo was domestic and not international in nature. The objective was to control rapidly skyrocketing domestic soybean prices, restore some semblance of order to a jittery and chaotic domestic market, and to stave off a threatened shortage of a vital commodity. Like these other attempts at export controls, however, the soybean embargo's consequences were largely negative. It was also, as is now apparent, an unnecessary measure as well as a costly one. An analysis of this episode is instructive for the light it sheds on the potential effectiveness of any embargo, including one instituted for foreign policy reasons.

When the Nixon administration announced a total ban on further export shipments of soybeans regardless of destination, it did so in response to a perceived domestic shortage. Still shell-shocked in the wake of the 1972 Soviet sale, Washington watched anxiously throughout the first quarter of 1973 as feedgrain prices, only then registering the full effects of the massive Soviet purchases in the preceding year, increased steadily and then began to climb more rapidly in the second quarter. Although soybean cash prices, the prices received by farmers, remained fairly stable throughout the 1972-73 marketing year, hovering in the range of $5.60 to $6.35 per bushel, Chicago spot prices were nearly 50 percent higher during this period. By early June, contracts on the 1973 soybean crop were virtually unobtainable and soybeans had become the price leader in the spot market as the price reached $12.35 per bushel.

These market gyrations strongly suggested the imminence of a critical shortage. A variety of explanations were offered for this development. The consensus among experts was that the situation resulted from a drastic reduction in the Peruvian anchovy catch, anchovies being a widely used soybean substitute, coupled with a poor 1972-73 American crop. What seemed clear was that there were too many buyers for too small a supply of soybeans and that the resulting price increases not only presaged shortage but threatened the administration's anti-inflation program. Cattlemen, poultry farmers, soybean processors, and consumers were alarmed. Many called for government intervention. That no one was entirely certain who was buying and for what purpose seemed a moot point.

Government intervention came in stages. On June 13 the administration announced a freeze on soybean prices and the establishment of a new export reporting system, although just how that system was to work had not been determined at the time of the announcement. Two weeks later, perceiving that the earlier announcement had only fueled rumors of eventual controls without stopping the export flow, the administration announced a total ban on all soybean exports. While the total embargo did not last long—it was replaced on 2 July by a licensing system—it was perceived by virtually all parties as a drastic measure. Such a ban affects friend and foe alike and can be expected to have particularly adverse consequences for the largest and most reliable foreign buyers. The only possible justification for the embargo, therefore, was the by then widespread fear of an imminent shortage.

Ironically, if there is one thing that is now clear about the soybean embargo of 1973, it is that it was enacted in response to a shortage that never existed. The rapid surge in spot soybean prices in early 1973 was the result of a rash of overselling by American grain giants to their overseas affiliates. These sales were mainly hedging tactics undertaken against the risk of an embargo. Their net effect was to push Chicago prices up and distort seriously the true supply/demand picture. Through such transactions, the price ranges which were pegged to the prior month's f.o.b. prices, the companies sought to avoid being caught short of grain without risking overexposure in a bullish futures market that would crumble at a moment's notice if the government ordered export controls.

The events leading to the 27 June embargo are a classic case of the government and private sector working at cross purposes, making an embargo inevitable in the process. Acting in anticipation of an export cut-off, the large grain houses called on their international network of affiliates to cover themselves by buying more than their normal requirements. White House advisors, determined to keep a lid on domestic prices even if it meant undermining the traditional U.S. policy of nurturing foreign markets, were caught up in the rush of events.

President Nixon's 13 June announcement regarding a new export system, and the universal embargo on all raw and semiprocessed soybean exports that followed on 27 June, could have been avoided. In early June, there was still significant disagreement among experts over the available supply of grains and soybeans. Herbert Stein, Chairman of the Council of Economic Advisers (CEA) of the Department of Commerce, received a memorandum from Assistant Secretary of Agriculture Carroll G. Brunthaver indicating that, even though he was required by law to do so, the Secretary of Agriculture could not furnish a short-run estimate of available supplies for those commodities being monitored by the CEA as potentially in need of export controls, because the picture was so unclear.[1] Only a week before Nixon's 13 June speech, a consensus had emerged from an interdepartmental meeting that the immediate imposition of export controls would be unwise given the lack of conclusive supporting data.

There were, in fact, sharp discrepancies in the figures gathered by various agencies. The figures on soybean inventories furnished to John Dunlop, then director of the Cost of Living Council, ranged from 245 million to 265 million bushels with roughly the same spread for soybean crush. The Commerce Department had concluded on 15 June on the basis of its own analysis, that carryover stocks would be depleted by 31 August and that there would be a shortfall of 1.26 million metric tons in soybean meal. The Department of

Agriculture, on the other hand, estimated the end of August soybean inventories at a relatively comfortable 45 million bushels and the corresponding soybean meal inventory at 765,000 metric tons, while forecasting a bumper crop in September. Such discrepancies produced nine different estimates of the quantity of soybeans available for export and might, in a different atmosphere, have challenged the need for an embargo. What they served to highlight, even then, was the inadequacy of the government's information about exports and its nearly complete dependence on the industry for that information.

What were the large international grain houses doing prior to the president's inquiry about their export commitments? The Department of Commerce tabulated the initial returns of reported anticipated exports as of the close of business on 13 June and found substantial double counting, especially in the soybean reports.[2] Aside from the inherent difficulties in deciphering the ultimate purpose of interaffiliate transactions, strings of such transactions were equally perplexing because each transaction in the string was considered a separate contract, even though it applied to the same foreign sale. Since each company involved in the string then reported an export sale on the same soybean contract, the actual quantity of grain committed to enter the report stream was greatly overestimated.

To add to the confusion, the Department of Commerce found that shippers were reporting a large number of soybean and meal contracts with unknown destinations. On 22 June, a joint Commerce and Agriculture Department calculation of the size of shipments to unknown destinations compared to the total was:

TABLE 8.1   Estimated U.S. Soybean Exports by Destination as of June 1973 (metric tons)

Soybeans 9/72–8/73 Metric Tons		Soybean Oil Cake & Meal 10/72–9/73 Metric Tons	
Unknown	1,056,233	Unknown	1,463,676
Total	2,510,710	Total	2,035,338

SOURCE: Official and trade sources, confidential.

In an audit conducted by the Agriculture Department on 26 June (the day before the embargo became effective), investigators found that Cargill had 26 contracts of unshipped soybeans, all but five of which were listed as "destination unknown" for sale to Tradax, Panama, care of Tradax, Geneva. Continental and Bunge also held a high ratio of unknown destination contracts and Netherlands deliveries for transshipment often to unidentified destinations.

Any effort to isolate bona fide sales for future shipment from paper transactions designed to hedge against possible quotas in exports became futile. Late reporting of destinations and double counting of contracts utterly distorted the picture. By 20 June, a Department of Agriculture audit demonstrated that Washington's original calculations significantly overstated actual exports. Cook, Mitsubishi International, and Continental Grain, it was shown, had over-reported their soybean sales, and Anderson Clayton double-counted its soybean and meal contracts. Each had duplications in the range of 130,000 metric tons, roughly half of their total transactions for the time period under review. Cook bought back over 50,000 metric tons of its contracts with Mitsubishi without subtracting the same amount from total sales commitments reported to the Department of Commerce. Continental had substantial cancellations with other Japanese firms; the Sogo Shosha reported these contracts as sales commitments from American affiliates to their parents in Tokyo.

Had these facts been more clearly established at the time, it would have been readily apparent that there was little, if any, need for a total embargo on soybean exports in June 1973. Nonetheless an administration anxious to avoid at all costs a repeat of the 1972 experience with the Soviets felt compelled to halt soybean exports altogether. Predictably, the chief effect of such an action was to place a severe strain on U.S. relations with foreign buyers, especially Japan. However the U.S. government cannot be entirely faulted for the tension which beset U.S.-Japanese relations after the embargo. The actions of the trading companies, and particularly those of the Sogo Shosha, contributed much to the ensuing difficulties.

In June 1973, the Japanese giants registered more confirmed shipments of U.S. soybeans to Japan than in any other month of the marketing year. Mitsubishi and Mitsui reported almost twice their normal amount—275,000 and 240,000 metric tons.[3] This was explained by trade analysts in Japan as part of preemptive strategy to cover import requirements in advance of any shutdown of the American supply lines. Whatever the explanation, the Sogo Shosha clearly overbought, leaving them in a comfortable position during the chaotic summer of 1973. Subsequently, however, they resold a substantial portion of their contracts at peak prices rather than retaining them as a hedge against future shortages. Thus, although the Sogo Shosha reported confirmed shipments of 1.4 million metric tons of U.S soybeans as of 6 June 1973, only about 25 percent of this amount ever cleared customs into Japan. One need look no further than the discrepancy between soybean prices in Tokyo and Chicago to seek an explanation. In May of 1973, the arrival price of soybeans in Tokyo was an average of $220.5 per metric ton, or approximately $6 per bushel, while quoted prices in Chicago and Rotterdam were in the $11-to-$12 range per bushel.

The Sogo Shosha found the temptation irresistible. With their associated processors and feed manufacturers at home well-supplied and a minimum spread of $100 per ton between current market prices and their original purchase price, the Sogo Shosha went for the windfall. They had no trouble finding customers: American companies were only too happy to buy back their contracts from the Japanese at a price below what they would have had to pay on the U.S. spot market prior to the embargo, had they been able to find so much as a seller. U.S. buybacks from the Sogo Shosha in May were on the order of 70,000 metric tons per week. This volume of purchases continued at roughly the same level until the embargo.

In the short term the Sogo Shosha and their American counterparts such as Cook and Continental benefited from this swap but at considerable expense to public and national economic interests and not without some risk. Had a complete cut-off remained in effect, Japanese supplies remaining from 1972 purchases would not have lasted much beyond the beginning of the new season. When the embargo was lifted on 2 July and was replaced by a system of validated licenses, U.S. soybean export levels were cut 50 percent and exports of soybean oil cake and meal by 61 percent. By choosing to resell their contracts, the Japanese traders had elected to operate on precariously thin margins which in turn precipitated a crisis. The strain began to show by the end of July as Japanese carryover supplies fell below 130,000 tons. Import prices rose and supplies dwindled.

Thus it was that the American embargo was in relatively short order followed by a Japanese counter-reaction. In July the Japanese government slapped on a price freeze and export restriction. These, however, had only limited effect. Limited in their access to soybean imports from the United States by the U.S. imposition of quotas, Sogo Shosha affiliates and independent buyers began clamoring for supplies. The companies were forced to buy on the open market and look for substitutes. They tapped Canada for more than their usual take of rapeseeds, but by the time they entered the market for more, they found that the pandemonium in Chicago had hit Winnipeg too, forcing the Canadian government to clamp on its own export controls. And there were no other alternative suppliers. In 1973 Brazil had yet to become a major supplier of soybeans while China was in no position to make up the difference.

The result was the biggest shock to date in contemporary U.S.-Japanese relations. Soybeans in the United States and Western Europe are essentially a feed item, but in Japan they are also a staple food. Hoarding of tofu (soybean cake) and edible oils set in among Japanese consumers. The Japanese export-import association for oils and fats called for government-to-government negotiations, and Japanese consumers and officials openly suggested that the United States could no longer be counted on as a reliable supplier. What went unnoticed was the extent to which the private sector, particularly the Sogo Shosha, had contributed to the near disaster. Had the trading companies not opted for windfall profits from heavy reselling of contracts that were registered but never shipped, Japanese consumers would almost certainly not have experienced a near cut-off in supplies. Had the Japanese government been more observant and dealt with the companies at arm's length, they could have foreseen the outcome and prevented resales before such action became meaningless in the face of a universal cut-off in shipments from both the United States and Canada. Through their own operations, Japanese and American-based companies alike helped bring on the embargo. They continue to refer to this as a low point in American agricultural policy.

Unlike Japan, Western European traders, including U.S. affiliates, played it safe. Independent buyers and affiliates of American grain companies in Western Europe played a more conservative strategy than the Sogo Shosha by not operating so close to the margin. Instead of reselling, they bought U.S. soybeans heavily on the presumption that the embargo would be lifted and a portion of existing contracts honored under some form of licensing system. Their informed hunch proved correct. Initially Rotterdam c.i.f. soybean prices climbed from $12 on 7 June to over $14.20 bushel three days after a licensing system went into effect on 27 July. Within the next five days, however, Rotterdam prices fell faster than Chicago's to the point that soybeans purchased in Europe were cheaper (minus transportation costs) than those purchased in the United States, where they were produced. This new twist was a firm indication that the European processors were well taken care of by their heavy advance purchases and could afford to cancel a sizable share of these contracts, as they did. With a licensing system in place, buyers and sellers stood to gain by terminating their original contracts and repurchasing whatever they needed to cover their requirements with new crop soybeans at a much reduced price.

Cargill, in particular, had heavily oversold to its European soybean-processing affiliates, advising them to buy at a level to cover their "maximum theoretical crushing capacity for crop year 1973/74."[4] Having oversold with contracts for new 1973/74 crop soybeans,[5] Cargill could afford to withdraw a portion of these commitments[5] once assured that the U.S. government would recognize the validity of its sales in 1972 soybeans. Thus Cargill's affiliates ultimately cancelled over 28 million bushels of soybeans, while the parent company bought back almost 25 percent of the contracts it had originally sold. Cargill contended these cancellations had no bearing on the temporary cut-off of shipments in 1972 beans. Even so Cargill's futures position in 1973 soybeans was substantial enough to distort government estimates of available supplies from the 1972 crop as well.

That Cargill and other companies subsequently cancelled such a large proportion of their 1973 crop commitments is a further indication of the companies' efforts to secure a hedge against the likelihood of export controls. Forward buying in the spring of 1973 was so heavy that the Commerce Department reports showed over 80 percent of the 1973-74 soybean crop scheduled to be harvested in September and 100 percent of soybean meal production were already listed as anticipated exports prior to the 13 June announcement.[6] Export controls applied only to the 1972 crop, for it was considered to be in precipitously short supply; the next year's crop, for which the Big League (with the possible exception of Cook) was so comfortably positioned, was exempt. Under the circumstances, the companies could feel free to cancel a large share of their previous paper purchases once the situation cleared, and it became obvious that even with license quotas, they had more than enough supplies to fulfill their export commitments. When the dust settled, the needs of the largest traders, including the Sogo Shosha, were met at considerable expense to public interests in Japan and the United States.

In the days leading up to the 13 June decision, the U.S. government was a bystander. When it intervened, it lacked the requisite information and capability to cope appropriately with the situation. The only recourse was to turn to the leading representatives in the trade.

> I was presented with a choice of attempting some consultation with the Trade, and running the risk of criticism for the very fact of having consulted with the Trade, and insulating myself from the criticism, but having to move forward in the position of vast ignorance or only the knowledge that we in Government could put together.[7]

In effect, the government was caught in an embarrassing bind, seeking expert advice on a future licensing system from executives of the same firms whose profits would be directly affected by the government's acceptance of their recommendations. It was clear conflict of interest, but not without precedent as demonstrated by the handling of credits and subsidies in the 1972 grain sales to the USSR. In 1973, as in 1972, an unschooled American bureaucracy was forced to rely almost exclusively on industry advice as it sought to regulate the commercial activities of the industry on behalf of a larger national interest. That the American government was unable, at a time when the United States held a near-monopoly in global soybean exports, to determine with accuracy what proportion of the domestic crop was slated for the export stream—let alone the destinations of many of the resulting shipments—and consequently was unable to effect an appropriate response is evidence of the significance of one major obstacle to the effectiveness of any attempted U.S food embargo—the government's reliance upon the industry for accurate export information.

This lesson was sufficiently obvious as to have been noted even at the time. As a result, Congress in 1973 expanded the Department of Agriculture's jurisdiction and responsibility for the export-reporting system, prompted in part by the results of several investigations and outcries from public interest groups.[8] These new measures, however, were short-lived. By 1975 the impetus for tight federal supply management had slowed considerably as the prospect of global food scarcities dimmed. Exports leveled off in that year and forecasts pointed to record production levels. Under these circumstances the government was persuaded by the private sector that a relaxation of reporting requirements was in order and might even contribute to a resurgence of foreign business. The trade found the new export reporting system too restrictive, a perception shared by foreign buyers who also preferred to function under strict confidentiality. The companies maintained that the reporting system, which required prior approval of individual foreign sales above 50,000 metric tons or weekly amounts over 100,000 tons, introduced unnecessary risks because a supplier might not be able to conclude an expected transaction if it failed to obtain official authorization. Further, if news of the transaction should be disclosed during the course of the government's review, an exporter's hedging position might be jeopardized.

Washington backtracked in the face of such arguments. In the end the prior approval system proved unworkable not only because it cramped industry's free-wheeling style but also because even a voluntary enforcement system raised questions about preferential treatment of certain companies and certain business practices. And there is no doubt that some of the majors were on occasion burned while the system was in effect. There is, for example, the case of a hastily organized 1974 White House breakfast with President Ford, Secretary of Treasury Simon, and members of the Big League in attendance.[9] The table conversation concerned sales to the USSR, which the Ford administration feared might create a repeat of the 1972 situation, and the outcome of the breakfast was a request that Cook and Continental suspend their sales of over 3.5 million metric tons of wheat and corn to the Soviet Union until the United States could review sales commitments to other foreign buyers, its own domestic consumption requirements, and the potential inflationary effects of any additional Soviet purchases.

At this meeting, Secretary Butz explained that the government was asking the companies' indulgence until a compulsory prior approval system was put into effect for shipments to the Soviet Union. The executive officers of the two companies, however, went away with different interpretations of the government's order. Cook maintained that what had been requested was a universal sales suspension. Steinweg of Continental claimed that the agreement affected only sales to the Soviet Union. Their different understandings resulted in a big loss for Cook and a windfall for Continental, since the latter, according to Ned Cook, executed a sale to Iran that Cook had refrained from making in an effort to keep its part of the gentlemen's agreement worked out in the White House. Whichever version of the White House meeting is correct, the incident underscores the fact that in 1974 the system was working no better than it had in 1972-73. Moreover, the absence of uniform treatment for export sales and adequate information left the government open to charges of a bias in favor of one exporter or buyer over another.

PL 480 AND THE JOHNSON ADMINISTRATION

The real history of the American food weapon, however, begins not with the 1973 soybean embargo, instructive though that episode is, but with PL 480, and, more specifically, with the Johnson administration. Although its declared purpose was often extolled as humanitarian, PL 480 has, since its inception, been designed more to accommodate U.S. political and economic objectives than the concerns of recipient countries. Although not always successful, efforts to synchronize PL 480 allocations with foreign policy interests led the way to subsequent and more explicitly acknowledged efforts to employ the food weapon. The first notable example of this phenomenon was President Johnson's "short tether" policy that attempted to link U.S. food aid allocations to changes in development policies and political actions in recipient countries.[10] India and Egypt were test cases. Both must have seemed promising grounds for the new weapon. Yet it failed both tests.

Clearly, India was in trouble in 1965. A series of production setbacks had put the country in a state of dependence on American concessional food transfers. The time seemed ripe, therefore, to effect certain changes in Indian policy desired by the Johnson administration. Accordingly, Secretary Freeman met with the Indian minister of Food and Agriculture in 1965 to hammer out new conditions for American assistance. The quid pro quo was to be American food in exchange for more emphasis in India on agricultural development, as well as greater hospitality for U.S. investments there, particularly in the fertilizer industry. The moral of the story was clear. The short tether was to be a prodding iron applied for both economic and political purposes. In part the Johnson administration sought to gain aid-recipient countries' acceptance of an increased role for U.S. business, a role subsequently institutionalized through new development criteria in the 1966 amended version of PL 480. In more political terms, Johnson sought to withhold aid from India in response to the Gandhi government's outspoken disapproval of American involvement in Vietnam.

Likewise, the Johnson administration sought to extract political obeisance from Egypt in exchange for American food aid. This scheme was triggered by a series of events beginning on Thanksgiving Day 1964 with Egyptian riots protesting U.S. actions in the Congo that resulted in the destruction of American property in Cairo. In December an American oil company plane belonging to Johnson's close friend John Micham of Texas was shot down. Egyptian President Nasser gave little heed to Washington's protests and stepped up his anti-American rhetoric. Johnson's response was swift—a cutoff in food aid just when Egypt needed it the most.

The Egyptian move backfired. Ironically, this occurred because many members of Congress applauded the administration's action and attempted to secure a legislative ban on further PL 480 allocations to Egypt. This was not quite what the White House had wanted, and it stepped in to stave off passage of the measure, fearing that such legislative action would limit the president's flexibility and do more damage than good to U.S interests in the Middle East and the Congo.[11] Johnson was concerned that he would lose the power to decide when to shorten or lengthen the tether. Quickly the issue escalated into a power struggle between the White House and Congress, while PL 480 was held hostage. Popular sentiment opposed Nasser's effrontery toward the United States but was not in favor of the blatant use of food for reasons of state-craft. PL 480's constituency was strong and broadly based. Farmers appreciated its contribution to holding up the floor under agricultural prices. The grain trade and agribusiness valued its role in developing new markets and investment opportunities. Humanitarians and internationalists were sensitive to the program's multiple uses in terms of social and economic development. And in the mid-1960s, virtually no one, least of all PL 480 supporters, was prepared to endorse an explicit use of the food weapon.

The Johnson administration's attempts to wield the food weapon failed. Neither Gandhi nor Nasser shed their anti-American posture when the flow was cut off, any more than they did when it was turned back on, while the domestic PL 480 lobby worked against any long-term cut-off. As a result, the flow of food aid from the United States to India and Egypt was interrupted only briefly and with little perceptible effect. The continuing strength of PL 480 supporters coupled with the White House's highly subjective approach toward food aid blunted the food weapon strategy during the Johnson years. Nor was there, in these years, any prospect of manipulating commerical sales rather than food aid. In the 1960s, America was actively competing for sales with other suppliers in a relatively small commercial export market that had not yet taken off, as it did in the 1970s. The food weapon, and the rhetoric in its behalf, may have first appeared under the Johnson administration, but it did not become a major element in American foreign policy.

THE NIXON AND FORD ADMINISTRATIONS

Nixon, Kissinger, and Butz changed all that. The period from 1968 through 1976 was one in which the administration in power seized upon the food weapon as a particularly useful tool for implementing its own vision of global *realpolitik*. During these years, U.S. decision making concerning food aid and commercial sales was effectively transferred from the Department of Agriculture to the State Department where it was dominated by Kissinger and the notion of linkage. These were the years that witnessed the waning of PL 480 and the rapid growth of commercial sales, the great Soviet sale of 1972 and its aftermath, the 1974 U.S. embargo of grain sales to the Soviet Union, and the U.S.-Soviet grain accord of 1975. And these were also the years of Secretary of Agriculture Butz and his continuing rhetorical defense of the administration's determination to make diplomatic use of American food supplies. There was, for example, the following:

> . . . I took two days (from the World Food Conference in Rome, November 1974) and went down to Cairo "with a little wheat in my pocket." They had the red carpet out for me there. I went to Syria. I got a royal welcome—not because I was Secretary of Agriculture; I was speaking the language of food, and they understand.[12]

The statement above was issued in the wake of an effort to bring about an Egyptian/Israeli peace agreement through an offer of increased food aid. This was, however, not an isolated incident. Less than a year after the 1972 presidential elections, PL 480 wheat transfers to Vietnam, Cambodia, and Iran soared. At the other end of the spectrum, some countries were denied American food aid for political actions that ran counter to the Nixon-Kissinger definition of American interests. Chile, a traditional recipient, was cut off after the election of President Allende, a leftist. Shipments of food to Bangladesh were delayed when the United States discovered that that nation had sold jute to Cuba.[13] Washington found further justification for this action in Bangladesh's strained relations with Pakistan, a nation with whom the United States was nurturing its relations as part of a larger effort to improve relations with China and counter Soviet influence in India.

The most glaring misuse of food aid for political purposes occurred in connection with Vietnam. As Congress was trimming military and security assistance in protest over U.S. foreign policy in Southeast Asia, Kissinger latched on to various loopholes in PL 480 as means to continue American support of the South Vietnamese regime. The peak years for food transfers to Vietnam, Cambodia, and South Korea (the only American "ally" to send combat troops into South Vietnam) were 1972 to 1974. During this period, when pressure was mounting for American withdrawal and just when massive credit-assisted grain sales were supposed to make the Soviets turn a deaf ear to the raid on Cambodia and the mining and bombing of Haiphong, food aid to Southeast Asia was being used to help keep the bullets flying. The administration desperately needed a way to circumvent congressional constraints in order to conclude its version of an acceptable peace settlement.

As a result, responsibility for administering food aid transfers devolved exclusively upon the Department of State during this period.[14] Secretary Butz was preoccupied with downgrading food aid to develop commercial exports, and the new Secretary of State, Kissinger, was only too happy to take the remaining morsels and craft them into a food weapon. By 1973, in part as a result of Secretary Butz's emphasis on commercial sales, PL 480 represented only 3 percent of total U.S. grain exports, a sharp drop from the high of 43 percent a decade before. But the administration managed to make maximum political use of this dwindling resource.

The same team adopted similar tactics with respect to large commercial sales. A major thrust of Nixon-Kissinger détente strategy was to encourage a more moderate Soviet defense and foreign policy stance through the prospect of increased U.S./Soviet trade, particularly grain exports coupled, when necessary, with CCC credits. As Kissinger later noted, it was

> . . . the White House's determination to have trade follow political progress and not precede it. Nixon and I agreed that it was best to proceed deliberately on grain sales (by delaying a trip to Moscow by Secretary of Agriculture Earl Butz until April). . . . We would, in short, make economic relations depend on some demonstrated progress on matters of foreign policy importance to the United States.[15]

Nixon and Kissinger substituted linkage for the "short tether" of President Johnson. Butz went along enthusiastically and brought the farm bloc with him. Exacting favorable commercial terms from the Soviets, however, seems to have taken on a lower order of importance. One result of this oversight was the disaster of 1972. The resulting losses to the United States were viewed as a major setback for U.S. agripower, at least by some, who viewed as naive the attempt to control such a substantial commercial grain transaction from within the inner sanctuary of the White House. The administration, however, was undeterred. Instead of recognizing the fundamental weakness in their approach, Kissinger and Nixon drew the opposite conclusion: "From then on (after the 1972 Soviet grain sale), all such transactions were treated as foreign policy matters and subjected to interagency monitoring."[16] Nor was Secretary Butz dissuaded of the correctness of a policy he had helped to fashion.

> Food has been a valuable tool in our strategy of peace—a lever that more than any other single factor has brought back into the world economy some 1.1 billion people—almost a third of the human race. Think of it! Within a few short months, the USSR and the PRC (the People's Republic of China)—with their old and valuable cultures—their large and growing populations—have returned to the world community.[17]

Others were less approving. While Nixon administration officials were extolling the virtues of U.S. agripower, resentment ran high among foreign buyers, especially developing countries. Yet, in the administration's view, conditions seemed to favor an even stronger-handed approach. In the wake of the huge 1972 Soviet sale and the 1973 soybean embargo, both commercial buyers and food aid recipients clamored for scarce American grain. One contemporary CIA study forecast the emergence of a form of agricultural Darwinism in which the United States would evolve as the breadbasket of the world: "The disparity between the rich and poor is thus likely to get even wider. And the world's dependence on North American agriculture will continue to increase."[18]

The 1972-73 string of disasters was followed by a spate of bilateral agreements that only reinforced the impression that the United States was intent on translating its agricultural wealth into political advantage. In 1975, when Butz returned from a world tour that impression was further bolstered by the line of countries waiting to sign long-term purchasing agreements with the United States. As Butz noted then, "The Minister of Agriculture of Romania told me that you have something more powerful than the atomic bomb—soya."[19] Nevertheless, Butz also continued to expound the virtues of free trade and demonstrated his desire to achieve this goal by declaring war against the protectionism of Europe's Common Agricultural Policy. Thus it was that while Washington was developing its own form of controls to be wielded against the USSR, it launched a frontal attack against certain European trade barriers, in particular those which impeded imports of U.S. grains to EC member countries.

The U.S. campaign against the EC was motivated in large part by the

Flanigan Report associated with the USDA and White House economic adviser, Peter Flanigan. Flanigan's report recommended that the United States seek to liberalize European and Japanese trade regulations with regard to feedgrains and livestock in return for the elimination of Amèrican protectionist programs in other sectors. Congress was outraged, not at the prospect of gaining a greater foothold in the rich markets of Europe and Japan, but at the thought of having to give up anything to attain it. The Flanigan strategy was shelved, but the effort to lower the EC's trade barriers was not.

There were, in fact, at least two subsequent attempts to negotiate a deal with the EC. In 1973 a high-level State Department official suggested to the European Commissioner for Agriculture, P.J. Lardinois, that the United States would be willing to refrain from increasing its oil imports from the Mideast in exchange for a commitment from the EC to modify CAP, so as to ease the entry of U.S. grain imports into Europe. This initiative also failed, but two years later, Lardinois and Butz allegedly struck a deal on soybeans according to which the United States was to withdraw its GATT complaint against the Commission's new levy on milk powder in exchange for an increase in European imports of American soybeans. Whether agreed to or not by Lardinois and Butz, this agreement too was never effected. Taken together, however, the two initiatives demonstrate the Nixon-Kissinger-Butz commitment to agricultural *realpolitik*.

The primary target of Nixon and Kissinger's attention, however, was not Europe but the Soviet Union. And it was against the USSR that the food weapon was wielded with the greatest vigor. Presumably it was in this diplomatic arena that the new doctrine of agricultural realpolitik was expected to yield the greatest gains for the United States. If so, the early results, notably the great Soviet "grain robbery" of 1972 in which the massive but well-concealed Soviet purchases were carried out with the unwitting assistance of the administration, must have been extremely disappointing. The administration was undeterred, however, by this early setback and remained steadfast in its resolve to use American food as a means of leverage in dealing with the Soviets. Thus the 1972 incident was followed, in rapid succession, by the 1974 and 1975 Soviet embargoes, abortive efforts to barter American grain for Soviet oil in Moscow, and, finally, the five-year U.S.-Soviet agreement.

The 1975 embargo, as already noted, was prompted in part by administration uncertainty over Soviet purchasing intentions. Memories of the trauma which followed in the wake of the 1972 sale undoubtedly played a part in the administration's thinking. So too did the realization that, left to their own devices, the Soviets were unlikely to conduct their grain purchases in a manner compatible with American interests. In addition, there was another reason for the embargo, namely the administration's interest in negotiating a long-term food-for-crude deal in which American grain would be exchanged for Soviet oil, thereby striking a bargain that would both advantage the United States in its dealings with OPEC and fend off any repeat of the 1972 experience with the Soviets.

Both the embargo and the food-for-crude effort, the latter very much a Kissinger initiative, were destined to fail. Yet the prospects for success, at least on the surface, could hardly have seemed brighter. In the summer of 1975 forecasts of Soviet grain production for the 1975-76 marketing year projected a decrease of almost 30 percent from the previous year while U.S. supplies were ample. And these forecasts were largely correct.

The failure of the food-for-crude initiative was implicit in the failure of the embargo. Announced in August 1975, ostensibly in response to pressure from the Longshoremen's Union then seeking a renewal of the Maritime Agreement on terms more favorable to ILA workers, the embargo quickly fell apart. The White House, working with scanty information, assumed that turning off the grain spigot would bring the Soviets to their knees. This was an unlikely scenario at best, but it was particularly unlikely in that the spigot could not, as was soon demonstrated, be turned off. More aware of the weaknesses in the American marketing system than U.S. authorities, the Soviets had managed, even before the embargo was announced, to obtain sales commitments of over 10 million metric tons of U.S.-origin wheat and corn through European affiliates of subsidiaries of American firms. By the time the American government attempted to close the gates, "the horse had left the barn."[20] This was a realization which came to Secretary Kissinger and Labor Secretary John Dunlop somewhat belatedly. When it did, they turned to George Meany and Ted Gleason, president of the International Longshore-men's Association (ILA), to block further shipments of Soviet grain. This, it was clear, was something the traders were unwilling to do and the govern-ment seemed incapable of doing on its own. As a further measure, the United States tried to turn the screws tighter against the Soviets in September 1975 by blocking their access to American food resources through Poland.

Although an attempt to show strength, the U.S. strategy was also a demonstration of the underlying weakness of the government vis-à-vis the private trade. Under questioning before Congress, government authorities explained the necessity of broadening the embargo to Poland because of commercial ambiguities that made it virtually impossible to distinguish the ultimate destination of shipments.[21] It was an admission that the government was effectively unable to carry out its own policy.

In the midst of these developments, the administration was carrying out its plans for the food-for-crude initiative. In September 1975, Undersecretary of State Charles W. Robinson led an American delegation to Moscow minus Earl Butz, who had fallen into disfavor because of his approval of 10 million metric tons in sales to the Russians in the summer of 1975, before the transaction had been approved by a special interagency review committee.[22] Amidst a widespread perception that major foreign policy issues were at stake, Kissinger took charge. The prospective grain agreement with the USSR quickly became a State Department show. Kissinger kept such a tight rein on developments in Moscow that USDA members of the delegation were often the last to see messages from Moscow to Washington or obtain any substantive information on behind-the-scenes negotiations. Kissinger, it seems, was not about to surrender responsibility for future Soviet purchases of American grain, thus abandoning his grand strategy and failing to stage a diplomatic coup after the 1972 calamity with which he was also closely associated.

Robinson delivered to Moscow the Kissinger-inspired plan of crude-for-food: The Russians would obtain large quantities of American grain over an extended period in exchange for selling a fixed amount of their oil at prices discounted below the OPEC cartel price. It did not work. Kissinger once again misjudged the Soviets and the grain trade. Based upon U.S. intelligence estimates of shortfalls in Soviet production and stock drawdowns, Kissinger believed the Soviet Union to be in a bind. The assumption was that the Soviet Union would be forced to accept a certain degree of humiliation and assent to U.S. demands for discounted oil. But the U.S. definition of what the Soviets would accept was wrong, particularly as U.S. information on Soviet stocks and access to U.S. grain via third markets like Poland was still at a stage of sophisticated guesswork. The Soviets continued to purchase grain on the international market in 1975 from the same companies that were bound by law to suspend American grain sales to them. Cook, Toepfer, Tradax, Louis Dreyfus, and others continued to sell grain to the Soviets.[23] In the 1975 crop year, the Soviet Union imported almost 16 million metric tons of grain with more than half coming from Australia, Argentina, Brazil, contracted in part by the Big League traders.

These purchases confounded earlier official estimates of how much U.S. grain the Soviets would buy in 1975/76. Determined to win this round, Kissinger and Robinson had vainly tried to score on two fronts simultaneously—grain and oil. The requirements for success in such an endeavor, however, were an American monopoly of the world's supply of wheat and feedgrain and Soviet dependence on imported grain. Neither requirement was present. The failure to gain more than a vague commitment to talk further about a matching five-year agreement on Soviet oil cast doubt upon the claim that the American food weapon could be used successfully against the Soviets.

The oil deal fell through, but when in October 1975 the United States and the Soviet Union signed the five-year bilateral grain agreement for wheat and corn, the moratorium on sales to Poland was lifted. With the resumption of much needed exports, further criticism of the government's management of agricultural export controls was muted. The agreement was hailed as a victory; any plan for reforming the reporting system was quickly replaced by a display of confidence in the government's management capabilities. Thus, although the administration's Moscow initiative failed, the administration's food weapon proponents suffered little setback. Secretary Butz, for example, attributed Russian good behavior during the Sinai negotiations in 1975 to the suspension of sales in the fall of the same year. President Ford extolled the bilateral grain agreement of 1975 as an important factor in the general improvement of American-Soviet relations.

Not everyone was convinced. Groups like the National Association of Wheat Growers thought that the moratorium and the agreement that followed did more harm than good. In a draft suit the Association challenged the legality of both the President and the Secretary of State's actions, and leveled allegations of anti-trust violations against the grain companies. Other producer groups echoed the charge that the agreement was biased in favor of the Big League. And Undersecretary Robinson's denials notwithstanding,[24] elements of the farming community still suspected that one of the agreement's entailments was a quota system in which fixed shares of the USSR sales, within a predetermined price range, were allocated to individual companies. At best, these farm groups viewed the agreement as likely to restrict rather than increase U.S. grain exports.

While the Soviet scenario was unfolding, so too were other diplomatic efforts. On occasion these involved a modest abandonment of the Nixon administration's hard line. The administration softened its attack on Japan's trading policies, for example, after the soybean shoku. Ironically though, the signing of the Butz-Abe agreement of 1975 ought to have disproved the notion that the United States had an effective food weapon but seemed only to foster support for the idea. That agreement, informal in nature and reached only with difficulty, was obtained with a nation totally dependent on the United States for wheat, feedgrains, and soybeans, in short an ideal target for manipulative agricultural strategy.

The Butz-Abe agreement was interpreted by some as a confirmation of American agricultural power and Japanese vulnerability. But it ought also to have served as a reminder that vulnerability is a two-way street. America may have been Japan's biggest supplier, but Japan was also one of America's biggest customers. Japan's imports represented nearly 15 percent of total American grain exports in 1975-76. As oil imports tilted the U.S. balance of payments into the red, exports of agricultural commodities became increasingly important. The loss of the Japanese market was too great a risk, particularly as U.S. agricultural prosperity became more reliant on foreign sales. Japan, as America's best agricultural customer, had its own form of leverage, its apparent dependence on American supplies notwithstanding. In addition, the United States could ill afford to offend Japan politically. Under the Nixon-Kissinger regime, there had been a series of shokus preceding the soybean embargo, and a failure to remedy the food supply picture would have threatened longer-term bilateral relations. The Butz-Abe agreement satisfied both sides and reduced political tensions between the two countries. So it was that the administration's loyalty to the food weapon idea remained intact.

It remained so until the end. Undeterred by opposition or the impractical, offensive aspects of its food weapon strategy, the Nixon administration stubbornly adhered to this policy in its handling of both concessional and commercial exports. A weakened president, hounded by the Watergate investigation, found himself faced with mounting dissension, even within his own ranks, over the failure to curb agricultural prices in the campaign against inflation. Developing countries protested vociferously over their second-class treatment in comparison to the Soviet Union at a time when several were facing serious crop damage. Vietnam's army did no better when it was well fed, and President Thieu, fortified by the continued flow of PL 480, could better resist American pressure for a negotiated end to the war. Heavy grain and military sales to Iran were hardly sufficient to compensate for the astronomical oil hikes frequently inspired by the shah nor to building support for his regime.

Kissinger's efforts to placate developing countries' food concerns were equally unsuccessful. When Kissinger tried to rally the have-nots around the world against the OPEC cartel[25] with the enticement of American food aid, there was hardly a stir. When he tried to use food aid as a means of preventing the Soviet Union and OPEC countries from chipping away at American influence in the Third World, the response was just as unrewarding. Nevertheless, the White House persisted in its efforts to utilize agripower for foreign policy purposes until disaffected interest groups in the United States spurned the idea decisively.

As long as Kissinger and the State Department dominated the making of American food policy, it could be generally assumed that international politics would be injected into U.S. agricultural export policies. Thus a major issue in the presidential campaign of 1976 was the administration's suspension of sales to the Soviet Union in 1974, and again in 1975, as well as its callous handling of food aid. In response, President Ford tried to disavow a manipulative approach to commercial and concessional food exports.

> The linkage of grain [with] diplomacy would mean disruption and hardship for you, the farmer, a serious increase in tensions between the world's two super-powers, and no effect whatsoever in Angola.
>   . . . We have heard much in the 1970s of "Petropower," the power of those nations with vast exportable petroleum resources. Today, let us consider a different kind of power—agripower, the power to grow. Agripower is the power to maintain and to improve the quality of life in a new world where our fate is interdependent with the fate of others of this globe.[26]

But he failed to convince the electorate in the American grain belt.

THE CARTER YEARS

In contrast to his predecessor, candidate Carter pledged that he would never initiate another embargo. Further, he proposed that the United States become the breadbasket rather than the arms merchant of the world. What distinguished the Carter promise from the practices of Nixon and Ford was an implicit commitment to reduce the emphasis on political objectives in favor of export promotion and development assistance.

At the outset of the new administration, market conditions and international diplomatic events seemed to work against a revival of the food weapon idea. Because of world surpluses in wheat and coarse grains, along with a slowdown of economic growth rates in Japan and Europe, the United States was anxious to sell its excess production to any interested buyer. As a result, the start of the Carter administration was marked by an apparent return to export promotion where handling food aid and commercial sales was sufficiently ambiguous to cloak any apparent political motivation. The improvement in agricultural trade relations with China was less the result of U.S. food diplomacy than a manifestation of changing political forces within China, and the Chinese government's extreme concern regarding Soviet expansionism. During this time the politics of food aid was equally ambivalent. In cases such as Pinochet's Chile and Nicaragua under Samoza, PL 480 was cut off to reinforce America's human rights stance. On the other hand, several countries with undemocratic governments—Indonesia, Korea, Morocco, and Haiti—were among the largest recipients of American food assistance.

Nonetheless, in some instances the Carter administration did link PL 480 grants and Title I sales with foreign policy concerns. Sensitivity to Vietnam's occupation of Cambodia and establishment of a puppet regime at first took precedence over concern for massive human suffering and starvation in Cambodia. Both Congress and the administration were reluctant to take steps that would appear to legitimize Vietnamese aggression. The opposing roles of the Soviet Union and China also figured into the equation. Eventually U.S. food assistance was forthcoming under international auspices, but political criteria weighed heavily in the extended delay.

In the case of Egypt, the Carter White House chose to follow its predecessor's example. Sadat's signing of the Sinai agreement, drafted by Kissinger, brought the first big wave of food aid. With the signing of the Camp David accord, in which President Carter was deeply involved, Egypt became the recipient of 23 percent of the entire volume of American food aid under the Title I program of PL 480. As the political stakes climbed, so did PL 480 aid to Egypt, reaching a value of $300 million in Title I commodities by 1980. The Agency for International Development's commodity import loans program (CIP), dormant since the ERP, provided additional incentives for purchases of U.S. agricultural commodities and American-made capital equipment. In fact, by 1979 Egypt was receiving as much aid through the CIP program as under Title I. Israel was receiving more.

Congress endorsed these initiatives, and several members responded by advocating a bolder use of the weapon against oil-rich countries in the Middle East. In so doing they were in large part picking up on Kissinger's food-for-crude idea, the failure of that initiative notwithstanding. As frustrations mounted over the rising energy bill imposed by the oil cartel, the idea that American grain exports could be used to pay for foreign oil gained wider currency. It was an idea that President Carter ultimately blessed with a certain messianic zeal.

One of the most important gifts that God has given us is fertile land and a free enterprise system, which gives us food and grain and other products to sell to others. . . . We have a better advantage in producing food, which will last, hopefully, forever, than the oil producing nations overseas have with depleting oil supplies. The greatest strategic advantage that I see that our country will have in years to come is food, which can be made available in a very beneficial way to all the people on Earth who need food.[27]

Simultaneous with the reemergence of the food weapon idea in administrative circles was the resurgence of interest in establishing a cartel among grain producers to counter OPEC. To some, it seemed an attractive, realistic alternative: the proposed grain cartel would charge OPEC members higher prices than the world food market for foodstuffs, just as OPEC was in effect charging oil-deficit nations above market prices for oil. Such an initiative would not have been without precedent. Efforts to establish a wheat cartel far antedate the so far more successful undertaking of the oil-producing countries. Canada was particularly anxious to revive high-level meetings of the old Exporters Group, primarily because of the precipitous drop in 1978-79 wheat prices. Argentina and Australia, although less enthusiastic, were willing to go along for similar reasons. But the United States demurred. Nonetheless, Washington publicized its discussion with the group in a manner that constituted a veiled threat to OPEC: "If we can do something about the oil cartel, fine. I'd be willing to drop these talks . . . when the oil cartel is dissolved. But until such a time as that occurs, I don't intend to back down."[28]

OPEC's actions were so unpopular with the American public that reservations about brandishing the food weapon were overcome by the popularity of a counter-cartel strategy.[29] Farm groups, attracted by the promise of higher export prices, and a greater return on their production, rallied around the idea.[30] American consumers, pinched by the price gouging of OPEC, joined forces with the farm interests in the Congress, where support grew for the Canadian proposal. Eventually, support for the formation of a grain cartel reached the point that a reluctant administration found itself under public pressure to adopt what had heretofore been an unpopular policy.

Starting in the spring of 1979, Bergland met with Australian, Argentinian, and Canadian ministers of agriculture, who agreed to coordinate wheat-marketing and -production policies in their respective countries. At the same time, Bergland floated the idea of a barter agreement, exchanging U.S. grain for Mexican petroleum. But the pressure for even more forceful action from Congress continued. Ranking senators from large wheat-producing states met periodically with their counterparts in Canada to keep the cartel idea alive. At a loss for pat formulas to get the U.S. economy out of its doldrums, some politicans turned to grain, prodding the Carter administration into a more aggressive posture.

In the end, higher agricultural prices and chaos in Iran saved the Carter administration from being effectively forced to swallow a congressional directive to pursue a bold counter-cartel strategy. An effective floor for grain prices was maintained through domestic programs until the Soviet Union, and to a lesser extent China, came to the rescue by placing purchase orders for 1979-80 that surpassed all previous orders. A gas deal was signed with Mexico, which in turn purchased record quantities of U.S. grain. Thus by late 1979 the forecast was for a surge in exports with attendant increases in farmer receipts, a forecast that quieted the voices of those who favored a hard-line grain strategy toward petroleum producers.

And then came Afghanistan. Even as support for a food cartel was dwindling and the direction of food policy had been returned to the Department of Agriculture, President Carter announced the cancellation of all outstanding wheat, corn, and soybean contracts with the Soviet Union on 4 January 1980. In previous months the administration had moved hesitantly in this direction and had undertaken a review of a possible food embargo against Iran to pressure for the release of American hostages there. But even though a food embargo had been high on the list of contingencies as the Iranian tragedy dragged on, circumstances and events conspired against such an initiative. In theory, the United States was in an ideal position to wield the food weapon against Iran. America supplied the shah's Iran with roughly 90 percent of its wheat and a majority of its other food imports. Not only had Iran been a regular buyer of American grain, but also wheat was an important part of the daily Iranian diet. Further, the Longshoremen's Union, in a burst of partriotic fervor, announced a boycott of shipments to Iran. Still, Washington was in no position to halt delivery of food supplies to that country.

In 1980, there was, in fact, no reason to believe that the United States could conduct an embargo any more effectively than the 1974 and 1975 efforts to shut off Soviet supplies. As with earlier attempts, it was too late. While the boycott was on, subsidiaries of American grain companies were allegedly shipping Australian wheat and Canadian barley to Iran.[31] And even had Australia and Canada joined forces with the United States in a food embargo, Iran would in all likelihood have made cash purchases from Europe or on the high seas through the same subsidiaries. Nothing short of a naval blockade in the Persian Gulf against all commercial traffic, including foreign-flag ships under charter from American and other international grain companies, could have sealed off Iran from food imports.

It seems likely that all this was known by the administration and deterred any efforts to wield the food weapon against Iran. But in January 1980 a different set of calculations applied. Although it was a clear renunciation of candidate Carter's pledge in 1976, the Carter administration, like those of Nixon and Ford, eventually undertook to cut off Soviet grain for political purposes. There was, however, one difference between the 1980 embargo and the embargoes of 1974 and 1975. The earlier embargoes were part of a grand design. The 1980 initiative was by contrast a desperate, symbolic attempt to rebuke the Soviets for invading Afghanistan.

Apparently emboldened by the decisiveness of the action—a quality many critics had found lacking in earlier foreign policy actions undertaken by the

Carter White House—administration officials, apparently assuming that the embargo would inflict significant damage on the Soviets, later tended to exaggerate the embargo's potential as an economic and diplomatic weapon. Believing that the embargo would make it more difficult for the Soviets to sustain their occupation of Afghanistan, the administration made the embargo's removal virtually conditional on a Soviet withdrawal. In due course, however, the negative effects of the embargo on the United States became more evident while the hoped-for Soviet retreat failed to materialize, and it became increasingly apparent that continuing the embargo over an extended period would be more costly to the U.S. than to the Soviets. Such an outcome could conceivably have been avoided had the original decision and later implementation of the embargo been handled differently. Taken off guard by the Soviet invasion, the administration was under considerable pressure to respond quickly and forcefully. The small cluster of presidential advisors involved was also extremely dependent on sound intelligence. Chief responsibility for this kind of information and analysis lay with the USDA and the Central Intelligence Agency. In conjunction with the Council of Economic Advisors, the USDA was asked, but less than two days before the president announced the embargo, to produce an impact evaluation. The CIA, however, had already prepared a comparable document prior to the first meeting—on 2 January—of the Special Coordinating Committee (SCC), a Cabinet-level, interdepartmental grouping under the National Security Council. Accordingly, the CIA's study was effectively the only show in town and received the greatest weight. By all accounts, the CIA predicted that a cut-off of grain would have a serious impact on the Soviet Union and would lead to at least a 12 percent reduction in meat production due to a forced increase in slaughtering.

The biggest flaw in the CIA's analysis, according to its critics, lay in its working assumptions. The study focused on projected shortfalls in production within the USSR while largely ignoring the prospect that the Soviets might obtain access to supply sources outside the United States which they were able to do. The Soviets were, in fact, able to import at least 31.2 million metric tons of their expected grain (and soybean) import total of 37.5 million metric tons during the 1979-80 marketing year. Further, they were, according to USDA calculations, able to replace over 6 million metric tons of American grain with supplies obtained from Argentina and Canada and transshipments from Eastern Europe. Soviet grain and soybean imports from these outlets in the 1979-80 marketing year ultimately accounted for all but 2.5 million metric tons of the 34 million tons they were able to purchase in that year.

High prices did not deter the Soviet buyers in making these purchases. As demonstrated in their purchase agreement with Argentina, the Soviets were prepared to buy above the international price. Argentina's corn prices went up as a result from $162 per ton in December 1979 to $202 per ton in February 1980. In the same period the U.S. export price of corn dropped $7 per ton to $132. This disparity produced windfall profits for buyers holding Argentinian contracts that could be sold to the Soviets and replaced at the lower U.S price. As for the United States, it was only too anxious to dispose of whatever portion it could of the 17 million metric tons in cancelled commitments. The result was a buyers' market for American grain that served as an open invitation to switch to U.S.-origin contracts and in turn freed Argentine supplies for the Soviets. Within a brief period there was a dramatic realignment of export and import relationships that significantly reduced the embargo's effectiveness.

The Soviets were able to import as much as they did by purchasing forward. Their heaviest American buying actually occurred during the fall of 1979, allowing enough time to ship roughly 13 million metric tons before the embargo was announced in January 1980 and another 2.5 million tons thereafter, this as part of the guaranteed annual minimum of 8 million metric tons due them under the 1975 U.S.-USSR accord. In addition, the Soviets immediately went on a global tour in the wake of the embargo announcement, buying crops in advance of harvest. Finally, during the period of the embargo they continued to receive grain from Canada and Australia under the terms of previously negotiated annual purchasing agreements with these two countries. This too served to keep supply lines open.

None of these developments were anticipated in the CIA study. In projecting the embargo's impact upon Soviet meat production, CIA analysts appear to have discounted the Soviet's ability to adjust to a poor harvest. Predictions of severe cut-backs in meat consumption and distress slaughtering of livestock herds proved unfounded. Whereas the initial CIA analysis predicted a 5 to 14 percent decrease in available Soviet feed supplies as a result of the embargo and a 7 percent reduction in meat consumption, revised USDA figures published in 1981 indicated that there was at most a 2 percent cut-back in available feedgrains and no perceptible effect on meat consumption.

In the absence of reliable information about Soviet stock levels, the United States was effectively unable to evaluate accurately the short or long-term effects of an embargo. Official estimates of 1980 stocks in the USSR were in the range of 23 million metric tons, 19 million of which were wheat and 4 million coarse grains. Allowing for additional national security stocks, these figures could have been off by as much as 15 million metric tons. The higher these levels, the less significant the impact of an embargo. In addition, the Russians may well have been buying heavily in 1979-80 in anticipation of a crisis. It seems certain in any event that they had stocks upon which to draw that were beyond the calculus of American intelligence analysts.

The Department of Agriculture's analysis, ordered in January 1980 but not completed until almost six months thereafter,[32] suffered from similar weaknesses. Unrealistically low projections of wheat, corn, and sorghum available from suppliers other than the United States gave Washington an inflated estimate of the embargo's eventual impact. The USDA experts, like their counterparts in the CIA, seemed ignorant of many facts of life in the grain trade, facts which would have altered their assessments of the embargo's effectiveness. In particular, there was and could have been no certainty about how much grain had already been sold to the Russians and who was holding the contracts. Further, in the month prior to the 4 January deadline, companies changed the declared destination of over 30 percent of their total shipments, or 4.5 million metric tons of wheat and corn, to the USSR. This action was taken in anticipation of a possible embargo and, while clearly beneficial to the companies, was most unhelpful to Washington's effort.

Despite the embargo's ineffectiveness, it was continued by the administration, largely for political reasons. The Republicans, however, were quick to grasp the growing discontent with this policy in the farm states and to call for lifting the embargo. This was one of the issues on which Ronald Reagan hammered away during the 1980 presidential campaign and for which he ultimately gained bipartisan support in the Senate after taking office. Candidate Carter, on the other hand, appeared to be boxed in, unable to disavow a policy that had boomeranged at home and abroad. The longer the embargo remained in effect, the harder it was to demand even minimal cooperation from other exporters. Good crops worldwide and stagnating demand in 1980-81 only increased the pressure to find export outlets wherever possible. Nor did the United States offer any real guidance to other exporters. On the one hand, the United States prevailed upon other members of the Exporters' Group to impose and maintain restrictions on sales to the Soviets. At the same time, Washington took steps that raised questions about its sincerity.

Less than six months after the embargo was announced, the United States began issuing export licenses to companies on a first-come, first-served basis to contract for shares of the 8 million metric tons of American grain guaranteed to the USSR under the 1975 grain agreement. The prospect that additional amounts might be sold later, depending on the Soviet response, was deliberately left open. In June 1980 the government began allowing subsidiaries of American grain firms to service Soviet contracts with non-U.S. grains and soybeans, thereby further softening the U.S. position and encouraging other exporters to sell on their own. By November, foreign support for the embargo was eroded almost completely by the signing of the U.S.-PRC grain agreement. Australia and Canada, each faced with growing pressure from domestic producer groups to end the embargo, were strongly critical of what seemed to be a deliberate attempt by the United States to intrude upon one of their traditional markets. Bitterness surfaced in the EC over leakages from other countries ostensibly supporting the embargo.

The overall effects of the embargo proved damaging to the United States on all fronts. A majority of American farmers were hurt, despite the costly relief measures instituted by the government. Some companies holding canceled contracts suffered more than others, the well-intentioned federal rescue effort notwithstanding. Consumers were left to wrestle with the residual inflationary effects of the government's intervention plan. And in the international arena, the Soviets were little damaged nor were they forced out of

Afghanistan, while traditionally faithful importers of American grain grew increasingly distrustful over the inconsistency in U.S. agricultural export policy. Within the Exporters' Group, discontent threatened to bring on a trade war. From the U.S. perspective, the positive effects of the embargo were few indeed.

Confronted in the spring of 1981 with a bumper crop at home, good harvests is the Soviet Union, and an ineffective embargo, President Reagan lifted the embargo and subsequently attempted to entice the Soviets back into the American market. Secretary of State Alexander Haig argued convincingly but briefly for the extension of the embargo as a punitive action against the Soviets for their implicit threat to Poland and alleged meddling in El Salvador.[33] Nonetheless, in the end, domestic pressure persuaded President Reagan to carry out his campaign pledge and lift the embargo. Significantly, however, this was done without disavowing a possible future cutoff as a sanction against Soviet behavior in Poland and elsewhere. Washington's romantic attachment to the food weapon seems unlikely to end with the Reagan administration.

THE EMBARGO PROBLEM REVISITED

On at least three occasions within the past decade, the United States has imposed an embargo on grain sales to the Soviet Union. All had a painful impact upon American producers. Yet despite claims to the contrary from Washington, none of these efforts to wield the food weapon had the desired effect on Soviet behavior. Perhaps even more important, none succeeded in shutting off Soviet access to grain. Why not? A large part of the answer is to be found in the behavior of grain companies and the government's inability to control that behavior. And the government's lack of regulatory capability is in turn largely a function of inadequate information.

As was noted earlier, one of the basic difficulties confronting American policy makers when they turn their attention to food export policy is the absence of reliable data concerning the proportion of domestic supplies committed to the export stream. At present, such information as can be amassed must come from the companies themselves. For a variety of reasons having to do with the structure of the grain trade, notably the dominant position of a half dozen firms whose operations are multinational in scope and its manner of operation, overcounting of export orders is almost inevitable. Thus it becomes almost impossible for Washington to determine, at any given time, precisely what proportion of available U.S. supplies has been contracted for foreign sale. This can in turn lead, as it did in 1973, to the imposition of a wholly unnecessary embargo with all the negative consequences thus implied.

The aforementioned is, however, only one dimension of the information problem that results from Washington's reliance on a reluctant industry, accustomed to and in some sense dependent upon secrecy, for basic information about the industry's operations. A second aspect of the problem, one that is particularly acute in the case of a selective embargo directed against a specific country, is the government's lack of access to reliable information about the acutal destination of overseas grain transshipments.

Transshipments pose a dilemma. When a large vessel arrives in Rotterdam, its cargo is often destined for transshipment points eastward in smaller lots, which are difficult to track. The terminals on the St. Lawrence Seaway are also transshipment depots that, despite their handling efficiencies, confound accurate export accounting. There are myraid ways in which transshipments can be deceptive. One illustration of this involved Toepfer Grain of Hamburg's diversion of a PL 480 shipment to Eastern Europe. A cargo of coarse grains, whose destination was marked Austria, was diverted to Hamburg, Bremen, and Rotterdam for transshipment as a commercial sale to Eastern Europe. Austrian importing firms certified receipt of the shipments and paid American exporters through a Swiss bank account on behalf of Toepfer and other German companies.[34]

ARA (Amsterdam, Rotterdam, and Antwerp) and Hamburg are the main transshipment centers because of their convenience as distribution points for the entire European continent. Generally, ARA arrivals not imported into European Community countries go to Eastern Europe and the USSR. Roughly 150,000 metric tons per month enter the Soviet Union via Rotterdam. In 1975, for example, Cargill explained that the Soviets had stored approximately 50,000 metric tons of U.S. grain in Tradax, Amsterdam's elevator, until congestion in the Baltic ports was relieved.[35] Industry representatives have maintained that such an occurrence does not go unrecorded because the transshipment is based on an already reported export sales. However, as long as the Soviets retain ownership of the grain based on a sale whose destination is registered as the Soviet Union, they can decide at a future date to ship the grain to another country without detection by the U.S. government of the destination change. Moreover, a country like the Soviet Union, which may be subject to limitations on the amount of grain it can import from the United States, can exceed these levels with the assistance of international grain shippers who can provide the necessary space in one of their elevators outside the United States or the USSR and declare the cargo "destination unknown."

Hamburg, one of the world's largest free ports for the grain trade, is ideally situated for handling the flow of grain destined mainly for the German Democratic Republic (GDR) and neighboring Eastern European countries. East Germany, due to its special status vis-à-vis the Federal Republic, has what amounts to preferred access to transshipments via Hamburg. At present, the amount of grain entering Eastern Europe via Hamburg is considerable. Official West German statistics indicate that in 1976 total grain and oilseed shipments with the Eastern bloc handled out of Hamburg were over 4.2 million metric tons, of which approximately 3.7 million originated in the United States[36] via the St. Lawrence Seaway. Of this total, more than 75 percent was handled in open bonded warehouses where grain deliveries could stay in West Germany on a levy-free basis for 45 days before transshipment to the GDR and Czechoslovakia. East Germany accounted for the largest share—64 percent—and the U.S. portion of the country's total was almost 90 percent, or more than 70 percent of all American grain and oilseed imports into the German Republic.[37] These percentages remained roughly the same throughout the 1970s, variations in the total amount of imports notwithstanding.

On the one hand, this arrangement facilitates the flow of traffic in grains, but, on the other, it constitutes an effective smokescreen against government efforts to ascertain the ultimate delivery point. Shipments of U.S. grain leaving the Great Lakes via the St. Lawrence transfer elevators are equally difficult to monitor.[38] Records of this traffic remain limited to customs forms, belated export sales reports, and random inspection certificates. The USDA has an informal understanding with the Canadian Grains Commission, an official Canadian agency for monitoring grain inspection and transportation, whereby the Commission sends to Washington summaries of its periodic checks on transfer elevators at Canada's Georgian Bay and lower lake ports. Commission officials admit, however, that the system is far from foolproof, especially regarding the verification of the final destination of a cargo in transit.

Enforcement of any system of export controls is, thus, virtually impossible. As such, foreign buyers like the Soviet Union and Eastern European countries are to a significant extent assured of access to the U.S. grain market regardless of governmental restrictions. When necessary, the St. Lawrence-ARA-Hamburg corridor provides a detection-proof channel for a black market in grain. Aware of this potential problem, Secretary Bergland announced the establishment of Operation Sting to detect any illicit transshipments to the USSR during the 1980 embargo. This initiative, however, proved largely a symbolic act.

The reasons for Washington's inability to implement effectively any grain embargo were described in a little publicized 1977 USDA audit of the 1974 and 1975 Soviet embargoes. In its report, the USDA staff identified real weaknesses in the system and advised that a task force be established to "evaluate data accumulated through the export sales reporting system"[39] and consider a number of recommendations based on a review of the three principal reporting forms for: (1) optional-origin sales; (2) export sales and shipments against sales; and (3) sales for an exporter's own account (shipments that remain unsold or unassigned to a specific export sale). The USDA report suggested that these forms had serious deficiencies respecting the usefulness of the information gathered. The basic problem was the relevance of the forms to the workings of the trade.

> . . . several exporters we visited were not maintaining complete records in accordance with the Export Sales Reporting Regulations. The exporters were unable to provide sales contracts because their U.S. offices only purchased and arranged shipment of commodities. As a result, we were unable to trace the applicable sales contract to the reported transactions for verifying the accuracy of submitted reports.[40]

The audit also determined that the reporting forms' identification of an export sale was virtually meaningless. The problem lay both with the disclosure requirements, in that they allowed for a declaration by the shipper of unknown destination, and the elusiveness of interaffiliate transactions.

> The Department cannot rely on export reporting destinations. In our review we could not determine final destination of commodities because of (1) the vast network of resellers; (2) commodities may change hands many times before they reach their final destination; and (3) U.S. grain often is commingled with foreign grain, and it would be impossible to distinguish U.S. grain from foreign grain from reseller records.[41]

The 1977 audit did not lead to significant reform. A USDA advisory committee on export sales was established as a result of the audit and conducted roughly six months of investigation, public hearings, and analysis. When it issued its report in 1979, however, its findings contradicted those of the earlier document. Despite more than a little evidence to the contrary, the committee reported that the existing system was "performing reasonably well."[42] In comparison with the 1977 audit, the authors of the 1979 report saw a need for only modest reform. Recognizing the need for timely reporting of sales, the Committee did call for a change in the USDA's deadline for data utilized in its weekly export sales reports received from the grain companies. It offered no recommendations concerning means of enforcing the new deadline.

The rationale for the new deadline was based on data from the earlier audit which indicated that 32 of 49 reported sales for a given week, several of which involved large contracts with the Soviet Union, were called in after the three o'clock Tuesday deadline and, as a result, did not appear in USDA's report issue on Thursday.[43] Without this information, the Thursday news was not only incorrect but misleading. Exporters who had withheld sales information until after the deadline were effectively securing an extra four to seven days in which to hedge their position before their sales would be made public in the following week's report.

Whereas the audit and earlier investigations had concluded that foreign company sales of U.S. commodities often go unreported, the Advisory Committee in its final report did not think the problem serious enough to warrant drastic revision of the law. The first draft of the Committee's report had contained a stronger recommendation. It had called for all firms, including those incorporated abroad, to be required to provide the Department of Agriculture with weekly sales records in addition to large daily transactions.[44] In the final document, however, this recommendation was sanitized, once again leaving the application of such a provision to the "discretionary authority" of the Agricultural Secretary,[45] and thereby effectively exempting foreign-based firms or affiliates of American-based companies from the more stringent reporting requirements applied to their U.S. counterparts.

The potential cost to Washington of this failure to tighten reporting requirements for foreign-based firms was underscored only one year later. In the wake of the 1980 embargo, the Carter administration announced a relief program for traders designed to offset any losses resulting from the embargo. The administration pledged that this program would be so designed as not to underwrite windfall profits for any of the firms involved, but the government had no way of realizing such an objective. Thus it was that when those grain companies holding USSR sales contracts scrambled to convert the destination of orders for more than 4.5 million metric tons of wheat and corn from "destination unknown" to the USSR they were able, by carefully structuring their interaffiliate transactions, to obtain the maximum possible coverage under the government's CCC reimbursement plan.[46] Precisely what proportion of the reported contracts with the USSR were, in fact, originally destined for shipment to that country was something that the government was in no position to judge. Ironically, given that it is Washington which has so often suffered from the trade's reluctance to report on its operations, the government has, on more than one occasion, effectively shielded the Big League from public scrutiny. When I sued the Department of Agriculture and Secretary Bergland for sales reports of shipments that had already taken place,[47] the government claimed that the commercial information contained in such reports, if released, "could cause substantial competitve harm to the exporters" for three main reasons: (1) current purchasing and selling practices would be disrupted, permitting domestic companies, who would not normally do so, to sell directly to the foreign buyer; (2) release would allow sellers in possession of what was heretofore confidential information to withhold sales for the export market until the price is driven up; or, conversely, (3) permit domestic and foreign buyers to take advantage of this same information in an effort to drive the selling price down.[48] Because of traditional buying and selling patterns, the government argued in the suit that ". . . the release of such individual forms could provide those companies normally selling to domestic buyers who purchase for subsequent export sale with an opportunity to sell instead for export directly to the foreign purchasers."[49]

Confidentiality of the reports was granted the USDA (for an undefined but not indefinite time period) in deference to fair competition and export promotion. Supposedly it was not for the protection of "traditional buying and selling patterns" (which could have been construed as an official sanction of anticompetitive practices).[50] In response to my proposed compromise of deleting the names and identity of exporters filing export and optional-origin sale forms, the government maintained that "there are certain instances in which it is generally known that a particular exporter consistently maintains a significant share of exports to a foreign market and/or for a given commodity.[51] The Department reasoned that with or without the exporter's name, I would be able to ascribe export sales, quantities, and destinations to individual companies, presumably on the basis of a knowledge of customary trading relationships and individual firms' specialization in certain commodities.

The importance of this request for information is that it placed the government in a position of openly endorsing conspicuous inadequacies in current policy and law. To date the U.S. government has stepped up its intervention in the export sector without a qualitative improvement in its management capability. Although the Big League may not be sanguine about this turn of events, they continue to hold a monopoly on information, which remains the key to their success.

CONCLUSION

Historically, manipulation of American grain exports has proven highly impractical as a foreign policy tool and actually damaging to the interests of virtually everyone other than the Big League. At best, American food supplies offer Washington an amount of leverage that is of some use in international negotiations. The consequence of this, however, is the introduction of politics into grain policy. PL 480 itself evolved from a surplus disposal to both a foreign policy and development vehicle. An increasing portion of commercial exports is now handled under bilateral sales and purchasing agreements between governments which often take into consideration a wide range of diplomatic priorities. Large foreign purchases are no longer devoid of political implications, even when handled exclusively by private traders whose operations have become so intertwined with governmental bodies.

Periodic government interventions in the marketplace for foreign policy purposes have done nothing to strengthen the U.S. agricultural economy. Governmental efforts to regulate or control grain exports have been frustrated by contradictory policies designed to promote exports, by American agriculture's increasing dependence on foreign demand, and by the oligopoly that dominates the grain trade. To date these complexities seem to have confounded the American bureaucracy. U.S. agripower thus remains nothing more than an inchoate mass of agricultural wealth, the strength of which is converted by the global grain market and national policies into something of a weakness.

To continue to entertain the use of food for foreign policy purposes without preparation and adequate knowledge of the grain trade is not merely an exercise in futility; it is a justification for unnecessary and damaging forms of export controls that could otherwise be avoided. Paradoxically, past applications of such controls on agricultural commodities suggest that they are measures of last resort to be taken when the government finds itself bereft of appropriate alternatives. Bridging the information gap and curbing the excesses of the grain trade business are appropriate steps to avoid a crisis that invites ill-considered embargoes. Otherwise, the U.S. government will be once again forced, whether for domestic economic or foreign policy purposes, back into export controls, abandoning with each such occurrence free market principles. The answer to domestic shortages generally lies elsewhere than with export controls, and U.S. foreign policy and overall economic interests would be best advanced by a disavowal of the phantom food weapon.

NOTES

1. Under the Export Administration Act of 1969 the Secretary of Agriculture had the sole authority to determine shortages in agricultural commodities.

2. U.S. Department of Agriculture, "USDA Auditors Report: Comments." (Manuscript FOIA material.)

3. Confirmed shipments: Unpublished reports prepared by M. Omori for the American Soybean Association, Tokyo.

4. U.S. Congress, Senate, Committee on Foreign Relations, *Multinational Corporations and United States Foreign Policy, Hearings before the Subcommittee on Multinational Corporations*, 94th Cong., 2d sess., 18, 23, and 24 June 1976, Pt. 16, p. 244.

5. Ibid., pp. 244-248.

6. U.S. General Accounting Office, *Impact of Soybean Exports on Domestic Supplies and Prices*, B-178753 (Washington, D.C.: Comptroller General of the United States, 22 March 1974). Also refer to U.S. Congress, Senate, Committee on Banking, Housing and Urban Affairs, *Export Priorities Act, Hearings*, 93d Cong., 1st sess., 26 and 27 September 1973, pp. 191-92.

7. U.S. Department of Commerce, *Conference*. Remarks of Mr. Stephen Lazarus from the original transcript, p. 3.

8. Section 812, *Agricultural Act of 1970*, amended by the Agriculture and Consumer Act of 1973 (PL 93-86).

9. U.S. Congress, Senate, Committee on Government Operations, *Sales of Grain to the Soviet Union, Hearings before the Permanent Subcommittee on Investigations*, 93d Cong., 2d sess., 8 October 1974, pp. 13-32.

10. Mitchel B. Wallerstein, *Food for Peace–Food for War: U.S. Food Aid in a Global Context* (Cambridge: MIT Press, 1980), p. 189.

11. Refer to John G. Merriam, "U.S. Wheat to Egypt: The Use of an Agricultural Commodity as a Foreign Policy Tool," in *The Role of U.S. Agriculture in Foreign Policy*, Richard M. Fraenkel, Don F. Hadwiger, and William P. Browne, eds. (New York: Praeger, 1979), pp. 95-99.

12. "Food: Potent U.S. Weapon, Interview with Earl L. Butz, Secretary of Agriculture," *U.S. News & World Report*, 16 February 1976, pp. 26-28.

13. Emma Rothschild, "Food Politics," *Foreign Affairs* 54 (January 1976): 296.

14. Joseph Gleason Gavin III, "The Political Economy of U.S. Agricultural Export Policy, 1971-1975: Government Response to a Changing Economic Environment," Ph. D. dissertation, Faculty of Political Science, Columbia University, 1979, p. 339.

15. Henry A. Kissinger, *White House Years* (Boston: Little, Brown, 1979), p. 1134.

16. Ibid., p. 1270.

17. U.S. Congress, Senate, Committee on Government Operations, *Russian Grain Transactions, Hearings before the Permanent Subcommittee on Investigations*, 93d Cong., 1st sess., 1973. Testimony of Earl L. Butz, Secretary of Agriculture, p. 92.

18. U.S. Central Intelligence Agency, *Potential Implications of Trends in World Population, Food Production, and Climate*, OPR-401, August 1974, p. 25.

19. Earl L. Butz, quoted in U.S. Department of Agriculture, *NEWS*, USDA 3472-75, 1 December 1975.

20. Dan Morgan, *Merchants of Grain* (New York: Viking, 1979), p. 268.

21. "Privileged and Confidential Advice of Counsel" (memorandum to the Board of Directors of the National Association of Wheat Growers, 16 January 1976).

22. Refer to I. M. Destler, "United States Food Policy 1972-1976: Reconciling Domestic and International Objectives," *International Organization* 32 (Summer 1978): 648-649.

23. U.S. Department of State, Bureau of Intelligence and Research, memorandum, "Soviet Wheat Purchases Confirmed," Report No. 33 (18 July 1975); and Dan Morgan, *Merchants of Grain* (New York: Viking, 1979), p. 275.

24. Charles W. Robinson, former Undersecretary for Economic Affairs, U.S. Department of State, in conversation with Richard Gilmore, per correspondence from the latter dated 27 October 1978.

25. Leslie H. Gelb and Anthony Lake, "Washington Dateline: Less Food, More Politics," *Foreign Policy*, no. 17 (Winter 1974-75): 179-181.

26. President Gerald R. Ford, "Remarks at the Annual Convention of the American Farm Bureau Federation in St. Louis, January 5, 1976," *Public Papers of Presidents of the United States, Gerald R. Ford, 1976-77*, Bk. I, 1 January and 9 April 1976 (Washington: U.S. Government Printing Office, 1979), p. 17.

27. Jimmy Carter, National Public Radio, Call-Out Program, 13 October 1979, printed in *NPR Selected Statements 79-6*, ed. Robert Rudney, 1 November 1979, p. 31.

28. Secretary of Agriculture Bob Bergland, quoted in "Wheat Cartel Modeled on OPEC Is Urged by Some American, Canadian Politicians," *Wall Street Journal*, 31 August 1978, p. 26.

29. As in the popular recording by Brent Burns and Bobby "Sofine" Butler, "Cheaper Crude or No More Food," IBC Record, 1979.

30. The average from members of all farm organizations polled was 88 percent in favor of establishing a wheat cartel. Richard Gilmore, Producer Questionnaire.

31. Richard Gilmore, "Why a Food Embargo Won't Work," *Washington Post*, 27 December 1979, p. A17; "Four Shiploads of U.S. Wheat Diverted to Iran in 1980," *Journal of Commerce*, 31 February 1981, p. 9; and "U.S. Company Pleads Guilty in Violation of Iran Trade Embargo," *Wall Street Journal*, 25 February 1981, p. 42.

32. Individuals directly involved in the embargo decision have made this claim; and U.S. General Accounting Office, *Report on Lessons to be Learned from Offsetting the Impact of the Soviet Grain Sales Suspension*, p. 9.

33. Richard Gilmore, "Reagan Right in Lifting the Grain Embargo," *Journal of Commerce*, 1 May 1981, p. 4.

34. Norman C. Miller, *The Great Salad Oil Swindle* (New York: Coward McCann, 1965), pp. 52-53.

35. U.S. Congress, Senate, Committee on Foreign Relations, *Multinational Corporations*, Pt. 16, p. 155.

36. Data obtained in 1978-79 from the Regional Statistical Office of the Port of Hamburg (Statistisches Landesamt der Freien und Hansestadt Hamburg) on Transit of Grain, Oil Plants and Oil Cake via Hamburg. Manuscript.

37. Ibid.

38. U.S. General Accounting Office, *Report on Irregularities in the Marketing of Grain. An Evaluation of the Inspection and Weighing of Grain, Prepared for the U.S. Senate, Committee on Agriculture and Forestry and the House, Committee on Agriculture*, 17 February 1976 (Washington: U.S. Government Printing Office, 1976), pp. 29-30.

39. U.S Department of Agriculture, Office of Audit, *Export Sales Reporting Program*, FAS, Audit Report No. 60207-13Hy (Washington, D.C., January 1977), p. 8.

40. Ibid., p. 5.

41. Ibid., p. 21.

42. U.S. Department of Agriculture, "Report of the Advisory Committee on Export Sales Reporting to the Secretary of Agriculture Bob Bergland," 27 February 1979, p. 9. Mimeographed.

43. U.S. Department of Agriculture, Office of Audit, *Export Sales Reporting Program*, pp. 32-33.

44. U.S. Department of Agriculture, "Draft Report of the Advisory Committee on Export Sales Reporting to Secretary of Agriculture Bob Bergland," 15 February 1979, p. 15. Mimeographed.

45. U.S. Department of Agriculture, "Report of the Advisory Committee," p. 2.

46. U.S. General Accounting Office, *Report on Lessons to be Learned from Offsetting the Impact of the Soviet Grain Sales Suspension*, CED-81-110 (Washington, D.C.: Comptroller General of the United States, 27 July 1981).

47. The lawsuit was dismissed by stipulation with prejudice, 10 August 1979. For further information see United Press International (UPI) stories of 9 December 1979 and 16 July 1979.

48. "Affidavit of George S. Shanklin," filed 23 April 1979 in *Gilmore* v. *Department of Agriculture et al*. Civil action No. 79-0863, U.S. District Court, District of Columbia, pp. 2-3.

49. Ibid., p. 3.

50. Ibid., pp. 2-3.

51. "Affidavit of Dr. Kelly Harrison, General Sales Manager, U.S. Department of Agriculture," filed 23 April 1979 in *Gilmore* v. *Department of Agriculture et al, p. 2*.

9

Multilateral Agreements: History and Prospects

Joseph was the original Secretary of Agriculture. He invented the ever-normal grain rate [granary] thousands of years ago and it is a pretty good lesson.
—ROBERT BERGLAND, *Secretary of Agriculture*

The history of international efforts to create an ever normal granary is one of successive failure. Exporters too often have attempted to boost prices without offering in return an adequate commitment on supplies; importers' purchasing commitments have been purposely vague on amounts and price levels. Foreign assistance plans grafted onto recent international accords have been strictly voluntary and too frequently linked to surplus positions of exporting countries.

Despite the international proportions of food issues, most countries have sought and continue to seek refuge from their problems unilaterally. Food deficits or surpluses are seen as short-term problems. Dwindling returns to efficient producers are considered aberrations. Expensive, inefficient agricultural systems are too often viewed as necessary to self-sufficiency and national food security. Given such reasoning, the establishment of adequate food reserves and multilateral coordination of agricultural policies have generally not been given serious consideration. Even so, there have been numerous efforts to solve the food problem, in whole or in part, through international agreements. The debate, it seems, is never ending and unchanging as are the results: international reserve and price plans doomed, almost from their inception, to rapid disintegration and failure.

Multilateral agreements, generally involving the withholding of wheat supplies from the market in order to keep a floor under international prices, have been particularly appealing to surplus producers whose agricultural prosperity is so closely linked to foreign consumption patterns. Their numbers have decreased to the point that there are now only five major wheat suppliers, notwithstanding intensive national self-sufficiency programs worldwide to reduce other countries' dependence on these few supply sources for such a staple food item. Demand for wheat, nonetheless, has nearly doubled in the last 20 years, mainly in response to rapid population growth, rising incomes, and accompanying changes in nutritional standards. Under present circumstances, general economic and agricultural conditions worldwide now have a direct, vital impact among this small group of suppliers. They have consequently a built-in incentive for a coordinated approach to their agricultural policies, particularly regarding exports, and yet an agreed, practical formula has consistently eluded them.

Importers, too, have an incentive to join in a concerted strategy for handling their purchases. Multilateral schemes have offered the promise of stabilized prices and food security through assured access to foreign supplies over an extended period of time. Many in this group have recognized periodically that self-sufficiency in wheat production is a costly if not an unachievable goal. Like exporters, however, their willingness to participate in any joint plan of an international scope has not been sustained for a long duration.

Wartime has been the exception to the rule. Under such conditions, food concerns become a matter of shared strategic interest that cuts across the traditional divisions between importers and exporters. During war conditions distributional and pricing requirements take priority over ideological commitments to an unregulated market or national aversion to multilateral coordination of the handling of food supplies. In his letter to President Wilson in July 1917 Herbert Hoover, as the U.S. government's first food administrator during World War I, painted a dire picture of the domestic wheat market and called for government controls.

> The experience this year in the rampant speculation, extortionate profits and the prospect of even narrower supplies than the 1916 harvest and carry-over, must cause the deepest anxiety. . . . the producer received an average of $1.51 per bushel for the 1916 wheat harvest and yet wheat has been as high as $3.25 at Chicago . . . so that through one evil cause or another, the consumer has suffered from 50 to 100 percent, and the producer gained nothing. After much study and investigation, it is evident that this unbearable increase in margin between producer and consumer is due not only to rank speculation, but more largely than this to the wide margin of profit naturally demanded by every link in the chain to insure them from the great hazards of trade in the widely fluctuating and dangerous price situation during the year when all normal stabilization has been lost through the interruption of world trade and war.[1]

Amid the disruption of war, even the archbishops of the trade accepted the wisdom of government intervention to correct those grave disturbances that an unregulated market was unable to handle.

> We realize that our Country is at war, and that under war conditions, many measures are necessary in the public interest, which would, under ordinary circumstances, be unwise and unnecessary. . . . direct Government control of the transportation of foodstuffs is absolutely necessaary for their better distribution.

. . . In all justice to our Allies, we must conserve all (wheat) supplies, distribute them economically and apportion them fairly between our own needs and those of our Allies . . . This control of wheat prices may be in such form that the trading in futures on the public exchanges . . . may be, for the time being, discontinued.[2]

The result was the establishment in 1917 of the Food Administration Grain Corporation (later known as the United States Grain Corporation). Its assignment was to dislodge bottlenecks created by wartime demands in the purchase, pricing, storage, and distribution of American wheat and wheat flour, and to restore order to a system thrown out of joint by Allied food requisitions. Grain exports, long secondary in importance to domestic consumption requirements, suddenly assumed primary importance by 1917. For perhaps the first (but certainly not the last) time, exports of American grain exceeded domestic sales.

The Allies also recognized that normal commercial practices would not ensure access to adequate supplies and found it necessary to consolidate their wartime purchasing in the United States and Canada under a public corporation known as the Wheat Export Company. The creation of its American counterpart, the U.S. Grain Corporation, served to balance the economic power of Europe's new monopolistic purchasing agency. Canada shortly followed suit and established the Board of Grain Supervisors, a body analogous to the U.S. Grain Corporation.

The wartime Wheat Executive Agreement of 1916 provided the international framework to coordinate allied shipments among these newly established government sales and purchasing agencies. The United States, Canada, and Australia were anxious to compensate for Europe's shortages and in the process induce an upswing in export prices. The inter-allied Wheat Executive sat in London, delegating responsibility for food deliveries to the British Royal Commission on Wheat Supplies.[3] This was no simple task because it involved chartering vessels to run Germany's tight blockade of the Continent. Nevertheless, the Royal Commission proved equal to the challenge and was effective at both allocating supplies and ensuring deliveries under a quota system, which temporarily pulled wheat export prices out of their slump. At the conclusion of the war, however, the accepted view was that the agreement's purpose had ended. And so it seemed. Without the aid of a Wheat Executive or an international agreement, Europe's agricultural economy recovered rapidly. In less than six years Europe became a wheat surplus region rather than a major importing area. And with the general economic prosperity of the 1920s came high commodity prices, which took the edge off pressures for a wheat agreement.

When the Crash ended the economic prosperity of the 1920s, many countries other than the United States clamored for a return to a multilateral agreement that would restore order in the wheat market. No such agreement was forthcoming. In 1931 surplus-ridden Central European countries sought preferential access to markets in Western Europe.[4] The importing nations of Western Europe, the U.K., Germany, the Netherlands, Italy, and Austria were in turn willing to accept a quota system provided the United States would also accept the idea of limiting its exports. At that time, the United States rejected any agreement containing quotas or fixed international wheat prices.[5] It argued that a quota system without production controls was misguided[6] and further that adherence to a system of export quotas would be inherently inimical to the U.S. economy.[7]

Two years later, however, the United States was prepared to accept some of the things it had eschewed in 1931. The Agricultural Adjustment Act (AAA) ushered in an epoch of federal agricultural programs designed to protect farmer incomes and an international policy of multilateral production controls and export quotas to bolster prices. The Depression years of economic disarray underlined the necessity for public participation in the agricultural sector both at the national and international level. The New Deal's AAA of 1933 gave birth to the Commodity Credit Corporation (CCC), which became the buyer and seller of last resort for American producers plus the creditor of domestic agricultural programs. Canada and Australia established national wheat boards with monopoly powers in the export sector. Importers and exporters developed more centralized marketing systems at home and turned with renewed interest to a multilateral wheat agreement to remedy some of their immediate domestic economic requirements.

Secretary of Agriculture Henry Wallace argued on behalf of an accord among the world's largest wheat exporters. Without such an agreement, he suggested, the United States would be prepared to undercut the other major suppliers, whose agricultural economies were more dependent than America's on high export prices.

> We have the legal authority and the economic resources to engage in competitive export dumping to an extent which would drive world market prices of wheat in Australia and Argentina down to zero. We hope such action will not be necessary. Unless other exporters will cooperate with us in correcting the present situation, we may be forced to take such steps to protect our own interests in world markets, and to bring other countries to the realization of the eventual need for world cooperation.[8]

This American hard line plus a succession of two good European harvests finally helped produce the International Wheat Agreement of 1933, the first of its kind. Under its terms, producers accepted export quotas in exchange for importer purchasing commitments. National market shares were to be assigned on the basis of average production minus domestic consumption with any remaining surplus subject to an agreed export limit. In the first year of the agreement, Canada received the largest export share, 5.4 million tons, and the United States one of the smaller shares, 1.3 million tons. Argentina's share was 3 million tons and Australia's 2.8 million tons; the share of the Eastern European states (the "Danubian group") was 1.5 million tons. No 1933 quota was established for the USSR, which was dissatisfied with the quota negotiations and, in fact, never did accept the production targets assigned to it.[9]

Aside from the establishment of export quotas, the treaty's other major feature was a uniform pricing system. The international price of wheat was pegged to gold and different prices were assigned to different types of wheat, all of which were thereby made convertible into universally accepted units of exchange. Once the average minimum price of any wheat had been sustained over a period of 16 weeks, importers were to begin adjusting their tariffs downward, on the theory that a higher average international price would obviate the need for high tariff walls to protect their agricultural production. These prices were, of course, predicated on a continuation of the gold standard, to which all participants were committed when the treaty was signed. Production restraints among exporters, and importers' obligations to reduce their tariff rates, were linked to higher prices. Quotas, in turn, depended on production and consumption levels. Each of the objectives set in the agreement was linked so tightly to the others that when one went unmet, the others faced the same fate. So ultimately did the entire structure. Before the ink was dry, most signatories abandoned the gold standard. Argentina had a bumper crop in the spring of 1934, which it did not store but moved onto the world market in violation of the quota system. A good European harvest made export quotas all the more unappealing and worsened the prospects for adherence to the agreement.

Although overly detailed, the 1933 agreement's main weakness lay with an inadequate commitment by its members. Argentina, which joined reluctantly, clung to an expectation that private intermediaries, such as Dreyfus and Bunge which dominated the nation's export sector at that time, would do more for the country's economy in sales than any wheat agreement could do.[10] Russia was dissatisfied from the start. Canada was burdened with surpluses, which created great pressures at home that the agreement could not relieve. Indeed, in the 1930-31 round of negotiations, Canadian millers and wheat traders were opposed to any quota plan and were hurt severely by the surpluses that followed acceptance of the 1933 version. Canada was subsequently in no mood to change the rules to accommodate Argentina's problem when its own endorsement of the agreement had already entailed such substantial political and economic costs.

Under these circumstances, the 1933 agreement proved inadequate. International regulations to control the flow of trade were meaningless so long as the principal wheat suppliers looked to exports as the preferred way to relieve their stock burdens. Demands placed on importers to reduce their protectionist policies were ineffective in the face of a market cycle for wheat that produced brief periods of cheap grain with plentiful harvests. A uniform pricing system dependent on governmental enforcement was inadequate when export markets were dominated by a few companies. The 1933 plan demanded too much in some respects and too little in others. Its failure was preordained. By 1935 the agreement was virtually inoperative, the need for it having been preempted by a fortuitous balance between global wheat production and consumption.

Such a state of affairs, however, could only be transitory. When prices showed signs of plummeting again in 1939, governments once again convened to work out a new international wheat agreement. Secretary Henry Wallace spearheaded an effort to come up with a stabilization plan—"the ever normal granary," which was to be the international counterpart of the New Deal's domestic agricultural program. Under the Wallace plan, food resources would be built up through a joint system of international reserves and production controls, balanced by an "equitable" formula for distribution of supply worldwide.

> As part of the effort to win the peace, I am hoping that what might be called the "ever normal granary principle" can be established for a number of commodities on a world-wide scale. It will be remembered that the fourth point of the eight points agreed upon by Roosevelt and Churchill in the Atlantic Charter mentioned the enjoying by all states, great and small, victor or vanquished, of access on equal terms to the raw materials of the world. To give this lofty ideal a more definite substance should be one of our chief objectives in the months that lie immediately ahead.[11]

It was a noteworthy proposal. To be sure, beneath the rhetoric lay the classic motivation of a country seeking multilateral assistance to help its own agricultural economy out of a slump. At that time, the United States was still plagued by depressed prices from an ailing agricultural sector and had not yet recuperated from the losses of the Great Depression. Accordingly, under the Wallace plan, stabilization was construed to mean higher export prices and a distribution formula that allocated market shares among suppliers.

The U.S. proposal for a new wheat agreement in 1939 certainly reflected its own economic interests, but the absence of an agreed export-import system led the United States to resort to accelerating its export subsidy program unilaterally. Other producers laden with surpluses pursued a similar course. With the outbreak of World War II in Europe the situation changed considerably, harkening to the period of 1916. In 1941, another drafting session took place in Washington, where Wallace attempted to revive and harden the evernormal granary concept. By this time, the U.S. position linked reserves and food aid to a mutually acceptable quota and pricing plan. The Secretary's proposals were somewhat out-of-step with influential American groups, which sought higher export prices and a greater share of the market for the United States. Importers were equally skeptical. Consequently, the 1942 draft memorandum of Agreement that had adopted much of the original Wallace idea was never warmly endorsed and wartime conditions altered priorities long enough to delay a final agreement until 1949.

Under the 1942 agreement, the U.S. quota was 16 percent of the total, a share that was above its actual share of the world market at the time.[12] Lord Keynes reacted to the U.S. and other exporters' allocations by calling the original 1942 plan "a fantastic piece of chicanery."[13] He viewed it as a deck stacked in favor of the exporters and was upset over the reserve and pricing provisions. A realistic stabilization scheme, he maintained, would require larger reserves and pricing provisions more accommodating of importers' requirements. The private grain moguls were also vehemently opposed to the 1942 draft agreement.[14] Needless to say, their objections were different from those of Lord Keynes. Any tinkering with the market along the lines of the proposed agreement was, in their estimation, a dangerous precedent.

The problems of 1933 haunted the 1942 initiative. Importers, led by the U.K., had sought lower prices and higher quotas to ensure access to wheat supplies at reasonable prices. Exporters, such as the United States and Canada, sought agreed higher prices at the highest possible total export-import quotas in an effort to maximize their revenues and thereby underwrite the costs of domestic programs associated with their surpluses. In the eyes of European importing countries, the plan was more an exporters' cartel than an ever normal granary for the world.

A more fundamental issue, however, was the question of enforcement. This was to be provided by the International Wheat Council (IWC) established in 1942. That body, however, was constrained from the outset by insufficient market information. To monitor prices effectively, the IWC needed timely, accurate price reports from member governments, which was virtually impossible as long as members continued to rely exclusively on the private sector for export news. The Council was twice removed from the source of information. And such information as was available was undoubtedly colored by the private sector's opposition to a uniform pricing system or official inquiries of any kind concerning their activities. The plan's own defects, world crop conditions, and a lack of total cooperation from the public and private sectors hampered the 1942 initiative.

For American and Canadian agriculture, the years between the trial balloon of 1942 and the next major grain agreement in 1949 were generally prosperous times due, in no small part, to the fact that Europe was temporarily unable to satisfy its own substantial food requirements under war-torn economic conditions. During this period, the United States willingly filled the breach by becoming the world's breadbasket and moved more wheat and wheat flour into the export stream than ever before. The Economic Recovery Program (ERP) succeeded in providing much needed food relief to Europe and offered U.S. producers, and the government, a welcome opportunity to dispose of mounting grain surpluses, making them available for European consumption at less than commercial rates.

With the conclusion of ERP and the prospect of slackening exports came renewed pressure for an international agreement. Work on such a new agreement was concluded in 1948 when the Washington conference of the IWC issued a new draft agreement. Although less comprehensive than the 1942 initiative, it was more realistic and faithful to traditional concerns of exporters. In selling the benefits of the agreement to the U.S. Congress in 1948, government officials stated:

> We have the picture before us of competition for markets by exporters. You will have a lot of bilateral agreements sent up. The United States might find itself here

with no outlets except for the occupied zones and a few small ones we could pick up. The other people would be practically taking the markets. (*Secretary [Acting] of Agriculture,* NORRIS DODD.)

The principal attraction of the agreement . . . namely that it assures a definite export market for United States wheat at prices not lower than the minimum price which it provides . . . It is a choice as to whether we would be content to see the more desirable markets signed up on a bilateral basis by other countries or whether we would be prepared to enter into competition in terms of trying to pre-empt those markets through bilateral agreements ourselves. . . . In that circumstance it would seem to me that the possibility, without some arrangement like this wheat agreement, of having a return to a fairly free flow of wheat among the markets of the world just has to be written off.[15] (*Assistant Secretary of State,* WILLARD THORP.)

Although Congress was unconvinced at the outset, the Truman administration portrayed the plan as a means of maintaining and even increasing U.S. grain exports. It was the administration's hope that the U.S. export quota, which was to apply only when prices were within a predetermined minimum-maximum range, would be set at an even higher level than the nation's average export market share at the time the agreement was to be signed.

One of the plan's provisions was the establishment of a modest reserve to be either released onto the world market or built up as circumstances required. The function of the reserve was to reduce price fluctuations associated with changes in supply and also to reinforce the quota allocations. But despite the lure of potentially great export sales under the quota system, and despite the precedent of government-owned domestic reserves held by the CCC, opponents of the 1948 proposal argued that it was an open invitation for more government intervention and thus a structural distortion of the commodity market: "If this gigantic cartel is carried into effect with respect to wheat, it will only be a question of time until other commodities such as corn, cotton, sugar, and so forth, will follow."[16]

In 1948, this argument prevailed. Legislators still accepted the popular view that the United States could do better on its own. But by 1949 market conditions were less favorable for the United States and the Congress came to realize that going it alone was too costly. The year was a sour one for American agriculture and Secretary of Agriculture Charles Brannan took advantage of the altered situation to win acceptance of an agreement: "You know how much the world wheat situation has ·changed within the past year. The severe shortage that prevailed a year ago has been modified. The price has dropped sharply. These changes weakened our hands and strengthened those of the importers."[17]

A modified version of the 1948 plan was thus ratified by the United States in 1949, but not before each of the domestic groups with a vested interest in the proposal had a hand in watering down its original language. American millers, for example, succeeded in modifying the proposed price range to avoid making exported grain too cheap and thereby placing European millers at an advantage. Representatives of the grain trade lobbied to maintain a minimal level of governmental interference with their role as principal handlers of global wheat sales.[18] And in deference to farm groups concerned with the potentially depressing price effects of the proposed reserve, the precise levels of national stocks to be assigned to the international reserve were deliberately left unspecified. In addition, the U.S. government launched the large wheat export subsidy program in 1949 to help meet its obligations by bridging the gap between high domestic prices and the agreement's lower export price range.

Despite its limitations, the 1949 agreement was generally viewed as a success. Signatories included three of the major exporters—Australia, Canada and the United States—as well as a substantial number of importing countries. Importers estimated that they were better off because under the terms of the agreement, they were able to purchase wheat at less than the open market price. Accordingly, they increased their purchase commitments, which assured exporters more sales than they could otherwise reasonably expect. Further, since Argentina and the USSR did not sign the agreement, the three principal exporting nations which did sign saw their participation as an opportunity to lock up as much of the world market as possible via quotas. From their perspective, the Wheat Agreement was a device for channeling more wheat into the export stream at subsidized prices and was preferable to a unilateral export subsidy that might provoke a trade war and further disruption of the world market.[19] The arguments in favor of the agreement were decisive. It placed limited demands on members in exchange for long-term benefits, a feature sufficiently persuasive to attract 46 participating countries by 1952.

The agreement's first four years demonstrated that it was to have only a minimal impact. Shrinking harvests in Europe and a war in Korea, which together served to depress supply and increase demand, did more to bolster world wheat prices than the agreement's quota system. In 1953, when quantities guaranteed to importers under the treaty were at an all-time high, 40 percent of world wheat transactions occurred on the free market. This black market wheat trafficked at prices above the agreement range, which in turn made wheat purchases under the agreement more attractive to importers and kept these purchases at ceiling levels. Throughout this period, the exporting countries, particularly the United States, profited from an expanding market. As a result, in 1953 the United States sought a renewal of the 1949 agreement timed to take advantage of the then higher world prices. Assuming that production would not exceed demand worldwide and that shortages would continue, U.S. officials reasoned that surplus holders, primarily the United States and Canada, could now command a higher price for their exports. Others saw the future differently, notably the U.K., which decided, either out of foresight or good guesswork, to withdraw from the agreement, citing the new higher price range. The withdrawal of the world's largest wheat importer was a major blow to the effectiveness of the treaty, which had already been undermined by the continued refusal of Argentina and the Soviet Union to join.

In the end, the result of the U.S. initiative was the revised agreement in August 1953, which proved even less effective than its predecessor. Transactions between 1953 and 1956 under the treaty accounted for an average of only 26 percent of world trade.[20] With fewer participants, the guaranteed import levels also fell sharply. American, Canadian, and Australian stocks grew as demand slackened after the Korean War. Between 1953 and 1959, Canada and the United States held close to 90 percent of the world's stocks, and accounted for almost 70 percent of total trade in wheat.[21] They were hurt most by the sharp downward shift in demand and resulting lower price levels, which the 1953 agreement's loose quota-pricing system failed to alleviate in any way.

Unable to rely on the agreement to support prices at a time of world surplus, the United States spawned its food assistance program, PL 480, as a means of drawing down stocks and keeping a floor under U.S. grain prices. With the prospect of PL 480 becoming a vehicle for massive dumping of U.S surpluses, which would undermine competing countries' traditional shares of the global grain market, other exporters insisted on a common set of groundrules. Members of the UN Food and Agricultural Organization (FAO) convened in 1953 and agreed upon a set of principles and mechanisms for coordinating all food assistance efforts. To curb the threat of PL 480, they accepted three main FAO guidelines on surplus disposal: (1) disposal should occur when it is increasing consumption rather than restricting supplies; (2) it should be conducted in an orderly manner; and (3) it should not interfere with "normal patterns of production and international trade."[22] Leading exporters and importers joined the Consultative Subcommittee on Surplus Disposal (CSD) established in 1954 for purposes of enforcing these guidelines.

To the extent that CSD was effective at all, it was due to a sense of shared interest among participants that was harder to discern in the larger, more heterogeneous setting of the International Wheat Council. CSD offered a UN-sanctioned forum for suppliers to discuss elements of maintaining orderly markets in the grain trade through the coordinated handling of their food aid and commercial exports. Although accepted under the General Agreement on Tariffs and Trade (GATT) code for free trade,[23] critics labeled CSD a rich man's club, an incipient wheat cartel.[24] In fact, CSD was little more than a weak shell. The real axis for any successful orderly marketing in wheat during the 1950s and 1960s was Canada and the United States, which accounted for roughly 65 percent of the world's total wheat exports. Their synchronized export strategy did more than either the CSD or the Wheat Agreement to keep the international price of wheat from plummeting, but the 1953 agreement at least served to legitimize their efforts to control the market.

Eventually the costs of U.S.-Canadian management of the world wheat system grew as rich harvests continued unabated in the absence of an international reserve system to absorb surpluses. In 1965 Australia, Argentina, and

France found themselves in a surplus position and could afford to attempt to undercut the Canadian-American price. The two giant exporters slashed prices as a means of defending their market position. What began as an international wheat war ended swiftly with a successful but costly blitz by the two-nation cartel of Canada and the United States.

They could not, however, sustain over an extended period of time a monopoly position in the global wheat market. By the late 1960s the EC, namely France, was developing into a residual supplier of wheat on the world market. Europe's Common Agricultural Policy (CAP) was viewed as a major disruptive force, since its export restitution system could undercut U.S. and Canadian prices for both wheat and wheat flour. Some accommodation had to be reached with the EC and neither the CSD nor the smaller grouping, the Wheat Utilization Committee (WUC) which was established in 1959, proved to be the appropriate forum. The Kennedy Round of Trade negotiations that began in 1962 offered an ideal opportunity to tame some of the worst effects of CAP and the common market system in exchange for a new wheat agreement that took greater account of EC member country interests. Although certain sensitive areas like agricultural export subsidies were left untouched, all parties to the trade negotiations recognized the need to avoid an agricultural trade war that depended on a successful outcome of the Kennedy Round as well as a new wheat agreement.

Initially, private exporters had advocated an end to U.S. participation in the 1962 agreement,[25] complaining, once again, about the restrictive nature of a wheat accord, particularly with respect to set prices. But by 1965, they were willing to accept a watered-down extension as the prerequisite for removal of more onerous trade restrictions in the Kennedy Round. Exporting countries feared that, unless subjected to international controls, an unbridled CAP would be adopted by the EC, resulting in the restriction of member grain imports and the dumping of European surpluses on the world market. From the European standpoint, there was general apprehension that without some formal understanding, the food producing Goliaths—Canada, Australia, and the United States—acting in common, would try to undercut CAP. Importers, such as Japan, were concerned about the effect of any export control strategy on their access to foreign food resources. Together, these factors led to the signing in Geneva of a memorandum on the basic elements for negotiation of a world grain arrangement at the end of the Kennedy Round.

Pursuant to the Kennedy Round memorandum, a conference was held in Rome in the summer of 1967 to agree upon the text. The timing was ripe for the signing of the Wheat Trade Convention (WTC) (to replace previous wheat agreements) and the Food Aid Convention (FAC), both of which were instruments of the International Grains Arrangement (IGA). In that year the supply picture was uncertain. U.S. wheat production was off, while its year-end stock position during the previous year had reached an all-time low. Price levels had risen. Exporters were in the enviable position of negotiating under bullish conditions. Larger importers such as Japan, which had accepted a sharp reduction in its import duties during the Kennedy Round, and the U.K., which had dropped altogether its soybean tariff during those negotiations,[26] were willing to accept an agreement with a higher price floor in exchange for guarantees of a higher minimum level of food imports, especially since the pricing formula proposed was sufficiently flexible to allow importers to profit during a bearish market.

The EC was likewise acquiescent. From the perspective of its member governments, the WTC represented a means of stabilizing wheat prices at a level higher than would have been obtained in a completely unregulated market. As a result, relatively expensive European wheat would become more competitive in price with that of the largest exporters, which would work to the EC's advantage in both export and domestic markets. In effect, the IGA established a cartel-like arrangement among exporters, and sacrificed the open trade principles reaffirmed in the Kennedy Round in exchange for more orderly world trading conditions in wheat. Despite the higher prices, developing countries accepted the scheme because it offered the prospect of price stabilization coupled with a commitment to food assistance on the part of the major exporters.

Under the FAC, donors agreed to commit fixed quantities of wheat, wheat flour, or cash equivalents to LDCs. This was welcomed by the United States as a way of keeping a floor under world wheat prices and absorbing a portion of the European wheat, which might otherwise have been used for feed. In an institutional sense, the FAC explicitly tied an international agreement for commercial grain sales to worldwide food aid commitments. Such a principle had first been implicitly espoused in Wallace's ever-normal granary plan.

Besides the FAC, the new IGA contained a number of innovations designed to avoid the pitfalls of the past. Rather than imposing unrealistic uniform prices for a variety of wheats, the 1967 WTC provided for different pricing schedules for each of 14 wheat types. A Price Review Committee was established within the IWC and given power to monitor prices and make temporary adjustments in minimum prices under exceptional market conditions. Both provisions were intended to introduce more flexibility than earlier arrangements and thus enhance enforcement prospects for a minimum set of groundrules.

In 1967 IGA also eliminated explicit export quotas in an effort to accommodate changing supply patterns and avoid rigid regulations, which members had repeatedly breached in the past. It included instead an ambiguous concept of market shares, which in reality did more to recognize traditional regional trading relationships of the major exporters than to assign fixed export quantities to each country. Quotas had proved to be an unworkable means of supporting export prices. The new arrangement offered a more flexible way to attain a long sought objective. The importance of this aim was publicly acknowledged by the U.S. Secretary of Agriculture, Orville Freeman: "But make no mistake about one key point. We are as determined to maintain our markets abroad as we are to make the Arrangement work."[27]

Despite its innovations, the ultimate effectiveness of the new system still depended upon mutual understanding among the principal wheat supplying countries and stable market conditions. In times of surplus, for example, the regulations once again proved unenforceable, and these times arrived quickly indeed. In a rapid turnaround from the previous year, the 1968 global wheat crop was beyond member governments' expectations. Countries outside the pact—among others the Soviet Union, Hungary, and Yugoslavia—were more than willing to sell below minimum prices to interested buyers. Under such conditions, although the agreement provided that the price of imports from nonmember countries should conform to the Council's schedules, importers quickly found reasons to renege on that portion of their commitment.

Exporters proved equally disloyal. As world prices dropped, American complaints about the pricing formula rose. The United States claimed the system worked in favor of higher-priced Canadian and Australian wheat. It also singled out and charged Australia with violating the agreement by concealing sales prices below the agreed minimum through inflated shipping rates. Under the agreement, those rates were to be based on a Gulf f.o.b. standard minus shipping and related services. Since rates from Sydney to London or Rotterdam were normally the cheapest in the world, Australia could reduce the f.o.b. Gulf price by artificially hiking these rates as part of its final export price quotation. In subsequent years, the United States never forgot Australia's alleged tampering with the system and used this case to support its opposition to any fixed pricing scheme. The United States also complained that several classes of foreign wheat were not covered by the agreement, whereas four American types had fixed prices. In effect, this loophole permitted nonagreement wheats to be traded on an unregulated basis, thereby underpricing standard types for which prices were set.[28]

In addition to its complaints about pricing under the agreement, the United States also protested invasions into its traditional markets by other exporters, notably France. France, the Americans complained, had intruded on American turf in 1968 in the Francéréales group's sales of milling wheat to Japan and Taiwan at subsidized prices in violation of both GATT rules and the 1967 IGA. Canada and Australia concurred. From the Canadian standpoint, such unilateral price-cutting devices threatened the effectiveness of a wheat producers' cartel blessed by the 1967 Wheat Agreement, whose enforcement was essential to Canadian farmers' incomes. In a closed-door session with U.S. Secretary of Agriculture Clifford Hardin, the Canadian minister of External Affairs argued that: "The collapse of the IGA would be a very serious matter. No one is blameless in this; there are intense pressures. We would be back to a dog-eat-dog situation. *It [IGA] is a sanctified cartel.*"[29]

The Australian producer's position was not much different from that of his Canadian counterpart. Both were highly dependent on a central wheat board, which could not long have stayed afloat in the face of plummeting wheat prices. Upset over the prospect that the United States could lower its prices unilaterally in reaction to other countries selling below the IGA minimums, Australia was persuaded, in response to Canadian and U.S. pressure, to join in a proposal to restore an Exporters' Club that would combat the threatened collapse in world wheat prices. By 1968, an informal caucus of wheat exporters—the United States, Canada, Australia, Argentina, and the EC—emerged with the governing purpose of making the IGA work and thereby avoiding a wheat war.

With its main objective to establish orderly marketing in wheat and secondarily in feedgrains, the Exporters' Group, as it was called, hosted private meetings where members exchanged extensive information weekly concerning the status and terms of export transactions. Members used these meetings, and continue to do so, to assert their "traditional markets" for grain exports. The Exporters' Group was in effect a rudimentary wheat cartel, more so than the CSD or WUC, sanctioned both by importers and exporters adhering to the WTC of 1967. Canada and Australia indicated a preference for using the Group for this very purpose. The Australian representative echoed the thoughts of Canadian Agricultural Minister Sharp at the June 1969 meeting of the Group on the cartel-like function of the assembly to maintain uniform, compatible export prices for members of the Group.

The United States, on the other hand, was prepared to abandon common pricing in exchange for a realistic export quota system, since its traditional interest was more in disposal of surpluses than in high export prices and lower volumes. In the estimation of U.S. government officials, quotas were likely to be a more permanent solution than vain attempts to sustain high fixed prices. Thus, the U.S. delegation to an earlier exporters' meeting in Canberra, Australia, in 1968, had proposed that the major exporting countries agree "on a system of informal market shares."

> The U.S. would not favor the establishment of specific quotas for each exporter, but rather a percentage share which would be consistent with each exporter's normal market participation, and would serve as a continuing guideline permitting each exporter to know at all times whether and what degree of sales restraint is incumbent upon him.[30]

As was perhaps inevitable given the American position of strength, the new proposal carried the day with the support of both Canada and Australia. Europe was reluctant. CAP had brought them the mixed blessing of surplus wheat stocks, and the EC members had their own trading partners—remnants, for the most part, of the colonial period. A quota system, especially one under U.S. leadership, threatened to disrupt these established trading relationships. On the other hand, France, Europe's principal wheat producer, could not fight the big three alone. As a result, the EC agreed to accept the de facto quotas created by the new arrangement and became a nonparticipating member of the Exporters' Group.

The working subgroups of the Exporters' Group, the price and monitoring group, did include the EC and served potentially as an important information resource for the Wheat Council. The whole purpose of this substructure outside the IGA was to cope with technical matters that the International Wheat Council and Price Review Committee were not equipped to handle.

Effective implementation of any quota scheme required that participating governments confer on the basis of accurate and timely commercial information. This had not been possible under the original IGA framework because the members themselves were not forthcoming.

In contrast to previous agreements, the new system was hampered less by an absence of governmental consensus than by faulty and inadequate information. Most of the governments of the five major exporters, in fact, were in the dark regarding prices and shipments. As other exporters had noted, the American system contained loopholes that worked to the advantage of the private trade and hindered U.S. fulfillment of its international obligations.[31] In an effort to keep its export prices within the range specified by IGA, the United States established a program of export subsidies. However, under the existing system, the private trade could sell American grain below the established subsidy price and still make a profit. When the firms did so, they undercut the international price. There were a number of ways in which this could be done:

> Since the United States Government has no control over individual transactions, it is occasionally possible for a U.S. exporter to sell below the minimum if he is willing to forego his normal or speculative profit. Thus, a U.S. exporter may offer wheat below the computed f.o.b. price plus export certificate for one or more of the following reasons: (1) a long position based on purchases when the domestic market was lower; (2) fixing of the export certificate when the cost of the export certificate was lower; e.g., after the sale was made; (3) hedging on the futures market; (4) purchases of distressed wheat at below the market price; (5) the need to clear elevator space by the firm making the sale.[32]

Other governments recognized that they, too, had difficulty gathering reliable commercial sales information. As the regular EC representative admitted at one meeting of the Exporters' Group, "Offer prices for grains were in fact sometimes lower than the prices quoted by the traders."[33] For each of the major exporters, the dilemma was roughly the same. Each suffered from a dependence on unverifiable information received from the trade. There were repeated instances when this sales information, as officially reported to the Wheat Council and the Exporters' Group, did not accurately reflect contract terms. The net effect was to limit considerably the utility and effectiveness of the weekly confidential report, shared by the United States, Canada, Australia, and Argentina, which detailed the quantities committed for export, monthly shipments, and the destination of these shipments, and which—in conjunction with updates on total commitments for shipment to unknown destinations to be supplied by the trade—was intended to provide a full accounting of each country's trade position at any given time.

The combination of haphazard information and sporadic cooperation among participants made the prospects for the Exporters' Group to establish a wheat exporters' cartel no more promising than those of the IGA. Success would have required that member countries respect one another's definition of traditional markets and collectively control global grain traffic. They were unprepared to meet either precondition. The United States, for example, was willing to recognize the legitimacy of Canadian and Australian interests in China, as well as a special European interest in Africa, but viewed these countries' efforts to trade with other Far Eastern nations as intrusions. On the other hand, the United States saw Eastern Europe as open territory, contrary to the interpretations of other members. Under these circumstances, differences quickly emerged as to what constituted sovereign limits for each member of the cartel, especially between the United States and Europe, particularly France, which the Nixon administration saw as a disruptive element.[34] Nonetheless, the EC refused to discontinue its special export restitutions for shipments to the Far East.

The stability of the new arrangement was also threatened by conflicts between the domestic and international interests of the members. The successful functioning of a wheat cartel entails restraints on production and withholding supplies from the world market. Australia and Argentina, however, were in no position to hold large stocks. As world surpluses mounted in the late 1960s, they buckled under pressure and sold large quantities of wheat below the agreed price range. The CAP, left very much intact by the Kennedy Round, could maintain increasingly high internal prices only through heavy export subsidies in the new era of excess European production in wheat. The United States, confronted with surpluses in 1969, the first year of the quota agreement, resorted to food aid to siphon off the excess supplies, so much so that in that year shipments under PL 480 accounted for 46 percent of total U.S. wheat exports. The American performance, in turn, did little to encourage other members to exercise restraint.

By 1971, the original Exporters' Group folded, undone, like its predecessors, by the pursuit of self-interest, public and private. Only the IGA remained, and only the IGA, in its watered-down 1971 version, remains today. Stripped of a fixed pricing system, the current Wheat Trade Convention contains only a vague commitment to examine this item at an "appropriate time."[35] As it stands, the agreement does little more than ratify the status quo, including the present pattern of gyrating grain prices. That it stands at all, that it remained in place longer than any of its predecessors, is perhaps because it does so little and makes so few demands on its signatories.

Others may have hoped for more, for an agreement that would provide something more substantial than an international forum for discussion of the grain trade, but few had anything to lose in signing the 1971 proposal and successive renewal agreements. Importers, including the EC, could hedge their risks in the event that the wheat cycle produced another period of scarcity with minimal obligations under the terms of the treaty. For developing countries, a formal coupling of food aid with successive Wheat Trade Conventions, begun under the IGA of 1967, has both a symbolic and practical appeal. If nothing else, it integrates the need to coordinate food assistance with commercial transfers to achieve more orderly marketing conditions, beneficial to LDCs and the commercial buyers who are often substantial food donors. And for the exporters, the motivation remains the same as ever. They seek an international forum within which they can pursue the available means of controlling export prices and supply. If that international forum is acceptable under the current GATT Agreement, then so much the better.

Since 1971, there have been at least two major initiatives, both involving the United States, on behalf of a more comprehensive international grain agreement. The first of these, unveiled by Henry Kissinger at the fall 1975 meeting of the Preparatory Group of the Wheat Council, was a belated response to heated protests from Third World food aid recipients and commercial customers heard at the 1974 World Food Conference in Rome.[36] However, the Kissinger proposal was stillborn. It was adamantly opposed by Secretary of Agriculture Butz, who objected to any agreement that included a compulsory international grain reserve. Interestingly, Butz had earlier suggested in a private conversation at Camp David with EC Commissioner of Agriculture Lardinois that he could accept some price-trigger mechanism as part of an eventual, suitably loose, international grain reserve agreement. The Kissinger proposal, it would appear, was too restrictive in the eyes of the influential agricultural clique in the United States. Butz and other domestic critics argued that "the only real food reserve in this world lies squarely where it always has: with the productivity of the individual farmer."[37] Thus 1975 came and went without a major new agreement.

In 1975, Europe and the United States were at loggerheads about agricultural protectionism and remain so today. To be sure, the focus of the dispute has shifted somewhat. The Nixon administration had launched a campaign to reform CAP outright. The Carter administration was content to work on promoting a more comprehensive trade package, leaving a grain agreement to be taken up as a separate and isolated issue by negotiators meeting in London. This shift in strategy reflected in part a change in the U.S. view of the importance of the EC's agricultural markets and export potential: "In the grains area there are bigger and plumper fish to fry, and fixing on the EC may be distracting some of the attention away from them."[38]

Nonetheless, each side retains an apparent interest in reforming the other's policies to the maximum extent possible while giving up the minimum in return. The United States has consistently sought to bring the EC into conformity with uniform international guidelines regarding export price levels and marketing, while the EC has linked any concessions on these issues to other, larger issues of international trade and, of course, to an acceptance of CAP's protectionist tools. Not even a country as dependent on outside food resources as Japan was prepared to register enthusiasm over the Kissinger proposal for a new international wheat agreement. The rise of OPEC apparently had the dual effect of inspiring cartel supporters in Canada and the United States and discouraging importers, afraid of the treatment they would receive at the hands of another exporters' club.

Nevertheless, discussions have continued since the 1975 proposal's demise. The United States unveiled yet another proposal in 1977 when surpluses had once again reached a point sufficient to encourage multilateral cooperation. The 1979 draft text of this proposal rivaled its 1933 and 1949 predecessors for complexity, reviving in many respects the ever-normal granary proposal of Henry Wallace. The central feature of this proposal was to be a system of nationally held reserves that assigned specific quantities to member nations.[39] These stocks were to be either accumulated or released at minimum and maximum "trigger price" levels, respectively, to be established in the treaty. It would have imposed certain obligations on exporters who were committed to withholding surpluses from the market, and on importers who agreed both to purchase the grain at prescribed price levels and to refrain from stepping up their own more expensive domestic production. Developing countries, heretofore not involved in multilateral agreements of the sort proposed, would be offered special incentives to build up their reserve stocks.

The 1977 plan contained a bit of something old and something new. The concept of an indicator price had been first floated in the Kissinger plan of 1975. Reserve allocations were a New Deal-Henry Wallace notion. The indicator price mechanism utilized the same basket of wheats (with one additional Canadian type) as the 1967 plan. The Advisory Subcommittee on Market Conditions of the IWC was to have been given a new lease on life and responsibilities identical to those it was assigned when established under the 1971 accord. An entirely new feature was a provision for consultations on coarse grain. Commitments to regulate production in conjunction with reserve allocations were to be more stringent than ever. For all the ambition and ingenuity that may have gone into its creation, this latest effort remained the archetypal wheat agreement, much discussed but never enacted. As to why this should be so, a variety of reasons have been offered.

The official American explanation has been that the Europeans were unwilling to accept adequate reserve stocks as part of the plan and that the developing countries insisted on unrealistically low trigger prices for the accumulation and release of those reserves. The impression given by the U.S. negotiating team was that the LDCs expected too much in terms of special assistance to build up their reserves without exhibiting any willingness to make reciprocal commitments.[40]

Europe saw things differently. EC representatives complained about the American insistence on writing some form of flexible pricing into the agreement instead of predetermined floor and ceiling prices to be set periodically by the Council, an old formula which the Europeans found more acceptable because they felt that flexible, or notional, prices were too vaguely defined and thus too open to individual interpretation. Moreover, the target and indicator price levels contained in the proposal were higher than those the EC originally wanted. This was a major stumbling block from the EC's standpoint. The higher international wheat prices are set, the more difficult and costly it becomes for EC members to dispose of their surpluses through subsidized export sales. A further European objection was that the agreement applied only to wheat. Originally, EC negotiators wanted an agreement for coarse grains analogous to the Wheat Convention. Short of that, they were willing to accept reluctantly some vague consultative machinery to tie the two together.

There was considerable variance, and some confusion, in the explanations offered by LDC representatives and the United States as to why the former ultimately found the proposed agreement unsatisfactory. Some LDC representatives, and some Wheat Council officials, charged that the United States had extended, and then reneged upon, an offer to lower indicator price levels and increase the financial assistance to be given to LDCs for the purpose of building up their grain reserves in exchange for their approval of the agreement. U.S. officials maintained that such an offer had never been extended. The United States did not, however, speak with one voice on all matters. The major aspirations of the developing countries, from the beginning, had been for lower price levels, large grain reserves, and a variety of special provisions including a fund to be financed by the developed countries, which would be used to cover the grain storage costs incurred by LDCs. To the last of these proposals, the State Department apparently objected while the USDA did not. On the other hand, the USDA seems to have been unwilling to countenance a special price level for LDCs, whereas the State Department was receptive to the notion. What is clear, in the end, is that while the LDCs and Washington disagreed, the American bureaucracy was not of one mind on the matter.

To date, all the jockeying among governments and interest groups has produced little. The 1971 Wheat Trade Convention was extended once more in 1981 for a period of two years. So too was the Food Aid Convention, this time in a form that provided for increased food aid commitments from exporters, commensurate with their existing surpluses. Renewal and not reform continues to be the order of the day.[41]

Not everyone is upset by this turn of events. Mid-year marketing forecasts of reduced global production in 1979-80, and heavy buying by the USSR and China, greatly reduced the prospect of continued surpluses of the sort that had plagued most exporters in 1977-78 and encouraged their interest in yet another attempt at cooperation. With wheat prices back up to 1973-74 levels when Congress debated the one year renewal of the IGA in 1979, Senator Church downplayed the agreement's significance in order to ensure its passage.

> This treaty contains no provisions to establish wheat quotas, nor any provisions which have any impact on wheat prices, nor any provisions which establish wheat reserves. It is not in any sense an international commodity agreement like the tin agreement or the proposed sugar agreement, which contain economic provisions such as buffer stocks to stabilize prices.[42]

Given the cyclical nature of grain production, however, a return of the surpluses, such as occurred in 1981-82 is inevitable. With such surpluses will come, once again, the pressure on exporters to seek a cooperative agreement. Indeed, as the prospect of unexpected wheat surpluses surfaced in early 1980, in large part due to the Carter administration's embargo on Soviet grain sales, exporter negotiations resumed at a high level. Then enthusiasm fell with the news of climbing international prices. In times of ample harvests, exporters seek a means of sharing the financial burden of holding stocks at the international level. The pendulum swings to an importer's initiative when supplies are tight and prices become inflationary. For such agreements as are obtained, however, the pattern is that, with the exception of wartime, exporters' interests generally carry the day.

In the absence of a comprehensive international agreement, the exporters' only recourse remains yet another effort to establish a producers' cartel. The prospect for such a cartel today are no better than before. Indeed, the U.S. appeal for other exporters to follow its lead in withholding grain supplies from the USSR in 1980 was largely ignored by Argentina and Brazil, who seized this opportunity to sell their crops, at a premium, to the Soviets. Nor did the United States exercise significant restraint in withholding its supplies from the export market or coordinating its sales with other exporters.

In July 1981, the Reagan administration vetoed a Wheat Council initiative aimed at reviving the 1979 U.S. proposal with modest revisions. Secretary of Agriculture John Block indicated that the reserve issue was a matter for each exporting country to handle unilaterally or jointly on an informal basis. Washington did not reject outright the concept of reserves, but it did express skepticism over any possible successful outcome for a multilateral agreement. Token attention was paid to the need of developing countries to obtain greater food security, but no new initiatives were forthcoming on precisely how to address this problem. The official U.S. position was that the private sector and the dictates of the market were the best determinants of global food allocations. As such, it was a resounding rejection of a comprehensive, international reserve system that, in light of the record, was not totally without justification.

The record also suggests, however, that when the final crop production figures are registered for 1981-82 worldwide, the United States may shed some of its market rhetoric and return to the moral high road of a new wheat agreement. Neither option is extremely promising as long as the United States and other countries fail to deal with domestic production and distribution issues, which are equally relevant to the problems of food security and price stabilization. An international agreement can at best provide a conducive setting, but only participating members can guarantee effective results.

NOTES

(Notes cited as FOIA material are unpublished information received by the author from the U.S. government upon formal request under the Freedom of Information Act.)

1. Frank M. Surface, *History of the Food Administration Grain Corporation and the United States Grain Corporation* (New York: Macmillan, 1928), p. 570.

2. Ibid., p. 573.

3. Alonzo E. Taylor, "International Wheat Policy and Planning," *Wheat Studies* 11 (June 1935): 359-62.

4. Ibid., pp. 439-46.

5. The Secretary of the American Delegation (Cox) to the Ambassador in Great Britain, No. 1976, and Report of the Chairman of the American Delegation (McKelvie) to the Federal Farm Board, No. 166. In U.S. Department of State, "Participation of the United States in the Conference of Wheat Exporting Countries, London, May 18-23, 1931," *Papers Relating to the Foreign Relations of the United States 1931,* 1: 639-42; and International Wheat Council, "International Wheat Agreements—A Historical and Critical Background," EX (74-75) 2/2 (14 August 1974), p. 3.

6. Alonzo E. Taylor (a member of the delegation and director of the Food Research Institute of Leland Stanford University in 1931), "The International Wheat Conference During 1930-31," *Wheat Studies* 7 (August 1931): 458.

7. Joseph Davis, *Wheat and the AAA* (Washington: Brookings Institution, 1935), p. 307.

8. The Acting Secretary of State to the Ambassador in Great Britain, No. 161. In U.S. Department of State, "Agreement Among Wheat Exporting and Importing Countries, signed in London, 25 August 1933," *Papers Relating to the Foreign Relations of the United States,* 1: 799.

9. Paul de Hevesy, *World Wheat Planning and Economic Planning in General* (London: Oxford University Press, 1940), p. 861; and U.S. Department of State Treaty Division, *Treaty Information Bulletin* 48 (September 1933): 24-28.

10. Taylor, "The International Wheat Conferences," p. 453.

11. Henry A. Wallace, "Foundations of Peace," *Atlantic Monthly,* January 1942, p. 37.

12. Exchanges of notes between the governments of Argentina, Australia, Canada, the United Kingdom, and the United States of America following upon the conclusion of the wheat discussions at Washington, 24 April, 18 May, and 27 June 1942, "Memorandum of Agreement," Art. 4, Export Control (FOIA material).

13. Cited in Richard J. Hammond, *Food: The Growth of Policy: Studies in Administration and Control* (London: Her Majesty's Stationery Office and Longmans, Green, 1962), 1:351.

14. Joseph S. Davis, *Wheat Under International Agreement* (Washington: American Enterprise Association, 1945), p. 8.

15. U.S. Congress, Senate, Committee on Foreign Relations, *The International Wheat Agreement, Hearings before a subcommittee, on ratification by U.S. Government of International Wheat Agreement,* 80th Cong., 2d sess., 14, 15, and 17 May 1948, pp. 16, 30, and 32.

16. Ibid., Testimony of W. C. Schilthuis, vice president of Continental Grain Co., p. 133.

17. Statement by Charles F. Brannan, Secretary of Agriculture, "Significance of New International Wheat Agreement to U.S. Wheat Farmers." U.S. Department of Agriculture Press Release, 23 March 1949.

18. U.S. Congress, Senate, Committee on Foreign Relations, *International Wheat Agreement, Hearings before a subcommittee, on ratification by U.S. Government of International Wheat Agreement,* 81st Cong., 1st sess., 19 and 23 May 1949, p. 44.

19. Murray Benedict and Oscar Stine, *The Agricultural Commodity Programs* (New York: Twentieth Century Fund, 1956).

20. International Wheat Council, "International Wheat Agreements—A Historical and Critical Background," EX (74/75) 2/2 (14 August 1974), p. 12.

21. Ibid.

22. UN, Food and Agriculture Organization, "FAO Principles of Surplus Disposal and Consultative Obligations of Member Nations," General Principles (Rome 1972), p. 4.

23. UN, Food and Agriculture Organization Committee on Commodity Problems, "Role of Subcommittee (CSD) in Light of Current and Prospective Developments in Agricultural Surpluses and Food Aid," CCP 68/7/2 (26 July 1968), p. 6.

24. Robert L. Bard, *Food Aid and International Agricultural Trade: A Study in Legal and Administrative Control* (Toronto: Lexington, 1972), p. 166.

25. "Future of World Wheat Pact," *Southwestern Miller* 40 (19 January 1965): 29.

26. The United States had already secured an understanding that raw soybeans would be binded free of any tariff into the EC.

27. Orville Freeman, U.S. Secretary of Agriculture, to U.S. Ambassador to France, Robert Sargent Shriver, 9 October 1968 (FOIA material; confidential letter).

28. United States Delegation, Canberra, Australia, 17-19 September 1968, "Position Paper: Role and Concept of Minimum Prices" (FOIA material).

29. Remarks by Mr. Sharp, "Notes on U.S.-Canadian Ministerial Meeting," Topic—Agricultural Matters Including IGA, 25 June 1969, p. 6 (FOIA material).

30. U.S. Delegation, Canberra, Australia, 17-19 September 1968, "Position Paper" (The Necessity of an Exporter Sharing Arrangement), p. 1 (FOIA material).

31. Memorandum from John A. Schnittker, U.S. Undersecretary of Agriculture, dated 24 September 1968. Attachment, Item 1, "Review of the Current Price Levels of Scheduled Wheats in Relation to IGA, Minima," p. 4 (FOIA material).

32. Copy of State Department Note, dated 20 November 1968, delivered to the Government of Canada (FOIA material).

33. U.S. Mission to the European Economic Community in Brussels, 5 October 1969, p. 3 (FOIA material; confidential telegram).

34. Remarks by Mr. Hardin, "Notes on U.S.-Canadian Ministerial Meeting," Topic—Agricultural Matters Including IGA, 25 June 1969, p. 1 (FOIA material).

35. U.S. Department of State, *International Wheat Agreement, 1971: Wheat Trade Convention and Food Aid Convention 1971, Treaties and Other International Acts Series* 7144 (Washington: U.S. Government Printing Office, 1971), p. 62. Failure to settle on a new agreement led to the approval of a two-year extension in 1981.

36. United States Proposal for an International Grain Reserve System as Presented at a Preparatory Meeting of the International Wheat Council in London, England, 29 September 1975. (Unpublished.)

37. Earl L. Butz, U.S. Secretary of Agriculture, "Can the World Turn Itself?" (address before the Agribusiness Council, Washington, D.C., 25 February 1975).

38. Memorandum to Association members from Joseph Halow, Executive Director, North American Export Grain Association. Subject: Wheat Agreement Negotiations, 23 June 1978. (Unpublished.)

39. "Draft Text of an International Arrangement to Replace the International Wheat Agreement, 1971, as Extended," United Nations Conference on Trade and Development. TD/Wheat 6/R.5 (February 1979).

40. U.S. Congress, Senate, Committee on Foreign Relations, *International Wheat Agreement, Hearings,* 96th Cong., 1st sess. Testimony of Dale E. Hathaway, Undersecretary of Agriculture, 8 May 1979, pp. 15-25 and 47-54.

41. In May 1981, the International Monetary Fund introduced special compensatory financing for food deficits in developing countries. This new resource has not yet been widely tapped, but potentially will be of some assistance to LDC concerns over food security.

42. U.S. Congress, Senate, Senator Church speaking on Protocols for the fourth extension of the 1971 International Wheat Agreement, 96th Cong., 1st sess., 26 June 1979, *Congressional Record,* S. 8525.

10

Alternative Marketing Systems Among Major Exporters and Importers

Although less than 15 percent of total global production in grains is actually traded, this amount has a far-reaching economic and social impact worldwide. National marketing systems play a determining role in linking global production with consumption. In the process, 15 percent translates into more than 220 million metric tons per annum, and represents in terms of value approximately $35 billion. When considering all the capital and labor-intensive undertakings involved in production, distribution, and marketing, this sum would rank alongside energy resources in its proportionate share of every country's gross national product. Similarly, the 15 percent figure assumes much greater significance when the amount is viewed in terms of its end use. In the case of developing countries, imported grains are used to satisfy immediate consumption requirements. These low-income countries now account for close to 50 percent of all grain imports and are likely to surpass developed countries' imports within the next 10 years. In countries like the Soviet Union, where the daily meat diet is lower than most industrial countries, feed for livestock purposes is essential for raising the population's nutritional standards. And all countries share the need to develop a minimum level of stocks as a buffer against periods of shortages at home and abroad.

American agriculture has grown to appreciate the costs and benefits of an export-biased economy. Now that an average of 50 percent of all U.S. grain and oilseeds grown enters the export stream, the American farmer's livelihood is linked with foreign consumers via the major international grain houses. Chicago, Minneapolis, and Kansas register commodity prices that bear directly on every country's food prices. The vulnerability in this situation lies in the fact that major buyers, such as Japan, the EC, or the USSR, can create havoc through adverse purchasing strategies or overly protectionist agricultural policies. The Big League can in many respects distort market conditions through its own operations so as to siphon off profits from growers as well as other sectors, and confuse Washington into taking inappropriate, frequently harmful actions.

Other countries fall victim to the same problem which is rooted in how the world's grain-trading system has evolved to its present stage. Grain takes on real value when it is marketed, not when it is grown. The actual worth of food-related crops and products is thus an expression of political and economic forces interacting on the battlefield of the marketplace. Rarely are national food policies and marketing systems synchronized to the real beat of supply and demand. Instead, government and commercial interventions are conducted with immediate interests in mind that so frequently undermine the workings of the market. No matter what the degree of protectionism or structural concentration in the grain trade, however, no importing or exporting country can operate independent of the United States. In fact, the relatively open market economy of the United States is essential to the maintenance of controlled marketing systems in other countries. As a result, the American system and its commercial representatives help insulate other systems from the vicissitudes of the market while increasing their own vulnerability to shock waves from abroad. It is a curious form of interdependence where structural economic weaknesses as well as grain are exported to other shores.

A few importing and exporting countries serviced by an oligopoly of traders now determine the availability of grain on the world market and the terms of its access. All countries are affected in the process and frequently the biggest suppliers and buyers are the least immune. Notwithstanding this close interrelationship, they have followed their own independent course with one thing in common: their marketing systems all depend on the United States to function as intended.

EXPORTING COUNTRIES

Canada

Canada's marketing system rests on a philosophy that regards grain production as a public resource. For over 40 years, each new administration, irrespective of its political affiliation, has emphasized the importance of price stability for the Canadian farmer and consumer. The Canadian Wheat Board (CWB), an autonomous government organization responsible for grain marketing, is the force that drives Canada's agricultural economy. Its fundamental purpose is to "(1) market as much grain as possible at the best price that can be obtained; (2) provide price stability to 'prairie' (Western provinces)[1] grain producers; (3) ensure that each producer obtains each year a fair share of the available grain market; and (4) maintain through its operations a fixed domestic price for grain to ensure reasonable prices for Canadian consumers."[2]

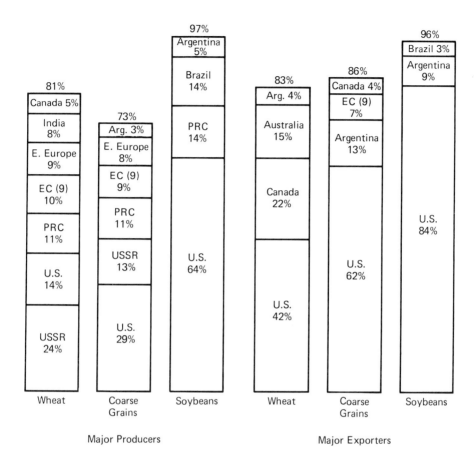

FIGURE 10.1 Global Market Shares of Major Producers and Exporters, Marketing Years 1978–79.

The present system is highly centralized. The Board's mandate covers everything from production and transportation to negotiating foreign sales for wheat and barley (wheat, barley, and oats for domestic consumption as well as other coarse grains like rapeseed, flax, and rye are sold on the open market outside the Board's jurisdiction). The Board charges a fee for its involvement and deducts this from its total receipts; anything left over goes to the farmer. The Board then takes ownership of the stored export grains and pays carrying charges to the elevator agent and interest on any capital it borrows from commercial banks.

One of the Board's major functions is to set a guaranteed minimum price, which it does in consultation with an interdepartmental body called the Grain Group, for the highest-grade hard red spring wheat, as well as durum, a more specialized, high-protein wheat. On delivery of their grain to primary elevators, 80 percent of which are owned by the three western provincial pools (regional grower cooperatives originally organized in the 1920s), producers receive an initial payment equivalent to the government's floor price. Any subsequent losses incurred by the Board for sales below this minimum, guaranteed price are covered by the Canadian government.

Domestic wheat sales are subject to price ceilings, in keeping with the system's objective of stabilizing prices to Canadian consumers while maximizing earnings abroad. In the Canadian system prices are both a market and a welfare mechanism in that they protect consumers and producers and at the same time offer a certain amount of inducement or disincentive in terms of production. The floor prices set by the Board, which determine a farmer's initial payment, influence but do not decide planting decisions as in the United States, where growers have little else to rely on than the market or loan and target price. With advance notice of the Board's prices, the producer can resolve how much acreage to seed and what to plant, with his choice limited to allocations for Board versus non-Board grains. The farmer then registers his plans in a permit book against which the Board sets delivery quotas for its grains based on its own forecasts for export levels, yields, and acreage allocations for wheat, barley, and oats. If the farmer believes there will be more profit in non-Board grains, he is likely to add acreage for these grains in his permit book and deliver less to the Board.

Critics regard the Board's production quotas and setting of prices as a major source of structural inefficiency.[3] Allowing the Board to fix prices at predetermined levels, they argue, may result in a loss of commercial sales, depending on the extent to which there are unanticipated changes in consumption or the price and availability of alternative supplies. Although this is theoretically a problem, the Board generally pegs its prices to prevailing prices in the United States. In this fashion, it gains all the advantages of its neighbor's marketing system without exposing Canadian producers to sudden dips in prices that may have little to do with true market forces. Thanks to the Board's price setting, the Canadian farmer assumes less risk than his American counterpart. In exchange, he is willing to sacrifice in part the possibility of extremely high earnings during good times that is the theoretical reward of efficient American producers.

The emphasis on production quotas via acreage allotments is a more serious weakness. In attempting to regulate production in this way, the Board is inherently ignoring the known relationship between technology and higher yields. As demonstrated by the American set-aside program, farmers can, and if possible will, grow the same amount of grain on less land by utilizing improvements in production technology.

The most serious and immediate problem that detracts from the efficiency of Canada's agricultural economy, however, is an inadequate transportation system. The CWB is saddled with the blame for the present situation, which it inherited and has tried to correct. Grain deliveries are notoriously inefficient.[4] Cars need replacement; tracks require modernization; rail rates, currently regulated by statute, may need modification to provide revenue needed to finance a major capital improvement program.[5] The Board's approach has been to accelerate public investments for modernization to improve the system's ability to move grain to ports and loading ships. The private sector, with Cargill, Canada among the more vocal firms, has argued in favor of eliminating statutory rail rates and substituting a tariff structure based on user fees to finance these improvements and provide revenues for railroads to upgrade their equipment. Under this proposal, larger, more modern elevators owned by the international houses would benefit, since they would pay reduced rates, while the smaller primary and "off-line" elevators closer to the farm and requiring shorter hauls would pay more and, perhaps, eventually atrophy. The pools, which own a majority of inland and off-line elevators, would be the biggest losers under such an arrangement. As a result, the pools and the companies are staging something resembling a pitched battle over user fees.

Despite the acid political tone of the debate, a middle ground is emerging. The Manitoba and Alberta pools have endorsed the notion that the rate, established in the Crows Nest Pass Agreement of 1897, should be raised by statute, but not adjusted on a volume base as suggested by the private sector. Meanwhile, the Wheat Board purchased over 10,000 hopper cars between 1973 and 1979 and has received special budgetary allocations for the purchase of another 10,000 cars by 1985. This modernization drive has muted some of the criticism concerning bottlenecks in the transportation system, but not that directed against the CWB itself. Whenever there is a downturn in export sales or prices, farmer discontent surfaces. The private sector, understandably, has been trying to drive a wedge between the Board and its natural constituency and, in slump periods, its campaign to trim the Board's power gains wider appeal. To fend off these attacks and improve its own operations, the Board periodically subjects itself to public review.

One such investigation occurred in July 1970 when the Board appointed a Grain Marketing Review Committee to assess its marketing practices in the light of the gradual erosion of Canada's position as the world's top wheat exporter. The overall thrust of the Committee's recommendations was that changes in the Board's techniques should be instituted in order to improve its commercial abilities.[6] Most notably, the Committee called for an aggressive sales strategy involving more direct transactions with foreign purchasers to supplant the Board's traditional reliance on international traders. At the same time, the consensus of the committee was that the private sector was best suited to assume the handling and shipping functions as agents of the Board.

Subsequent to this report, the Board upgraded its market development effort and inaugurated a global hard-sell campaign. A slew of long-term government-to-government purchasing agreements quickly followed. Guarantees and credit lines were thrown out to foreign buyers, and agents were welcomed as the Board's partners in promoting Canadian grain. The private sector went along willingly since it had little choice. Over time the "Canadian" grain houses, particularly the Big League, managed to carve out a role for themselves that now extends beyond the conventional role of handling agents. A marriage of convenience emerged between the Board and these firms with the grain houses acting as agent-brokers, buyers, and sellers of Board grains. With its hands full of managing the export sector and facing a constant onslaught of political opposition, the Board has opted to refrain from direct participation in the commodity markets. Instead, it takes a back seat, leaving its licensed agents at the wheel.

The Board's ventures into the commodity market, however indirect, have been at times controversial. In 1976, for example, the Board reportedly sold 4 to 5 million metric tons of wheat to the private trade, basing its decision on the expectation of an immediate decline in the international price. The anticipated decline would, of course, have made it more expensive for the Board to hold its unsold grain for an extended period of time. The private trade promptly hedged its cash position (its purchase of Board wheat) in Chicago and, as the Board expected, the exchanges reflected the surplus position in depressed prices. However, some critics pointed out that the Board's actions cost it dearly. By first selling at a price below the world market to the private trade and then subsequently having to sell its current crop at lower prices induced partially by its "open market" sale to the private firms, the Board, they argued, lost twice. In response, the Board commissioners countered that it would have been costlier to hold wheat off the market. The new sales, they contended, helped usher in a period of higher prices that the Board captured in subsequent export contracts.

The CWB's record in international arbitrage—a monetary hedge to protect the value of its export contracts—is harder to defend. The Board acknowledges only one time when it engaged in a currency "play." Until 1977, the People's Republic of China paid in sterling for Canadian grain. The last such purchase occurred when the British pound was being buffeted from pillar to post. As a result, the Board could afford to accept China's payments only by selling sterling short at tumbling prices. The problem was compounded by the fact that the terms of purchase were negotiated earlier with an allowance for deferred payment of up to 18 months from the time of shipment. The Board was caught. It was obligated to accept sterling for as long as a 30-month period, during which time sterling seemed likely to continue plummeting in money markets. China got a good deal, paying for expensive wheat in what was then the world's cheapest currency. Its trading partner, the Wheat Board, allegedly lost at least $81.5 million (the "net difference between spot Canadian dollar values at the time of sale and the Canadian dollar actually received").[7]

In light of these mishaps and a rising tide of criticism, the Board may choose to reassess strategies. Until now it has avoided entering the commodity markets to hedge its own grain inventories. Instead, it has left this task to the traders, a practice that is now open to question. The problem is that the interests of the companies do not always coincide with the interests of Canadian producers and the Wheat Board. Leaving the companies free to dispose of the grain as they see fit following purchase can adversely affect Canada's export prices and future sales just as easily as promote them. Moreover, the Board's inventories and commitments are so high that hedging in both money and commodity markets is almost a prerequisite to profitability. Should the Board attempt to deal with these problems by redefining its powers[8] and acting as a quasi-corporate grain trader as is now being discussed, the impact on the United States and international markets will be tremendous. The major pitfall with this option, of course, is that the economic benefits of direct hedging could become a political risk in terms of Canada's relations with the United States.

Facing such risks, to date the Board has chosen to maintain a relatively conservative marketing strategy. To obtain a dependable share of the world market, the Board has whenever possible opted for bilateral agreements, an area where it has a decided advantage over the United States. It can assume export commitments under defined contract terms whereas Washington's role is more limited. Further, the Board has counterpart organizations in a majority of importing countries that facilitate these arrangements, which have traditionally posed legal and political problems for the United States.

The Board's biggest bilateral customers are Ceroilfoods, China's purchasing agency, and the Soviet Union's Exportkhleb. The arrangements with these two buyers are handled differently. Ceroilfoods can order as much as 12 months in advance, subject to review only twice during an individual contract year no matter what interim changes may occur in the market. It also has access to credit at below commercial rates, repayable over the duration of the contract. The Board apparently believes these inducements are worth their cost because of the additional sales they generate.

Sales via the official Soviet grain trading company—Exportkhleb—are treated in a considerably different way. More conventional commercial procedures are followed, perhaps reflecting the fact that the USSR is an older and richer customer. The Board gives Exportkhleb no costly credits and has not found it necessary to do so since the big sale to the Soviet Union in 1963. Under its annual purchasing agreements, Exportkhleb supposedly accepts a card price—the daily f.o.b. price of grain reported on the Winnipeg Exchange—set at the time of shipment, but more skeptical observers in the trade suggest that the Board sweetens the price. Since the Board does not publish individual contract terms, any such understanding is a treasured secret shared only with Exportkhleb.

Today, Canada no longer enters into long-term sales agreements with the USSR, but has a "verbal" understanding about the level of annual purchases. Like those with China, Soviet contracts have an escape clause that allows Exportkhleb to divert shipments destined for the Soviet Union to other countries, upon notifying the Board. During the Vietnam War, North Vietnam's wartime apparatus was well fed by this indirect routing of Canadian grain, with or without the consent of the Canadian government. The U.S. government did not know of these shipments, although U.S. officials were aware of direct Board sales to North Vietnam. Similarly, it was common knowledge that the Soviets were diverting a portion of their Canadian grain imports to Cuba with the help of agents whose American affiliates were prohibited by law from doing so.

CWB sales to Japan work still another way. On sales of wheat and barley, the Japanese Food Agency negotiates purchase levels with the Wheat Board. Once the aggregate levels are worked out, it is up to the Agency to schedule shipments, an exclusive domain of the Sogo Shosha. The trading companies pick up weekly tenders after the Agency tidily approves their bids. With an Agency contract in hand, they acquire Board grain from official agents. Japanese firms are not members of the Winnipeg Exchange and therefore do not appear on the agent roster. The explanation for their limbo status in Canada is that to qualify as members requires reciprocal treatment for Canadian companies (including American and other firms of non-Canadian origin) in Japan. Given the Food Agency's exclusive relationship with the Sogo Shosha, Canada has opted to exchange one form of discrimination with another. Nonetheless, the Japanese firms seem content with their present status, which allows them access, albeit indirect, to Canadian grains via other Board agent firms.[9]

Canadian sales to the United Kingdom, although not formally negotiated between the two governments, are analogous in form to the bilateral agreements between the United States and Taiwan and Norway. Since 1972 the Board has entered into export understandings with the three largest British milling and trading houses—Spillers, the Western Group, and Ranks Hovis McDougall. This arrangement reportedly covers a joint commitment for purchases or sales within a predetermined price range. Although not as restrictive as the official bilaterals, in some respects it is more comprehensive and effective in preserving the traditional trading relationship between Canada and the U.K. Like the American arrangement with Taiwan and Norway, however, this agreement's preferential treatment of selected firms raises serious antitrust problems.

To a lesser extent, all members of the Big League are given special treatment by the Board. The mere fact that some firms are agents while others are not is an indication of the type of discrimination that can benefit a few firms. Moreover, a Board-like system will inevitably engender this type of treatment because transportation, storage, and grain sales for domestic and foreign markets are such politically charged decisions. The U.S. example does not, unfortunately, offer more equitable conditions for the private sector. In the United States, the problem is market imperfections, partially attributable to government favoritism or bias, whether intentional or otherwise. In Canada, the problem resides in a government-run marketing system that is ostensibly controlled by a public agency whereas, in fact, it is constrained by certain political objectives and by lack of cooperation from the private sector.

In recent years, Big League members in particular have stepped up their investments in Canada, which suggests that they estimate the tide to be turning in their favor there. In 1974 Cargill purchased National Grain, a medium-sized Canadian grain company, and by 1978 the company had constructed two large elevators in the interior of the country in addition to 231 primary elevators in the provinces. It now has a terminal elevator in Thunder Bay, Ontario, and a major transfer elevator at Baie Comeau, Quebec. Other Cargill investments include National Feeds and Livestock, a feed compound and fertilizer manufacturer; Nipigon Transport, which handles Cargill's vessels coming from the Great Lakes; and Shaver Poultry Breeding.[10] Bunge has its own transfer elevator in Quebec, and Continental Dreyfus and Range (the Canadian subsidiary of André) has leased-space arrangements.

This trend need not suggest the demise of the Board. The private sector has managed to chip away the edges of the Board's power. In such efforts as the rapeseed referendum of 1973, for example, farmers—spurred on by the private sector—voted to have this promising cash crop traded as a non-Board grain. Nevertheless, the Board's jurisdiction is firmly intact and the core of its support is faithful and strong. The days of the railroad monopoly and the syndicates that gave birth to the original Board are still tinged with emotion, as captured in a popular Canadian play: "When I first started farming, when they skinned the wheat they removed just the bran. Now when they skin the wheat they skin the farmer right along with it."[11]

The Board cannot, however, afford to take its support for granted. Each time it makes a mistake, particularly when the result is a substantial loss of income for farmers, the private sector, and more independent-minded producer groups, such as the Pallisers of Alberta, are poised to jump. This state of semi-siege requires an alertness and flexibility on the part of the Board. Most recently it has had a record of success, tarnished slightly by the depressing effect on Canadian grain prices of the 1980 American embargo against the Soviet Union. In recovering from this setback, the Board demonstrated aggressive commercial tactics and singular independence from the United States. The embargo motivated the Board to negotiate its largest bilateral agreement with the USSR, one for a minimum of 25 million metric tons (primarily in wheat) during 1981-86. Nevertheless, these internal and external pressures have not as yet forced the Board to change its overall strategy. For the moment, it prefers a posture of friendly coexistence with the private sector and competing suppliers, such as the United States on whom it is so dependent.

Australia

Australia's marketing system, like Canada's, is highly centralized and designed to accommodate the needs of an agricultural export economy dominated by wheat. Wheat and barley, as Australia's principal crops, require basically uniform growing conditions and their production is concentrated in a few regions of the country. These conditions, so unlike those in the United States where a highly diversified agricultural sector does not lend itself to centralized control, are well suited to an approach similar to the Canadian one.

The Australian analogue of the CWB is the Australian Wheat Board

(AWB). All wheat destined for export is handled by the AWB, which also conducts domestic sales except for intrastate transactions. In this respect, the Australian and Canadian Boards' functions are virtually identical. Nevertheless, important differences point up the higher degree of integrated operations in Australia. The AWB acquires wheat from producers directly at its own elevator facilities, through licensed private agents and processors, or from bulk-handling authorities that are licensed receivers in each state.[12] On delivery of the wheat, producers are paid an initial or advance payment, the level of which is a matter of negotiations between the federal government and the Australian Wheatgrowers' Federation (AWF). The Board deducts freight costs and discounts for wheat that does not meet official standards. Any subsequent payments are drawn from a pool of export sales deposited in a self-financing fund, newly redesigned to ensure against any short-run downturn in producer returns.

With the prevailing upturn in wheat prices since 1974, the Australian government departed from its traditional approach of uniform fixed prices for wheat sold domestically or for export purposes. Like Canada, it now has a two-track system, allowing export prices to float above the prefixed minimum while keeping a lid on domestic prices. Unlike Canada, however, Australia's home consumption price has been above the export price in 20 of the past 29 years[13] and was 40 percent higher in 1978-79.[14] Since 1972, export prices have exceeded domestic prices at wider margins than the reverse, leaving consumers in a more favorable position than farmers.[15] Under the old stabilization system, in effect until October 1979, producers had to contribute a portion of the export sales price into the stabilization fund, reducing their receipts. The new, seventh plan attempts to correct this discrepancy in favor of the consumer by pegging the domestic price of wheat to a freely fluctuating export price and to an index of production input prices. In this way, the consumer is tied more closely to market conditions than previously. The new Wheat Finance Fund also pays the farmer a guaranteed price at the time of production as opposed to the time of AWB export sales. Like the Canadian system, Australian growers now have additional income security, which they had lacked because of the time lag between production and repayment periods under the old system.

Such reforms, however, are relatively minor adjustments to the overall system that remains similar to its Canadian counterpart save in the treatment of domestic versus export prices. Because it often realizes more revenue on an individual domestic sale than on an export sale, the AWB has less incentive to seek maximum export prices than to maximize volume. Unlike Canada, which derives proportionately more revenue from high export prices, the AWB concentrates on keeping the supply line wide open with as little as possible in storage. Both Canada and Australia's domestic markets use roughly 30 percent of their total annual wheat production, but Australia's higher domestic prices make the costs of holding stocks that much greater and thus the motivation to dispose of them all the more attractive.

A second important distinction between Canada and Australia's wheat-marketing boards is that the AWB is more of a trader, with fully integrated, international operations. The Reserve Bank of Australia handles financing, offering the AWB credit at concessional rates as well as covering initial payments and other credit advances to producers; for shipping, the AWB has its own Chartering Committee with representation on the London Baltic Exchange, the central world pit for fixing ocean vessel charters;[16] and for market development, the Board uses its foreign offices as well as its agents in the private trade. Board sales account for an average of 60 percent of Australia's total export transactions with the remainder conducted by the private trade. It has no legal or policy injunctions against participation in foreign futures markets or engaging in arbitrage to protect its currency position and reportedly has hedged several small lot sales to China on the Board of Chicago.[17]

The international trading houses also have an important role to play. Although it is equipped to handle the total export package, the better part of the AWB's contracts, like the CWB, are on an f.o.b. basis. Big League members act as licensed receivers of Board grain and as agents of foreign buyers. As in Canada, the Sogo Shosha are not licensed by the AWB for sales to the Japanese Food Agency, presumably because of the Agency's preferential policy toward its own national traders, but the Board does sell to them directly for exports to countries other than Japan. For sales to the mother country, Japanese traders have to purchase from other international houses that buy directly from the Board. The AWB in the past has entered into exclusive agreements with individual companies for sales to select countries. Their explanation: "AWB considers it commercially prudent to offer exclusive trading rights for Australian wheat in some markets to particular merchants."[18] One probable advantage is that an individual company with traditional ties and a dominant market position in a given country can penetrate foreign markets that formerly were closed to Australian wheat. Bunge, for example, with its preeminent position in Brazil, is reported to hold an exclusive arrangement to handle Board sales to several Latin American countries.

The Board is in effect underwriting a cartel. Objections to this have come from unlikely circles. Tradax Australia, Ltd., raised the issue publicly during special hearings in 1978 to review the Board's operations. Questioning how the Board determines "exclusive geographic trading rights" for individual traders and places conditions "on the destinations to which traders can export wheat," Tradax was informed that Board decisions were a matter of its "commercial judgment."[19] The Board's general manager added that "the reaction of Tradax was surprising, particularly when they had earlier been granted exclusivity for Iran and a number of other markets in the Middle East. These arrangements have now lapsed."[20]

This disclosure came to haunt Cargill during the American hostage crisis in Iran from late 1979 to 1981. When Washington froze the government of

Iran's assets in American banks, it specifically excluded the option of a food embargo. Nevertheless, the U.S. International Longshoremen's Association boycotted any food shipments and Iran had to get its supplies elsewhere. As a traditional source, Australia continued to sell to Iran during this time and reportedly deferred to Cargill and others to act as agents for the government of Iran.[21]

The accuracy of this allegation is less important than its likelihood under exclusive dealerships, such as the AWB has designated in the past. In economic as well as political terms, it would appear that the gains do not balance out the costs. In allocating a portion of its sales under exclusionary terms, the Board may weaken its own profitability and inevitably surrender some of its market power to private grain merchants. Because of its relative position on the world market, Australia has a minimal influence on international prices. Siphoning off a portion of its sales to the private trade in this fashion simply reduces its ability to maximize its return. The AWB may have drawn the same conclusion, since it now contends such exclusive agreements are no longer in effect.

Whatever the status of these arrangements, the AWB's methods of operation offer more opportunities for the big international grain houses than do those of its Canadian counterpart. Like the CWB, the AWB still concentrates on negotiating deals with other governments, leaving the handling, shipping and delivery phases to the private sector. In lieu of assuming a daily hedge position, the AWB offers to the trade a special provision that, in the Board's estimation, reduces its own risks. Private grain merchants purchasing from the AWB are given the option, as agents or sellers of Australian wheat, to delay fixing a final contract price (the time between actual purchase from the Board and loading on a waiting vessel) for three months.[22] In theory, this is a no-lose proposition: the private trade gains because a fixed contract with the buyer is balanced by an open price with the Board—a built-in hedge; the Board buys time to hedge or reprice its sale commitment to avoid the kinds of losses sometimes experienced by the CWB.

The trade is given even more room to maneuver in barley, Australia's second export crop. Whereas the CWB retains control over all export grains in the western provinces, in Australia the state boards are supposed to perform the equivalent function for barley. In practice, their function is mainly as a clearing house. The state boards generally evince little ability or inclination to enforce a common set of rules and regulations for intraregional and export transactions. Bunge reportedly has an agreement with the New South Wales Board for "exclusive authority in northern New South Wales to collect and sell barley."[23] One firm which owns an elevator in bordering Queensland is reputed to engage in purchasing barley from New South Wales and transporting it across the border, undeclared to the New South Wales or the Queensland Barley Board. For sales to Japan and Taiwan, individual Japanese companies are free of the AWB's restrictions and have exclusive agent status with the barley boards of at least three states.[24]

The Australian method for sustaining a prosperous agricultural economy that encourages efficient production and provides equitable returns to growers and consumers is a mixed marketing system. For wheat, which accounts for over two-thirds of the country's grain production, central controls are seen as the best means of linking farmer income to export earnings. The private sector's assistance is enlisted, but sometimes such an arrangement not atypically reduces the profit for the Wheat Board and, hence, producers. Government control over barley is looser because of the smaller quantities involved.

In comparison with the Canadian Board, the AWB has tended to make slightly different mistakes in its dealings with the private trade, albeit often with markedly similar results. Both of these centralized systems, however, tend to produce a more equitable return to producers on export sales than does the U.S. system. Indirectly, the structure of the American marketing system and its role in determining international wheat prices allows smaller, residual supplying countries an opportunity to maximize their gains from exports artificially set above the U.S. selling price.

Argentina

Argentina now has a more market-oriented agricultural economy than that under the last Peron regime, but it, too, functions to some extext at the expense of the United States. The prime example of this one-sided relationship was in 1980-81 at the time of the U.S. embargo against the Soviet Union. Helped by Washington's inability to implement this initiative, plus remarkable strides in its own production, Argentina was able to capitalize on the situation by making significant inroads into the Soviet market under a new, long-term bilateral agreement. Argentina proceeded to sell out its bumper crop of wheat and corn at premium prices to the Soviets. At the same time, the Soviets agreed to purchase a 4.5 million metric tons of Argentine corn, sorghum, and soybeans from 1980 to 1985. Clearly, Argentina staged a commercial coup on a traditional and extremely important U.S. market.

Argentina's leaders and private sector representatives described these developments as the product of a natural evolution in which the market compensated for the cutoff of U.S. supplies. This explanation plays down the active role assumed by the government of Argentina, both in this particular episode and in general, since the Argentine marketing system does involve more government controls than its U.S. counterpart. The National Grain Board, JNG (La Junta Nacional de Granos), established during the same period as the Canadian and Australian boards, runs the country's export registration system. Although its role is now diminished in comparison to the years before 1976 when the Board was the sole authorized buyer and seller of Argentina's wheat, corn, and sorghum, its present limited functions certainly affect the flow of exports.

Exporters, for example, must submit weekly declarations to the JNG that include information on purchases from storage facilities in the interior of the country. These reports must specify the type of grain, the amount and the port at which the grain is to be delivered, and the estimated time of delivery. Export sales reports, submitted to JNG within 24 hours of an actual sale, must also contain such items as the shipping period, the name and number of ocean vessels scheduled to pick up the grain at the designated port of origin, and the price of the certified sale, which is legally required to be the minimum national price.[25] With this kind of information, the JNG could institute a licensing system for export quotas on a moment's notice. It has the machinery and government backing to do so whenever domestic shortages arise and could, therefore, have easily followed the U.S. lead in 1980 with respect to Soviet sales instead of undercutting the American position.

Argentina is, nevertheless, more hospitable to the private trade than most grain-exporting countries other than the United States. Opportunities for the private trade are extensive. There is, in fact, concern in some circles that the large multinational trading firms may obtain a stranglehold on the country's market.

> The inference from the current distribution of export markets is that a major market development program should be undertaken by Argentine grain interests to establish continuing outlets and to merchandise the projected increase in export supplies. . . Since so much of the Argentine grain export trade is not in the hands of multinational companies, which quite normally sell grain on optional-origin contracts (i.e., for sorghum, it could come from Argentina, United States, or Australia, whichever was most profitable to the trader at a particular time), such a promotional program should be undertaken by distinctly "national" entities, independent grain companies, cooperatives, and, particularly, by Government departments or agencies.[26]

At present, the export trade in Argentina is dominated by the Big League. Five of the six firms in the Big League group account for close to 40 percent of the country's exports in their own name and an incalculable additional amount as shippers and handlers in a c.i.f. transaction. André La Plata Cereal has been the number one handler of Argentina's grain exports, but Cargill and Continental have held the title for wheat. Bunge and Born and Cargill are the top soybean merchants, and in 1977 Feruzzi handled over 33 percent of Argentina's total exports. In addition to their dominant position in this sector, the giants of the trade play an extremely important role in the flourishing domestic market with integrated operations comparable in scale to their investment in the United States. Their presence has certainly contributed to the recent agricultural boom that Argentina has experienced, particularly in the export business.

This prosperity, however, does not come without certain costs that are much the same as those experienced in the United States. Although Argentina has, in the post-Peron era, thrown out the welcome mat to the Big League, it still retains a traditional bias in favor of cooperatives. Yet, as in the United States, the latter have been indirectly penalized by the operations of the Big League. Argentina's co-ops prevail in the domestic market like their American counterparts, but continue to hold a proportionately small share of the export market. In an effort to retain more of the profit from their production, the co-ops have entered into joint ventures with private firms, which only strengthens the hand of the Big League.

When thoroughbred Argentine firms and co-ops had a chance to assume a greater share of the export business, the U.S. government stepped in to avert this outcome without objection from Buenos Aires. Within six months of the U.S. embargo against the Soviet Union, Washington modified its regulations to allow Argentine subsidiaries of American companies to participate in sales of non-American grains and soybeans to the USSR. No doubt Argentina's neutral position stemmed from the fact that the Big League was best equipped to service these large-lot exports to the Soviet Union, which the government was so anxious to handle. In this instance, Argentina opted to profit from the embargo with assistance from the United States. Rarely have Canada and Australia received the same kind of direct help from Washington. Although the embargo exaggerated economic benefits to Argentina at the expense of the United States, similar results are likely to recur as long as Argentina's system runs on government interventions and an oligopoly in the grain trade, bolstered by the U.S. marketing system and Washington's own contradictory agricultural trade policies.

Brazil

Brazil's system is in some respects the most centralized of those in major grain-exporting countries. In other respects, it offers the most fertile field for the private sector, particularly the large international grain-trading houses. Government and choice private firms or individuals traditionally have been wedded together in a form of social contract to accelerate the development of Brazil's agricultural economy. As a result, private firms operate under conditions that reduce some of the investment risk but do not necessarily guarantee a satisfactory return. As perhaps the world's last and largest new agricultural frontier, Brazil offers much potential and peril to any foreign investor.

To date, the country's major success story is in soybeans. As a result of deliberate government policy, soybean production has soared. It moved from a low in 1960 of 206,000 metric tons to approximately 16 million metric tons by 1980-81.[27] Equally spectacular has been the increase in Brazil's soybean-crushing capacity, which has grown from approximately 500,000 tons in 1967 to over 13 million metric tons in 1980.[28] Current government policy is to build up Brazil's crushing capacity mainly for foreign consumption. The value added in this stage of processing is seen as a net plus to the Brazilian economy and a means of capturing the largest share of foreign currency possible.

This growth has been stimulated in large part through the actions of CACEX, the foreign trade arm of Brazil's Central Bank. CACEX, a joint venture in which 51 percent of the ownership is held by the government and the remainder by a consortium of private banks,[29] has offered an array of incentives to channel investment into soybean processing. Although complaints, such as the one filed by the European Community soybean association (FEDIOL), have moderated some of CACEX incentives held to be in violation of GATT rules, they have not deterred the Brazilian government from continuing to offer a wide range of favorable credit and tax treatments to producers and the trading companies. CACEX also administers the licensing program for soybean products, primarily crush. The licensing system is an arbitrary one in that quotas are often assigned for a combination of political and economic reasons, but the overall objective is to encourage exports of these products. Because of its excess plant capacity for processing soybeans, Brazil periodically imports beans from the United States, which are then exported as crush, meal, or oil. Such a strategy is economical because American soybeans are at present cheaper than those grown in Brazil, largely due to high capital costs for developing efficient production and a tax structure favoring exports of soy products. To carry out such assignments, COBEC, a semi-official trading company, hedges in U.S. commodity markets and acts as a speculator to influence Brazil's cash export prices.

COBEC consorts with the private trade in handling imports, while CACEX strives to direct as much export business to Brazil's cooperatives. When world soybean prices soared in 1973 and Big League shippers were accused of having covered their prospective sales by purchases of Brazilian beans at bargain prices, cooperatives subsequently won the majority of licensing concessions. A U.S. government official reported on the exporters' subsequent difficulty in receiving licenses in the following manner:

> CACEX arbitrarily disallowed licenses and later restored them in a discriminatory manner. During this period (July-August, 1974, sic.) Cargill and Cook Industries, among others, made known to the Department's Agricultural Officer at Sao Paulo their concern about CACEX's action and the Government of Brazil's soybean and products export policy. It was our Agricultural Officer's understanding, however, that all firms which had been dealt with arbitrarily eventually received the necessary documentation to export. What appeared particularly galling to some exporters, *was the fact that when CACEX began to restore export licenses, cooperatives received priority*.[30]

This situation, however, was a temporary one. As the political heat wore off in the period immediately following the price boom of 1974, the private companies once again obtained what they deemed their rightful quotas. It is unlikely that even in the worst possible case the veteran grain warriors were severely injured. Brazilian cooperatives, like all their foreign counterparts, are still effectively unable to execute international c.i.f. contracts. Inevitably they must turn to Big League traders to handle their quotas. Further, private Brazilian firms and multinational grain-trading houses together own 86 percent of the country's crushing capacity, with cooperatives controlling the remaining 14 percent.[31] Given such a position, cooperatives can seldom fill soybean meal and oil quotas in their own right. Nor can the smaller Brazilian firms, which may own the majority of crushing plants but are saddled with those that have the smallest capacity and most antiquated equipment.

These small, domestically based firms are, therefore, poorly placed in the export business. As a result, both the smaller local firms and the cooperatives channel most of their business through larger multinational companies. Thus, despite an official preference for cooperatives, the private sector has gained a warm reception in Brazil. In general, the government holds the view that these large firms serve as engines of growth in Brazil's agricultural leap forward. At a minimum, as in other marketing systems, the marriage is one of convenience in which government appreciation of the efficiencies of the grain giants is a key factor. Big League members, as a result, have achieved a degree of integration in Brazil that rivals their operations in the United States, Western Europe, and Argentina.

Nor has the Big League been the only source of outside investment. The Sogo Shosha are involved in a major joint venture with the Brazilian government for agricultural development of the Minas Gerais region. The scale of the project is enormous, coordinated by the Brazilian-Japanese corporate mutation called the Agro-Industrial Participating Company, established in September 1978. Reportedly this company has acquired approximately 50,000 hectares of land for corn and soybean production, partially financed by the government of Brazil and partially by Sogo Shosha in partnership with the Japanese government. Similarly, a holding company called the Agricultural Promotion Company (CPA) was formed in 1978 by 49 Japanese and 23 Brazilian firms. This venture will invest $78.5 billion toward production in central Brazil. Originally these projects were to be part of what the Brazilian government referred to as its "export corridor" program, which was a mammoth effort to attract investment in critical areas of transportation and port improvement. The joint ventures with the Japanese may fall short of this grand design, but they nevertheless are the most ambitious, integrated investment efforts to date in the nation's soybean sector. Both projects illustrate Japanese traders' search for secure alternative sources to the U.S. market. As such, they are viewed by many in the trade as the sleeper, the dramatic commercial initiative that could affect the world soybean market in a few years.

The picture that emerges from this panorama of the world's principal food exporting countries is that each country's marketing system is designed to satisfy national economic and political objectives, whose successful implementation depends to a large extent on the United States and the grain titans. From the perspective of the private traders, the greater the number of nations that welcome their services the better. Multiple sourcing is key to their profitability and, for that matter, a potential advantage from the standpoint of importing nations as well. Argentina and Brazil's success is a food buyer's bounty.

It can be argued then that the present set of circumstances benefits producers and consumers alike. One country's grain exports are another's imports. Potentially, the transaction offers a net return for both sides. Yet the system is hardly perfect and is flawed in at least one serious way. Its chief problem is that the self-interests of governments and the grain trade oligopoly, who are the system's key actors, are frequently at variance with the needs of developing countries and the encouragement of efficient production worldwide. One marketing system's smooth operation is often achieved at the expense of another's, particularly the United States. Often working at cross-purposes, national agricultural economies nevertheless do eventually intersect to make up the potpourri of an international agricultural trading system. The functioning of this system is as much determined by the role of importers as by exporters.

IMPORTING COUNTRIES

The importing group constitutes every deficit country or region, but as with exporters a few countries play a determining role in the market. Even though the developing countries together account for approximately one-half of all cereal imports, Figure 10.2 indicates that the largest individual buyers of wheat, coarse grains, and soybeans are industrial, rich countries like Japan, the EC, or the USSR. As a result, the scales are tipped in favor of big buyers with reserves of foreign exchange that guarantee them access to the world food market at virtually any price. Their dependence on foreign food resources, on the one hand, is a weakness and, on the other hand, a strength, as demonstrated by the experience of Soviet shopping excursions in the United States. Moreover, this relatively small cluster of nations has the power to influence the market on the demand side proportionate to the weight suppliers hold. Their efforts to develop their own agricultural production and achieve food security and price stability have inspired marketing systems that thrive on protectionism and the maintenance of an open market in the United States.

Europe

In agriculture, the European Community is today a victim of its own success. The dual objectives that spawned the establishment of its Common Agricultural Policy (CAP)—increased productivity with a reasonable return for farmers and stable prices for consumers—have been met. CAP has created a breadbasket in Europe to the point that by 1981 the EC had become a net exporter of grain by a margin of approximately 4 million tons. Hand in hand with increased production has come stable prices. EC member states do not experience the price gyrations commonly endured by American consumers and producers. European producers, in effect, have a guaranteed floor price for their crop and a ceiling defined by the target price. Consumers also have a price cushion; they know the cost of their purchases will range between the target and threshold prices. Essentially the EC has built an agricultural fortress whose strength depends on the market forces surrounding it, particularly those emanating from the United States. Across the Atlantic a

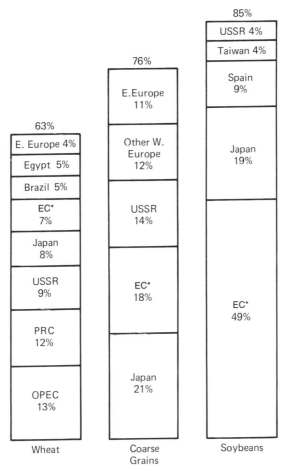

* Nine member countries.

FIGURE 10.2 Global Market Shares of Major Importers, 1977–78 Marketing Year.

relatively open market and freely fluctuating prices give foreign buyers and sellers the best approximation of market conditions worldwide, allowing the Commission to best gauge its own internal prices, levies, and export restitutions. Member countries can simultaneously cover their food import requirements at cheaper U.S. export prices than the cost of production within the EC.

The European Commission's biggest problem has been administering the increasingly cumbersome and expensive CAP system. In theory, its levies and export restitutions offer the maximum protection for a thriving domestic agricultural economy with the least amount of structural dislocation. The problem lies in the tremendous disparities among EC member countries in terms of production, specialization, and consumption requirements. Efforts to harmonize these differences, exacerbated by the addition of Greece and imminent membership of Spain, have placed an enormous burden on the CAP. Directing Europe's new-found agricultural prosperity into the most rational, efficient production possible has added to the strains on the system.

The Commission and its member countries are acutely aware of these problems. They recognize that the cost of CAP's subsidies have become excessive. In the 1981 report to the Council of Agricultural Ministers, the Commission recommended that internal EC prices be gradually lowered to a point more closely in line with the international export price. To compensate for the resulting reduction in subsidies to producers, the report recommended that the EC intensify its export program through bilateral agreements and coordination with competing suppliers. The suggested changes presume a continuation of the EC's surplus position that will necessitate a greater emphasis on exports. If the report's recommendations are accepted, it would mark a significant departure from the EC. Any such alterations, however, do not imply an end to the present system, but rather a refinement of export policy.

At present restitution levels, such as U.S. subsidy payments to shippers, are in theory calculated to cover the gap between EC and world market prices. A trader can prefix his export in the sense that he can bid on a Commission tender at the predetermined refund level and then, assuming his bid is accepted, hold the export certificate for the duration of his export license without any obligation to shop until the license period has expired. Generally, the export period is longer than the period of levy prefixation, allowing the trader greater opportunity to hedge his risk. Once the Commission issues an export certificate, it is good for any person or corporation in any member state. As a result, a lively secondary market in certificate trading exists. Certificates, which are not assigned to any named exporter, can be transferred any number of times. The ultimate holder is the one who receives the original restitution upon proof of delivery to the national intervention agency.

Setting payment levels under current procedures is a politically tinged process. A Management Committee, composed of member states with voting weighted according to their contribution to the EC budget, approves Commission proposals on the level of restitution payments. The Commission proposes the general export refund level to the Committee; upon approval, this figure is announced in the EC's *Official Journal*. Each member's Intervention Agency collects the bids from interested traders and submits them anonymously to Brussels. Concealed bidding is supposed to protect the Committee from approving contracts on political grounds. Nevertheless, approval of payment levels rests with Management Committee governments, not "Eurocrats" responsible for posting daily levies. The system may, as a result, minimize corruption, but not national political ambitions.

The Community has seven export zones for its wheat and flour. In theory, the restitution levels for exports to each zone correspond to freight rates calculated on the basis of distance and the volume of international shipping traffic. In practice, politics is a principal consideration in determining refund levels for each export zone. On occasion there have been no refunds for exports to Japan, while countries like Switzerland and Austria qualify for a modest refund, notwithstanding their proximity to EC countries. Japan is formally listed in Zone VII, along with China, both of which qualify for restitutions above the declared maximum. Generally, those countries receiving the highest export subsidies (or food aid) are "associates" of the Community, former French and British colonies, or countries vital to European foreign policy interests. In this sense, the system of export zones enables subsidy adjustments to reflect political and economic considerations toward traditional European markets and at the same time keeps EC grain and wheat flour exports competitive with larger, normally more efficient exporting countries.

Because France is Western Europe's largest producer of agricultural commodities, it gains proportionately the most under the present system. Other member states do less well. This imbalance is cause for considerable dissension within the Council of Ministers, particularly since the admission of the United Kingdom. CAP has its own monetary system designed to compensate other member states for any distortion in favor of an individual country. The main problem, however, is that it operates under supremely adverse conditions in that the EC lacks a truly uniform monetary system apart from agriculture and must rely in large part on the U.S. dollar, which still has a determining influence within the present international monetary system. The entire functioning of CAP hinges on a uniform currency-exchange system; otherwise, the internal pricing and external protectionist devices would vary in each member state as a function of the relative value of its own national currency.

In the absence of one all-purpose European currency, a special unit of account (u.a.) was set up for agricultural products based on the value of the dollar. By 1969, when France devalued the franc by 11 percent and Germany revalued its mark by 9 percent, the foundation began to shake. Both countries were unwilling to change the u.a. in keeping with their own currency realignments because it would have meant shouldering higher domestic food prices and lower farmer incomes. Instead, they agreed to maintain their earlier u.a. exchange rates for agricultural products with yet another agricultural currency to compensate for unequal burden sharing in each country. CAP thus got a new lease on life, resuscitated by the green rate—a monetary standard used as a means of converting (annually and intermittently) the u.a. into the currencies of the nine member countries. The green rate is the national currency equivalent that attempts to align each country's agricultural production prices with actual exchange rate valuations.

However ingenious, green rates compound the problem by exaggerating price divergences among members. They act as shields, protecting national agricultural economies from vicissitudes battering the international monetary system. When a member country witnesses a sharp depreciation in its currency, it cushions the effect on food prices by holding its green rate relatively constant. Alternatively, a country may devalue the green rate to raise agricultural prices for its farmers while its currency appreciates or remains relatively stable. In each scenario, the country needs the approval of all members. If a country pushes hard enough, it gains the Council of Ministers' consent, thus minimizing the effectiveness of this institutional check on unilateral initiatives.

Still another device was needed to achieve a uniform value for agricultural commodities among all members; monetary compensatory accounts (MCAs) are border taxes, or subsidies on goods traded within the Community, designed to equalize differences between green and market exchange rates. They act as a tax on exports and a subsidy on imports for member countries with devalued currencies, and in the opposite manner for states with appreciating or overvalued currencies. Similarly, in trade with nonmember nations, MCAs are used to keep levies and export subsidies uniform for every member country, adjusted according to the relative strength of its currency.[32] Introduced as a stop-gap measure in 1969 to moderate exchange rate differentials among member states, MCAs have proven more acceptable than has ending the system altogether, primarily because of the indisposition of member states to bear the full brunt of their own and other states' monetary and agricultural policies. MCAs, green rates, and u.a.'s have seemed to some a second-best rather than an ideal answer.

The advent of floating exchange rates in 1971 compounded the problem of maintaining uniform agricultural prices within the EC. Germany, Belgium, Luxembourg, and Denmark established a joint float, referred to as a "snake," that allowed fluctuations of individual country currencies within a prescribed range. The effort, however, failed to achieve its purpose of reducing price discrepancies for goods traded within the Community, in part because France, Italy, and the U.K. declined to join the snake. Their currencies were too weak to keep within the range enforced by the strong German mark.[33] Instead, they opted for the course of least resistance by floating their currencies independently; hence, their exchange rates were still on the dollar merry-go-round. By pegging their currencies to the performance of the dollar, the weak triumvirate added more dead weight to the system. For the MCA system, it also meant two sets of calculations—one for the "snake" group and one for the "free floaters."

The EC is no closer to price harmonization today than it was when CAP was put into effect. In late 1978, members agreed in principle to establish a common currency, the European Currency Unit (ECU), under a unified European Monetary System (EMS), but agricultural price variations abound much as before and may worsen with the accession of new members. In theory, EMS could obviate the need for MCAs, since there would no longer be the distortions that existed under the two-track system. The longer it takes to implement such a comprehensive system, however, the more it will need repair.

One of the side effects of such a complicated system is that it helps bolster the position of the largest international grain houses at the expense of greater competition. The MCA/levy-export refund system is not for the faint of heart. Only the majors can now afford to handle European transactions. Coordinating MCA and levy prefixations with export positions in the EC alone is a major undertaking. Fitting these factors into foreign grain purchases and shipments compounds the cost. The European market is too important to ignore, but CAP regulations militate against a rush for this business. Each year more small firms are driven into bankruptcy as the CAP system and predatory practices of the larger traders grind on.

Of the Big League traders, one of the most active in the EC is Cargill. Cargill's Tradax now has its highest concentration of subsidiaries within the EC where it was once considered an intruder. In fact, as late as 1967, just before the completion of the unified levy system under CAP, Cargill representatives maintained that its company in Hamburg was the brunt of exclusionary strong-arm tactics engineered by leading German companies. A similar claim is advanced by European representatives of Continental and Bunge. All three firms assert that a "millionaires' club," whose members included well-known German grain dealers like Toepfer, Beecher, and Kampfmeier, was established for the express purpose of preventing other companies from importing into Germany. If so, the tide has certainly turned. Now the Tradax group is very much at home in the EC, acting as one of Europe's largest grain-trading firms. The same is true for the rest of the Big League, none of whom are presently disposed to level charges of collusion to restrict their EC business operations against anyone. In fact, firms like Toepfer and Beecher have seen their market positions erode, with the slack picked up by the international superstars.

Despite its successes to date, CAP's future is problematic. To work, CAP needs to have a relatively open market functioning outside its borders. It is also heavily dependent on the Big League. Yet the mode of operations of these international firms has redefined the rules in the grain trade. In addition, their global position has reduced the openness of the system. Along with government monopolies, they are the prime determinants of the "market." As their influence grows, the effectiveness of CAP's form of protectionism diminishes. To date, recognition of this problem has commonly led the EC to impose additional restrictive measures. These, however, often serve only to complicate an already complex system, and, on occasion, to stimulate countermeasures among other importing and exporting countries. The question is, therefore, whether such a system can continue without major reform and, if so, for how long.

Japan

Japan's agricultural protectionism is built on a rice economy and a marketing system akin to corporate statism. The price of all edible grains, whether grown domestically or imported, is pegged to the price of rice.[34] There are also comprehensive government controls on the production and import of rice substitutes—wheat and barley. These are seen as a prerequisite for protecting domestic production.

The Japanese Food Agency, a government organ within the Ministry of Agriculture, exercises complete control over rice production, sales, and prices in domestic markets. The backbone of the rice program, however, is the Agency's manipulation of wheat and barley imports. The importation of cheap foreign wheat and barley sold at exaggerated prices for domestic consumption is a money-making proposition for the government and the private sector. The difference between what the Food Agency pays for imported wheat and barley "landed" in Japan and its resale price is revenue. On the Japanese market the Food Agency is a trader whose profit comes in part from the margin between the purchase (delivered c.i.f. import) and sale (resale on the local market) price.

Exchange rates between the yen and dollar have frequently proven to be an additional source of profit. In 1977-78, the Food Agency used overvalued yen to purchase American and Canadian wheat and barley quoted at depreciated dollars. It was a windfall. In the marketing year the Agency averaged 42.7 percent gross and 33.2 percent net profits on its wheat (U.S., Canadian, and Australian) transactions, equivalent to over $200 million. These profits represented the yen's advantage over the dollar in currency exchange rates plus the margin between the Food Agency's landed purchase and resale price. In 1977-78 the advantage was almost enough to cover the Agency's operating budget. It was a stroke of luck, but not permanent enough to counter the mounting costs and attendant inflationary effects of Japan's rice-based protectionist agricultural program.

Government policies and the agricultural marketing system in Japan protect both growers and merchandisers. In other principal importing and exporting countries, preferential treatment of the Big League is generally an outgrowth of the system itself rather than an intentional government policy. In Japan the role of the Sogo Shosha is consciously intertwined with the operations of the Food Agency. Except for foreign subsidiaries incorporated in Japan, only Japanese companies with "stable backgrounds" can qualify to handle wheat and barley imports. According to government officials, 28 companies are eligible; the actual number is closer to 12 because many companies listed officially belong to one of a few nuclear groups headed by the Sogo Shosha.

One of the Agency's functions is to establish annual import targets. The private trade is apprised of these targets, notwithstanding official government disclaimers. Since Agency projections are virtual commitments, the trading companies can position themselves well in advance of any contract to cover wheat and barley imports for the Japanese market. Every Wednesday at 2:00 p.m., the Agency puts out a tender for a fixed quantity of wheat and barley imports. When the Agency announces a tender, bidding companies indicate their price and the quantity they can ship. In reality, it is more like the finale than the overture in that the club of Japanese trading companies is already well informed. Trade sources assert that the Agency invites only certain companies, already informed in detail about the tender, to bid and awards them the right to import fixed quantities, allocated according to "merit of past performance." The same companies have been handling roughly the same percentage of Agency business for years.

Food Agency contracts are big business. The fact that they are awarded on a noncompetitive basis is particularly attractive to the lucky ones on the list. Once the contract is agreed on, there are additional benefits. The Agency pays 70 percent of the total before delivery of the cargo, which gives the companies ample cheap capital. Agency grains are shipped to designated warehouses, which are privately owned and generally affiliated with the Sogo Shosha handling the imports.

Non-Japanese companies complain that they are left with only the pickings. All the Big League traders are represented in Tokyo, but their share of the Japanese market is much less than their share worldwide. Excluded from handling Agency grains, companies like Tradax also face obstacles in dealing with uncontrolled commodities. If a Tradax confronts the Japanese giants head-on through direct sales to their customers of even non-Agency grains and oilseeds, it risks a complete cut off of the sizable business it does with these trading companies in the United States and elsewhere. Moreover, now that Tokyo has become one of the world's largest ship-chartering centers, the Big League would risk losing this business in a direct confrontation with the Sogo Shosha. Indeed, Tradax Japan's principal line of activity is ship brokering from Tokyo, especially in fixing charters for the Cargill/Tradax group worldwide. Under the circumstances, most members of the Big League have preferred to move cautiously in their grain sales operations much as the Sogo Shosha traditionally have done in the United States. As Japan evolves into the Netherlands of the Pacific, the Big League can only profit along with their Japanese counterparts by pursuing this conservative strategy. There is also potential for further inroads in the Japanese market as pressure mounts to reduce Japan's most flagrant forms of protectionism.

The USSR

The Soviet Union is the world's largest wheat grower and has evolved into the second largest grain importer in the course of the last decade. Its internal production and marketing system is the most centralized of all the major agricultural economies, but its procurement practices are identical in many respects to those of the most sophisticated privately owned grain firms. Exportkhleb, the official grain-trading arm, has free rein to exercise whatever commercial muscle it can to satisfy Soviet import-export requirements. When the United States canceled sales commitments for 17 million metric tons in January 1980, Exportkhleb had to do some fancy footwork to replace its

TABLE 10.1 Sogo Shosha Import Shares of Selected Grains (in percent)

Grain / Firm	Wheat Jap FY 1976 Total Imports 5,324,000 met. tons	Barley Jap FY 1976 Total Imports 1,687,000 met. tons	Soybeans Jap FY 1976 Total Imports 3,318,000 met. tons	Corn (feed usage) Calendar Yr. 1976 Total Imports 6,987,737 met. tons
Mitsubishi	9	12	19	16
Mitsui	12	13	15	13
Marubeni	8	9	14	12
Kanematsu-Goshu	12	12	4	4
C. Itoh	7	11	15	10
Nichimen	11	7	3	3
Nissho–Iwai	8	6	7	5
Toshoku	7	13	4	4
Sumitomo	5	5	9	3
Toyomenka Kaisha (Tomen)	4	3	3	6
Yuasa	3	4	—	—
Ataka	3	2	—	1
Sanyo	.63	2	—	—
TOTAL	90	99	93	77

orders from other sources and cover the losses that undoubtedly occurred. In the five years prior to 1980, the Soviet Union had imported an average of 15.6 million metric tons of grain (9.6 of which came from the United States) valued at roughly $1.7 billion. Exportkhleb has had paramount responsibility for these transactions. It is a tough merchant, using monopoly powers to play off governments and companies against one another.

Soviet commercial strategy involving grain has evolved over time. As the Soviet Union moved from a state of self-sufficiency to become a heavy importer of wheat in the 1960s, it locked up most of its business through purchasing agreements with Canada and Australia. At that time the U.S., European, and Latin American markets served as residual suppliers of wheat and corn. These transactions were relatively straightforward because of government participation in contract negotiations with a limited role for private traders.

The USSR was unaccustomed to being an importer and was not yet committed to building up its livestock herds to levels that would require foreign resources. When there was a shortfall in these years, there was no certainty that the USSR would shop abroad. Frequently, Soviets opted for distress slaughtering of their stocks to cut down on the demand for feedgrains rather than stepping up of imports. Without precise figures on Soviet stocks, it was hard to predict how much the government could draw from its own reserves before it would have to resort to imports for food grains. There were sharp drawdowns on their stocks in 1963, 1965, 1971, and 1972, but only in 1972 was the severe loss balanced by heavy imports.[35] Exporters were falling over themselves in their efforts to lure the Soviets to buy. The miscalculation on the part of both the companies and the supplying countries, however, was their assumption that Soviet import needs would harmonize with their exporting and marketing capabilities to the point of mutual gain.

Exportkhleb learned too much too soon and was well prepared by 1972-73 when it purchased almost two and one-half times as much grain as in the total previous eight years—30 million metric tons, or 75 percent of all grain traded commercially throughout the world. The shift in strategy was handled with a commercial prowess that has now become legend. The Soviets successfully traded when there was an outstanding surplus among major exporters, particularly in the United States where the USSR bought over 19 million metric tons. By concealing their plans from most of the trade and from governments of supplying countries, they were able to buy when the exchanges registered low grain prices (largely wheat and corn) in response to the assumption that existing surpluses would remain unsold. Acting under the same assumption, Washington offered the Soviets special credit and subsidized prices to firm up the deal expeditiously.

The companies were duped as well. Cargill stated publicly in 1973 that its estimated profit after taxes on its Russian grain sales would be less than 1 percent.[36] Subsequently, representatives of the company have maintained that Cargill actually lost money on these 1972 transactions. Continental, the largest seller of American grain to the USSR at the time claimed that it was completely unaware of the extent of Soviet buying intentions: "Had we known that we were about to sell millions of tons of corn to the Soviet Union and that the price of corn was going to rise, we would have been buyers, not sellers."[37] Big League representatives asserted that they were uninformed about the scale of Soviet purchases and equally in the dark about the cutoff date for U.S. export subsidies applicable to Soviet sales. U.S. government officials blamed the entire fiasco on poor information. Despite regular conferrals with Washington, and ongoing negotiations with the Soviets during which one company executive traced another's footsteps in Moscow, the private sector's position is that no one had precise knowledge about the size of the package and who was selling what.

Since 1972 changes in Soviet trading practices have been negligible. The 1975 bilateral treaty did little to curb Exportkhleb's sharp trading practices. In an atmosphere of surpluses, which again characterize the opening of the 1980s, the United States has exhibited little interest in limiting either American traders' or their Soviet counterparts' freedom to maneuver. As long as surpluses last, the market will also remain relatively insensitive to Soviet purchases. When the production cycle returns to scarcity, the same tactics left unmonitored by the U.S. government today are bound to create grievous disturbances and consequent economic losses.

China

China's import strategy has changed significantly in conjuction with the volume of its imports. Although Ceroilfoods (National Cereals, Oils, and Foodstuffs Import and Export Corporation) is, like Exportkhleb, a government trading arm that operates as a private company, it has exercised more restraint than its Soviet counterpart. Traditionally it imported under long-term purchasing agreements with prearranged financing from supplying countries. The main objective was to buy high-quality wheat specified as opposed to optional in origin. With adverse climate conditions in the 1980 and 1981 growing seasons and sweeping political changes, the government assigned Ceroilfoods the broader task of competing with other buyers for the most favorable export prices.

Ceroilfoods has, nevertheless, interpreted its mandate conservatively. It has refrained from large spot purchases that distort the market and has not engaged in either reselling or speculative activities such as have been ascribed to other government trading agencies like Brazil's COBEC. As a result, its entry as a big buyer in the U.S. market has been greeted as a welcome development.

The picture could change if China's dependence on foreign food resources mounts and Ceroilfoods is forced by necessity to resort to the tricks of the trade. As an increasingly price-conscious government monopoly, it could, with the assistance of the omnipresent Big League, disrupt the world markets in much the same manner as has Exportkhleb. This is the great unknown in any effort to assess the future role of Ceroilfoods.

Centralized government agencies have grown in number so that in 1973-77 they accounted for an average of 91 percent of the world's grain imports.[38] They behave as monopsonists—buyers with monopoly powers—which enables them to regulate prices and supplies more effectively for their national purposes than if they were to rely strictly on the private sector. If they were to coordinate their strategies effectively, presumably they could become an effective grain-importing cartel. Two essential factors discount this prospect in the immediate future: (1) there is no common strategy among the world's major importers, although they share common goals of cheap supplies at stabilized prices; and (2) they all rely on an oligopoly of traders that in varying degrees handles their purchases, whether they are under concessional or commercial terms.

Dependence on the majors to execute grain transactions increases as the relative international importance of a country's economy declines. Lacking real market power and relevant commercial skills, governments in this situation, primarily LDCs, turn to the most sophisticated international companies—the Big League—to conclude the best deals in their behalf. They generally entered into preferential relationships with particular firms over an extended period of time, making it extremely difficult for others to compete. Among LDCs the emerging pattern is one in which Big League members have secured their traditional markets with each specializing in a particular region or country. An analogous trend exists among developed countries.[39]

At this juncture, governments need the major trading firms to make their own marketing systems work; and the giants of the trade need governments as clients, protectors, and competitors vying for immediate fulfillment of national food objectives. The positive effects of this symbiotic relationship are reduced by the costs to producers and consumers worldwide. Some marketing systems have been more successful than others in insulating a national agricultural economy from supply and price instabilities that take place on the world market. In the process, however, other problems arise—witness the experience of the EC or Japan. Canada and Australia have achieved better results, but inherently their strength depends on existing weaknesses in the American marketing system. Inevitably there are costs for all concerned and the degree of loss mounts as the demand for food resources rises. Given present policies and marketing systems, the United States is least exempt from such economic ill effects.

NOTES

1. The Board's jurisdiction applies to the western provinces: Saskatchewan, Manitoba, and Alberta produce 96.1 percent of wheat, 79.3 percent of barley, 94.2 percent of oats, and 8.7 percent of other feedgrains in Canada.

2. Andrew Schmitz and Alex McCalla, "The Canadian Wheat Board," in

Agricultural Marketing Boards: An International Perspective, Sidney Hoos ed. (Cambridge, Mass.: Ballinger, 1979), p. 82.

3. Schmitz and McCalla, "Comparison of Canadian and U.S. Grain Marketing Systems" (paper prepared for the National Grain and Feed Association, March 1976).

4. The Commission on the Costs of Transporting Grain by Rail, *Report*, vol. 1 (Ottawa: Supply and Services Canada, 1976); and Grain Handling and Transportation Commission (Hall Commission), *Grain and Rail in Western Canada*, vols. 1-3 (Ottawa: Supply and Services Canada, 1977).

5. The Hall Commission recommends "the difference between the statutory rate and the cost of transporting grain to be paid directly to the railways." *Grain and Rail in Western Canada*, p. 545.

6. The Canadian Grain Marketing Review Committee, *Report Submitted to the Canadian Wheat Board*, 12 January 1971, p 17.

7. Canadian Wheat Board, "Grain Matters: A Letter from the Canadian Wheat Board," April 1978, p. 7.

8. *Canadian Wheat Board Act*, F.S., c. C-12, 1972, p. 5.

9. Mitsui reportedly deals most often with Cargill, Canada Kanematsu with Parrish and Heinbecker Ltd., Marubeni with XCAN, a pool exporting company, and C. Itoh in a joint venture with the Alberta pool of a rapeseed processing plant.

10. In 1977 Cargill purchased a portion of the Panco Poultry Company from the British Columbia Government for approximately $3.3 million. Panco had been purchased by the government in 1974 when the Social Democrats were in office, but sold in parcels when the Social Credit Party took office.

11. *Paper Wheat*, a play produced by the 25th Street House Theatre that played in Canadian provinces in 1977 and was filed as a documentary by the National Film Board of Canada in the same year.

12 New South Wales, Victoria, Tasmania, and Queensland.

13. Industries Assistance Commission, *Wheat Stabilization* (Canberra: Australian Government Publishing Service, 30 June 1978), p. 18.

14. Bureau of Agricultural Economics, *Wheat Stabilization, BAE Submission to the Industries Assistance Commission Inquiry* (Canberra: Bureau of Agricultural Economics, August 1977), p. V-31.

15. Industries Assistance Commission, *Wheat Stabilization*, p. 18.

16. The Australian Chartering Committee operates through John Darling Proprietary Ltd. and Gilbert J. McCaul (Overseas) Ltd.

17. U.S. General Accounting Office (GAO), *Grain Marketing Systems in Argentina, Australia, Canada, and the European Community; Soybean Marketing System in Brazil* (Washington: GAO, May 1976), p. 24.

18. Industries Assistance Commission, *Wheat Stabilization*, p. 50.

19. Ibid.

20. From John H. Williams, General Manager of the AWB, to Richard Gilmore, 9 January 1979, in reply to the author's correspondence of 15 December 1978.

21. Richard Gilmore, "Why a Food Embargo Won't Work," *Washington Post*, 27 December 1979.

22. GAO, *Grain Marketing Systems*, p. 25.

23. Ibid., p. 27.

24. Ibid., pp. 26-27.

25. Confirmation of these procedures has come from trade sources and confidential reports.

26. The World Bank, Regional Projects Dept., *Staff Appraisal Report: Argentina, Grain Storage Project,* Report No. 1749b-AR (26 January 1978), p. 21.

27. U.S. Department of Agriculture, Foreign Agricultural Service, *Foreign Agriculture Circular,* FOP 10-81, p. 13.

28. Ibid.

29. E. E. Broadbent and F. Perry Dixon, *Exploratory Study of Brazil Soybean Marketing,* AERR144 (Champaign-Urbana: Dept. of Agricultural Experiment Station, University of Illinois, n.d.), p. 46.

30. Internal U.S. Department of Agriculture document. Italics added.

31. USDA, FAS, "Brazil: Soybean Crushing Capacity," BP-8015, p. 3.

32. MCAs are calculated by translating the difference between market and green rates into the EC's agricultural unit of account which, in turn, is pegged to the dollar. Export contracts are expressed in dollars and the refund payments plus the original purchase price are in a European currency. Prefixation of MCAs, therefore, allows the trader to hedge against a possible devaluation by moving into a strong currency and applying for MCAs on the basis of the original contract quoted in dollars.

33. France was originally a member of the snake, but quickly dropped out in January 1974.

34. Refer to Richard Gilmore, "Growing Food for Japan," *Mainichi Newspapers* (Tokyo), 12 January 1981 (published in Japanese); and Richard Gilmore, "National Food Stabilization—At What Price?" *Trends* (Japanese magazine of the U.S. International Communication Agency), February 1981 (published in Japanese).

35. U.S. Central Intelligence Agency, *The Soviet Grain Balance 1960-1973,* A (ER) 75-68 (September 1975), p. 20.

36. U.S. Congress, Senate Committee on Government Operations, *Russian Grain Transactions, Hearings before the Permanent Subcommittee on Investigations,* 93d Cong., 1st sess., 1973, pt. 2, p. 299.

37. Ibid., Statement of Bernard Steinweg, Senior Vice-President of Continental Grain Co., New York, pt. 1, p. 55.

38. Schmitz, "The Establishment and Operation of a Grain Export Cartel," U.S. Department of Agriculture Contract 697-ASCS-79, 24 September 1979, p. 7. Refer to Appendix, "National Grain Trading Organizations."

39. "Affidavit of George S. Shanklin," filed 23 April 1979 in *Gilmore v. Department of Agriculture et al.,* Civil Action No. 79-0863, U.S. District Court, District of Columbia (action dismissed by stipulation with prejudice, 10 August 1979), p. 4. Dan Morgan, "A Nation Comes to Terms on Wheat," *Washington Post,* 7 December 1977, p. 1; Emma Rothschild, "Food Politics," *Foreign Affairs* 54 (January 1976): pp. 285-07; and Emma Rothschild, "Is It Time to End Food for Peace?" *New York Times Magazine,* 13 March 1979, p. 15.

11

Prognosis and Prescription: An Agricultural Manifesto

Let Pharaoh proceed to appoint overseers over the land, and take the fifth part of the produce of the land of Egypt during the seven plenteous years. And let them gather all the food of these good years that are coming, and lay up grain under the authority of Pharaoh for food in the cities, and let them keep it. That food shall be a reserve for the land against the seven years of famine which are to befall the land of Egypt, so that the land may not perish through the famine—   GENESIS, 41:34–36.

Now we propose to survey the situation in regard to surpluses and shortages in each circuit as a whole, to sell when grain is dear and buy when it is cheap, in order to increase the accumulation in government storage and to stabilize the prices of commodities. This will make it possible for the farmers to go ahead with their work at the proper season, while the monopolists will no longer be able to take advantage of their temporary stringency.
                            WANG AN-SHIH, *"Memorial"* to Emperor Shen-tsung, 1069.

What both farmers and consumers want is a more uniform price and a more uniform supply from year to year. The ever-normal granary legislation is designed to iron out the peaks and fill up the valleys.
                            HENRY WALLACE, *U.S. Secretary of Agriculture*, 1937.

No marketing system or set of food policies is perfect, but the present system's imperfections darken the horizon. U.S. wheat harvests in 1981 surpassed all records and the corn crop was the third largest in U.S. history. Global wheat production was at an all-time high, increasing 5 percent over the previous year. Prices, although declining in the face of apparent surpluses, still remained as much as 30 percent above 1980 levels in feedgrains and 5 percent over healthy 1980 wheat prices. At the same time, 1981 grain carryover stocks were down to a low of 14 percent of consumption requirements. Food shortages persisted in a majority of African countries, and food prices were outdistancing the rate of overall inflation in most developing countries. Soaring interest rates made U.S. and other foreign grains prohibitively expensive for all but the wealthiest countries. And stagnating foreign demand, coupled with the high cost of capital, constituted a serious blow to U.S. farmers only just recovering from the effects of the 1980 Soviet grain embargo.

The Big League, on the other hand, was suffering no seeming decline in earnings. The volume of grain traded in the export market had reached a peak level of approximately 25 percent of annual world production, which assured the major grain houses of more business. Between 1979 and 1981 these companies made some of their largest acquisitions, which required vast capital resources derived from high earnings along with long-term borrowing. Grain merchandising remained the most profitable part of their operations, facilitating their drive toward expansion and integration.

Today, the structural evolution in agriculture has reached a point where concentration in production and merchandising worldwide has become fact. U.S. food production and that of a satellite group of supplying countries is now essential to satisfying basic global food consumption requirements. The Big League is the confirmed vehicle to carry out these transfers, having gradually displaced growers as an influential market force. The mode of operations of these firms, reinforced by the actions of monopolistic, state-run organizations, has reduced the significance of traditional market indicators and transformed the trade arena. Futures or export prices and reports of current stocks are of transparently little importance as opposed to sales commitments to affiliated foreign companies, their cancellation, optional contracting, and shipments to unknown destinations. Cash prices, which previously received only passing attention on the grounds that they moved up or down solely in relation to spot prices, are now as meaningful an indicator of price trends as futures thanks to current grain trade practices. European levies, Winnipeg transactions with Canadian Wheat Board "agents," or Japan's Food Agency tenders tell more about available supplies than any official stock figures.

Changes in structure and groundrules have not produced equivalent adjustments in public institutions and policies in the agricultural sector. On the contrary, governments have demonstrated an inability to track these developments and grasp their significance in terms of national economic interests. The United States in particular has deferred to the grain trade oligopoly not only to promote exports but effectively to determine the outcome of U.S. agricultural export policies. The implementation of these U.S. policies is dependent on the accuracy of information Washington culls from the trade. The real business of commodity exchanges revolves around transactions that elude government agencies responsible for their surveillance. And American producers are resigned to a government life insurance policy underwritten by the moguls of the grain business who thrive on exporting as much of the annual crop production as possible.

Whatever the weaknesses of its institutions and agricultural programs, the United States continues to toy with a food weapon strategy. Other exporting and importing countries are likewise prone to manipulating food issues for their own political and economic gain. The end result is a unilateral approach to the problem, the importance of which transcends national boundaries. Protectionism abounds, sustaining inefficient forms of production and obstructing the flow of trade. Plans for an accelerated growth of the agricultural sector in developing countries are inevitably retarded when food aid for foreign policy purposes is substituted for economic development objectives. The risk of long-term economic dislocations, such as the effects of the 1980 Soviet grain embargo, are ever present. Under these circumstances the future is grim for producers and consumers worldwide, but Big League traders can look forward to good times. The evidence is conclusive that current national policies and commercial practices will give rise to increasing economic and political disruption. Moreover, past experience demonstrates that when breakdowns have occurred, producers and consumers, both in the United States and other countries, have been seriously affected. Government remedial measures have tended to worsen the situation from a public welfare standpoint and, conversely, strengthen the influence of a few international grain houses. To reverse this trend so as to maximize the efficiencies of the private sector without ignoring the joint interests of producers and consumers worldwide, there are a number of corrective remedies the United States can take unilaterally.

Introducing a well-managed export licensing plan could offer producers and consumers a means of capturing a greater proportion of the gain from production and high-volume foreign sales. Such a system, under proper administration, could allocate supplies more equitably—an especially important task in times of emergency—and remit a greater share of profits from export sales to U.S.-based operations, as opposed to the current practice of disbursing these returns to nonproductive investment centers in Panama or Switzerland. Tightening export reporting requirements in conjunction with a comprehensive licensing program would provide Washington with the supply management controls it now lacks without adding another burdensome layer to the bureaucracy.

Government participation in the agricultural sector is an irrefutable fact accepted by every vested interest in the grain business. Interests do not, of course, concur over the form this intervention should take, but the principle of public and private coparticipation in agriculture is no longer contested, except at the level of rhetoric. Neither farmers nor the trade objected to government credits and export subsidies for the 1972 Soviet sale. Government surveillance of these transactions met a cooler reception, however, particularly from the grain houses. Despite the gross misreading of the market in 1972, and in the major events thereafter, Washington still hesitated to move in this area. It was one thing to bestow export incentives, a role welcomed by most of the interest groups directly affected, and quite another to assume a more direct agricultural management role.

The Carter administration in 1980 moved unwittingly in this direction when it instituted contractual auditing procedures for holders of Soviet contracts willing to accept the Commodity Credit Corporation's conditions for reimbursement. In exchange for liquidating these contracts, the government secured access to corporate books for a period of up to three years, which was deemed necessary to certify that exporters were acting in good faith in carrying out their agreement with the CCC.[1] Although limited to transactions with the USSR for a defined time span, this initiative could easily have served as the basis for a revised export reporting and, conceivably, an umbrella licensing system. If applied, the auditing provision could have given the federal government meaningful insights into the workings of the trade.

Any such notion was scotched by the Carter administration's handling of the canceled contracts. In an all-out effort to avoid the expense of holding these sales and reselling them at what was then considered the relatively high legislated price, the CCC painstakingly delayed until there were enough additional foreign sales to turn the contracts back to the private sellers. The whole process was sufficiently rapid to allow auditors at best only a glimpse at the company books. The opportunity was then lost, and the Reagan administration gives no hint of an interest in reconsidering the issue. The need for tighter export reporting requirements and an evaluation of a possible export licensing system remains. A combination of the two within a single administration could coordinate enforcement functions with export sales and shipments information.

The destination of shipments has proved to be a problem in the handling of past sales suspensions, particularly the most recent one against the Soviet Union. As long as shipments remain indeterminate until final delivery, the government has no way of knowing where cargoes are headed. This knowledge gap becomes crucial in times of scarcity and emergency political situations, such as the Soviet invasion of Afghanistan. The rush to switch contracts with foreign affiliates into bona fide Soviet purchases was typical for the trade and a costly headache for the government. An export license for the Soviet Union would require confirmation of final delivery. Without this certification, exporting firms would risk losing their permits for future shipments.

As long as the United States intends to reserve the right to initiate grain embargoes for political or domestic economic purposes, a full-fledged export reporting-licensing system would minimize the harmful effects by spreading losses more equitably than under the present system, which is too loosely run to do more than tolerate an uneven distribution of gains and forfeitures. The arguments in favor of such a plan are not that it would facilitate a food weapon strategy and export restrictions but that it would help prevent recourse to an extreme, generally unwise measure. The more accurate the government's sales and, hence, current supply information as well as its enforcement powers, the less possibility for misunderstandings such as the soybean embargo of 1973, which, in retrospect, was both unnecessary and exceedingly damaging.

Cancellations, buy-back provisions, optional contracting, and concealment of large-scale foreign purchases become less attractive under a licensing arrangement. Everything hinges on the issuance of a license. If a seller negotiates a handsome contract with a foreign buyer via a non-American affiliate, the sale remains problematical until an appropriate license is approved. Sales on non-U.S.-origin grain under an optional contract are always possible, but, again, sudden shifting into U.S. grain would not necessarily mean that a given contract could be consummated with American grain. The final hurdle—transforming a paper contract into a firm contract for delivery—could come only with the approval of a license.

Even commodity speculation by the majors would be reduced, thereby enhancing the balancing function of hedging in the market. Licenses can bridge the gap between a sales commitment and an actual shipment and thus moderate the degree of uncertainty about daily or longer-term supply positions. Under current CFTC regulations, sales count as hedgeable inventories even though they may never materialize. This distinction, albeit practical from a regulatory and legal standpoint, significantly distorts the supply picture. A licensing system would reduce the margin for error by treating a sales commitment as a bona fide contract only upon receipt of a licensed stamp of approval. As a result, exporters and importers would be hedging only their exposure for a specific contract, bringing hedging operations on the exchanges more closely in line with actual market conditions. With less risk, producers might return to the futures market to exercise their rightful market power in hedging their own transactions.

The direct price effects of an evenhanded licensing system could also translate into higher public and private revenues without undue harmful effects for foreign buyers. License fees would generate public income and act as an export tax, which would result in higher prices for exported U.S. grains. Properly administered, the fees could be remitted to growers, who have experienced a relatively low rate of return during the last decade. Given the nature of current and future import requirements and relatively inelastic world import demand, higher prices for U.S. grain are not likely to induce a significant downturn in export volume, and therefore the earnings would be greater than at current international prices (it is probable that other exporting countries, which already sell higher-priced grain than the United States, would follow suit). With severe foreign currency constraints placed on developing countries, which are unable to produce enough cereals to cover their immediate food requirements, the United States could attempt to implement a variable fee structure, akin to the EC zone system, with lower prices for qualified buyers or regions. The drawback, of course, is that such a plan is extremely hard to enforce uniformly and could contribute to even greater market convulsions than more open market conditions, as demonstrated by EC restitution fiascos.

Although every option under a variable fee plan is subject to abuse, it is conceivable that import coupons issued to developing countries would create the least difficulty and would ensure LDC access to the American grain market. Coupons, in essence, would provide a discount off the higher international price, but the floor still would be above some of the low U.S. export prices during the last ten years. The tradeoff for LDCs would be greater market stability, since the coupon rate would be pegged to an international price known far in advance of their purchases, introducing an opportunity for more cost savings over time than offered by the present, highly erratic trend in prices.

Short of this kind of reform in the U.S. export sector, there are more modest initiatives that the United States could undertake with disproportionately positive results. The preferential treatment now accorded foreign subsidiaries and affiliates of American firms is a loophole that permits extraordinary profits for Big League traders, while at best offers little productive return to the rest of the economy. Other informational gaps are of equal disservice to the public interest. Failure to synchronize reports to the CFTC on futures contracts with export sales reports to the USDA is another profit opportunity for the largest international grain houses and a hindrance to government analysis and the dissemination of market information. Because of a time lag, the material Washington gets is stale and the substance misleading. Lack of hard-core data on cash markets results, at best, in a half picture of current market conditions. The 24-hour reporting rule for sales of over 100,000 metric tons is an abused regulation, according to trade sources. Soviet sales, for instance, still go undetected until it is convenient for the trade to report them from their foreign subsidiaries. Strict confidentiality of such information provided to the government has not ensured either the quality or timeliness of the export sales reports.

Surveillance of cash markets is in a worse state, widening the information gap to the point that official assessments of the market are based on faulty or partial indicators of actual conditions. To make the picture more complete and up to date, the government could tighten reporting regulations and expand its oversight of the cash markets, both of which it has the power and mandate to do under current laws. These steps would be a more moderate response to recurrent breakdowns in the present system rather than a shift to an overkill in regulatory controls. In fact, an improvement in the information base should lead to less need for frequent, direct government interventions in the market and more equitable protection of all U.S. agricultural interests.

Government cannot resign from its role in policy direction and efforts to ensure that the American marketing system remains as nondiscriminatory as possible. Regulatory involvement has its place in the endless task of balancing public against private interests. Transportation problems in the United States, although minor by comparison to neighboring Canada, are significant and not subject to the quick and superficial solution of complete deregulation. The initial rail bill proposed by forces in Congress and the Carter administration ignored the demands of efficient, smaller producers. The final rail deregulation legislation paid some attention to these special concerns, but probably not enough. Moreover, the present approach risks an emphasis on easing investment opportunities in the railroad industry for the sake of modernization, which coincidentally will buttress the position of the Big League vis-à-vis potential competition from smaller private exporters and cooperatives. And transportation is only one illustration of how this problem can arise from an overly categorical approach to the issue of regulation in agriculture.

Indecision about the role of the CFTC has severely limited its contribution toward making the commodity exchanges function reliably. In the last few years, there have been too many breakdowns or close calls that underscore the need for government to exercise its oversight responsibilities, working with the exchanges to establish more reliable, neutral price discovery and hedging mechanisms (including closer monitoring of cash markets). The alternative is to allow the status quo—equivalent to a passive, ad hoc approach to regulation—to foster a continuation of anticompetitive practices that corrode the system's principal value. In the absence of a government initiative, the trade is certainly capable of introducing appropriate reforms along these lines, which, after all, are in its own interests.

Fiscal reform is another area downplayed in terms of its effects on American and foreign agricultural economies. Current liberal tax treatment of corporate earnings abroad fortifies the position of the Big League with negligible positive effects for the rest of the economy. The U.S. government gives special tax breaks to exporters on the theory that they bring substantial increases in foreign grain sales. In actuality, they are superfluous as an incentive for improving the U.S. position as the global grain giant because of the comparative advantage it holds in agriculture. No country is likely to displace the United States from its predominant position as supplier of food and feedgrains worldwide by undercutting its prices. At best, such competitive practices can result in temporary market lows, generally unsustainable because of the thinner margin of excess supply among residual producers other than the United States. The greater threat to American exports is U.S. policies themselves. Allowing a tax break for foreign subsidiaries' earnings on sales of American grain and maintaining DISCs for grain sellers are two immediate means by which the return to producers or the government in terms of higher exports is nonexistent, but the return to international grain houses is considerable.

Fiscal reforms are extremely delicate, with broad implications for international trade and commerce. Eliminating the DISC for grain companies is an easy step, but treatment of foreign corporate profits is not. Other options could prove equally constructive and avoid the pitfalls of the United States' extending changes in its tax laws for application in other countries. If the uniform treatment of American grain companies and their foreign subsidiaries' corporate earnings produces inequitable results, such as double taxation, the government alternatively could seek to have such foreign tax payments put to better use. Under revised tax treaties, foreign affiliates of American grain trade houses could, for example, direct their tax payments into special reserve and food aid funds established by the United States and other governments. Isolating tax payments for a specific use should be of no concern to corporations as long as their tax obligations do not grow more burdensome and inequitable. At the same time, such payments could introduce more stability into the global grain market.

Without the concurrence of other countries, the United States, as the world's largest food aid donor, could still modify its policies and achieve some of the same objectives, as in the above-mentioned areas of fiscal reform. The simplest step would be to make long-term supply commitments on a quantitative basis to aid-worthy countries, much as it already does with bilateral commercial grain agreements. Until developing countries achieve a higher degree of self-sufficiency, they will continue either to depend on outside food resources or to face shortages affecting large segments of their populations. Cheap concessional food does not in itself discourage a recipient's intensive development of its own agricultural production as much as do the continual variations in supply and price these countries have experienced to date.[2]

A long-term food aid commitment (as opposed to the pledge arrangement under the Food Assistance Convention) also could benefit American farmers by providing an assured foreign outlet for production and opportunities for new entrants into the export business, other than members of the existing oligopoly. When PL 480 accounted for the largest portion of American wheat exports, it was important business for the big grain houses, both from a volume and market development standpoint. Now, spokesmen for these corporations downplay the program's significance as far as their own commercial operations are concerned. Cooperatives, on the other hand, are in search of low-risk export business, which PL 480 still offers. Under the circumstances, the government could well require aid recipients to contract exclusively with American cooperatives for PL 480 sales. As a result, cooperatives could gain a foothold in foreign markets with commercial growth potential. Judging from the Big League's reaction to the Carter administration ruling in favor of export pool access to CCC loans, the warlords of the business are not likely to welcome this initiative. But they once had the privilege of handling most of the PL 480 business, whose importance as a profit source they now disclaim. Exclusive contracting with cooperatives would reintroduce on a much smaller scale (because of the lower level of food aid compared to commercial sales), an opportunity that the private sector in effect already enjoyed.

In so doing, the government would be introducing an element of competition, which the United States and world grain market now lack. Contracting with cooperatives having U.S. government backing is both a supplementary food security guarantee for aid recipients and a means of linking American farm interests directly with agricultural development concerns in these countries. In fact, producer members of export cooperatives have valuable skills for LDCs, which could be utilized more easily as co-ops became exclusive handlers of their U.S. food aid imports. Recipient countries could contract with cooperatives for technical assistance as part of a total PL 480 agreement, which would have beneficial effects for all parties. Implementing such a program, of course, means allocating a certain portion of existing stocks for food assistance purposes. The United States already has a security reserve of 4 million metric tons of wheat, established to soak up unforeseen surpluses resulting from the 1980 sales cancellations with the USSR. As the law is currently written, this reserve is isolated from the market and can only be tapped under tightly defined conditions of shortages that would otherwise force the United States to reduce its obligations under PL 480. With only a slight modification in the law, these stocks could be used to supplement the U.S. food aid program over the long term. One such use would be to extend the life of U.S. commitments to individual countries rather than to augment the annual allocation. The net effect would be to avoid depressing domestic prices and at the same time enhance food security for chronically deficit aid recipient countries.

Traditionally, American farmers have been opposed to reserves because of their fear that the government would use such reserves to hold down prices. This legitimate concern deals with their use, but not the concept of reserves itself. Additional measures to compensate for eroding farm incomes, for instance indexing loan and target prices, would help assuage farm group objections to a national reserve system. Coupling price supports with reserves was part of the ever-normal granary equation once so well received by national farm groups.[3] As Secretary Wallace noted, the two go hand in hand: "He (the American farmer) believes he can achieve balanced abundance for both the consumer and himself if the soil is sensibly handled, if the farm income is fairly maintained, and if highly variable weather is offset by a workable ever-normal granary policy."[4]

But the United States never really developed an ever normal granary. The Wallace approach was, in fact, an incomplete idea rather than a systematic plan. At no time has the United States attempted to fashion a program that would integrate domestic and international concerns. A lop-sided emphasis on internal concerns could be justified when only a small portion of annual production moved into the export stream. Today, the dependence of the United States on exports requires a comprehensive outlook in which export policies and domestic programs are handled as one and the same. The United States would do well to adopt an integrated approach to current agricultural problems, designing, in the process, a comprehensive agricultural plan. While any such plan would have limitations, it would be nevertheless an appropriate exercise for any reform effort. Most importantly, it serves as a means of assessing the usefulness of any modification to present policies and programs. The partial measures outlined thus far merit this kind of test to separate the wheat from the chaff.

A food bank system offers one model to relate the parts to the whole with useful guidelines for comprehensive structural change. Domestic (U.S.) and international food banks for wheat and wheat flour would introduce a greater degree of stability and equity than now exists in the market for these crops.[5] Once the fundamental arrangements had been sufficiently well tested, the system could be expanded to include other essential feedgrains and oilseeds, which are frequently substituted for feed quality wheats. The overall purpose for both banks would be to establish a system that links production more closely with farmer income and integrates supply with global demand generated from poor as well as rich countries. In effect, the banks would be designed to redress the structural problems that now distance the farmer from a fair return for his production; the buyer (American and foreign) from available supplies; the aid-recipient country from a constant minimum level of food resources; and all governments from adequate knowledge of the market and, hence, from sound agricultural management policies. It would attempt to combine the efficiencies of the private sector with government representation of public interests.

Ideally, the two banks would be established jointly, since they are by definition highly complementary. The United States could very well set up the Domestic Food Bank (DFB) on its own, and because of its predominant position vis-à-vis other suppliers, could still have a significant impact on wheat markets worldwide. Apart from its potential contribution internationally, the DFB would remedy many of the most serious problems plaguing American agriculture. It would provide a means of capturing the maximum rent possible for the farmer from high export volumes while avoiding the sponsorship of increasingly inefficient forms of production. In addition, it would offer growers an assured minimum level of income and consumers a fixed noninflationary price for wheat sold via the Bank. Above all, it would insulate the U.S. economy from an omnipresent vulnerability to sharp swings in food prices that have less to do with available supplies than with commercial practices among buyers and sellers. Having such a system in place would address these interrelated issues with deliberation, unlike the inevitable stop-gap approach that is characteristic of Washington's contemporary agricultural policies, which tend to be more responsive to political issues than to underlying causes.

In many respects the Bank would build on a mandate already written for the CCC, a New Deal remnant. CCC responsibilities are sufficiently broadly based to include major government programs in agriculture ranging from storing to selling grain. But it is primarily a master plan to service domestic agricultural programs rather than an autonomous policy and enforcement agency. The DFB, on the other hand, would put flesh on the CCC skeleton.

The DFB, as a banking institution, would function on the basis of wheat deposits, thereby building a national agricultural program that turns fixed reserves into real resources. Unlike a centralized board system, it would not operate as an exclusive monopoly for the purchasing and selling of wheat and wheat flour but as an alternate marketing organ for such transactions. Its weight in the market would depend on the extent of producer participation determining the size of the Bank's wheat deposits available for export, food aid, and domestic reserves. There would be incentives for selling to the Bank designed to counterbalance the normal attractions to farmers and their member cooperatives of selling to the private sector. The end result would be to introduce an element of competition in the domestic market, which does not exist at present.

The main attraction of the DFB is that in exchange for a certain quantity of wheat, it would offer the farmer minimum prices, fixed at regular intervals in conjunction with significant changes in international prices, and high enough to ensure a level of income competitive with other sectors of the economy. There would at the same time be a ceiling on individual purchases and prices to protect against the weakness of current programs in oversubsidizing the largest farms and accumulating undisposable stock levels. In effect, the Bank's bidding price would be higher than the current loan-target, farmer-held reserve level, but kept to a maximum payment for each participating grower.

On the export side, the Bank would resell its wheat deposits to the private trade at a higher price than the original purchase price. The export price inevitably would reflect this increase, and the difference between these two prices would result in a profit for the Bank, a portion of which would be returned directly as profits for member banks of the DFB and indirectly to farmers. The Bank's role in handling exports is confined to this resale function and handling of export license registrations, but the net effect is to offer U.S. grain at more stable prices, albeit higher than the present average prices. The DFB, in effect, would distribute the return from production and high volume export sales to producers and consumers at relatively constant prices.

Equally appealing to producers should be the fact that the DFB, unlike existing governmental bodies, would be an autonomous institution working directly with the farming community whose participation at all levels, including the administration of the Bank, would be absolutely essential. It would counterbalance the declining political influence of this element of the American economy and simultaneously join consumer and agricultural interests on a working level. The Bank would be self-financing, in contrast to current agricultural programs, which represent an increasing budgetary expense exaggerated by revenue losses to the public and attributable to the structure of the trade. In this respect and in a general institutional sense, it would be styled after the example of the Federal Reserve.

Like the "Fed," the DFB would be empowered to acquire and release wheat stocks to ensure the availability of supply at stable prices. The Bank's assets are its reserves. When a participating farmer comes to a branch of the federal bank, he has the choice of receiving direct payment for his wheat deposit based on a set minimum and maximum price range for different quality crops; or he can accept a DFB-backed wheat certificate in exchange for this deposit. The advantage of the financial instrument as opposed to cash is that the farmer can earn interest on it that is exempt from federal taxes or he can sell it at a premium to any interested buyer. He can improve his earnings at a minimum risk because the wheat currency has a par value—a minimum fixed price—established by the federal bank's own board of governors, composed of a broad spectrum of interest groups from producers to cooperatives, private firms and consumers (see Appendix C, The Domestic and International Food Bank: Charters and Balance Sheets).

The wheatgrower does not limit his options by participation in the Bank system. If his harvest is greater than the quota for his deposit, he can do just what he does now: he can sell the remainder on the open, private market or store it in a facility of his own choice in the expectation that he will receive a better price in the near future or that the Bank will later accept more deposits at a higher price, competitive with bids from the private sector. He has still another alternative of dealing exclusively with buyers outside the banking system. This choice encompasses the most risk, but also the possibility of the greatest return. By withholding all of his harvest from the DFB, he would be abandoning the income insurance which this facility offers. The Bank pays grower-depositors a fixed price, which is calculated to guarantee them a minimum income level corresponding to the American median income. The DFB price, however, may be below the going rate which the farmer could capitalize on by selling independently. He has to decide, but at least he has a wider range of options (including a reduction of wheat plantings in favor of another higher income-producing crop) than is now available.

Food assistance would become part and parcel of the DFB-administered reserve system. Currently, food assistance represents less than 1 percent of total U.S. budget outlays but is a major preoccupation of the Department of Agriculture and the Agency for International Development, as well as other executive branch agencies concerned with security and foreign policy issues. U.S. food aid programs invariably suffer from this infinite division of labor. In addition, the levels of food commitments are unpredictable, depending upon the availability of domestic supplies and, frequently, upon shifting political objectives.

The DFB, on the other hand, would calculate the amount of reserve deposits it is willing to accept in terms of producer income, price stability, and a liberal assessment of food requirements from lesser-developed countries with chronic food deficits. It would issue separate food aid bonds, which, again, would be exchangeable for wheat or the equivalent wheat flour at par value, just like the reserve certificates. They would be held by qualified recipient countries or an international food bank, convertible at any time into food aid.

Whether concessional or commercial, export contracts would be handled by the private sector with the Bank assuming a more neutral role. The USDA would still have a mandate for promoting U.S. exports and negotiating government-to-government deals, but the companies alone would have responsibility for executing the sales. They would be left to do what they do best: act as international grain merchants distributing supplies efficiently around the globe. All companies would have to register with the Bank in order to conduct any transactions involving U.S. grain. They, in turn, would receive

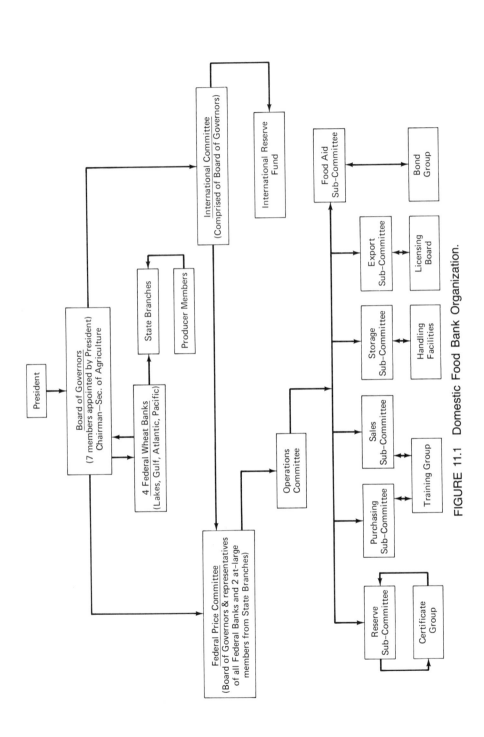

FIGURE 11.1 Domestic Food Bank Organization.

general licenses, which would be renewable periodically. Should they choose to handle contracts under the Bank's jurisdiction, they must in addition get authorization from the DFB to serve as its agents. These procedures would provide the same benefits as the option of a licensing system and would have the additional value of assisting the Bank in its supply management and pricing functions.

Registration and licensing would be one source of income available to the Bank and interest on its certificates another. The DFB would deposit its issues in interest-bearing accounts of the U.S. government. The Bank's "Operations Committee" could earn profits as well as stabilize prices through its hedging operations. It would keep DFB guarantees within a fixed price ban corresponding to an actual price trend in the market. Acting in this limited way as a trader, the DFB would be protected from the occasional and costly mistakes of a Wheat Board restricted to cash transactions. Bank prices would not only reflect the market but also influence it to maintain prices within the DFB's own defined range. The Bank's resales would be an additional source of earnings, assuming it played the market correctly. Potentially, the return from these transactions would be large enough to be remitted to holders of DFB certificates.

The International Food Bank (IFB) would reinforce the role of the DFB by performing in other markets much as the DFB would do in the United States, and would also reduce the cost of operating a national reserve stabilization system unilaterally. The IFB would be an appropriate mechanism to avert major disruptions in the world's wheat market, redirecting conflicting national agricultural policies into one mutually beneficial scheme to (1) stabilize supplies through the accumulation of nationally held reserves; (2) establish a floor and ceiling for wheat prices; (3) introduce greater equality in distribution by modifying procurement practices; and (4) establish a reliable, internationally coordinated food assistance program.

The function of the IFB in the food sector would be similar to that of the International Monetary Fund regarding capital questions. Each member country's subscription would be in the form of a food reserve quota. For donors, there would be an additional allotment to cover food aid allocations. DFB's reserve and food aid certificates could be used to fulfill U.S. participation requirements. The Bank's assets would be national quotas. Its liabilities would be the subscriptions which serve as a call on IFB country-held reserves and aid commitments. Like the DFB, the international bank would guarantee a par value for its reserve and aid certificates based on a minimum-maximum price range for wheat and wheat flour. Like any buffer stock mechanism, the IFB would acquire and release reserves in the open market to keep prices within the agreed band. Participating countries would have preferred access to these stocks until they had redeemed all their certificates. Then the decision to dip below the minimum subscription level and raise the price would be taken by a consensus of all members.

Food aid certificates would also be redeemable. Countries that qualify for

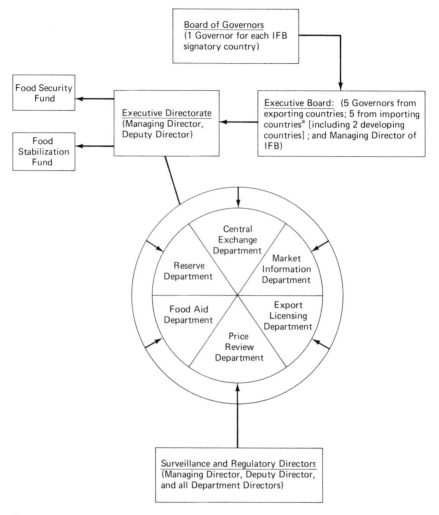

FIGURE 11.2 International Food Bank Organization.

such assistance would hold these instruments, which they could cash in to compensate for a shortfall in production or to increase their level of imports. Such countries would have the full understanding that access to this portion of IFB's reserve would last only as long as they did not exhaust their food aid certificates. Alternatively, they could trade their certificates at a premium, increasing their foreign currency position, which might be more valuable than food assistance, depending upon relative market conditions. To avoid the age-old problem of dampening incentives for these countries to become masters of their own food fate, the IFB could participate with other international organizations in providing financial assistance for agricultural development within the aid recipient country. IFB's greatest service, however, would be to establish and enforce a price band that could facilitate long-range planning and investment in LDCs.

For aid recipients, the appeal of the proposed IFB lies in its assurance of food security along with the range of choices it provides, leaving ultimate responsibility to the countries themselves. Importers joining such a system would secure a hedge against the lean years, which most forecasters agree will characterize the next decade. Even wealthy buyers, strapped by energy-import requirements, could appreciate noninflationary food prices in the light of their present slow-growth economies. The most efficient producers, like the United States and Canada, would gain from IFB prices pegged above their internal, domestic levels.

Generally, the United States has struggled through production controls and joint export strategies with other suppliers to bolster international prices. Usually, the climate or the Soviet Union has had more impact in this regard than any policy initiative, leaving the United States and other countries with all the negative effects of higher prices and scarcities, and without a systematic approach to improving the return from exports to producers. Under an IFB pricing mechanism backed by working stocks, the EC would have a tougher time dumping any significant portion of France's wheat surpluses, which have in the past been so disruptive to agricultural markets in developing as well as exporting countries. IFB price levels, while above the trend of the past few years, would be below CAP levels to avoid a situation where the international price would actually underwrite the world's least efficient producers.

Without adequate participation, the system would be doomed from the start. But, unlike past initiatives, the IFB would be sufficiently comprehensive and balanced in terms of varying importer and exporter interests to gain broad-based support. If, on the other hand, a structurally deficit producer such as the Soviet Union chose not to join, it could risk a virtual cutoff from foreign supplies. Its access to foreign markets would be severely restricted if world production were tight, leaving IFB reserves as the main source of relief. Even if the global bin were overfilled, the spigot of cheap wheat would be turned off for nonmembers, assuming enough influential countries joined the Bank system. Under the new rules of the game, even bilateral agreements between IFB participants and nonparticipants would be impossible.

It would be extremely difficult under such circumstances for a nonparticipating foreign buyer to use internationally based trading companies for black market purchases outside the IFB system. The Bank's enforcement powers would stem from the registration and licensing system, which would be in force, applicable to government and private trading companies alike. Although not foolproof, this small amount of paperwork, under new procedures, would give governments a monitoring capability over the trade and an information base, which is critical to agricultural policy design and management. By introducing this degree of regulatory duties in the public sector, the IFB, as well as its American counterpart, could have the positive effect of maximizing the efficiencies of the trade and curbing its all too frequent social and economic costs. There would, of course, be strength in numbers so that the greater the number of participants, the less chance the IFB would be undermined by veterans in the business of playing one country against another for profit.

The banks are by no means a panacea, but they do offer one way to address the needs of producers and consumers, importers and exporters, and developing and developed countries. In the past, agricultural decisions usually have been the outgrowth of a victory by one or more of these feuding factions rather than a growing consensus based on shared interests. The banks' premise is that a political and economic common denominator exists and that, potentially, it even extends beyond national limits to encompass a far-reaching international proposal. Worse times ahead are, perhaps, the most persuasive argument for a sharp departure from the past.

Whatever the future holds, it seems clear that some action is required. Unilateral action by the United States represents a second best alternative, but it is better than no action, which is an invitation to disaster. Present trends, if unarrested, can only ensure the disinheritance of productive American farmers and the cartelization of the most important links in the U.S. agricultural chain. Reform is not only necessary, it is imperative for American interests and those of the international community.

NOTES

1. "The Exporter agrees that CCC and the Comptroller General of the United States . . . shall, until the expiration of three years after final payment under the Agreement, have access to the premises of the Exporter and its affiliates during regular business hours to inspect, examine, audit, and make copies of such books, records, and accounts including, but not limited to, financial records and reports pertaining to purchases, sales, inventory positions, hedging, transportation costs, administrative costs, and incidental costs both normal and unforeseen of the Exporter or its affiliates involving transactions relating to the Agreement, or any other transactions which may bear on CCC's determination of appropriate reductions in the contract price." *CCC-Exporter Agreement,* Art. 8, A, "Audit of Records and Access to Premises," p. 19.

2. John W. Mellor, "Third World Development and the Demand for Agricultural Exports—The Role of the United States," IFPRI working paper 78/20 (presented at a symposium sponsored by the Federal Reserve Bank of Kansas City, "World Agricultural Trade: The Potential for Growth," 18-19 May 1978).

3. "Farm Leaders Ask Regulated Market," *New York Times,* 10 February 1937.

4. Henry Wallace, "Wallace Urges 'Balanced Abundance,' " *New York Times Magazine,* 14 November 1937, Sec. S, p. 1.

5. See Richard Gilmore, "Grain in the Bank," *Foreign Policy,* no. 38, (Spring 1980): 168-81.

Appendix A

National Grain Trading Organizations

IMPORTERS	
EUROPE	**FAR EAST**
Bulgaria Hranexport *Czechoslovakia* Koospol *East Germany* Dianahrung *Finland* Finnish State Granary *Hungary* Agrimpex *Norway* Norwegian Grain Corporation (Statens Kornforretning) *Poland* Rolimpex *Portugal* Institute of Cereals *Rumania* Agroexport *Spain* Spanish Grain Service (SENPA) *Sweden* Swedish Agricultural Marketing Board *Switzerland* Swiss Cereals Administration *U.S.S.R.* Exportkhleb *Yugoslavia* Granexport	*Bangladesh* Ministry of Food and Civil Supplies of the Government of the People's Republic of Bangladesh *Burma* Myanma Export & Import Corporation *Cambodia* Government of Cambodia *China* China Food (China National Cereals, Oils, and Foodstuffs Import & Export Corporation) *India* Food Corporation of India and Department of Food (Ministry of Agriculture & Irrigation) *Indonesia* Bureau of Logistic Affairs (BULOG) *Japan* Food Agency (wheat and barley) *North Korea* Korea Cereals and Foodstuffs Export & Import Corporation *South Korea* Korea Flour Mills Industrial Association (wheat) (private organization subject to government control) National Agricultural Cooperative Federation (barley, sorghum, millet, and corn) (quasi-government organization) Office of Supply of the Republic of Korea (rice)

(FAR EAST Cont'd.)

Malaysia
National Padi and Rice Authority (rice)
Pakistan
Ministry of Food and Agriculture,
Government of Pakistan
Philippines
National Grain Authority
Sri Lanka
Sri Lanka State Flour Milling
Corporation under authorization from
the Food Commission (wheat)
Taiwan
Taiwan Supply Bureau
China Trade & Development
Corporation
Central Trust of China
Vietnam
Agrexport, Hanoi

LATIN AMERICA

Brazil
Superintendencia Nacional do
Abastecimento (SUNAB)
Chile
Empresa de Comercio Agricola (ECA)
Colombia
Instituto de Mercadeo Agropecuario
(IDEMA)
Cuba
ALIMPORT
Mexico
Compania Nacional de Subsistancias
Populares (CONASUPO)
Venezuela
Corporacion de Mercadeo
(CORPOMERCADEO)

MIDDLE EAST AND AFRICA

Algeria
Office Algerien Interprofessionel des
Céréales (OAIC)
Angola
Instituto dos Cereais de Angola (ICA)
ARE (Egypt)
General Authority for Supply
Commodities
Iran
Foreign Transactions Corporation (FTC)
Iraq
Grain Board of Iraq
Lebanon
Cereals and Sugarbeets Office—
Ministry of National Economy
Libya
National Supply Corporation (NSC)
Morocco
Office National Interprofessionnel des
Céréales et des Légumineuses
(ONICL)
Nigeria
Nigerian National Supply Company
(NNSC)
Saudi Arabia
Grain Silos and Flour Mills
Organization
Syria
General Establishment for Cereals
Processing and Trade
Tunisia
Office des Céréales (ODC)
Turkey
Toprak Mahsulleri Ofisi (TMO)
Zambia
Industrial Development Corporation
(INDECO)

EXPORTERS

Argentina
Junta Nacional de Granos
Australia
Australian Wheat Board (AWB)
Australian Barley Board
Queensland Graingrowers Association
Grain Sorghum Marketing Board of
New South Wales
Yellow Maize Marketing Board of
N.S.W.
N.S.W. Barley Marketing Board
N.S.W. Oilseeds Marketing Board
Grain Pool of West Australia

Canada
Canadian Wheat Board (CWB)

South Africa
Wheat Board
Maize Board

Thailand
Department of Trade
Department of Commerce

Appendix B

PL 480 Data

TABLE B.1 PL 480 Title I[a]: Twenty Largest Exporters of Grain[b] from Inception Through December 31, 1960 (dollar value of commodities exported by each supplier)

Exporter	Amount Financed through 12/31/60
Continental Grain Co.	597,792,683
Cargill, Inc.	521,903,886
Louis Dreyfus Corp.	358,475,060
Bunge Corp.	134,508,799
Garnac Grain Co.	113,938,228
Robin International, Inc.	80,883,321
Producers Export Co.	69,386,552
Pillsbury Mills	49,671,361
Interoceanic Commodity Corp.	47,173,513
Balfour, Guthrie and Co.	45,578,271
Kerr Grain Corp.	41,607,410
Archer-Daniels Midland Co.	28,078,983
Mitsui and Co.	20,765,743
Tricerri Grain Corp.	18,619,381
Sinason-Teicher Inter-American Grain Corp.	16,548,794
C.B. Fox Co.	12,729,107
Nichimen Co., Inc.	11,565,746
Uhlmann Elevator Co.	11,285,981
Tidewater Grain Co.	8,971,617
General Mills, Inc.	8,858,100
TOTAL	2,198,342,536

[a]Title I prior to 1967 represented sales for local currencies only.
[b]Grain consists of barley, corn, grain, sorghum, wheat, and wheat flour.

Source: Data supplied by ASCS, USDA.

TABLE B.2 PL 480 Title I[a]: Twenty Largest Exporters of Grain[b] during Calendar Years 1961 Through 1967 (dollar value of commodities exported by each supplier)

Exporter	Amt. Financed 1961	Amt. Financed 1962	Amt. Financed 1963	Amt. Financed 1964	Amt. Financed 1965	Amt. Financed 1966	Amt. Financed 1967	Rank of Top 10
Cargill	131,281,312	140,698,415	195,560,624	184,625,185	130,608,767	150,552,833	97,045,213	1
Continental Grain Co.	171,133,396	190,323,346	150,367,566	175,993,910	128,574,317	128,713,462	69,415,649	2
Bunge Corp.	52,874,982	122,240,198	89,249,572	74,494,284	51,482,504	49,782,815	50,336,242	3
Louis Dreyfus Corp.	33,440,827	26,949,832	51,032,450	53,780,140	32,326,764	74,544,031	48,101,636	5
Cook Grains Inc. (Cook & Co., Inc.)	15,347,923	25,456,497	38,459,466	19,679,496	37,897,886	54,907,345	45,764,350	8
Garnac Grain, Co.	9,582,383	7,871,042	11,994,291	50,221,968	20,967,563	14,769,077	16,261,433	7
Mitsui and Co.	18,587,998	9,944,631	16,865,646	7,150,860	3,351,459			
Archer-Daniels-Midland Co.				9,883,322	8,690,007	15,599,583	12,285,176	
Producers Export Co.	32,076,036	24,812,384	47,650,914	61,993,520	67,449,638	65,160,795	45,143,463	4
The Peavey and Co.	7,300,518	18,217,724	15,961,143	7,834,003	8,167,745	19,557,158	16,672,661	9
Burrus Mills, Inc.	5,631,140	11,212,936	9,056,802	10,490,302	4,605,632	2,725,143		
Marubeni American, Inc.		1,845,354			3,897,543	1,848,770		
Toshoku Ltd.			6,552,642		4,124,957	2,396,768	3,787,712	
Nicheman Co., Inc.	4,029,621		4,077,906		4,924,414			
The Nissho Pacific Corp.						1,764,632		
Pillsbury Mills (Pillsbury Co.)	20,490,739	16,940,071	20,097,028	17,717,249				
Kerr Grain Corp.	10,801,345	6,256,080	10,781,315		8,751,021	6,863,459	2,001,353	10
General Mills, Inc.	5,748,586	6,333,640	4,909,085	7,772,208				
Goodpasture Grain & Milling Co.				25,108,124				
Bartlett & Co.	17,248,335	4,636,726	21,986,756	34,160,973	35,635,622	19,870,721	6,179,102	
Harlin Mills, Inc. (Harlin Mills Grain Co.)			54,433,729	81,094,072	45,524,459	21,330,945	5,600,737	6
Pike Grain Co.		4,914,887	6,342,795	13,134,627		5,595,500	4,972,403	

Company						
Goffe & Carkener Inc.	4,971,845	5,316,310	6,901,555	4,717,592		
Dixie Portland Flour Mills		5,284,966		5,517,625		
Mitsubishi Int'l, Corp.					3,972,812	1,720,866
American Trade Sales Co.					3,058,226	3,701,210
Olavarra & Co., Inc.	38,714,292					2,261,950
J.A. Goldschmidt Trading Corp.						
Balfour, Guthrie & Co.	6,524,840					
Sinason–Teicher Inter-American Grain Co.	5,515,452					
(Teicher Int'l. Ltd.)				5,763,949		
West Coast Grain Corp.	3,705,934	3,131,080				
Standard Milling Co.		3,128,785				
Tucker International			5,219,748			
Kerr, Gifford & Co., Inc.					3,755,402	
Tidewater Grain Co.						
Toyomenka, Ltd.						
Fisher Flouring Mills Co.						
Centennial Mills, Inc.						
Int'l. Milling Co., Ltd.						
Kerr, Gifford & Co., Inc.						3,830,168
						1,872,588
						1,652,644
						1,643,759
						1,173,902
						1,132,488
TOTAL	595,007,504	635,514,904	767,500,033	851,133,049	607,766,738	643,677,063	434,872,679
	(Represents 95.4% of all Title I sales of grain.)	(Represents 96.4% of all Title I sales of grain.)	(Represents 95.6% of all Title I sales of grain.)	(Represents 95.9% of all Title I sales of grain.)	(Represents 96.4% of all Title I sales of grain.)	(Represents 97.2% of all Title I sales of grain.)	(Represents 98.3% of all Title I sales of grain.)

aTitle I prior to 1967 represented sales for local currencies only.

bGrain consists of barley, corn, grain sorghum, wheat, and wheat flour.

SOURCE: Data supplied by ASCS, USDA.

TABLE B.3 PL 480 Title I: List of Exporters of Wheat and Products During Fiscal Years 1969 Through 1975 (dollar value of commodities exported by each supplier in thousands of dollars)

	1969	Rank	1970	Rank	1971	Rank	1972	Rank	1973	Rank	1974	Rank	1975	Rank
ADM Milling Co.	5,073	10	0		1,775		169		1,723		1,291		3,208	
Ataka America, Inc.	0		0		0		0		1,227		4,616	5	2,816	
Bunge Corporation	16,221	5	11,924	7	20,037	5	8,517	10	7,344	7	1,282		33,375	5
Burrus Mills	5,323	9	4,768		6,608		2,516		908		0		0	
California Milling Corp.	0		153		13		0		0		0		0	
Cargill, Inc.	28,956	2	39,377	1	46,567	2	49,260	2	27,536	2	20,314	3	64,927	3
C.B. Fox, Co.	1,893		307		3,031		6,453		8,763	6	2,417	10	0	
Centennial Mills, Inc.	679		179		1,845		204		0		0		0	
C. Itoh	0		0		0		0		0		0		2,264	
Continental Grain Co.	22,438	3	27,604	3	42,875	3	50,166	1	21,887	4	4,714	4	68,300	2
Cook Industries, Inc.	29,214	1	33,720	2	47,412	1	37,709	3	25,191	3	26,943	1	56,500	4
Crete Mills	638		0		0		0		0		0		0	
Dixie Portland Flour Mills	2,367		1,577		2,945		2,086		0		667		4,279	
Equity Export Corp.	861		9,525	8	0		0		0		0		0	
Far-Mar-Co., Inc.	0		122		0		0		0		0		0	
Farmers Co-op Commission	1,270		0		158		0		0		0		0	
Fisher Flour Mills	8,837	7	1,508		3,941		2,904		3,186		2,985	9	0	
Fort Garry Milling Co.	139		0		0		0		0		0		0	
Garnac Grain Co.	1,711		3,923		9,620	9	7,927		6,028	9	3,680	7	18,349	6
General Mills, Inc.	89		162		536		55		301		0		0	
Goodpasture, Inc.	2,673		809		8,734	10	2,615		433		0		2,310	
Helix Milling Co.	0		0		118		0		0		0		0	
Int'l. Dairy Eng. Co. at Asia	0		0		593		0		0		0		0	
Int'l. Milling Co., Ltd.	365		805		103		86		0		0		0	
Int'l. Multifoods Corp.	0		0		159		706		944		0		2,021	
Int'l. Proteins Corp.	0		0		579		0		0		0		0	
J.A. Goldschmidt Trading Corp.	3,650		0		0		0		0		0		0	
J.P. Stevens and Co., Inc.	0		0		855		0		0		0		0	

Company	1	2	3	4	5	6	7
Kansas Milling Co.	4,381	748	2,483	4,651	0	0	0
Lauhoff Grain, Co.	0	955	275	0	212	0	0
Leger Mill Co.	132	331	109	0	0	0	0
Louis Dreyfus Corp.	7,253 (8)	13,767 (6)	14,257 (6)	14,216 (5)	38,255 (1)	26,875 (2)	89,658 (1)
Marubeni America Corp.	0	0 (4)	1,421	10,550 (7)	2,376	0	0
Mitsubishi Int'l. Corp.	0	0	2,641	1,347	2,319	0	0
Mitsui and Co.	229	0	6,260	2,186	3,544	1,551	13,692 (7)
Morton Milling Co.	785	0	0	263	0	0	0
Nichimen Co., Inc.	949	886	3,070	3,863	2,448	0	0
Nissho-Iwai America Corp.	0	0	0	0	0	3,888 (6)	0
North Pacific Grain Growers	0 (6)	6,177 (9)	5,931	1,252	0	0	0
Pacific Int'l. Grain Co.	0 (4)	0	0	0	3,057	1,518	0
Peavey Company	4,647	6,156 (10)	3,084	5,136	2,129	454	8,786 (9)
Pillsbury Company	13,999 (6)	14,307 (5)	10,057 (8)	9,115 (8)	7,081 (8)	0	0
Producers Export Co.	18,020 (4)	0	0	0	1,257	0	0
Producers Grain Corp.	0	4,043	10,939	1,367	3,380	0	0
Ross Industries, Inc.	925	4,717	0	4,235	0	553	2,592
Royal Milling Co.	22	22	10	5	0	0	0
Rozel Packing Corp.	2,439	742	1,631	3,025	850	0	2,106
St. John Int'l., Inc.	1,977	195	1,035	420	0	0	0
Sumitomo Shoji America	0	0	3,022	9,039 (9)	4,579 (9)	0	7,521 (10)
Thomas P. Gonzales	0	0	0	0	0	0	3,642
Toshoki, Ltd.	0	3,238	1,219	1,980	1,294	0	9,744
Toyomenka, Inc.	3,313	1,884	1,038	1,723	3,676	458	3,845 (8)
Union Equity Cooperative Exchange	0	25,981 (4)	34,994	18,395 (4)	4,751 (10)	3,261 (8)	0
United Grain Corp.	0	2,175	3,223	593	8,886 (5)	929	6,636
Washburn Crosby Co.	127	71	72	2	0	0	0
West Coast Resources	0	1,191	3,358	11,676 (6)	8,287 (7)	0	0
Wilcox Hayes Company	0	0	0	0	181	0	0
TOTAL	191,593	224,048	308,634	276,412	203,933	108,396	406,571

SOURCE: ASCS, USDA.

TABLE B.4 PL 480 Title I: List of Exporters of Feed Grains and Products During Fiscal Years 1969 Through 1975 (dollar value of commodities exported by each supplier in thousands of dollars)

	1969	Rank	1970	Rank	1971	Rank	1972	Rank	1973	Rank	1974	Rank	1975	Rank
Ballard and Ballard	0		0		0		0		0		0		700	2
Bunge Corporation	4,373	3	4,302	4	8,920	2	3,065	7	7,318	5	6,592	2	0	
Cargill, Inc.	4,824	1	11,113	1	8,314	3	14,396	1	16,239	1	350	10	0	
C.B. Fox Co.	0		0		641		273		0		414		992	1
Continental Grain Co.	4,258	4	2,787	7	10,064	1	9,133	3	12,482	2	0		0	
Cook Industries, Inc.	2,467	7	9,364	2	1,189	10	7,651	4	8,545	4	10,848	1	0	
Farmers Export Co.	0		3,207	6	1,192	9	509		1,989		0		0	
Garnac Grain Co.	455		2,040	9	5,203	4	1,187	10	3,482	7	5,049	3	0	
Goodpasture, Inc.	2,863	6	5,595	3	1,901	8	1,226		2,114	10	0		0	
I.S. Joseph, Inc.	0		0		0		0		0		298		0	
Krause Milling Co.	0		0		0		0		0		151		0	
Lauhoff Grain Co.	0		0		0		0		0		167		0	
Louis Dreyfus Corp.	3,087	5	2,447	8	2,945	6	3,868	6	5,604	6	4,124	4	571	3
Marubeni America Corp.	0		0		0		12,623	2	10,626	3	863	8	0	
Mitsubishi Int'l. Corp.	0		0		770		2,266	8	1,192		1,293	7	0	
Mitsui and Co., Ltd.	0		0		0		575		745		0		0	
Nichimen Co., Inc.	0		0		0		1,166		0		789	9	0	
Owens Milling Co.	109		0		0		0		0		0		0	
Peavey Company	491	10	1,344	10	3,939	5	1,421	9	0		0		0	
Pike Grain Co.	861	9	0		0		0		0		0		0	
Producers Export Co.	4,544	2	4,084	5	2,330	7	5,602	5	3,012	8	2,861	5	0	
Producers Grain Corp.	1,009	8	0		0		0		0		0		0	
Sumitomo Shoji America	0		0		0		611		0		0		0	
Tabor and Company	0		0		0		0		0		2,240	6	0	
Toyomenka, Inc.	0		0		0		564		0		0		0	
Union Equity Cooperative Exchange	0		0		0		0		2,316	9	0		0	
West Coast Resources	0		0		0		783		252		0		0	
Woodward and Dickerson	664		1,173		0		0		0		0		0	
TOTAL	30,010		47,456		48,209		66,919		75,916		36,039		2,263	

SOURCE: ASCS, USDA.

TABLE B.5 PL 480 Title I*: List of Exporters of Cottonseed and Soybean Oil During Calendar Years 1961 Through 1967 (dollar value of commodities exported by each supplier in thousands of dollars)

	1961	Rank	1962	Rank	1963	Rank	1964	Rank	1965	Rank	1966	Rank	1967	Rank
A.E. Staley Mfg. Co.			6		7		9							
Allied Crude Veg. Oil Ref. Co.	11,694	2	1,574	7										
Amata Agency, Inc.	155		291											
American Trade, Inc.					783	10	538	10	1,482	9				
Amertrade, Inc.	121		64		1,545	6								
Anderson, Clayton & Co.	1,676	6	794				10,271	3	3,327	5	2,157	6	2,042	5
Archer-Daniels-Midland Corp.									3,815	4	2,844	4	328	8
Arkansas Grain Corp.							319		2,554		6			
Atkins Kroll & Co.							176		275					
B.N.S. Int'l. Sales Corp.	368		1,372	8	838	8	566	9	325		392	7		
Balfour, Guthrie & Co., Ltd.	17													
Bauer Int'l. Corp.											165	9		
Bernard Bowman Corp.	367		444		776									
Berns & Koppstein, Inc.	371		821		205									
Bunge Corporation	11,928	1	53,116	1	22,927	1	15,831	2	26,195	1	6,263	3	16,053	2
C. Pappas Co., Inc.	748	9												
Cargill, Inc.	1,309	7	3,178	5	1,196	7	6,699	4	6,593	3	13,245	2	20,692	1
Central Soya Co.	821	8	432		234		3,130	6	1,765	7			2,545	4
Chemoleum Corp.	65													
Continental Grain Co.					16,089	3	29,019	1	23,263	2	16,145	1	14,158	3
D.S. Hawkins & Co.													125	9
Daniel M. Hicks							4							
Drew Chemical Corp.			94		29		4,105	5	91					
Drew Food Corp.											149	10		
E.F. Drew & Co.	90													
Empire Steel Trading Co., Inc.					10									
Fehr Bros. Manufactures, Inc.					28		33							
Garnac Grain Co., Inc.	5,587	4	8,744	3	4,280	4	27		240					
Garsony-Strauss Co., Inc.	5,027	5	4,759	4	18,156	2								

TABLE B.5 (continued)

	1961	Rank	1962	Rank	1963	Rank	1964	Rank	1965	Rank	1966	Rank	1967	Rank
Honeymead Products Co.											55			
Hunt Wesson Sales			176		798	9	2,852	7	1,565	8	170	8		
Lever Brothers Co.							237	9	242					
Liberty Steel & Metals Corp.			290											
Manufacturers Foreign Trade Co.					96									
Marubeni America, Inc.							1		317					
Monarch Trading Co.	52		823	9	231									
North American Continental Co.	8,534	3	10,170	2	3,910	3								
Overseas Credit Corp.						5								
Pacific Vegetable Oil Corp.	400	10	556		132		177				2,231	5	478	7
Pasternak, Baum & Co.			1,746	6	115								1,618	6
Roberts Food Corp.							26							
Skytex Chemical Co.			145											
Skytex Mercantile Co.					213				12		85			
Spencer Kellog & Son, Inc.	377													
The Titan Industrial Corp.									138					
Theobold Industries														
Vegetable Oil Export Corp.					11		1,385	8	1,024	10				
White Trading Corp.														
TOTAL	49,881		89,594		72,615		75,413		73,223		43,902		58,038	

*Title I prior to 1967 represented sales for local currencies only.

SOURCE: Data supplied by ASCS, USDA.

TABLE B.6 PL 480 Title I: List of Exporters of Vegetable Oil Products During Calendar Years 1969 Through 1975 (dollar value of commodities exported by each supplier in thousands of dollars)

	1969	Rank	1970	Rank	1971	Rank	1972	Rank	1973	Rank	1974	Rank	1975	Rank
Amato Int'l., Inc.	0		0		0		1,235	6	893	7	396	9	0	
Anderson, Clayton Co.	261	5	0		451	8	456	10	0		596	7	0	
Archer-Daniels-Midland	0		0		0		0		954	6	565	8	0	
Arkansas Grain Corp.	2,119	4	1,012	4	0		0		0		0		0	
Balfour MacLaine, Inc.	0		0		0		0		512	8	224	10	0	
Bunge Corporation	7,122	2	7,063	3	22,234	1	11,201	3	3,802	4	9,395	2	3,893	1
Cargill, Inc.	4,926	3	10,651	2	21,221	3	12,270	2	4,074	3	6,924	3	3,576	2
Continental Grain Co.	8,004	1	11,224	1	22,105	2	22,188	1	10,287	1	10,032	1	3,093	3
Cook Industries	0		0		4,580	5	2,280	4	0		4,449	4	608	5
Garnac Grain Co.	0		0		1,297	7	509	9	0		0		0	
I.S. Joseph Co., Inc.	0		86	6	0		598	8	0		0		0	
Leviant Int'l., Inc.	0		0		0		0		0		0		0	
Mitsubishi Int'l. Corp.	0		0		0		0		9,047	2	0		0	
Mitsui and Co.	0		0		0		110		0		0		0	
Nestle Trading Corp.	0		0		2,066	6	0		0		0		0	
Pacific Molasses Co.	0		0		0		917	7	0		0		0	
Pasternak Baum and Co.	204	6	183	5	13,593	4	0		174	9	0		2,698	4
Riceland Foods	0		0		0		0		0		2,746	5	0	
Wilbur Ellis Co.	0		0		0		1,983	5	2,087	5	863	6	0	
TOTAL	22,636		30,219		87,547		53,747		31,830		36,190		13,868	

Source: ASCS, USDA.

259

TABLE B.7 PL 480 Title I: Exporters by Destination for Selected Recipient Countries* During Fiscal Years 1969 to 1978 (in thousands of dollars)

	FY 1969	1970/71	1972	1973	1974	1975	1976	1977	1978	Total	Rank
Bangladesh											
Wheat											
Bunge						9,856			5,982	15,838	6
Cargill					3,949	11,100	22,435	2,174	11,350	51,008	2
Continental						19,723	18,370	2,330	6,843	47,266	3
Cook						5,291	3,218	11,068		19,577	5
Dreyfus					10,999	30,090	8,561	3,816	11,221	64,687	1
Farmers Export								2,743		2,743	9
Garnac							3,945	4,381	17,992	26,318	4
C. Itoh						2,264				2,264	11
Sumitomo-Shoji						3,956				3,956	8
Toepfer								2,332		2,332	10
Toshoku						6,042				6,042	7
TOTAL					14,948	88,322	56,529	28,844	53,388		
Veg. Oil Products											
ACLI Soya Co.									3,599	3,599	5
Bunge						1,756			2,522	4,278	4
Cargill						3,576	4,498	6,818	2,094	16,986	2
Continental					3,953	3,093	17,337	2,433		26,816	1
Cook						608				608	7
Dreyfus								1,956	7,712	9,668	3
Pasternak Baum						2,698				2,698	6
TOTAL					3,953	11,731	21,835	11,207	15,927		

Brazil

Wheat

Bunge	1,652	10,903	12,555	2
Cargill		1,675	1,675	8
Continental	2,716	5,299	8,015	4
Cook	9,970	7,611	17,581	1
Garnac	1,653	2,313	3,966	5
Mitsubishi		983	983	10
Mitsui		969	969	11
Nichimen		648	648	12
Producers Grain	3,153		3,153	6
Sumitomo-Shoji		2,131	2,131	7
Toyomenka		1,322	1,322	9
Union Equity		12,092	12,092	3
TOTAL	19,144	45,946		

Chile

Wheat (and Products)

Bunge		9,932	4,022	13,954	3
Cargill			5,817	5,817	6
Continental	3,663	16,027	12,114	31,804	1
Cook		3,231	6,536	9,767	4
Dreyfus		12,281	13,012	25,293	2
Garnac		197	7,511	7,708	5
Gonzales, Thomas P., Corp.		3,642		3,642	7
Goodpasture		2,310		2,310	8
TOTAL	3,663	47,620	49,012		

TABLE B.7 (Continued)

	FY 1969	1970/71	1972	1973	1974	1975	1976	1977	1978	Total	Rank
Chile (cont'd)											
Feed Grains											
Cargill		2,254								2,254	2
Continental	537	1,038								1,575	3
Cook		6,153								6,153	1
Garnac	1,500									1,500	4
TOTAL	2,037	9,445									
Veg. Oil Products											
Continental	1,431									1,431	1
TOTAL	1,431										
Columbia											
Wheat (and Products)											
Bunge		2,724								2,724	4
Cargill		1,158		3,693	4,373					9,224	2
Continental		1,366	1,258							2,624	5
Cook	1,217	4,849	1,243	2,369	2,250					11,928	1
Garnac		785	1,281							2,066	7
J.H. Goldschmidt Trading Co.	3,975									3,975	3
Nichimen			2,503							2,503	6
Sumitomo Shoji		1,377								1,377	8
TOTAL	5,192	12,259	6,285	6,062	6,623						

Dominican Republic

Wheat

								Total	
Bunge		1,268						1,268	5
Cargill		2,766	3,403	610	543			7,322	2
Continental Grain	512	3,829	264					4,605	3
C. B. Fox		710	134	1,693	1,431			3,968	4
Garnac		681						681	6
Peavey		1,137	3,066	1,697	1,518			7,418	1
TOTAL	512	10,391	6,867	4,000	3,492				

Feed Grains

								Total	
Cargill			362					362	5
Continental			490					490	4
C. B. Fox			296	469	414	273		1,452	2
Goodpasture							1,500	1,500	1
I. S. Joseph				370	298			668	3
TOTAL			1,148	839	712	273	1,500		

Veg. Oil Products

								Total	
Bunge		1,214						1,214	2
Cargill		626						626	5
Continental Grain	474	1,163	1,190	1,064	957			4,848	1
I. S. Joseph			630					630	4
Pacific Molasses			1,008					1,008	3
TOTAL	474	3,003	2,828	1,064	957				

TABLE B.7 (Continued)

	FY 1969	1970/71	1972	1973	1974	1975	1976	1977	1978	Total	Rank
Egypt											
Wheat (and Products)											
ADM/ADM Milling Co.							18,093	9,786	24,633	52,512	5
Bartlett and Co.								2,762	1,478	4,240	18
Bunge						10,774	19,640	29,189	25,686	85,289	2
Burrus Mills (Cargill)							3,288	3,241		6,529	15
Cargill						9,145	25,542	16,020	33,034	83,741	3
Continental						18,532	20,268	20,944	13,478	73,222	4
Cook						8,444	25,478	8,661	3,108	45,691	7
Dixie Portland							7,681	4,757	4,502	16,940	9
Dreyfus						11,787	18,281	27,731	41,008	98,807	1
Farmers Export								4,455		4,455	17
Garnac						3,696	10,547	2,477	7,866	24,586	8
Int'l. Multifoods							2,833	2,469	1,493	6,795	13
Koppel							4,093	2,450		6,543	14
Peavey							1,080	7,848	3,895	12,823	10
Pillsbury							20,139	13,157	18,381	51,857	6
Ross Industries (Cargill)									9,496	9,496	12
Rozel							1,071			1,071	19
Toepfer							3,409	4,922	3,707	12,038	11
Toshoku								5,000		5,000	16
TOTAL						62,378	181,443	165,849	191,965		
Feed Grains											
Bunge Corp.								5,582		5,582	2
Cargill								4,317		4,317	3
Garnac								1,537		1,537	5
Koppel								5,591		5,591	1
Toshoku								2,881		2,881	4
TOTAL								19,908			

Ghana

Wheat						
Cook	100				100	2
C. B. Fox	1,459	3,215			4,674	1
TOTAL	1,559	3,215				
Veg. Oil Products						
Cook	64				64	1
TOTAL	64					

Haiti

Wheat (and Products)						
Cargill				4,063	4,063	3
Farmers Export			4,199		4,199	2
Pillsbury	2,254	3,583			5,837	1
TOTAL	2,254	3,583	4,199	4,063		
Feed Grains						
Goodpasture			1,058		1,058	1
TOTAL			1,058			
Veg. Oil Products						
Burrus Mills (Cargill)				233	233	3
Cargill		1,478		2,069	3,547	2
Flota Export, Inc.			3,379	1,012	4,391	1
TOTAL		1,478	3,379	3,314		

TABLE B.7 (Continued)

	FY 1969	1970/71	1972	1973	1974	1975	1976	1977	1978	Total	Rank
India											
Wheat (and Products)											
ADM/ADM Milling Co.	3,690									3,690	14
Ataka America						2,816				2,816	15
Bunge	8,450	947	1,664				7,169			18,230	6
Cargill	24,594	5,236	2,385			28,692	3,724			64,631	1
Continental	10,543	7,625	3,293			11,766	6,939			40,166	3
Cook	14,072	3,580	8,918			20,466	3,724			50,760	2
Dreyfus	2,854	891				8,468	7,451			19,664	5
Equity Export	9,944									9,944	9
Garnac		1,740				12,691	21,212			35,643	4
Goodpasture	2,074									2,074	16
Mitsui	976									976	19
Nichimen	901					10,289				11,190	8
North Pacific Grain	3,780									3,780	13
Peavey	4,670		946							5,616	11
Producers Grain	1,303									1,303	18
Sumitomo-Shoji							1,493			1,493	17
Toshoku	2,672						3,479			6,151	10
Toyomenka	2,491					2,801				5,292	12
Union Equity		9,727	6,296							16,023	7
TOTAL	93,014	29,746	23,502			97,989	55,191				
Feed Grains											
Bunge	4,289									4,289	1
Cargill	3,879									3,879	2
Cook	1,471									1,471	4
Goodpasture	2,889									2,889	3
Peavey	714									714	6
Producers Grain	1,147									1,147	5
TOTAL	14,389										

Veg. Oil Products

					Total	
ACLI Soya Co.				1,305	1,305	12
Beacham				1,317	1,317	10
Bunge	2,108	3,870	5,557	1,987	13,522	3
Cargill	4,521	2,828		11,499	18,848	1
Continental Grain	3,415	1,807	10,399		15,621	2
Cook		1,974			1,974	8
Dreyfus				3,333	3,333	7
Gersony-Strauss				3,950	3,950	6
Gold Kist				1,432	1,432	9
Mitsubishi				1,306	1,306	11
Mitsui			5,211		5,211	5
Pasternak Baum	951	3,737	4,832	1,672	11,192	4
TOTAL	10,995	14,216	25,999	27,801		

Indonesia
Wheat (and Products)

								Total	
ADM/ADM Milling Co.	1,949		1,425			1,663	1,133	6,170	13
Benson Quinn-Joseph						1,113		1,113	23
Breman Corp.						4,487		4,487	14
Burrus Mills (Cargill)	6,765		1,673	934		1,367	196	10,935	5
California Milling							747	747	24
Cargill		708	4,690			1,873		7,271	10
Continental Grain		3,172	1,292		4,006	5,325		13,795	2
Cook		1,382			8,162			9,544	6
Crete Mills (Lauhoff)						2,866		2,866	18
Dixie Portland	1,956			934				2,890	17
Dreyfus			12,663				1,844	14,507	1
Far-Mar-Co	162							162	27
Farmers Export Co.					3,532			3,532	16
Fisher Flour Mills	1,557		2,349			2,104	724	6,734	11
C. B. Fox		5,281	3,811					9,092	8
Garnac						2,226	1,946	4,172	15

267

TABLE B.7 (Continued)

	FY 1969	1970/71	1972	1973	1974	1975	1976	1977	1978	Total	Rank
Indonesia (cont'd)											
Wheat (and Products) (cont'd)											
General Mills		693								693	25
Koppel								2,153		2,153	21
Lauhoff Grain		275		212						487	26
Leger Mills		109								109	28
Marubeni			1,480	496						1,976	22
Mitsui								2,574		2,574	19
Peavey									12,747	12,747	3
Pillsbury		7,618	1,875							9,493	7
Ross Industries (Cargill)		11,556	474							12,030	4
Toshoku								6,357		6,357	12
Toyomenka								1,062	1,264	2,326	20
United Grain				5,199				2,902		8,101	9
TOTAL		32,640	16,240	33,810			15,700	38,072	20,601		
Iran											
Wheat											
Bunge				2,761						2,761	4
Cargill		1,801	5,172							6,973	1
Continental		1,833								1,853	5
Cook		913	1,501	2,028						4,442	2
Dreyfus		1,041	2,692	526						4,259	3
Goodpasture		1,144								1,144	8
Nichimen		948								948	9
North Pacific Grain			1,386							1,386	7
Pasternak Baum		515								515	10
United Grain		954	614							1,568	6
TOTAL		9,149	11,365	5,315							

Veg. Oil Products

					Total	Rank
Arkansas Grain	1,934				1,934	3
Bunge	2,463	744	4,037		7,244	1
Cargill			482		482	4
Continental		1,927	5,078		7,005	2
TOTAL	4,397	2,671	9,597			

Jamaica

Wheat (and Products)

					Total	Rank
ADM/ADM Milling Co.		174	1,848		2,022	1
Bartlett and Co.			577		577	3
Continental			878		878	2
Goodpasture			157		157	5
Pillsbury			533		533	4
TOTAL		174	3,993			

Feed Grains

					Total	Rank
Cargill		255		4,572	4,827	2
Continental			1,317		1,317	5
Goodpasture			5,068		5,068	1
Peavey				1,720	1,720	4
Pillsbury			1,010	1,704	2,714	3
TOTAL		255	7,395	7,996		

Veg. Oil Products

					Total	Rank
Cargill				389	389	2
Cook			300		300	3
Pasternak Baum			600		600	1
TOTAL			900	389		

TABLE B.7 (Continued)

	FY 1969	1970/71	1972	1973	1974	1975	1976	1977	1978	Total	Rank
Korea											
Wheat (and Products)											
ADM/ADM Milling Co.	2,806									2,806	18
Ataka America							2,180			2,180	20
Bunge		2,432	1,643	8,258	2,812			3,283	4,639	11,997	7
Cargill	2,914	12,389	20,191				16,246	16,687	11,276	90,773	1
Columbian Grain									5,391	5,391	14
Continental Grain	1,138	7,932	10,291	3,725			4,478	3,800	1,217	32,581	4
Cook	2,164	8,459	10,168	4,606	1,017		17,819	20,196		64,429	3
Dreyfus	2,567	5,717	7,884	10,223			8,476	31,274	1,290	67,431	2
Garnac							4,091			4,091	15
C. Itoh							4,047	5,343		9,390	8
Marubeni		1,475	9,722	1,234						12,431	6
Mitsubishi		284	1,368				3,882			5,534	13
Mitsui							4,253	4,763		9,016	9
Nichimen		1,641	1,312							2,953	17
North Pacific Grain		410							2,155	2,565	19
Pacific Int'l Grain	3,982			3,274						7,256	11
Peavey	999						2,179			3,178	16
Producers Grain	942									942	23
Sumitomo-Shoji			4,765				2,996			7,761	10
Toshoku			2,129					2,280	1,277	5,686	12
Toyomenka							2,042			2,042	21
Union Equity			1,200							1,200	22
West Coast Resources		3,095	12,591	9,024						24,710	5
TOTAL	17,512	43,834	83,264	40,344	3,829		72,689	87,626	27,245		

Feed Grains

							Total	Rank
Bunge		277				4,827	5,104	4
Cargill	552	4,569	2,936	3,983	350	12,864	25,254	1
Continental		3,805	2,347			11,945	18,097	3
Marubeni			10,233	10,206	127		20,566	2
Mitsui						2,707	2,707	6
Nichimen			1,272				1,272	7
Peavey	628	2,809					3,437	5
West Coast Industries			1,096				1,096	8
TOTAL	1,180	11,460	17,884	14,189	477	32,343		

Pakistan
Wheat and Products

									Total	Rank
Bunge	882	1,964	2,636	4,186			10,467	2,946	23,081	5
Cargill	6,848	4,466	14,734	5,181		13,913	29,277	14,875	89,294	2
Continental	1,554	2,902	20,576	11,052				1,840	37,924	4
Cook	1,796	7,805	11,093	4,063	5,119	11,162	5,317		46,355	3
Dreyfus	6,172	3,976	4,348	10,105	5,667	23,183	42,455	5,632	101,538	1
Garnac			1,751	2,855		1,765	6,215		12,586	7
Goodpasture		3,009	1,724						4,733	10
Mitsui			923						923	16
Nichimen			1,396						1,396	14
North Pacific Grain		2,337							2,337	13
Otaka				1,294					1,294	15
Peavey	1,774			2,313					4,087	11
Sumitomo Shoji						3,565			3,565	12
Toshoku				1,294		3,702			4,996	9
Union Equity		7,553	4,012	5,001					16,566	6
United Grain		714	2,074			6,271			9,059	8
TOTAL	19,026	34,726	65,267	47,344	10,786	63,561	93,731	25,293		

Feed Grains

		Total	Rank
Cook	4,093	4,093	1
TOTAL	4,093	4,093	

TABLE B.7 (Continued)

	FY 1969	1970/71	1972	1973	1974	1975	1976	1977	1978	Total	Rank
Pakistan (cont'd)											
Veg. Oil Products											
ADM/ADM Milling Co.	433									433	12
Arkansas Grain	470									470	11
Bunge	1,426		6,766	989	4,449		10,751	5,830	3,911	34,122	1
Calif. Veg. Oils, Inc.								1,248		1,248	9
Cargill	1,971		5,164		3,444		4,882	11,490	18,257	33,718	2
Continental	3,105		8,617	630			3,040		3,175	30,057	3
Cook			417		5,958		4,148	8,214		18,737	5
Dreyfus									2,903	2,903	7
Garnac			1,297							1,297	8
Koppel							763			763	10
Mitsubishi				9,561				7,579	6,744	25,884	4
Pasternak Baum			1,448				1,331	2,739		5,518	6
TOTAL	7,405		23,709	11,180	13,851		24,915	37,100	34,990		
Peru											
Wheat											
Granus									3,399	3,399	1
Alfred C. Toepfer									2,801	2,801	2
TOTAL									6,200		
Veg. Oil Products											
ACLI Soya Co.									3,319	3,319	2
Continental Grain									1,595	1,595	3
Dreyfus									8,882	8,882	1
TOTAL									13,796		

Portugal

Wheat

	1	2	3	4	Total	Rank
Cargill	4,595	3,545			8,140	2
Continental		7,734			7,734	3
Cook	2,366				2,366	5
Dreyfus		3,493			3,493	4
Garnac	7,639	11,228			18,867	1
TOTAL	14,600	26,000				

Feed Grains

	1	2	3	4	Total	Rank
Bunge	718				718	9
Cargill	2,329		8,948	7,662	18,939	1
Continental	3,840		13,795		17,635	2
Cook	5,448				5,448	5
Dreyfus	3,678	2,242			5,920	4
Garnac	2,786	5,049	1,775		9,610	3
Mitsui	807				807	8
Pasternak Baum				2,538	2,538	7
Tabor and Co.	2,457	2,240			4,697	6
TOTAL	22,063	9,531	24,518	10,200		

Sudan

Wheat (and Products)

	1	2	3	4	5	Total	Rank
Bartlett and Co.					376	376	10
Bunge					2,990	2,990	3
Burrus Mills (Cargill)					1,678	1,678	7
Cargill				2,409		2,409	5
Continental		1,790	768			2,558	4
Cook				2,391		2,391	6
Dixie Portland					1,308	1,308	8
C. B. Fox	2,223	986				3,209	1
Garnac					3,010	3,010	2
Int'l. Multifoods					192	192	11
Pillsbury					746	746	9
TOTAL	2,223	2,776	768	4,800	10,300		

TABLE B.7 (Continued)

Vietnam
Wheat (and Products)

	FY 1969	1970/71	1972	1973	1974	1975	1976	1977	1978	Total	Rank
Ataka America Inc.					4,616					4,616	6
Bunge		979	1,958	957						3,894	9
Burrus Mills (Cargill)		1,419								1,419	15
Centennial		1,143								1,143	16
Continental		372	2,145			1,482				3,999	8
Cook		1,346	2,074	3,765	8,160					15,345	1
Dreyfus				2,872	4,329	3,912				11,113	2
Fisher Flour Mills		2,241	808							3,049	11
C. B. Fox		506								506	18
Helix		118								118	21
Int'l. Multifoods		120								120	20
Marubeni			613							613	17
Mitsubishi		1,628	626	1,783						4,037	7
Mitsui		3,477	1,254	2,790						7,521	4
Nichimen			1,584							1,584	14
Nissho-Iwai American					3,888					3,888	10
Peavey		1,943								1,943	13
Pillsbury		1,166	923							2,089	12
Sumitomo-Shoji		1,069	4,266	4,078						9,413	3
Toyomenka		1,022	639	3,806						5,467	5
United Grain						365				365	19
TOTAL		18,549	16,890	20,051	20,993	5,759					

Feed Grains

Company					Total	Rank
Continental	1,950		2,055		4,005	3
Cook		2,318	675		9,993	1
C. B. Fox	673				673	7
Marubeni		607	730		1,337	5
Mitsubishi	1,508	1,194	1,352		4,054	2
Mitsui		607			607	10
Nichimen			789		789	6
Peavey	1,947				1,947	4
Sumitomo-Shoji		611			611	9
Toyomenka		612			612	8
TOTAL	6,078	5,949	5,601			

Veg. Oil Products

Company					Total	Rank
Continental	6,613				6,613	1
Cook	159				159	4
Mitsui	112				112	5
Riceland Foods			2,746		2,746	3
Wilbur Ellis	1,985	2,088	863		4,936	2
TOTAL	8,869	2,088	3,609			

Zaire
Wheat (and Products)

Company					Total	Rank
Burrus Mills (Cargill)		113	485		598	5
Cargill				6,624	6,624	1
Continental				1,031	1,031	3
Dixie Portland			287		287	8
Int'l. Multifoods		126	680		806	4
Peavey		179	315		494	7
Pillsbury	1,077	899	285		2,261	2
Rozel	469	119			588	6
TOTAL	1,546	1,436	2,052	7,655		

TABLE B.7 (Continued)

	FY 1969	1970/71	1972	1973	1974	1975	1976	1977	1978	Total	Rank
Zaire (cont'd)											
Feed Grains											
Goodpasture									556		556	1
TOTAL									556		

*Countries were chosen on the basis of the degree of participation in the PL 480 historically and to reflect a balanced geographical distribution.

SOURCES: Data for fiscal years 1969–1973 and 1976–1978 were compiled from records of individual Title I sales maintained in the "Sales Registration Books," by the Office of the General Sales Manager, U.S.D.A. The sales figures for those years in most cases include a 5% maximum tolerance. Thus, the actual sales figures may have been slightly less than indicated. Data for fiscal years 1974 and 1975 were supplied by the ASCS, U.S.D.A. and is based on actual payments made by the Commodity Credit Corporation to the individual exporters.

TABLE B.8 Selected Bilateral Long-Term Agreements and Contracts Concluded Thereunder Involving Grains[a] for Shipment From 1978/79 Onward

Countries Exporting/Importing	Date Announced	Quantity (million of tons)	Terms of Agreement/Sale
Argentina			
Algeria	October 1974	0.27–0.45 per year—wheat	A draft five-year agreement beginning with 1975 covering 0.1–0.2 m. tons of durum wheat and 0.15–0.2 m. tons of corn annually.
Chile	November 1976	0.5 per year—wheat	A three-year agreement commencing 1977.
China	May 1978	3.0 (wheat & corn)	A three-year agreement commencing 1979.
	September 1980	1.0–15 per year (wheat/corn/soybeans)	A four-year agreement commencing 1981.
Iraq		0.4 per year—wheat	A three-year agreement commencing 1981.
Mexico	December 1980	0.8–1.0—sorghum 0.25—soybeans	Agreement for shipment of these quantities between April & July 1981.
Peru	March 1976	0.61—wheat 0.1—corn/sorghum	A three-year agreement commencing 1976.
Venezuela	November 1976	0.2—wheat per year 0.1—maize per year 0.1—sorghum per year	An agreement providing for the shipment of these quantities annually between 1976 & 1980.
USSR	January 1980	4.0—feedgrains per year 0.5—soybeans per year	A five-year agreement providing for the shipment of these quantities annually commencing 1980.

TABLE B.8 (Continued)

Countries Exporting/Importing	Date announced	Quantity (million tons)	Terms of agreement/sale
Australia			
China	January 1979	7.5—wheat	A three-year agreement for total shipments commencing 1979. Contract under the above agreement. Credit terms covering 12 months.
	January 1979	2.5—wheat	Shipment December 1978–November 1979.
	January 1979	0.5—wheat	Contract, same as above.
	October 1979	1.5—wheat	Contract, shipment 1980.
Egypt	October 1975	3.0—wheat	A three-year agreement providing for the shipment of 1.0 m. tons annually commencing 1 January 1976.
	October 1978	1.0—wheat	A three-year agreement providing for the shipment of minimum 1.0 m. tons annually commencing 1 January 1979. Contract fulfilling the 1st year of the agreement. Shipment 1979 calendar year. Credit terms covering 24 months. To be continued December 1981 to November 1984.
	October 1979	1.5—wheat	Contract, shipment 1980.
Indonesia		0.6—wheat	Agreement for shipment of these quantities during 1981.
Japan		0.9—wheat	Agreement for shipment of these quantities during 1981.
Qatar		0.48—wheat	Agreement for shipment of these quantities over 10 years beginning in 1980.
Saudi Arabia	March 1976	0.6—wheat	A three-year agreement starting from 1976 to supply 0.2 m. tors annually.
USSR		2.46—wheat 1.4—coarse grains	Agreement expired 30 June 1981.
Yemen		0.35–0.50—wheat	Agreement providing for shipment of these quantities annually from December 1981 to November 1984.

Canada			
Algeria	May 1976	0.87–1.0—wheat	A three-year agreement with shipment commencing 1976.
Brazil	October 1975	0.9–1.5—wheat	A three-year agreement commencing 1976.
	May 1978	0.3—wheat	Contract. Shipment July–October 1978 to complete the above agreement.
		3.0—wheat	A three-year agreement, 1980–1982.
China	February 1979	13.2–15.3—wheat	Four different agreements covering 1979 to 1981.
Jamaica	January 1979	0.15–0.25—wheat	An agreement providing for the shipment from 1979 to 1981.
Japan		1.3—wheat 0.85—barley	Agreement providing for shipment of these quantities in 1981.
Mexico	February 1981	0.5—wheat	A two-year agreement for delivery of up to 0.15 m. tons in 1981 and 0.35 m. tons in 1982.
Norway	January 1977	0.06–0.12 per year—wheat	A three-year agreement commencing 1977.
Poland	April 1977	1.5–2.4 (wheat/barley/oats)	A three-year agreement providing for the shipment of wheat, barley, and oats from 1977.
	February 1978	0.75 (wheat/barley/oats)	Contract, shipment of above grains during 1978 calendar year.
	October 1979	4.5 (wheat/durum/barley/oats)	A three-year agreement providing for the shipment of 1.0–1.5 m. tons of wheat, durum, barley, and oats during 1980–1982.
USSR		4.5—wheat	Agreement for shipment during 1980–1981.
		1.1–1.4 (corn/oats/barley)	Same as above.
		25.0 (wheat & feedgrains)	Agreement for total shipments during 1981–86.
Sweden			
Norway	March 1975	0.15–0.25 (wheat & coarse grains)	A three-year agreement to supply grains including 0.1–1.2 m. tons of wheat covering the period 1975/1976–1977/78.
Poland	March 1977	0.6 (wheat/barley/rye/oats)	A three-year agreement to supply annually 0.2 m. tons of wheat, rye, barley & oats starting from 1977.

TABLE B.8 (Continued)

Countries Exporting/Importing	Date announced	Quantity (million tons)	Terms of agreement/sale
Turkey Libya	June 1978	0.3—wheat 0.1—barley/oats 0.1—flour	A five-year agreement from 1978 to 1983.
United States of America China	October 1980	6.0–9.0 (wheat & corn) per year	A four-year agreement for the shipment of these quantities annually commencing 1980.
Israel	November 1975	0.4—wheat per year 0.66—sorghum per year 0.25—corn per year 0.38—soybeans per year	Shipment of these quantities annually in 1975/76–1977/78.
Japan	August 1975	3.0—wheat per year 8.0—feedgrains per year 3.0—soybeans per year	Shipment of these quantities annually in 1975/76–1977/78.
Mexico	January 1980 September 1980 December 1980	4.76 (wheat & feedgrains) 7.2 (wheat & feedgrains) 6.5–8.18 (sorghum/corn/ soybeans)	Agreement for shipment in calendar year 1980. January agreement amended from 4.6 to 7.2 m. tons for shipment in calendar year 1980. Agreement for shipment in calendar year 1981.
Norway	November 1974	0.15–0.35 (wheat/rye/ corn/sorghum/barley) per year	Shipment of these quantities of wheat, rye, corn, sorghum & barley annually from 1 October 1975 to 30 September 1978.
	January 1979	0.5–1.0 (wheat/rye/corn/ sorghum/barley) per year	A three-year agreement commencing 1979 providing for minimum annual purchases of 0.15 and maximum of 0.35 m. tons of wheat, rye, corn, sorghum & barley.

Poland	November 1975	2.5—wheat per year	Shipment 1975/76–1980/81.
Taiwan[a]	September 1981	3.4 (wheat/barley/corn & soybeans) per year	A five-year agreement replacing the agreement of 1976. Shipment of 17.2 m. tons annually (8.6 mt corn, 4.8 mt soybeans, 2.85 mt wheat & 900,000 mt barley).
USSR	October 1975	6.0–8.0 (wheat and corn) per year	A five-year agreement for the shipment of at least 3.0 m. tons of wheat and 3.0 m. tons of corn annually commencing 1 October 1976. Sixth year in effect 1 October 1981 to 30 September 1982.

[a]Between U.S. private exporters and Taiwanese importers. U.S. participants: ADM Export Co., Agri-Industries, Bunge Corp., Cargill, Inc., Coast Trading, Inc., Columbia Grain Co., Continental Grain Co., Far-Mar-Co. Inc., Farmers Export Co., Garnac Grain, Inc., Gulf Coast Grain Inc., Koppel, Inc., Louis Dreyfus Corp., National Council of Farmer Cooperatives, Peavey Co., Philipp Bros.-Oceanic Inc., the Pillsbury Co., and United Grain Co.

SOURCE: International Wheat Council, Review of the *World Wheat Situation 1978/79*, p. 100; and Gilmore International Consulting for updated material.

Appendix C

The Domestic and International Food Bank: Charters and Balance Sheets

DOMESTIC FOOD BANK, FUNCTION

Board of Governors: *semi-autonomous,* implements agricultural policy as formulated within Department of Agriculture, but independent in the sense that self-financed.

                    Membership   Secretary of Agriculture to serve in dual capacity as Chairman of the Board and Secretary of USDA; others appointed from outside for 9-year terms with at least 2 producers, 2 from cooperatives, 2 from private milling, processing, or merchandising sector, and 2 consumer representatives.

                    Powers   determine minimum and maximum prices for different quality wheats* at parity levels which account for production costs and the need for an average farm income corresponding to national median income; the minimum price would be set and the maximum could be adjusted according to an index of consumer prices;

                                         determine reserve requirements;

                                         appoint Federal Wheat Bank directors;

                                         direct Federal Price Committee to

*Coarse grains and oilseeds could also be handled by the DFB.

(1) ensure convertibility of Domestic and International Reserve Certificates into wheat at prevailing prices on date of maturity established within the set price range plus interest exempt from federal taxes to bearer;

(2) ensure the convertibility of Food Aid Bonds into wheat at prevailing prices on date of maturity established within the set price range;

(3) purchase wheat on the open market for purposes of reserve or food aid creation;

(4) adjust interest rates on these redeemable certificates and bonds, adjusted according to Bank system's supply and demand requirements;

(5) engage in cash and futures transactions to keep supplies above the reserve threshold and maintain domestic prices within the established price range;

(6) store grain;

(7) coordinate domestic and international transactions;

(8) issue licenses for commercial and concessional export sales;

(9) invest revenues in U.S. government certificates;

(10) gather and disseminate market information;

retain fixed percent of earnings to cover cost of operations and contribute remainder to International Reserve Fund.

Federal Wheat Banks: four banks, located in the four principal regional distribution centers of the United States—the Great Lakes, Gulf, Atlantic, and Pacific—with responsibility to execute the directives of the Board of Governors.

Membership 9 directors in each bank appointed for 5-year terms, same member composition as board of directors;

Powers   implement all board of governor directives;

coordinate and oversee state branch operations;

approve directors of state branches;

intervene in the markets for purchases and sales of wheat or adjust bond and certificate interest rates with approval of Federal Price Committee in those instances when regional prices and supply positions are significantly at variance with established national minimum and maximum price range;

retain fixed percent of earnings to cover cost of operations and contribute remainder to International Reserve Fund.

State Branches: located with a minimum of one branch in every wheat-producing state.

Membership   9 directors, all nominated by producer members and approved by Federal Wheat Bank in the region where branch is located;

5-year terms;

Duties   provide the requisite services to execute the board of governors and Federal Wheat Bank directives;

management responsibilities for storage and grain-handling operations;

provide information and service to other governmental departments and agencies, particularly Department of Agriculture;

act as clearing agent for all producer member earnings and bearers of reserve certificates and food aid bonds.

Federal Price Committee:

Membership   Board of Governors plus representatives of all federal banks and 2 at-large members drawn from state branch directors with latter serving for a minimum of five years.

| *Duties* | direct and supervise "Operations Committee" to carry out responsibilities of board of governors which includes: |

(1) direct participation in domestic grain transactions;

(2) authorizing acquisition and rental contracting of storage and grain handling facilities;

(3) oversee the issuance of export licenses to individual grain trading companies;

(4) coordinate concessional and commercial transactions as part of overall effort to maintain uniform national price range;

gather market and financial information from all participants in the system to the extent necessary to carry out Domestic Food Bank functions properly.

International Committee:

| *Membership* | board of governors |

| *Duties* | act as liaison with International Food Bank (IFB); |

execute U.S. obligations to the International Food Bank (IFB);

clear all international transactions;

establish and supervise the International Reserve Fund, designed to cover U.S. budgetary expenses involved in participation in the IFB;

collect export license fees.

TABLE C.1   Domestic Food Bank Balance Sheet

ASSETS	LIABILITIES
Reserve stocks	Member reserve deposits
Domestic and international reserve certificates (purchased)	Domestic and international reserve certificates (sold)
Food aid bonds (purchased)	Food aid bonds (sold)
Member production loans	Member income guarantees
Commodity and futures purchases	Commodity and future sales
Handling fees (user charges, etc.)	Handling costs (storage, rental, etc.)

INTERNATIONAL FOOD BANK, FUNCTIONS

Board of Governors: approves all actions undertaken by the Bank with voting weighted according to reserve and food aid (or cash equivalent) quotas. For individual importing countries, quotas based on percent of average wheat and wheat flour imports paid for in purchases of reserve subscriptions. Less developed countries' quotas paid in part by food aid commitments from donors. Exporting country quota subscriptions equivalent to nationally held reserve quotas for wheat and wheat flour based on a percent of average exports.

Membership one governor for each signatory country to the International Food Bank (IFB) Treaty.

Powers authorizes and approves all actions of the executive directorate in semi-annual meeting, one of which must occur during wheat-marketing year;

delegates supervisory authority over executive directorate to the executive board;

exercises sole authority to initiate penalties against member countries for failure to observe treaty regulations upon recommendation of the surveillance and regulatory directorate;

exercises sole authority to deny any IFB privileges, including access to food aid, to nonmember countries.

Voting all voting, on a weighted basis, concluded by majority rule.

Executive Board: assumes responsibilities delegated by the board of governors to authorize and monitor the activities of the IFB.

Membership 5 governors from wheat-exporting countries, 5 from wheat-importing countries, 2 of which are from developing countries (European Community members collectively will have 2 governors), and managing director of IFB.

Powers		authority the same by delegation as the board of governors.
Voting		voting on technical issues by majority with one vote for each member and unanimous votes for all substantive issues. Any substantive vote may be referred to the Board of Governors, and, otherwise, all voting shall be conducted on a quarterly basis corresponding to the IFB fiscal year.

Executive Directorate: management authority.

Membership	executive director and deputy director appointed by board of governors for individual terms of seven years.
Duties	oversee all IFB operations and under direction of the executive board conduct the normal business of the Bank;

prepare quarterly reports to the executive board plus an annual report to the board of governors. |

Food Security Fund   interest-bearing account from an isolated portion of Bank earnings available for loans to qualified members for storage and wheat-handling facilities.

Food Stabilization Fund   interest-bearing account from an isolated portion of Bank earnings available for loans to qualified members for purchases of wheat at par values of wheat quotas determined by the IFB.

Surveillance and Regulatory Directorate   the IFB enforcement device, assigned the principal responsibility for monitoring adherence of all departments to IFB regulations and member countries to IFB obligations.

IFB Departments

Reserve Department	in charge of reserve quotas and subscriptions, the maintenance of reserves and clearing transactions which involve the release or acquisition of those reserves.
Food Aid Department	in charge of food aid quotas and subscriptions, and periodic review of the disbursement practices by donor members.

Central Exchange Department	determines cash equivalents of quotas and subscription tranches and handles receipts or payments of foreign currencies, special drawing rights and government securities pursuant to member obligations and activities.
Market Information Department	collection agency for all government and private sector reports on market conditions, responsible for market analysis and preparation of IFB reports on market conditions.
Export License Department	issues licenses semiannually to registered government and private agents for handling IFB wheat purchases, sales and shipments.
Price Review Department	sets the par value of IFB wheat transactions and determines the margin above and below par value for members. The par value may be adjusted periodically according to prevailing market conditions.

TABLE C.2   International Food Bank Balance Sheet

ASSETS	LIABILITIES
Wheat reserves with depositories*	Wheat reserve subscriptions and food aid subscriptions of members
Foreign currencies/special drawing rights of the International Monetary Fund	Capital subscriptions of members
Securities (including instruments like the proposed U.S. Domestic Food Bank International Reserve certificates)	Food security fund Food aid fund
Service charges receivable	Interest payable on indebtedness

*Reserves located in wheat surplus and deficit regions.

Selected Bibliography

NEWSPAPERS

Childs, Marquis. "The Mismanaged Soybean Embargo." *Washington Post,* 10 July 1973, p. 19.

"Four Shiploads of U.S. Wheat Diverted to Iran in 1980." *Journal of Commerce,* 13 February 1981, p. 9.

Gilmore, Richard. "Grain for Russia." *New York Times,* 10 December 1979, p. 27.

Gilmore, Richard. "Why A Food Embargo Won't Work." *Washington Post,* 27 December 1979, p. A17.

Rothschild, Emma. "Is It Time to End Food for Peace?" *New York Times Magazine,* 13 March 1979, p. 15.

"U.S. Company Pleads Guilty to Violation of Iran Trade Embargo." *Wall Street Journal,* 25 February 1981, p. 42.

PERIODICALS

Adjusting to Scarcity: Annals of the American Academy of Political and Social Science 420 (July 1975): 1-176.

Alaouze, Chris M.; Watson, A.S.; and Sturgess, N.H. "Oligopoly Pricing in the World Wheat Market." *American Journal of Agricultural Economics* 60 (May, 1978): 173-85.

Barraclough, Geoffrey. "Wealth and Power: the Politics of Food and Oil." *New York Review of Books* 22 (7 August 1975): 23-30.

Destler, I. M. "United States Food Policy 1972-1976: Reconciling Domestic and International Objectives." *International Organization* 32 (Summer 1978): 617-653.

Eberstadt, Nick. "Myths of the Food Crisis." *New York Review of Books* 23 (19 February 1976): 32-37.

"Food: Potent U.S. Weapon, Interview with Earl L. Butz, Secretary of Agriculture." *U.S. News & World Report, Inc.,* 16 February 1976, pp. 26-28.

Gelb, Leslie H.; and Lake, Anthony. "Washington Dateline: Less Food, More Politics." *Foreign Policy,* no. 17 (Winter 1974-75): pp. 176-89.

Gilmore, Richard. "Grain in the Bank." *Foreign Policy,* no. 38 (Spring 1980), pp. 168-81.

Harris, Simon and Swinbank, Alan. "Price Fixing Under the CAP—Proposition and Decision: The Example of the 1978/79 Price Review." *Food Policy* (November 1978): pp. 256-71.

Houthakker, H. S. "Do We Need a National Food Policy?" *American Journal of Agricultural Economics* 58 (May 1976): 259-69.

Johnson, Paul R.; Grennes, Thomas; and Thursby, Marie. "Devaluation, Foreign Trade Controls, and Domestic Wheat Prices." *American Journal of Agricultural Economics* 59 (November 1977): 619-27.

Luttrell, Clifton B. "Grain Exports and Inflation." *Federal Reserve Bank of St. Louis Review* 57 (September 1975): 2-4.

McCalla, Alex F. "A Duopoly Model of World Wheat Pricing." *Journal of Farm Economics* 48, Part I (August 1966): 711-27.

McCalla, Alex F., and Schmitz, Andrew. "Grain Marketing Systems: The Case of the United States versus Canada." *American Journal of Agricultural Economics* 61 (May 1979): 199-212.

MacLennan, Robert. "Food Prices and the Common Agricultural Policy." *The Three Banks Review* 119 (September 1978): 58-71.

Markov, P. "The World Food Problem." *International Affairs, Moscow*, no. 9 (September 1975), pp. 79-87.

Miguez, Daniel F. "Agricultural Co-ops—Farmers Band Together for a Larger Market." *Brazilian Business* 57 (June 1977): 20-23.

Morgan, Dan. "American Agripower and the Future of a Hungry World." *Saturday Review*, 9 November 1976, pp. 7-12.

Rojko, Anthony S. "The Economics of Food Reserve Systems." *American Journal of Agricultural Economics* 57 (December 1975): 866-72.

Rothschild, Emma. "Food Politics." *Foreign Affairs* 54 (January 1976): 285-307.

Sarris, Alexander and Taylor, Lance. "Cereal Stocks, Food Aid and Food Security for the Poor." *World Development* 4 (1976): 967-76.

"Secretary Kissinger interview for *Business Week*: Transcript of interview December 23, 1974." *Department of State Bulletin* 72 (January 1975): 97-106.

Taylor, Alonzo E. "International Wheat Policy and Planning." *Wheat Studies* XI (June 1935): 359-62.

"U.S. Food Power: Ultimate Weapon in World Politics." *Business Week*, 15 December 1975, p. 56.

Walters, Harry. "Difficult Issues Underlying Food Problems." *Science* 188 (9 May 1975): 524-30.

"What—And Who—Makes Cargill So Powerful?" *Forbes*, 18 September 1978, pp. 150-56.

UNITED STATES DEPARTMENT OF AGRICULTURE DOCUMENTS

U.S. Department of Agriculture. Commodity Credit Corporation. "CCC-Exporter Agreement," 1980.

U.S. Department of Agriculture. Economic Research Service. "The Freight Car Supply Problem and Car Rental Policies," April 1972.

U.S. Department of Agriculture. Economic Research Service. "Relationship Between Daily Grain Price Movements on Rotterdam and U.S. Markets and EC Levy." Report submitted to the Subcommittee on Multinational Corporations of the U.S. Senate Foreign Relations Committee, June 1976. (Unpublished.)

U.S. Department of Agriculture. Economics, Statistics, and Cooperatives Service. "A Study of Relationships Between Large Export Sales and Futures Trading," by Richard Heifner, Kandice Kahl and Larry Deaton, 8 June 1979.

U.S. Department of Agriculture. Economics, Statistics, and Cooperatives Service. *Another Revolution in U.S. Farming?* by Lyle P. Schertz et al. Agricultural Economic Report No. 441. Washington, D.C.: U.S. Government Printing Office, 1980.

U.S. Department of Agriculture. Food Aid Task Force. *New Directions for U.S. Food Assistance: A Report of the Special Task Force on the Operations of PL 480 to the Secretary of Agriculture.* Washington, D.C.: May 1978.

U.S. Department of Agriculture. "Report of The Advisory Committee on Export Sales Reporting to Secretary of Agriculture Bob Bergland." 27 February 1979. (Mimeographed.)

U.S. Department of Agriculture and U.S. Department of Transportation. Rural Transportation Advisory Task Force. *Agricultural Transportation Services: Needs, Problems, Opportunities, A Final Report,* January 1980.

HEARINGS AND OTHER UNITED STATES GOVERNMENT DOCUMENTS

Commodity Futures Trading Commission, Division of Economics and Education. "Inquiry Into Operations of Spot Price Committees on New York Coffee and Sugar Exchange, Minneapolis Grain Exchange, and Kansas City Board of Trade." June 1977. (Mimeographed.)

Commodity Futures Trading Commission, Office of General Counsel. *The Antitrust Implications of Spot Cash Quotation Committees.* Memorandum, 18 November 1976.

Presidential Commission on World Hunger. *Overcoming World Hunger: The Challenge Ahead.* Report of March 1980. Washington: U.S. Government Printing Office, 1980.

U.S. Central Intelligence Agency. *The Soviet Grain Balance 1960-1973.* A(ER) 75-68, September 1975.

U.S. Central Intelligence Agency. *Potential Implications of Trends in World Population, Food Production, and Climate.* OPR-401, August 1974.

U.S. Congress. House. Committee on International Relations. *Use of Food Resources for Diplomatic Purposes–An Examination of the Issues,* Congressional Research Service, Library of Congress. Committee Print. HD 9002 U.S. Washington: U.S. Government Printing Office, 1977.

U.S. Congress. Senate. Committee on Agriculture and Forestry. *Grain Inspection. Hearings before the Subcommittee on Foreign Agricultural Policy and the Subcommittee on Agricultural Production, Marketing, and Stabilization of Prices,* Part 1, 94th Cong., 1st sess., 19 June 1975.

U.S. Congress. Senate. Committee on Agricultural and Forestry. *Policies and Operations Under PL 480. Hearings,* 85th Cong., 1st sess., 1957.

U.S. Congress. Senate. Committee on Agriculture and Forestry. Subcommittee on Foreign Agricultural Policy. *Hunger and Diplomacy: A Perspective on the U.S. Role at the World Food Conference.* Committee Print, 94th Cong., 1st sess., 4 February 1975.

U.S. Congress. Senate. Committee on Agriculture and Forestry. *Who's Making Foreign Agricultural Policy? Hearings before the Subcommittee on Foreign Agricultural Policy,* 94th Cong., 2d sess., 1976.

U.S. Congress. Senate. Committee on Foreign Relations. *The International Wheat Agreement. Hearings before a subcommittee on ratification by U.S. Government of International Wheat Agreement,* 80th Cong., 2d sess., 14, 15 and 17 May 1948.

U.S. Congress. Senate. Committee on Foreign Relations. *USSR and Grain,* Richard Gilmore. Committee Print. Staff Report, Washington, D.C.: U.S. Government Printing Office, 1976.

U.S. Congress. Senate. Committee on Government Operations. *Grain Sales to the Soviet Union. Hearings before the Permanent Subcommittee on Investigations,* 94th Cong., 1st sess., 31 July and 1 August 1975.

U.S. Congress. Senate. Committee on Government Operations. *Russian Grain Transactions. Hearings before the Permanent Subcommittee on Investigations,* 93d Cong., 1st sess., 1973.

U.S. Congress. Senate. Committee on Government Operations. *Sales of Grain to the Soviet Union. Hearings before the Permanent Subcommittee on Investigations,* 93d Cong., 2d sess., 8 October 1974.

U.S. Congress. Senate. *Food and Fibre As A Force For Freedom.* Report by Sen. Hubert H. Humphrey to the Senate Committee on Agriculture and Forestry. Washington, D.C.: U.S. Government Printing Office, 1958.

U.S. Federal Trade Commission. *Report of the Federal Trade Commission on Methods and Operations of Grain Exporters,* 2 vols. Washington, D.C.: U.S. Government Printing Office, 1922.

U.S. General Accounting Office. *Federal Export Grain Inspection and Weighing Programs: Improvements Can Make Them More Effective and Less Costly.* Report to Congress by the Comptroller General of the United States. Washington, D.C., 30 November 1979.

U.S. General Accounting Office (GAO). *Grain Marketing Systems in Argentina, Canada, and the European Community: Soybean Marketing Systems in Brazil.* A Report to the Congress by the Comptroller General of the United States, Washington, D.C. ID-76-61, 28 May 1976.

U.S. General Accounting Office. *Impact of Soybean Exports on Domestic Supplies and Prices.* B-178753. Comptroller General of the United States, Washington, D.C., 22 March 1974.

U.S. General Accounting Office. *Issues Surrounding the Management of Agricultural Exports.* A Report to the Congress by the Comptroller General of the United States. 2 vols. ID-76-87. Washington, D.C., 2 May 1977.

U.S. General Accounting Office. *Russian Wheat Sales and Weaknesses In Agriculture's Management of Wheat Export Subsidy Program.* A Report to the Congress by the Comptroller General of the United States. B-176943, 9 July 1973.

U.S. Interstate Commerce Commission. *Ex Parte No. 270 (Sub-No. 9).* "Investigation of Railroad Freight Rate Structure—Grain and Grain Products." Decided 1 February 1979.

U.S. Interstate Commerce Commission. *Ex Parte No. 307.* "Investigation into the Distribution and Manipulation of Rail Rolling Stock to Depress Prices on Certain Grain Shipments for Export." Decided 18 July 1977, p. 16.

PAPERS, REPORTS, AND STUDIES

Berlan, Jean-Pierre. "Les Matières De Base Agricoles." Institut National de la Recherche Agronomique, Paris, December 1978.
Caves, Richard E. "Organization, Scale, and Performance In the Grain Trading Industry." Discussion Paper No. 546. Harvard Institute of Economic Research, Harvard University, 1977.
"Food Policy Options of the European Community for the 1990s: Part III Critical Policy Issues." Sussex European Research Centre, University of Sussex, 29 March 1979.
Gavin, Joseph Gleason III. "The Political Economy of U.S. Agricultural Export Policy, 1971-1975: Government Response to a Changing Economic Environment." Faculty of Political Science, Columbia University, 1979. (Unpublished Dissertation.)
Jones, Norman H., Jr.; and Ferguson, Allen R.; with Booth, James; and Yockey, Thomas. "Competition and Efficiency in the Commodity Futures Markets, Executive Summary." Prepared for the Commodity Futures Trading Commission by the Public Interest Economics Center, Washington, D.C., May 1978.
Krzyminski, James. "Agricultural Transportation: The National Policy Issues." National Planning Association Report No. 168. Washington, D.C., 1978.
McCalla, Alex F. "Structural Characteristics of International Grain Markets." University of California, Davis, 1979. Submitted to the U.S. Department of Agriculture. Office of the General Sales Manager, Contract 671-ASCS-79.
National Academy of Sciences, Washington, D.C. Committee on World Food, Health, and Population. "Population and Food: Crucial Issues." Washington, D.C., 1975.
Schmitz, Andrew. "The Establishment and Operation Of A Grain Export Cartel." Department of Agricultural and Resource Economics, University of California, Berkeley, 1979. Submitted to the U.S. Department of Agriculture, Contract 697-ASCS-79.
Smith, Topper; and Picard, John. "The Economics of United States Grain Stockpiling." A report prepared for the Council on International Economic Policy. Rand Corporation, R-1861-CIEP, March 1977.
Zachar, George. "A Political History of Food for Peace." No. 77-18. Cornell University Agricultural Experiment Station, Department of Agricultural Economics, Ithaca, May 1977.

U.N. AND OTHER INTERNATIONAL ORGANIZATIONS

Gilmore, Richard, with the assistance of Frederick Blott, "U.S. Food and Beverage Industry Report." United Nations Center on Transnational Corporations, United Nations, January 1978. (Mimeographed.)

International Wheat Council. "International Wheat Agreements—A Historical and Critical Background." EX (74/75) 2/2, London, 14 August 1974.

"Transnational Corporations and Food and Beverage Processing." ST-CTC-19, United Nations, 1980.

United Nations. Food and Agriculture Organization. Committee on Commodity Problems. "Role of Subcommittee (CSD) in Light of Current and Prospective Developments in Agricultural Surpluses and Food Aid." CCP 68/7/2, 26 July 1968.

FOREIGN DOCUMENTS

Grain Handling and Transportation Commission (Hall Commission). *Grain and Rail in Western Canada,* vols. 1-3, Ottawa: Supply and Services Canada, 1977.

Industries Assistance Commission. *Wheat Stabilization.* Canberra: Australian Government Publishing Service, 30 June 1978.

OTHER SELECTED BIBLIOGRAPY

Benedict, Murray; and Stine, Oscar. *The Agricultural Commodity Programs.* New York: Twentieth Century Fund, 1956.

Brook, Ezriel; Grill, Enzo; and Waelbroeck, Jean. *Commodity Price Stabilization and the Developing Countries.* World Bank Reprint Series: Number 66. Reprinted from *Banca Nazionale del Lavoro Quarterly Review.* No. 124 (March 1978).

Cochrane, Willard W.; and Ryan, Mary E. *American Farm Policy, 1948-1973.* Minneapolis: University of Minnesota Press, 1976.

Davis, Joseph S. *Wheat and the AAA.* Washington, D.C.: The Brookings Institution, 1935.

Davis, Joseph S. *Wheat Under International Agreement.* Washington: American Enterprise Association, 1945.

Debatisse, Michel-Louis. *Le Commerce International Des Céréales.* Paris: Centre Français Du Commerce Extérieur, 1979.

Destler, I. M. *Making Foreign Economic Policy.* Washington, D.C.: The Brookings Institution, 1980.

Fraenkel, Richard M.; Hadwiger, Don F.; and Browne, William P., eds. *The Role of U.S. Agriculture in Foreign Policy.* New York: Praeger, 1979.

Gilmore, Richard. "Wheat and Coarse Grains—Stabilization or Status Quo." In *A New International Commodity Regime,* pp. 77-85. Edited by Geoffrey Goodwin and James Mayall. London: Croom Helm Ltd., 1979.

Grennes, Thomas; Johnson, Paul R.; and Thursby, Marie. *The Economics of World Grain Trade.* New York: Praeger, 1978.

Hamilton, Martha M. *The Great American Grain Robbery and Other Stories.* Washington, D.C.: Agribusiness Accountability Project, 1972.

Harle, Vilho, ed. *The Political Economy of Food.* Westmead, Farnborough, England, Axon House, 1979.

Harmon, David P., Jr. "Return to World Grain Surpluses." Trends and Implications." In *Critical Food Issues of the Eighties,* pp. 323-339. Edited by Marylin Chou and David P. Harmon, Jr. New York: Pergamon, 1979.

Hathaway, Dale Ernest. *Government and Agriculture: Public Policy in a Democratic Society*. New York: Macmillan, 1963.

Heady, Earl O. "Productivity: Farm Policy and Income." In *Farmers in the Market Economy: Market Organization and Competitive Behavior in Relation to Farmers' Prices, Costs, & Incomes*. Ames Center for Agricultural and Economic Development, Iowa State University of Science and Technology. Ames: Iowa State University, 1964.

de Hevesy, Paul. *World Wheat Planning and Economic Planning in General*. London: Oxford University Press, 1940.

Johnson, D. Gale; and Schnittker, John A., eds. *U.S. Agriculture In A World Context: Policies and Approaches for the Next Decade*. New York: Praeger, 1974.

Lappe, Frances Moore; and Collins, Joseph. *Food First Beyond the Myth of Scarcity*. Boston: Houghton Mifflin, 1977.

McClintock, David W. *U.S. Food: Making the Most of a Global Resource*. Boulder: Westview, 1978.

Malott, Deone W. *Problems in Agricultural Marketing*. New York: McGraw-Hill, 1938.

Matusow, Allen J. *Farm Policies and Politics in the Truman Years*. Cambridge: Harvard University, 1967.

Morgan, Dan. *Merchants of Grain*. New York: Viking, 1979.

Norris, Frank. *The Pit: A Story of Chicago*. New York: Grosset and Dunlap, 1903.

Roll, Eric. *The Combined Food Board, A Study in Wartime International Planning*. Stanford: Stanford University, 1956.

Schmitz, Andrew; and McCalla, Alex F. "The Canadian Wheat Board," *Agricultural Marketing Boards: An International Perspective*. Sidney Hoos, ed. Cambridge: Ballinger, 1979.

Schneider, Stephen H. *The Genesis Strategy: Climate and Global Survival*. New York: Plenum, 1976.

Surface, Frank K. *The Grain Trade During the War: Being A History of the Food Administration Grain Corporation and the United States Grain Corporation*. New York: Macmillan, 1928.

Trager, James. *Amber Waves of Grain*. New York: Arthur Fields Books, Inc., 1973.

Wallerstein, Mitchel B. *Food For War–Food For Peace: U.S. Food Aid*. Cambridge: MIT, 1980.

Index

Agricultural Adjustment Act (AAA), 72, 181–87, 195–96
The Andersons, 52, 152
Archer-Daniels-Midland (ADM), 47, 49, 108
Argentina: bilateral agreements, 97, 103, 213–14; cooperatives, 214–15; government board, 97, 213–14; grain sales to USSR, 160, 166, 197; surpluses, 187–88; U.S. grain embargo against USSR, 213, 215
Australia: Australian Wheat Growers' Association, 210; bilateral agreements, 97, 103; export credits, 75; government board, 55, 97, 106, 181, 209–13; grain sales to Iran, 211–12; grain sales to Japan, 105, 211, 212; grain sales to Taiwan, 212; grain sales to USSR, 160, 167; and international reserve proposal, 6; and Iranian commodity agreement, 107, 211; national food aid program, 94; surpluses, 187–88; Wheat Trade Convention and, 190. *See also* AAA

Bergland, Robert, 78, 79, 81, 82, 109, 139, 140, 141, 164, 171
Big League grain traders, 58, 59, 60; Argentinean operations, 214–15; Australian operations, 211; Brazilian operations, 64–66, 216, 217; Canadian operations, 205, 208–209; Chinese operations, 228, 229; commodity exchanges and, 127, 128, 129, 131–32; and EC, 68, 223; federal indictments and, 124; food aid programs and 94–96; Form G, 140; influence on grain market prices,

69–70; Japanese operations, 224, 225; and market instability, 131–32; membership of, 24–47; Norwegian trade agreement, 108; protectionism and, 70; soybean embargo of 1973, 147, 148, 151; U.S. government protection of, 173–74; U.S./USSR agreement (1975) and, 161; USSR grain sales, 160, 227–28; vs. farmer cooperatives, 14, 141; windfall profits, 138
Brannon Plan, 73, 76
Brazil: CACEX, 65, 215–16; COBEC, 129, 216, 228; cooperatives, 216–17; as grain buyer, 92, 93; grain sales to USSR, 160, 197. *See also* Brazilian soybeans
Brazilian soybeans, 65–66; 215–16
Bunge and Born Corporation, 24, 41; Argentinean operations, 182, 214; Australian operations, 211, 212; barter exchange, 76; Canadian operations, 209; corporate structure, 42; debt, 41; and EC, 223; exports, percentage of U.S., 26–27; as foreign trader in U.S., 130; history, 40; markets for, 41; PL 480, 95; grain sales to Norway, 108; grain sales to Taiwan, 108; soybean embargo of 1973, 148; tax shelters for, 40–41
Butz-Abe accord, 104–106, 161
Butz, Earl, 65, 74, 75, 77, 78, 92, 94, 98, 153, 155, 156, 157, 158, 159, 160, 194

Canada: arbitrage, 206; bilateral agreements, 97, 103, 207; commodity markets and, 206; export credits, 75; export markets and, 5, 203; govern-

bean embargo of 1973, 148, 149, 150; tax harbors, 36; U.S. Soviet grain export cutback (1974), 99

Cook Industries, 59; Agri-Products Group, 43; barter exchange and, 76; debts, 43, 45; exports, percentage of U.S., 26–27; foreign markets, 43; the Hunts, 43, 59, 130; losses, 43; merchandising structure, 44; protests to USDA about, 123; purchase by Mitsui, 45; grain sales to Norway, 108; grain sales to Taiwan, 108; grain sales to USSR, 99, 131, 153, 160; soybean embargo of 1973, 149, 150, 151; soybeans, miscalculation of market (1977), 130; U.S. Soviet grain export cutback (1974), 99. *See also* Mitsui/ Cook

Cooley loan program, 96

cost, insurance, freight (c.i.f.), 16; Amsterdam-Rotterdam-Antwerp (A-R-A) and, 67, 68, 69; EC and, 66, 67; Farmers Export Company and, 54; influences on, 69–70; Rotterdam market and, 16, 69–70; U.S. reliance on, 69

Domestic Food Bank (DFB), 240, 241–45, 282–85

Domestic International Sales Corporation (DISC), 32, 40, 41

Eastern European satellites, 99, 100, 106; grain transshipments and, 170–71

European Commission: administration of CAP, 219–20; and c.i.f. grain prices, 66–67, 68; export restitutions, 68–69, 70, 188, 220–21, 223; export zones, 220–21; and GATT complaint, 158; prefixed levies and, 67, 68, 70

European Communities (EC): administration of grain trade system, 67, 69; Brazilian soybeans and, 64, 65; daily grain market information, 67, 68; European Economic Community, 4, 68; European Monetary System, 222–23; Flanigan Report and, 158; floating exchange rates, 222; food aid program, 94; grain imports and, 218–23; grain sales to USSR, 103; Kennedy Round memorandum and, 188–89; 221–22; manipulation of grain trade system, 68, 69; monetary compensatory accounts, 221–23; oil vs. grain, 158;

protectionism and, 6, 66, 157–58, 194; subsidized exports, 66, 68; subsidized farm programs, 3, 4; Wheat Trade Convention, 193. *See also* CAP; European Commission

European Recovery Program (ERP), 21, 75, 84, 85, 163, 184

Exporters Group, 190, 191–93

farmer cooperatives, 13–14, 16, 50, 51; anti-trust exemptions, 59, 141; Congress reviews status of, 141; and exports, 53; foreign aid programs and, 95; Justice Department and, 141; and PL 480, 239; price-support loans and, 140–41; vs. grain trading companies, 14, 141

Farmers Export Company (FEC), 59; and c.i.f. export business, 54; losses, 54; management, 54; grain sales, 54; soybean futures miscalculation, 131, 141

Feruzzi Serafino and Company, 51, 214

Flanigan Report, 157–58

Food Aid Convention, 188, 189, 196

the food weapon: Bangladesh and, 156; Chile and, 156, 163; China and, 157; Egypt and, 154–55; 163; and export licensing system, 235; ineffectiveness of, 145, 152, 154, 155, 158, 159, 160, 161, 162, 168, 174; India and, 154, 155; Iran and, 165; Israel and, 155, 160; PL 480 as, 153–69, 174; Soviet Union and, 158–61; soybean embargo of 1973, 145, 146–53

France: GATT and, 190; surpluses, 187–88. *See also* Francereales

Francéréales, 61–64, 70, 190

free on board (f.o.b): Gulf of Mexico market, 16; prices and, 116, 121

Futures Commission Merchants (FCMs), 30, 127, 128, 130

Garnac Trade Company, 24, 26–27, 46; André and Company and, 45–46; grain sales to Taiwan, 108

General Agreement on Tariffs and Trade (GATT), 65, 109, 158, 187, 190, 194, 216

German Democratic Republic (East Germany), 50, 107, 170–71

grain standards: cheating the system, 123–24; conflict of interest and, 124; Federal Grain Inspection Service, 20,

gentinean operations, 181; assets, 40; Canadian operations, 209; as a cooperative, 36, 51; corporate structure, 39; credit, 40; earnings, 40; exports, percentage of U.S., 26–27; as foreign trader in U.S., 130; operations, 40; grain sales to Norway, 108; grain sales to USSR, 36, 160; taxes and, 40

Maritime Agreement, 100, 106, 159
Mexico: gas deal, 165; oil for grain, 101, 164; U.S. grain exports to, 78
Minor League grain contenders, 47–52
Mitsui/Cook, 24–7; acquisitions, 45; grain trade, role in North American, 45; history, 41, 43; losses, 45; purchase of Cook assets, 45; mode of operation, 45; uniqueness, 41. *See also* Cook Industries

Nixon administration, 18, 92; analysis of Nixon-Butz policies, 77; barter exchange with Soviet Union, 75, 76; and CAP reform, 194; export credits, 76; export subsidy program, 138; farm policy, 74–75; the food weapon, 155–62; soybean embargo of 1973, 146, 147–49

oil for grain: EC and, 158; Mexico and, 110, 164; Soviet Union and, 110, 158–60
Organization of Petroleum Exporting Countries (OPEC), 78, 104, 158, 160, 162, 163, 194

parity, 72–74
Peavey, 52, 108
Philbro Corporation, 49
Poland: Carter visit, 109; as source of grain for USSR, 159, 160; U.S. grain sales, 106–107; U.S. moratorium threat, 106, 160; USSR cancels supply contract, 106
Private Trade Agreement (PTA) programs, 95, 96
Public Law 480 (PL 480): Bangladesh, food aid denied, 156; Cambodia and, 155–56; Chile, food aid denied, 156; concessional rates and grants, 22, 74, 87; Consultative Subcommittee on Surplus Disposal and, 187, 188, 191; Cooley loan, 95–96; cooperator pro-

grams, 95–96; cottonseed and soybean exporters, 257–58; domestic grain prices and, 87, 92, 94, 187; as economic development tool, 21, 86, 92, 94; Egypt and, 154–55; 163; export credits, 22; exporters by destination, 260–81; Export-Import Bank and, 75; export incentives and, 137; export subsidy program, 137; feed grains exporters, 256–58; Food and Agricultural Organization and, 187; Food for Peace, 85–86, 94; grain exporters, largest, 251, 252–53; grain exports and, 88–89, 97, 114, 239; Haiti and, 163; human rights and, 163; Humphrey and, 86; India and, 154, 155, 156; Indonesia and, 163; Iran and, 155–56; Johnson White House vs. Congress, 154–55; less developed countries and, 21, 22, 92, 93, 94, 104; market development and, 85, 86, 87, 92; Morocco and, 163; Nicaragua and, 163; price effects of, 87, 94, 187; private sector and, 95; Private Trade Agreement and, 95, 96; recipients become commercial buyers, 92; reduced storage costs, 86; South Korea and, 156, 163; supporters, domestic, 154–55; surpluses and, 21, 22, 73, 74, 78, 84–85; vegetable oil products exporters, 259; Vietnam and, 155–56; waning of, 155–156; wheat exporters and, 254–55

railroads: abandonment of lines, 121–22; advisory task force, 122; alternative transportation, 122; deregulation by Congress, 121, 123, 237; grain transportation and, 11, 12, 118–20; hopper cars, 119, 120, 121; ICC and, 120, 121; rates, 119, 120–21, 123; tariff adjustments, 121; unit trains, 119–21
Reagan administration: and international reserve system, 197; Poland export obligations, 106–107; and Soviet grain embargo, 102, 168
Roosevelt administration: farm policy, 72, 74, 84; Wallace and the ever-normal granary, 183–84, 195, 240

Sogo Shosha, 45, 54, 224, 225; Australian operations, 210; Brazilian operations, 105, 217; Canadian operations, 208; expansion of U.S. trade

with Norway, 108, 109, 208; as
patchwork, 111; with Poland, 106–107;
prices and, 111; and private preferential agreements, 109; with Romania,
107, 157; with Soviet Union, 63,
98–103, 106, 155, 158, 160, 228;
symbolic value of, 109, 111; with
Taiwan, 108, 109, 208; and U.S.
trade flow, 108. *See also* Butz-Abe
accord; Eastern European satellites
U.S. Department of Agriculture
(USDA): Agricultural Marketing Service, 123, 134; Cargill, Inc., complaint
against, 134; CCC and, 75, 132;
Cook Industries, formal protests
about, 123; credit for foreign grain
buyers, 78; daily price information
and, 132, 133; Domestic Food Bank
and, 243; export–reporting system,
152–53; export volumes and, 140;
food aid decisions and, 85, 94, 155,
156, 159–60; grain standards, role in,
125, 126; Humphrey report and, 87;
market news reports for, 134, 169,
171–72; mismanagement of, 76; registering export sales, 128; reserve
system, adapting regulations of, 81;

Soviet embargoes and, 165, 166,
167–68, 171–72; soybean embargo of
1973, 148, 149; special task force, 99;
storage facilities of, 124; subsidies
and, 22, 137–38; substandard shipments, complaints to, 123–24
U.S. Department of Commerce, 147,
148, 149
U.S. Department of State, 155, 156,
159–60
U.S. Grain Standards Act (USGSA):
(1916) 20; (1940) 124; (1968) 124;
(1976) 125, 126; (1979) 125

Van Stolk, 52
Vietnam: Cambodia, occupation of, 163;
funding restraints by Congress, 94;
PL 480 and, 155–56; Vietnam War,
85, 94, 154, 156, 207–208

Wallace, Henry, 181, 183, 195, 240
Wheat Executive Agreement, 180
Wheat Utilization Committee, 188, 191
Wheat Trade Convention, 188, 189–90;
193–94; 196
World Food Conference, 104, 155, 194